Oh!great

TRANSLATED AND ADAPTED BY
Makoto Yukon

LETTERED BY
Janice Chiang

BALLANTINE BOOKS • NEW YORK

Air Gear, volume 2 is a work of fiction. Names, characters, places, and incidents are the products of the author's imagination or are used fictitiously. Any resemblance to actual events, locales, or persons, living or dead, is entirely coincidental.

A Del Rey Trade Paperback Original

Published in the United States by Del Rey Books, an imprint of The Random House Publishing Group, a division of Random House, Inc., New York.

Del Rey is a registered trademark and the Del Rey colophon is a trademark of Random House, Inc.

Publication rights arranged through Kodansha Ltd.

First published in Japan in 2003 by Kodansha Ltd., Tokyo

ISBN 0-345-49279-X

Printed in the United States of America

www.delreymanga.com

9 8 7 6 5 4 3

Translator and Adaptor—Makoto Yukon
Lettering—Janice Chiang
Cover Design—Dave Stevenson

Honorifics Explained

Throughout the Del Rey Manga books, you will find Japanese honorifics left intact in the translations. For those not familiar with how the Japanese use honorifics and, more important, how they differ from American honorifics, we present this brief overview.

Politeness has always been a critical facet of Japanese culture. Ever since the feudal era, when Japan was a highly stratified society, use of honorifics—which can be defined as polite speech that indicates relationship or status—has played an essential role in the Japanese language. When addressing someone in Japanese, an honorific usually takes the form of a suffix attached to one's name (example: "Asuna-san"), is used as a title at the end of one's name, or appears in place of the name itself (example: "Negi-sensei," or simply "Sensei!").

Honorifics can be expressions of respect or endearment. In the context of manga and anime, honorifics give insight into the nature of the relationship between characters. Many English translations leave out these important honorifics and therefore distort the feel of the original Japanese. Because Japanese honorifics contain nuances that English honorifics lack, it is our policy at Del Rey not to translate them. Here, instead, is a guide to some of the honorifics you may encounter in Del Rey Manga.

-san: This is the most common honorific and is equivalent to Mr., Miss, Ms., or Mrs. It is the all-purpose honorific and can be used in any situation where politeness is required.

-sama: This is one level higher than "-san." It is used to confer great respect.

-dono: This comes from the word "tono," which means "lord." It is an even higher level than "-sama" and confers utmost respect.

-kun: This suffix is used at the end of boys' names to express familiarity or endearment. It is also sometimes used by men amongst friends, or when addressing someone younger or of a lower station.

-chan: This is used to express endearment, mostly toward girls. It is also used for little boys, pets, and even among lovers. It gives a sense of childish cuteness.

Bozu: This is an informal way to refer to a boy, similar to the English terms "kid" or "squirt."

Sempai/
Senpai: This title suggests that the addressee is one's senior in a group or organization. It is most often used in a school setting, where underclassmen refer to their upperclassmen as "sempai." It can also be used in the workplace, such as when a newer employee addresses an employee who has seniority in the company.

Kohai: This is the opposite of "sempai" and is used toward underclassmen in school or newcomers in the workplace. It connotes that the addressee is of a lower station.

Sensei: Literally meaning "one who has come before," this title is used for teachers, doctors, or masters of any profession or art.

[blank]: This is usually forgotten in these lists, but it is perhaps the most significant difference between Japanese and English. The lack of honorific means that the speaker has permission to address the person in a very intimate way. Usually, only family, spouses, or very close friends have this kind of permission. Known as *yobisute,* it can be gratifying when someone who has earned the intimacy starts to call one by one's name without an honorific. But when that intimacy hasn't been earned, it can be very insulting.

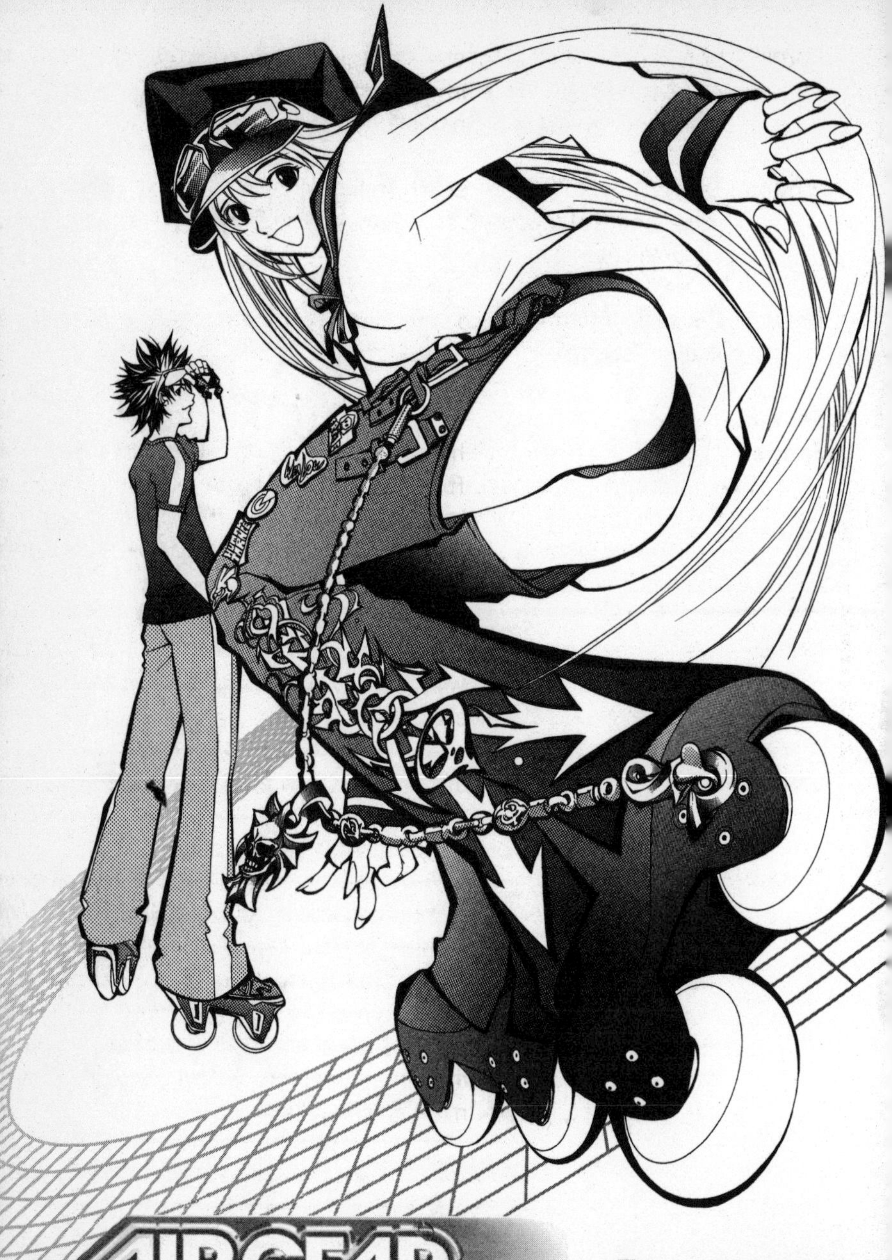

AIR GEAR

2 大暮維人

Oh!great

Sleeping Forest

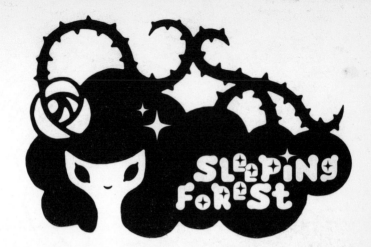

CONTENTS

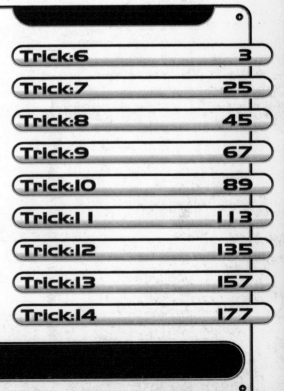

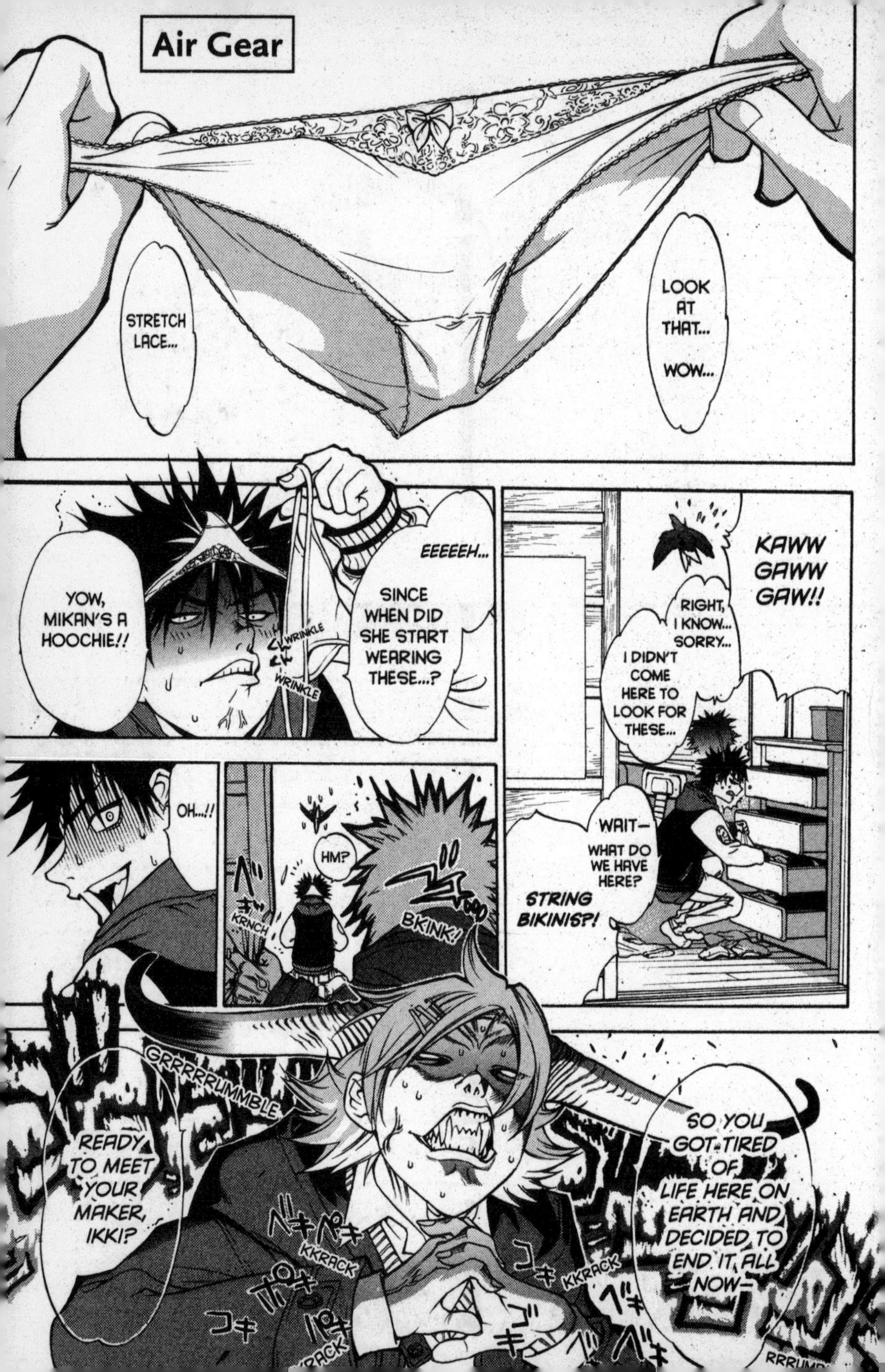
LOOK AT THAT... WOW...
STRETCH LACE...
KAWW GAWW GAW!!
RIGHT, I KNOW... SORRY...
I DIDN'T COME HERE TO LOOK FOR THESE...
WAIT— WHAT DO WE HAVE HERE?
STRING BIKINIS?!
EEEEEH...
SINCE WHEN DID SHE START WEARING THESE...?
WRINKLE
WRINKLE
YOW, MIKAN'S A HOOCHIE!!
BKINK!
HM?
KRNCH
OH...!!
GRRRRRUMMBLE
SO YOU GOT TIRED OF LIFE HERE ON EARTH AND DECIDED TO END IT ALL NOW—
READY TO MEET YOUR MAKER, IKKI?
KKRACK
KKRACK
KKRACK

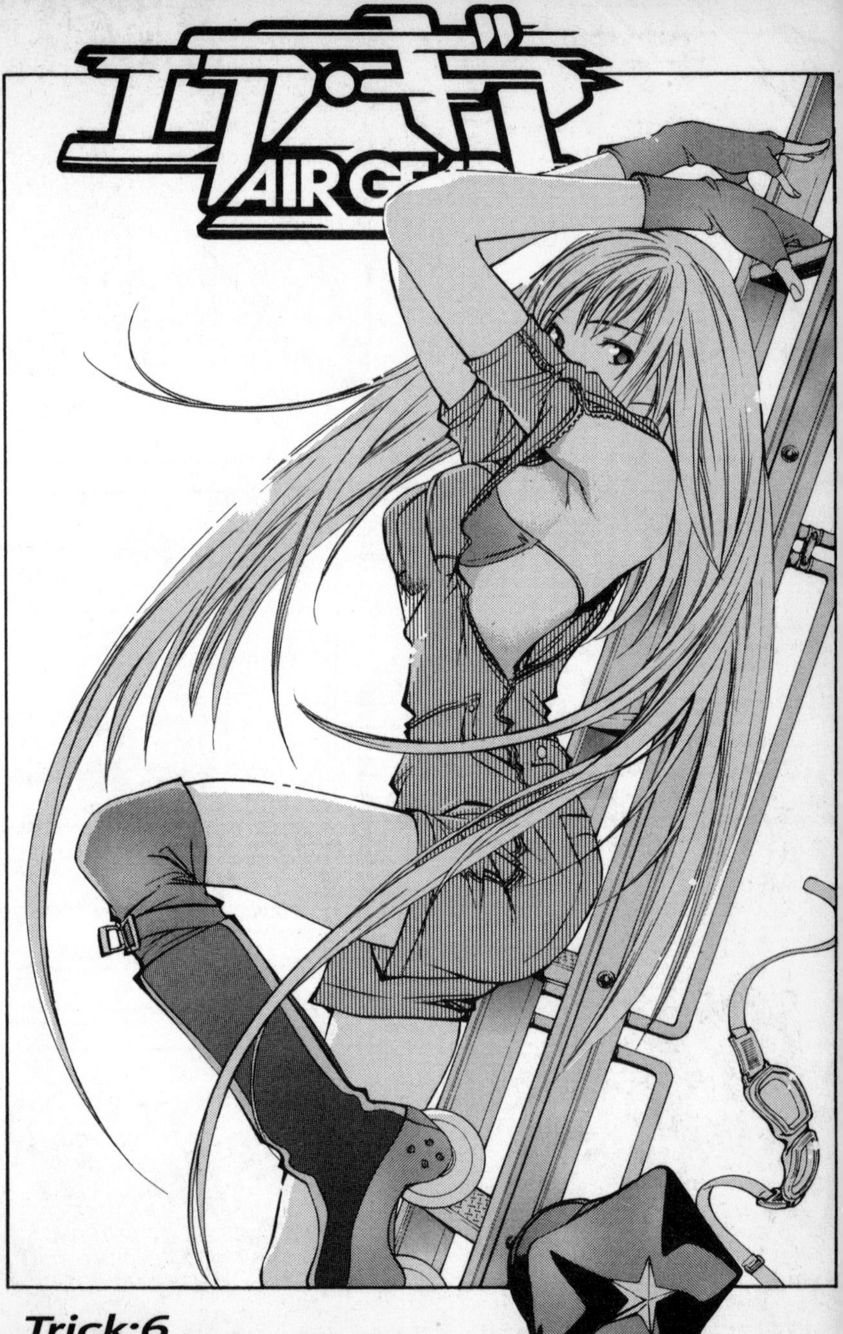

Trick:6

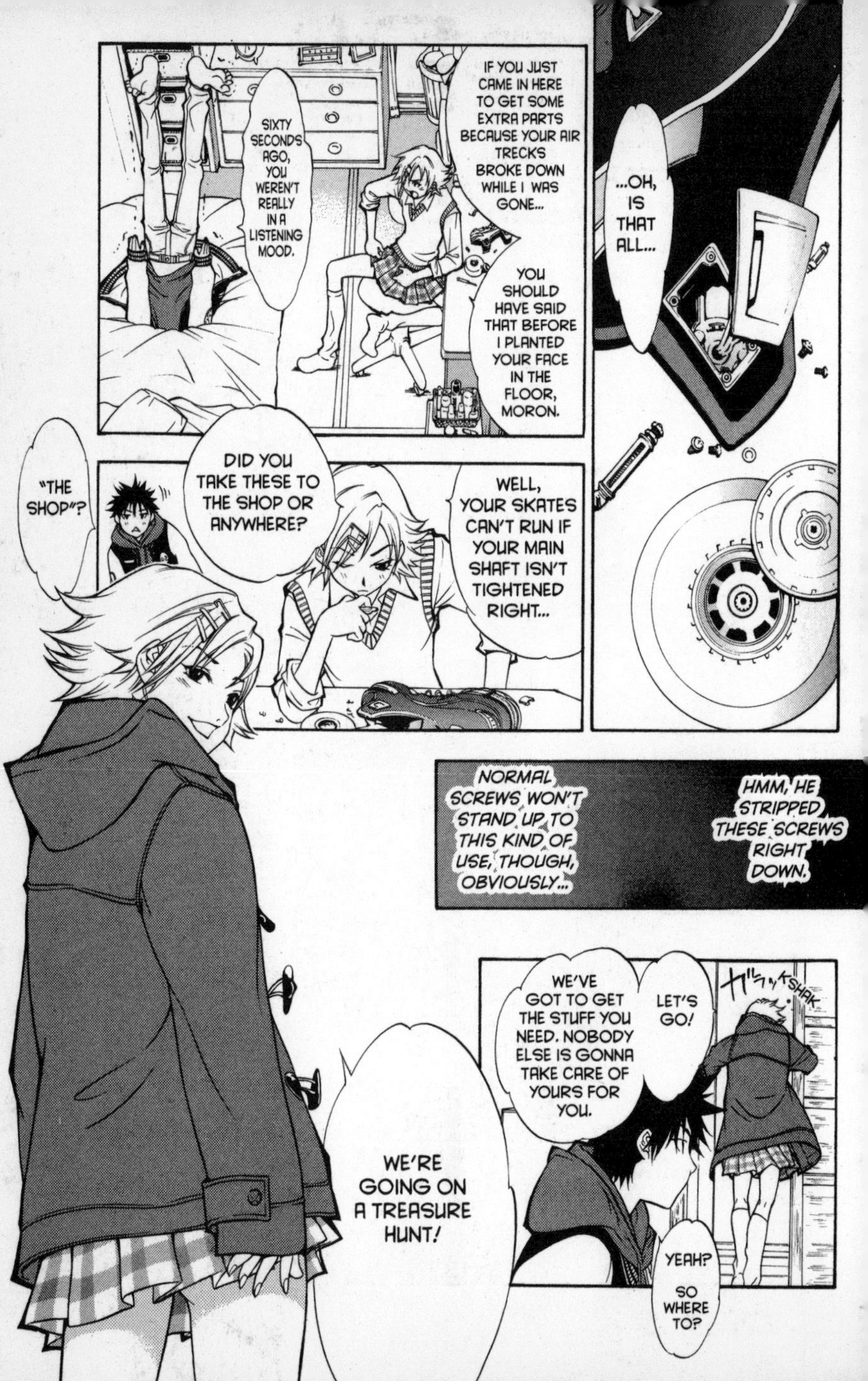
...OH, IS THAT ALL...
IF YOU JUST CAME IN HERE TO GET SOME EXTRA PARTS BECAUSE YOUR AIR TRECKS BROKE DOWN WHILE I WAS GONE...
YOU SHOULD HAVE SAID THAT BEFORE I PLANTED YOUR FACE IN THE FLOOR, MORON.
SIXTY SECONDS AGO, YOU WEREN'T REALLY IN A LISTENING MOOD.
WELL, YOUR SKATES CAN'T RUN IF YOUR MAIN SHAFT ISN'T TIGHTENED RIGHT...
DID YOU TAKE THESE TO THE SHOP OR ANYWHERE?
"THE SHOP"?
HMM, HE STRIPPED THESE SCREWS RIGHT DOWN.
NORMAL SCREWS WON'T STAND UP TO THIS KIND OF USE, THOUGH, OBVIOUSLY...
SHAK
LET'S GO!
WE'VE GOT TO GET THE STUFF YOU NEED. NOBODY ELSE IS GONNA TAKE CARE OF YOURS FOR YOU.
YEAH? SO WHERE TO?
WE'RE GOING ON A TREASURE HUNT!

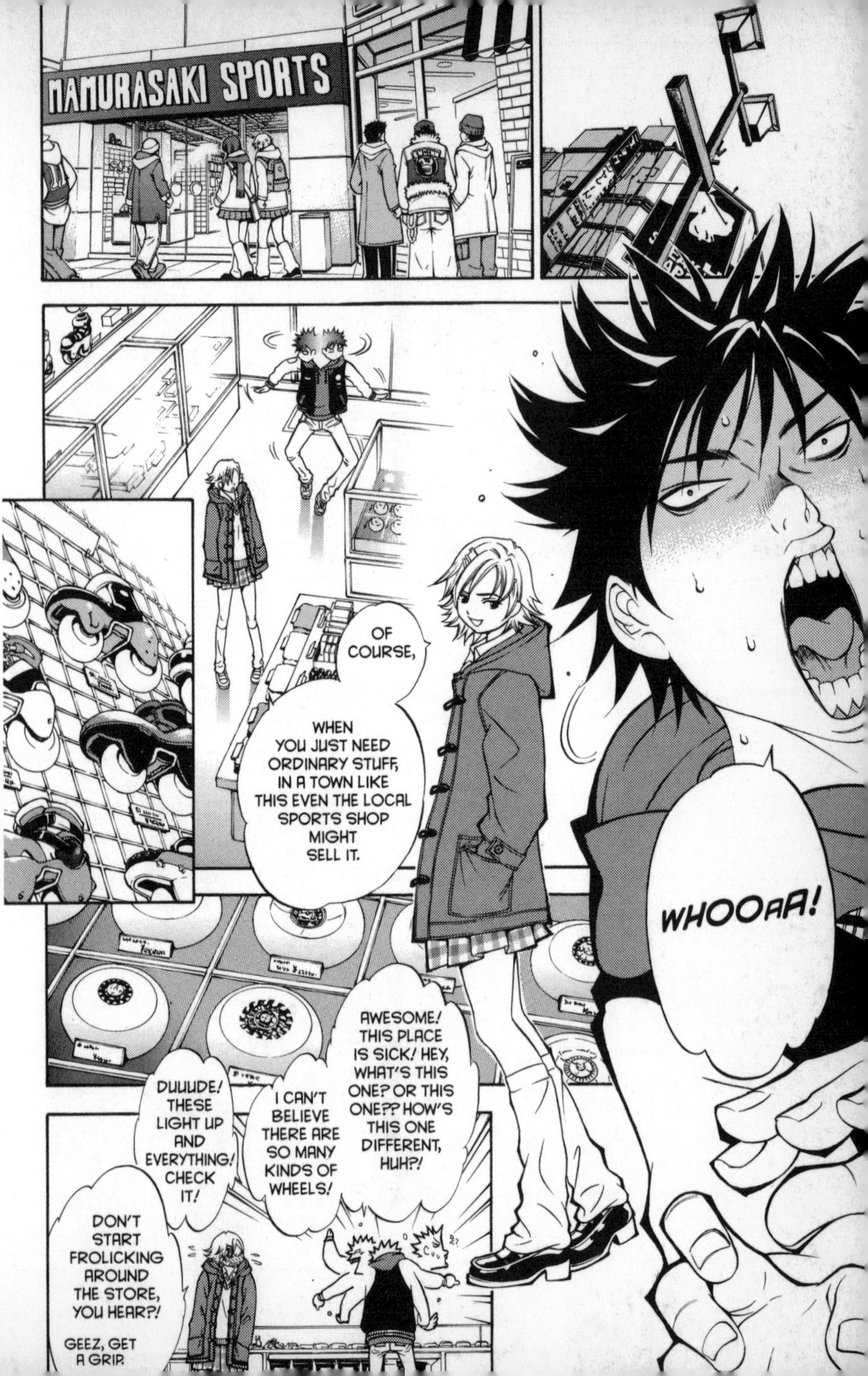
MAMURASAKI SPORTS
WHOOAA!
OF COURSE,
WHEN YOU JUST NEED ORDINARY STUFF, IN A TOWN LIKE THIS EVEN THE LOCAL SPORTS SHOP MIGHT SELL IT.
AWESOME! THIS PLACE IS SICK! HEY, WHAT'S THIS ONE? OR THIS ONE?? HOW'S THIS ONE DIFFERENT, HUH?!
I CAN'T BELIEVE THERE ARE SO MANY KINDS OF WHEELS!
DUUUDE! THESE LIGHT UP AND EVERYTHING! CHECK IT!
DON'T START FROLICKING AROUND THE STORE, YOU HEAR?!
GEEZ, GET A GRIP.

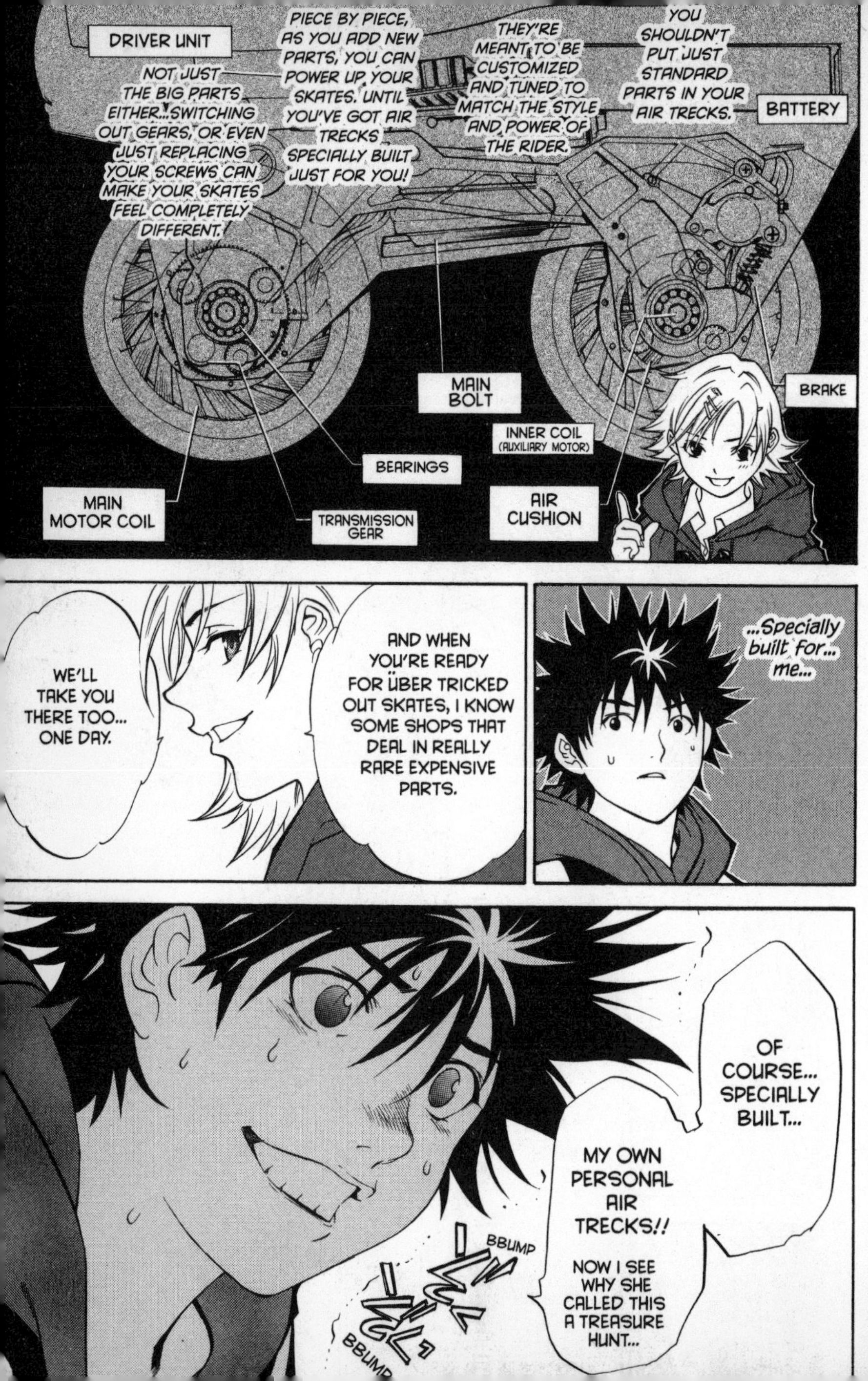
YOU SHOULDN'T PUT JUST STANDARD PARTS IN YOUR AIR TRECKS.
THEY'RE MEANT TO BE CUSTOMIZED AND TUNED TO MATCH THE STYLE AND POWER OF THE RIDER.
PIECE BY PIECE, AS YOU ADD NEW PARTS, YOU CAN POWER UP YOUR SKATES. UNTIL YOU'VE GOT AIR TRECKS SPECIALLY BUILT JUST FOR YOU!
NOT JUST THE BIG PARTS EITHER...SWITCHING OUT GEARS, OR EVEN JUST REPLACING YOUR SCREWS CAN MAKE YOUR SKATES FEEL COMPLETELY DIFFERENT.
BATTERY
DRIVER UNIT
BRAKE
MAIN BOLT
INNER COIL (AUXILIARY MOTOR)
AIR CUSHION
BEARINGS
TRANSMISSION GEAR
MAIN MOTOR COIL
...Specially built for... me...
AND WHEN YOU'RE READY FOR ÜBER TRICKED OUT SKATES, I KNOW SOME SHOPS THAT DEAL IN REALLY RARE EXPENSIVE PARTS.
WE'LL TAKE YOU THERE TOO... ONE DAY.
OF COURSE... SPECIALLY BUILT...
MY OWN PERSONAL AIR TRECKS!!
NOW I SEE WHY SHE CALLED THIS A TREASURE HUNT...
BBUMP
BBUMP

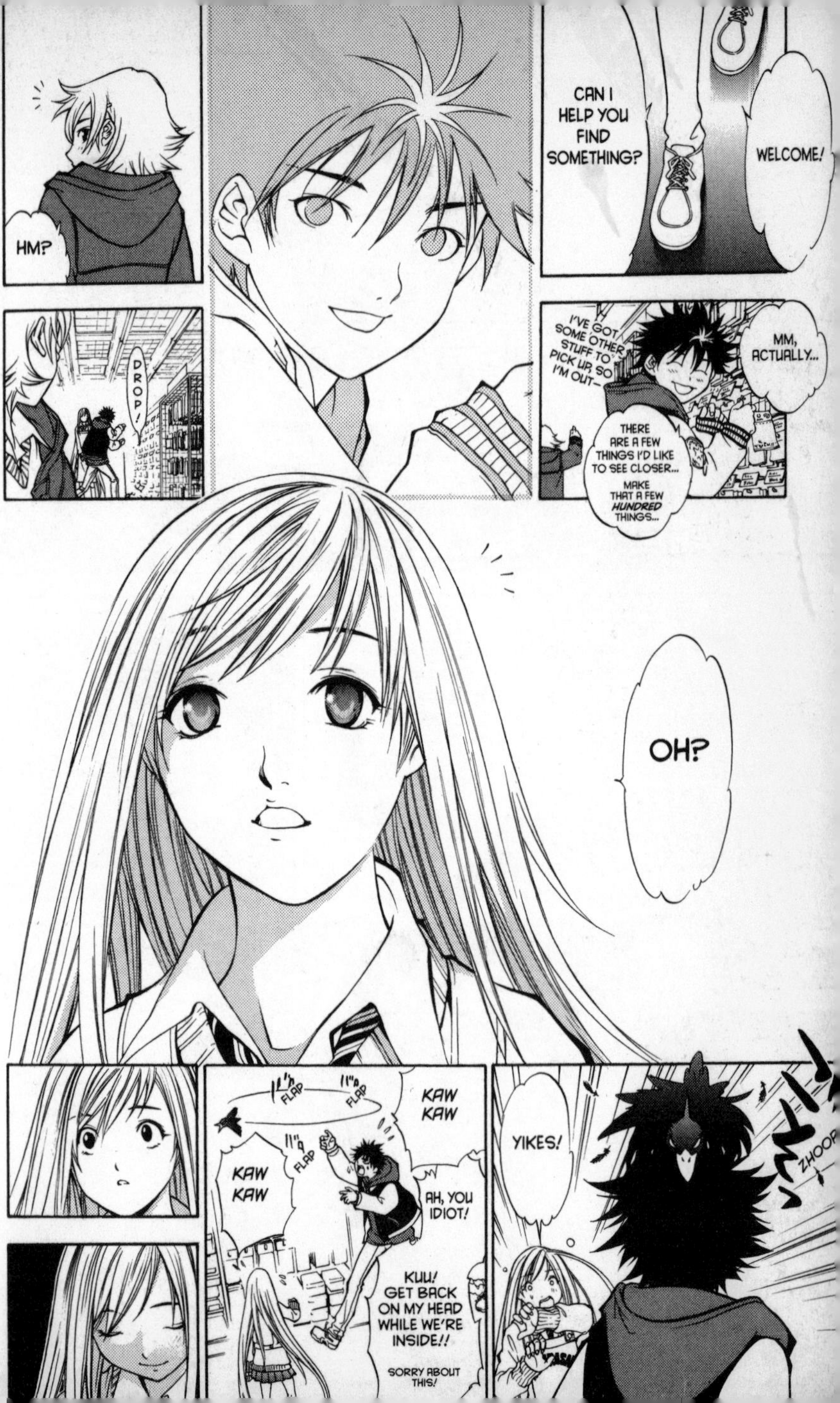
WELCOME!
CAN I HELP YOU FIND SOMETHING?
MM, ACTUALLY...
I'VE GOT SOME OTHER STUFF TO PICK UP, SO I'M OUT–
THERE ARE A FEW THINGS I'D LIKE TO SEE CLOSER...
MAKE THAT A FEW *HUNDRED* THINGS...
HM?
DROP!
OH?
ZHOOP
YIKES!
KAW KAW
FLAP
FLAP
FLAP
AH, YOU IDIOT!
KAW KAW
KUU! GET BACK ON MY HEAD WHILE WE'RE INSIDE!!
SORRY ABOUT THIS!

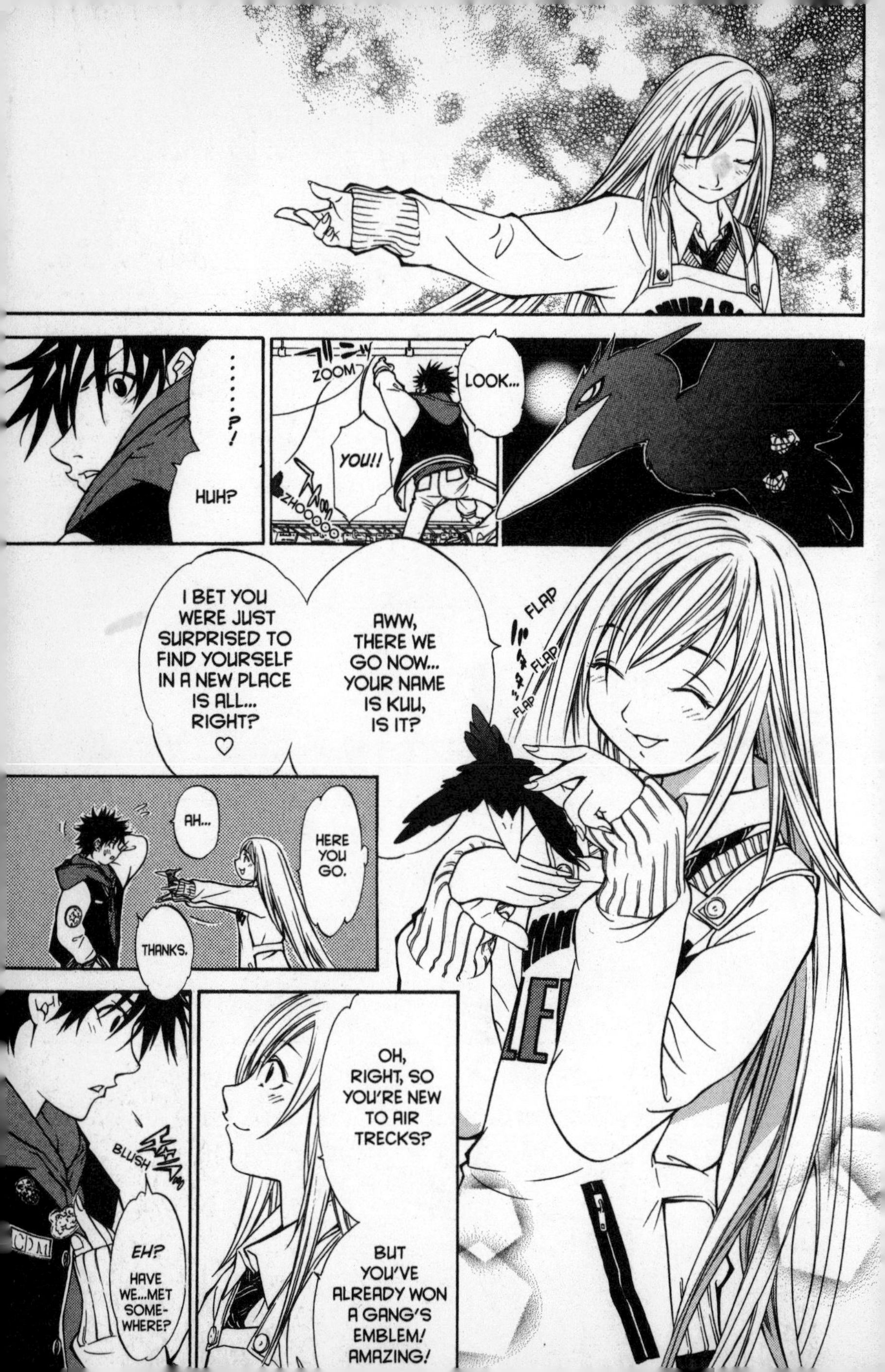
LOOK...
ZOOM
YOU!!
ZHOOOOOM
......?!
HUH?
AWW, THERE WE GO NOW... YOUR NAME IS KUU, IS IT?
I BET YOU WERE JUST SURPRISED TO FIND YOURSELF IN A NEW PLACE IS ALL... RIGHT? ♡
FLAP
FLAP
FLAP
HERE YOU GO.
AH...
THANKS.
OH, RIGHT, SO YOU'RE NEW TO AIR TRECKS?
BUT YOU'VE ALREADY WON A GANG'S EMBLEM! AMAZING!
BLUSH
EH? HAVE WE...MET SOME-WHERE?

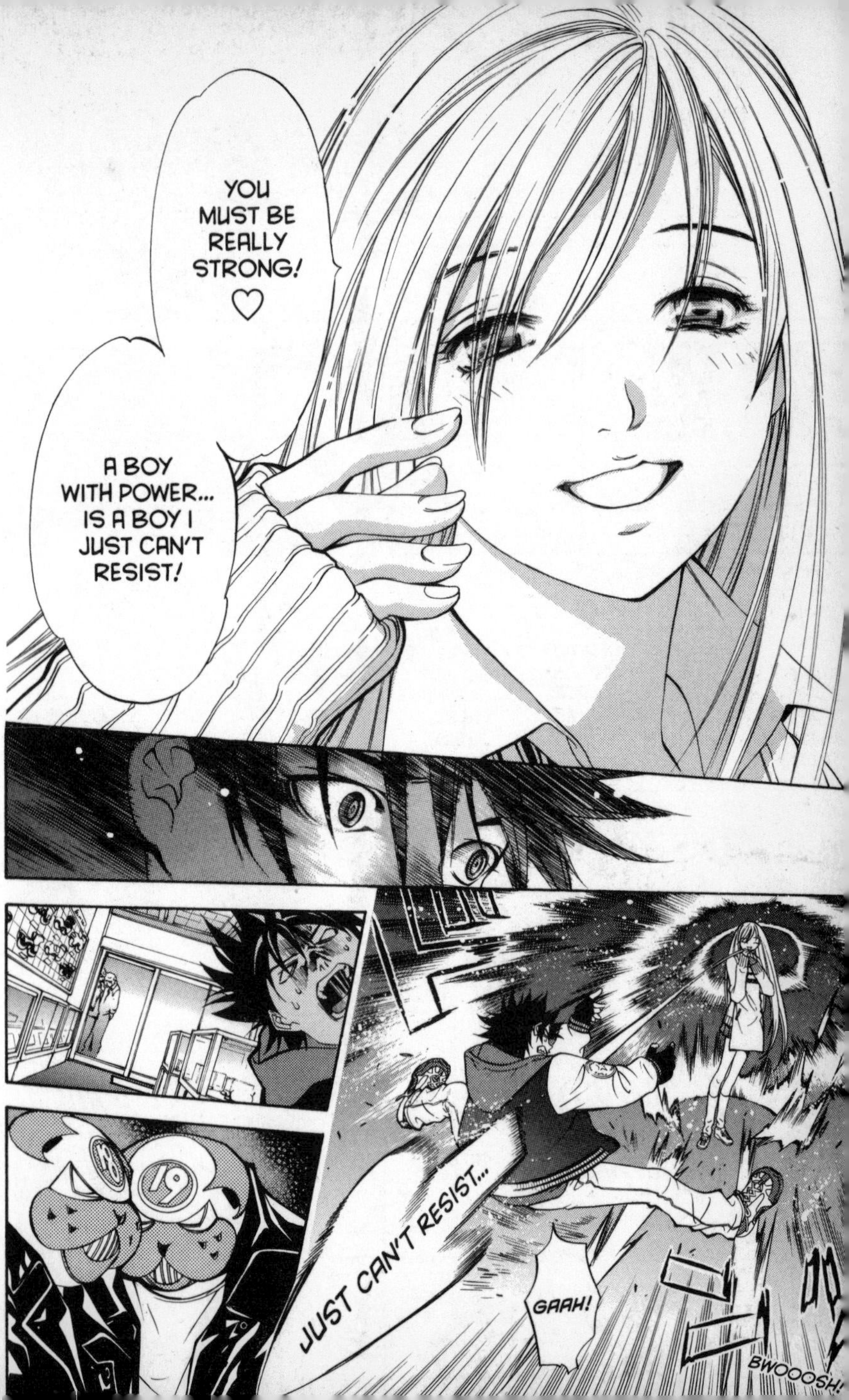
YOU MUST BE REALLY STRONG! ♡
A BOY WITH POWER... IS A BOY I JUST CAN'T RESIST!
JUST CAN'T RESIST...
GAAH!
BWOOOSH!

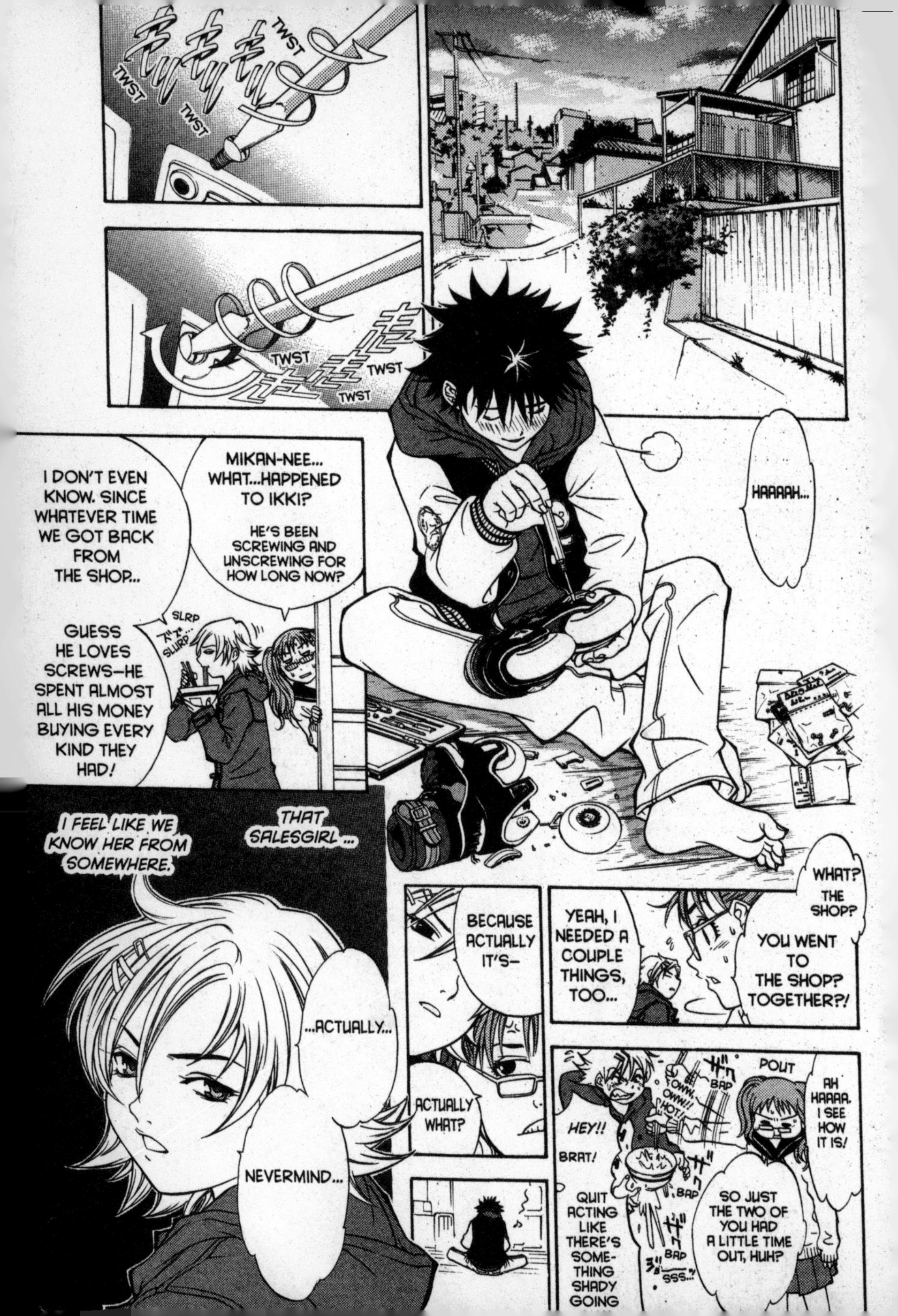
HAAAAH...
TWST
TWST
TWST
TWST
TWST
TWST
MIKAN-NEE... WHAT...HAPPENED TO IKKI?
HE'S BEEN SCREWING AND UNSCREWING FOR HOW LONG NOW?
I DON'T EVEN KNOW. SINCE WHATEVER TIME WE GOT BACK FROM THE SHOP...
SLRP
SLURP
GUESS HE LOVES SCREWS—HE SPENT ALMOST ALL HIS MONEY BUYING EVERY KIND THEY HAD!
WHAT? THE SHOP?
YOU WENT TO THE SHOP? TOGETHER?!
YEAH, I NEEDED A COUPLE THINGS, TOO...
BECAUSE ACTUALLY IT'S—
ACTUALLY WHAT?
AH HAAAA. I SEE HOW IT IS!
POUT
SO JUST THE TWO OF YOU HAD A LITTLE TIME OUT, HUH?
OWW, OWW!! HOT!!
BAP
HEY!!
BRAT!
BAP
BAP
SSS...
QUIT ACTING LIKE THERE'S SOME-THING SHADY GOING
THAT SALESGIRL...
I FEEL LIKE WE KNOW HER FROM SOMEWHERE.
...ACTUALLY...
NEVERMIND...

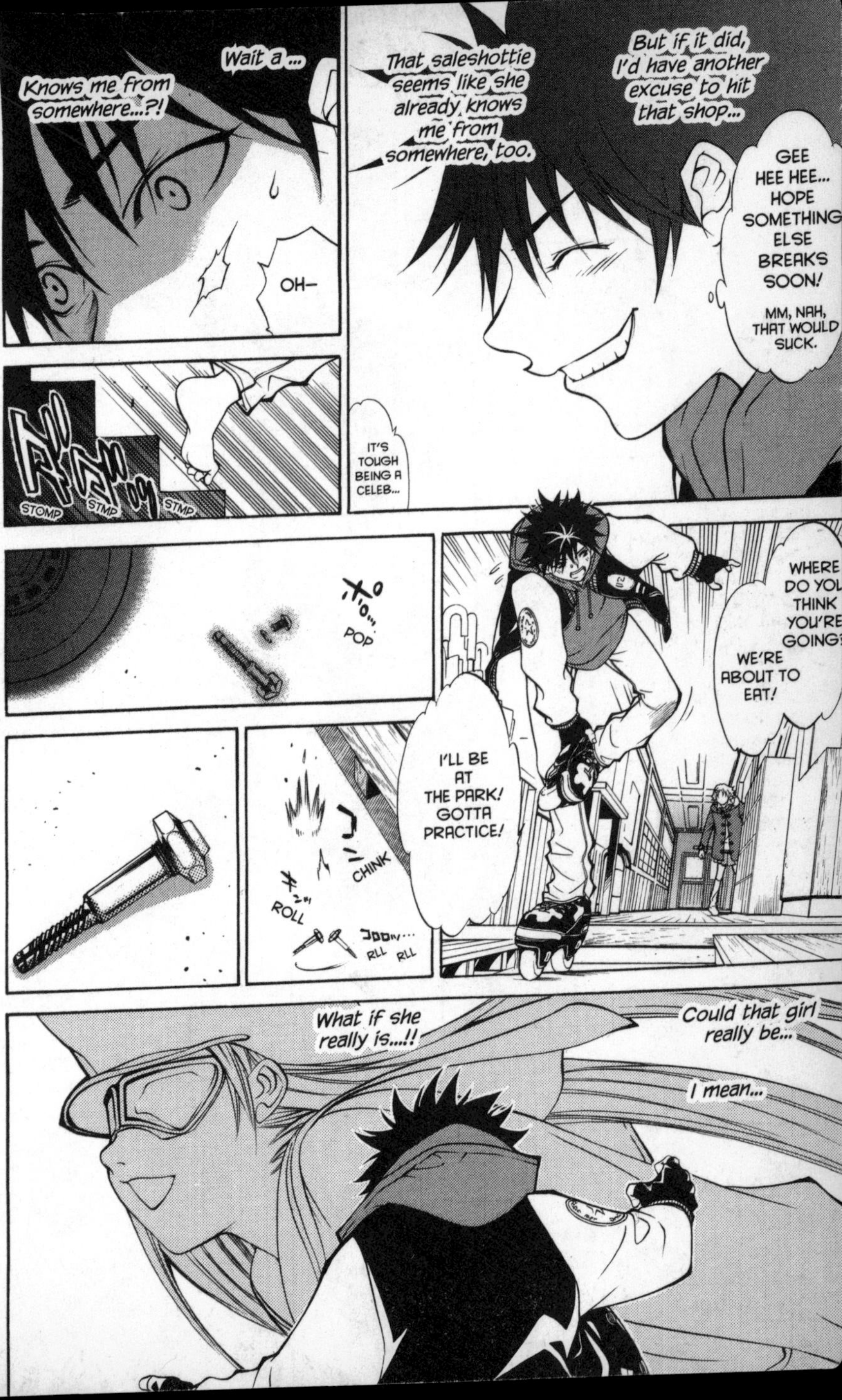
GEE HEE HEE... HOPE SOMETHING ELSE BREAKS SOON!
MM, NAH, THAT WOULD SUCK.
But if it did, I'd have another excuse to hit that shop...
That saleshottie seems like she already knows me from somewhere, too.
IT'S TOUGH BEING A CELEB...
Wait a ...
Knows me from somewhere...?!
OH–
STOMP STMP STMP
WHERE DO YOU THINK YOU'RE GOING? WE'RE ABOUT TO EAT!
I'LL BE AT THE PARK! GOTTA PRACTICE!
POP
CHINK
ROLL
RLL RLL
Could that girl really be...
I mean...
What if she really is...!!

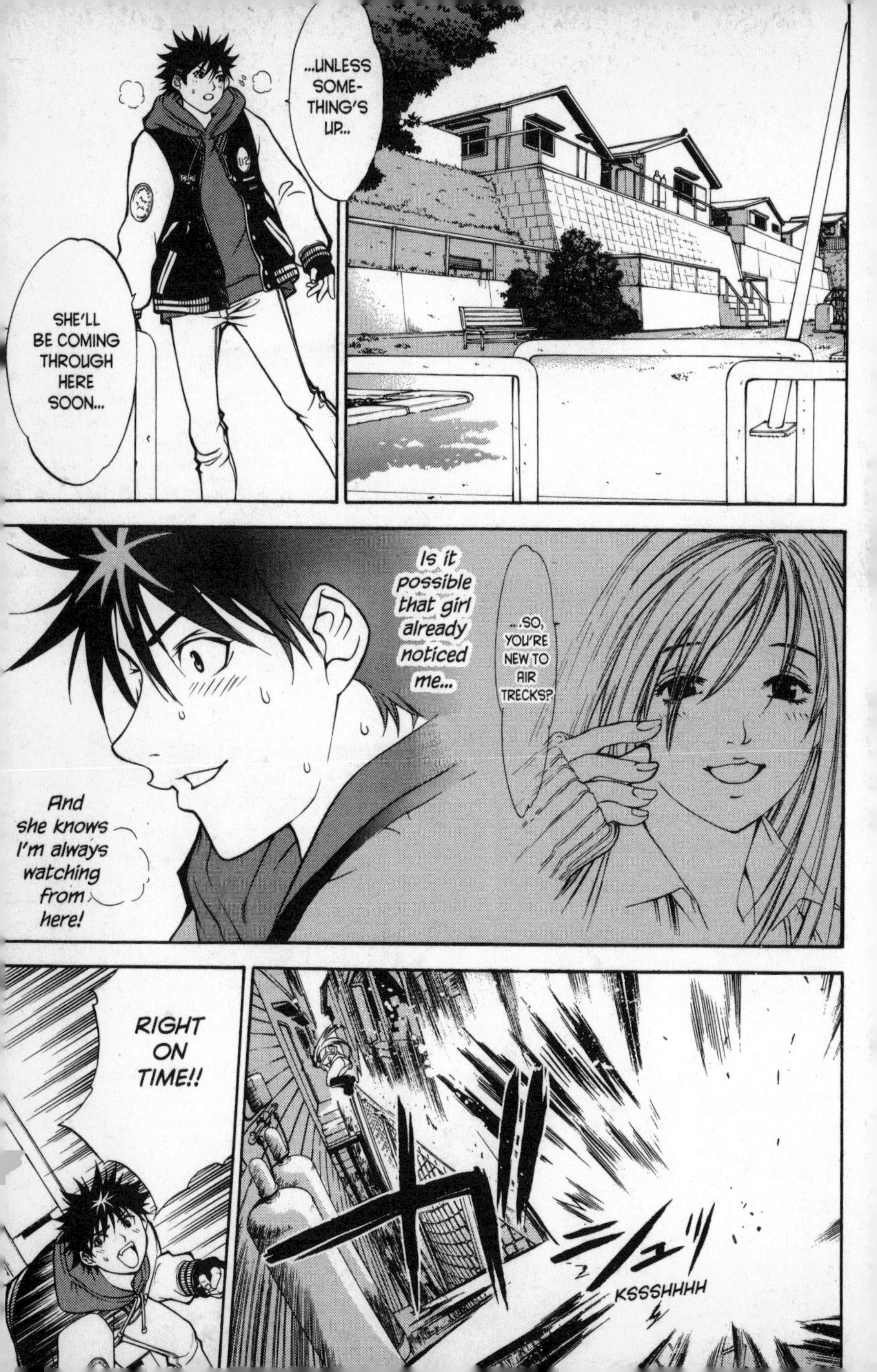
...UNLESS SOME-THING'S UP...
SHE'LL BE COMING THROUGH HERE SOON...
...SO, YOU'RE NEW TO AIR TRECKS?
Is it possible that girl already noticed me...
And she knows I'm always watching from here!
KSSSHHHH
RIGHT ON TIME!!

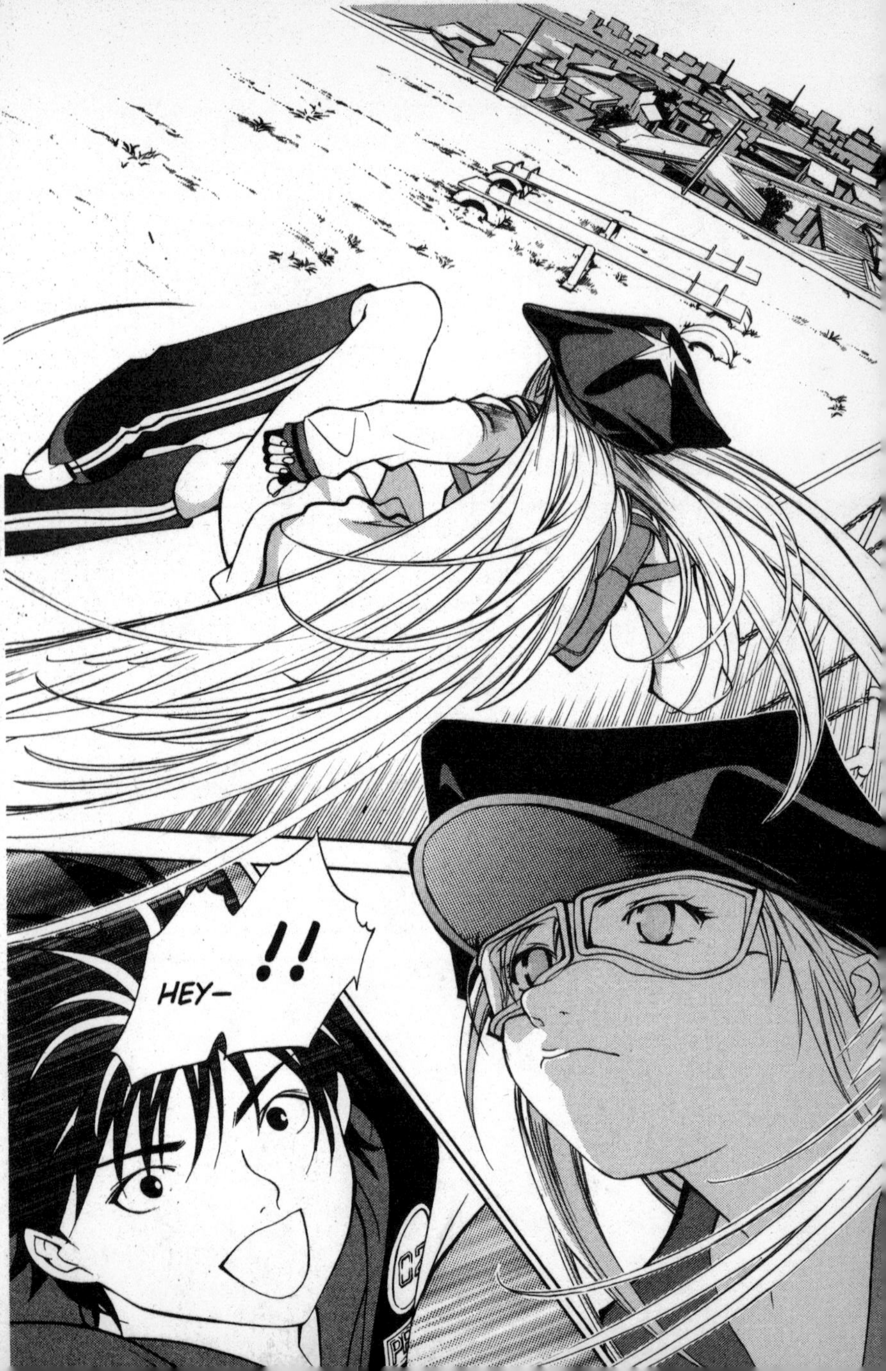
HEY- !!

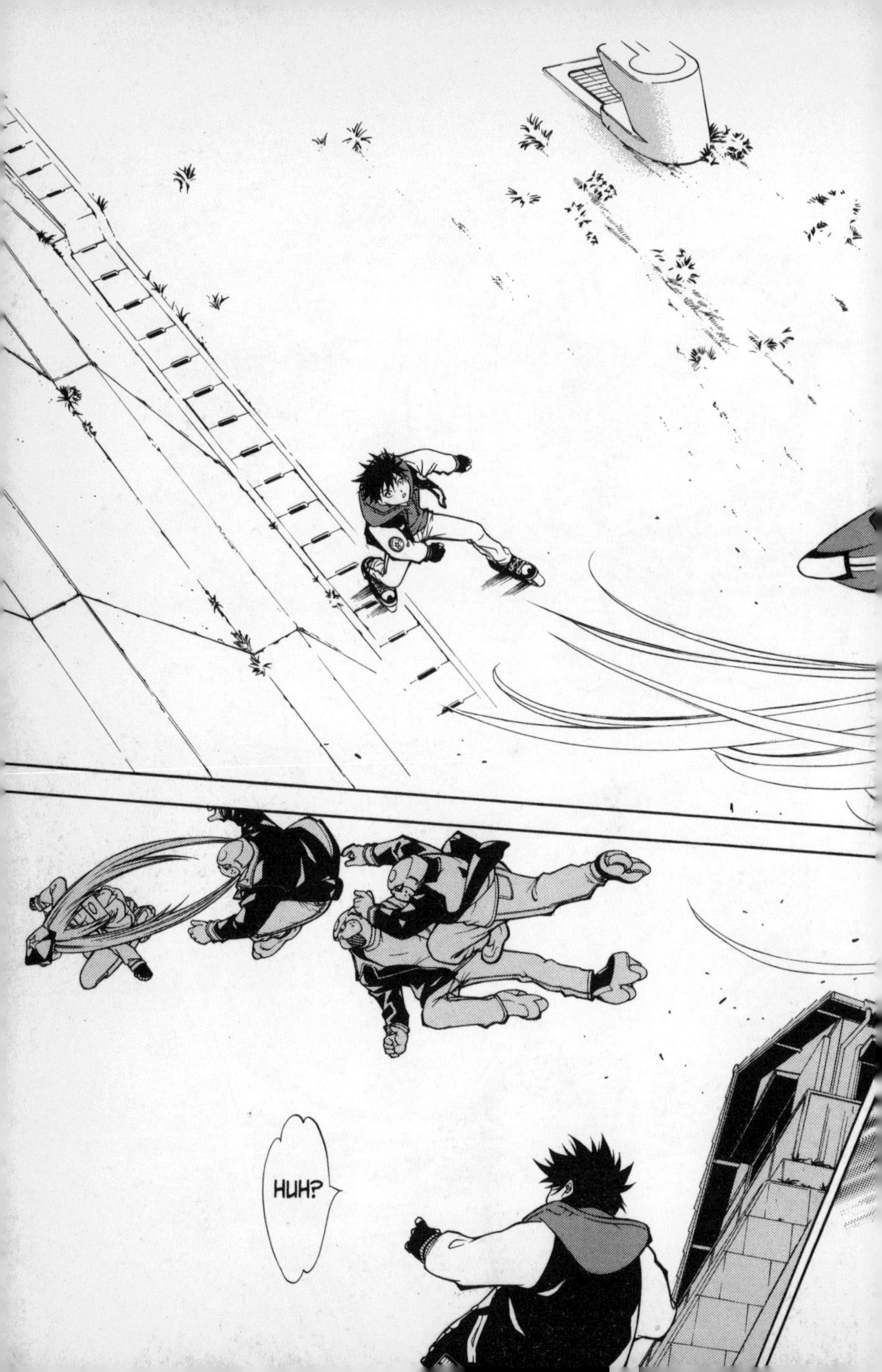
HUH?

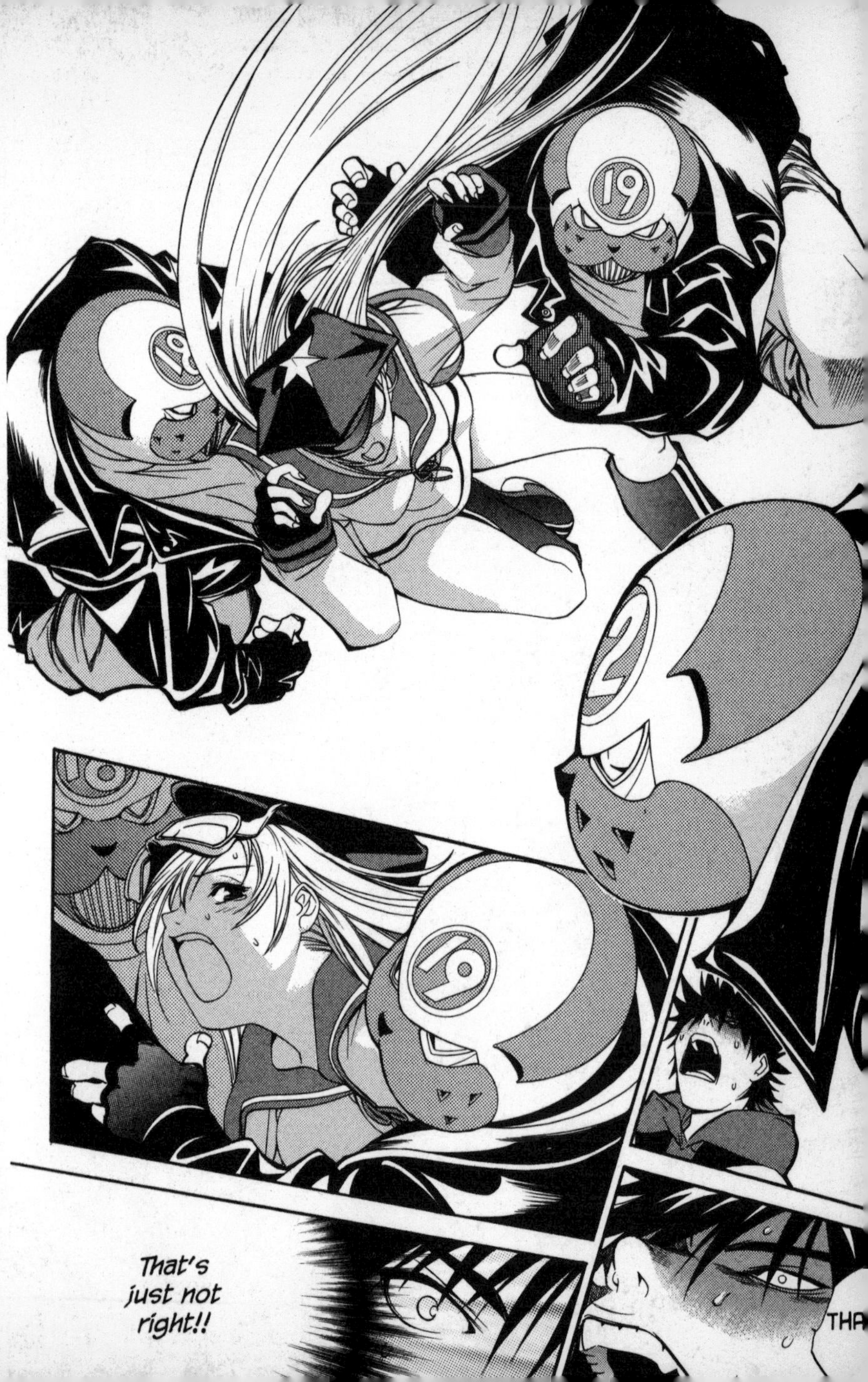
THA
That's just not right!!

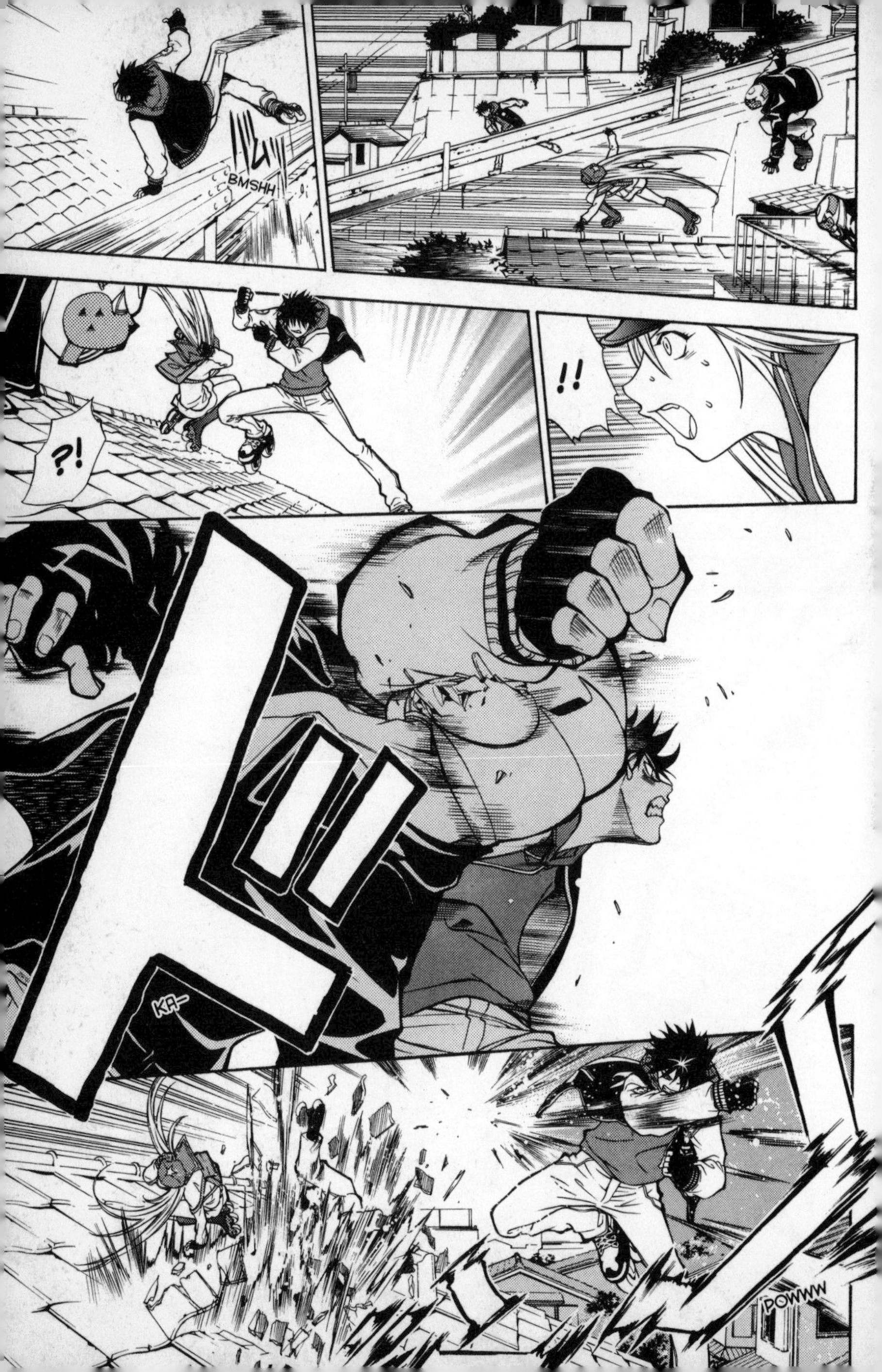
BMSHH
!!
?!
KA-
POWWW

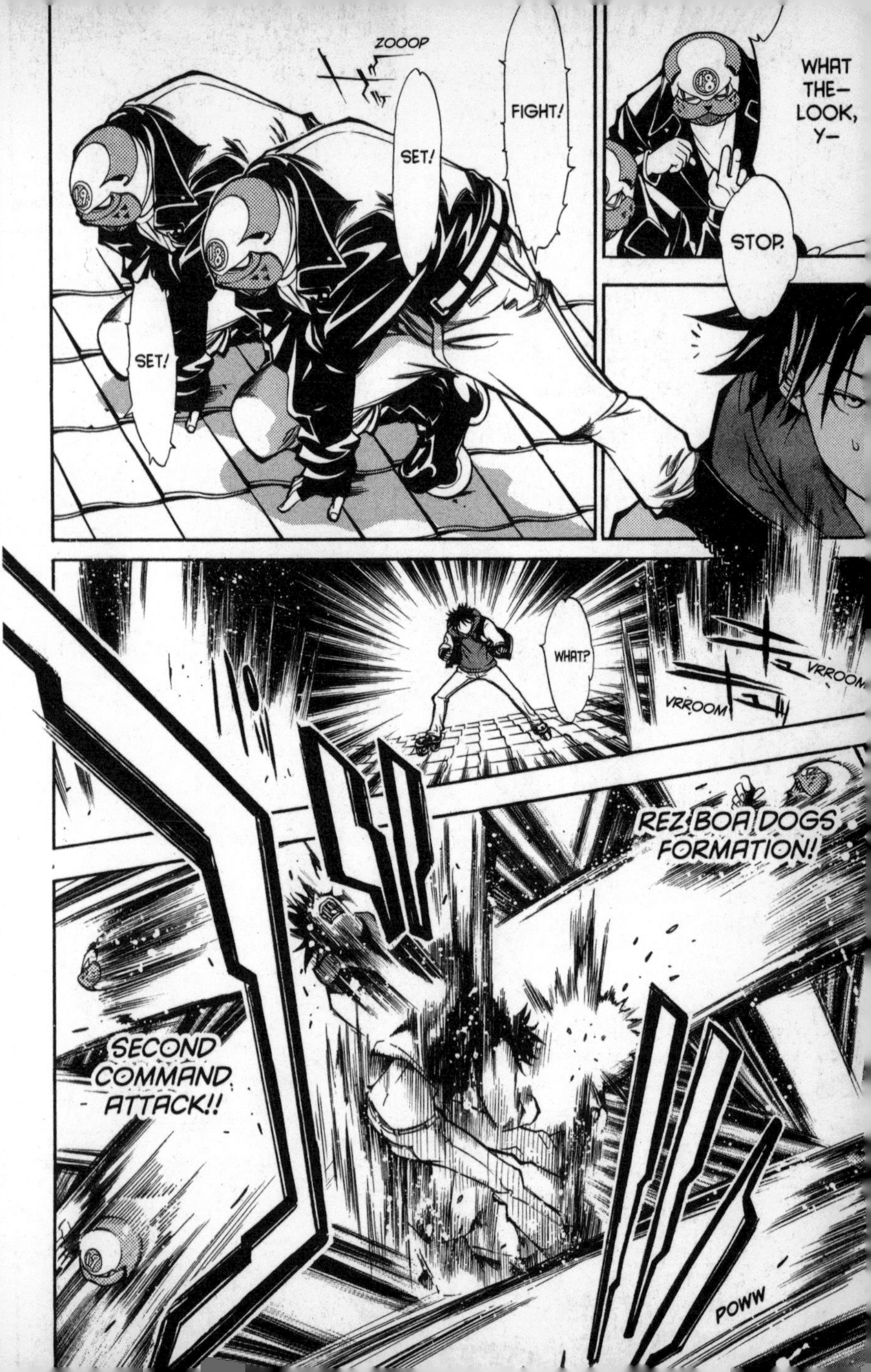
WHAT THE— LOOK, Y—
STOP.
FIGHT!
ZOOOP
SET!
SET!
VRROOM
VRROOM
WHAT?
REZ BOA DOGS FORMATION!
SECOND COMMAND ATTACK!!
POWW

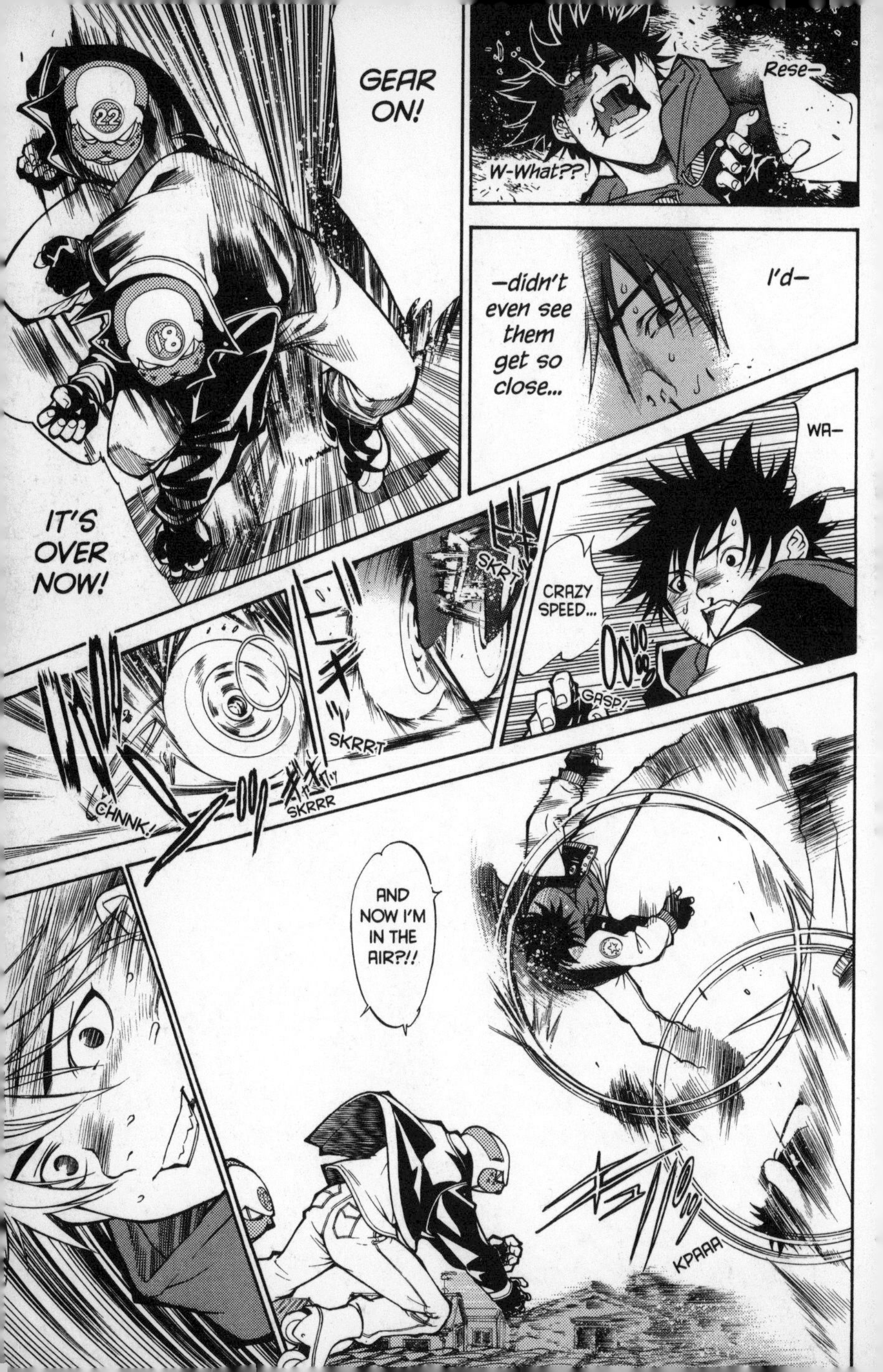
Rese—
W-What??
I'd—
—didn't even see them get so close...
GEAR ON!
IT'S OVER NOW!
WA—
CRAZY SPEED...
GASP!
SKRT
SKRRT
SKRRR
CHNNK!
KPAAA
AND NOW I'M IN THE AIR?!!

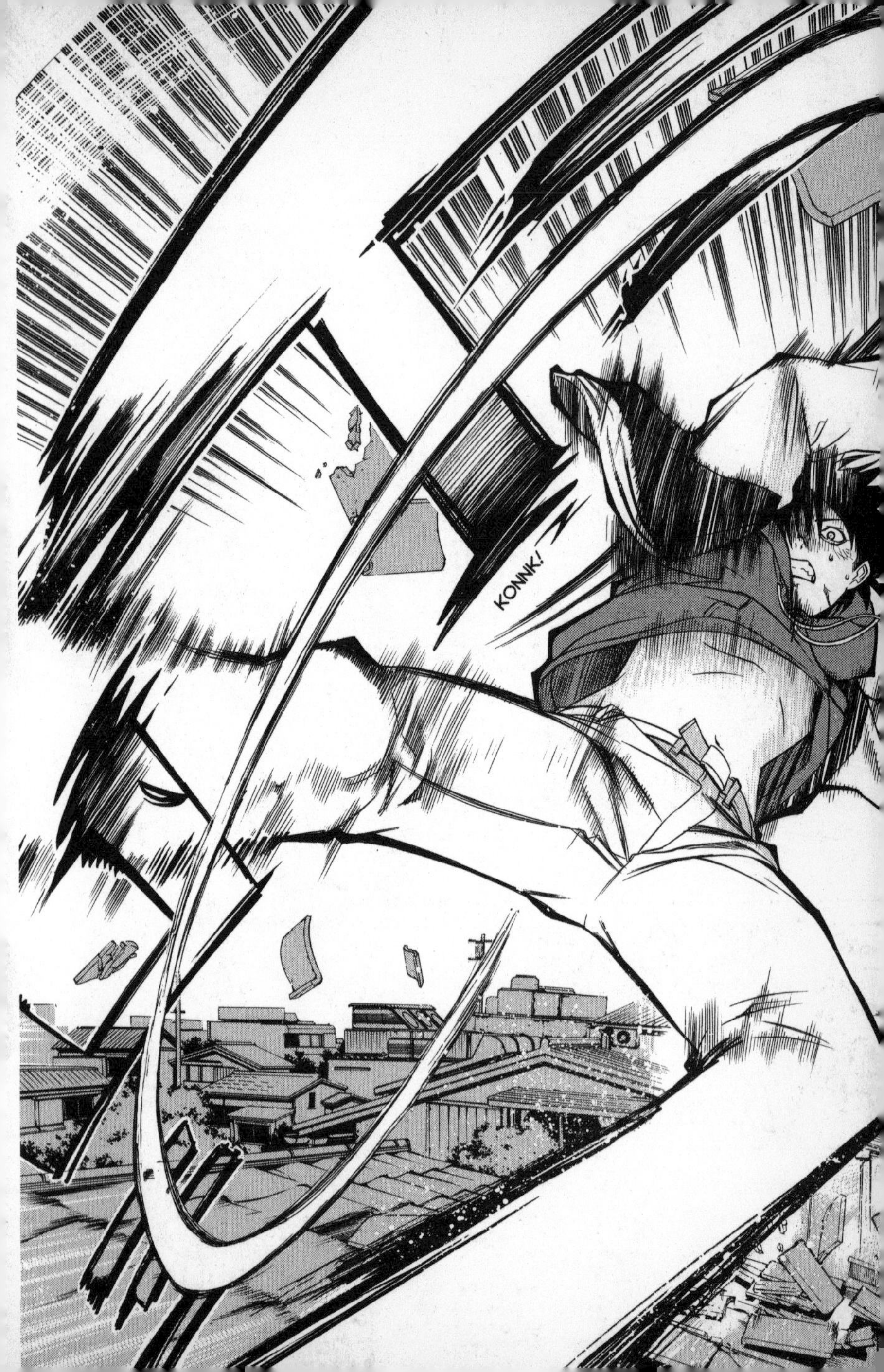
KONNK!

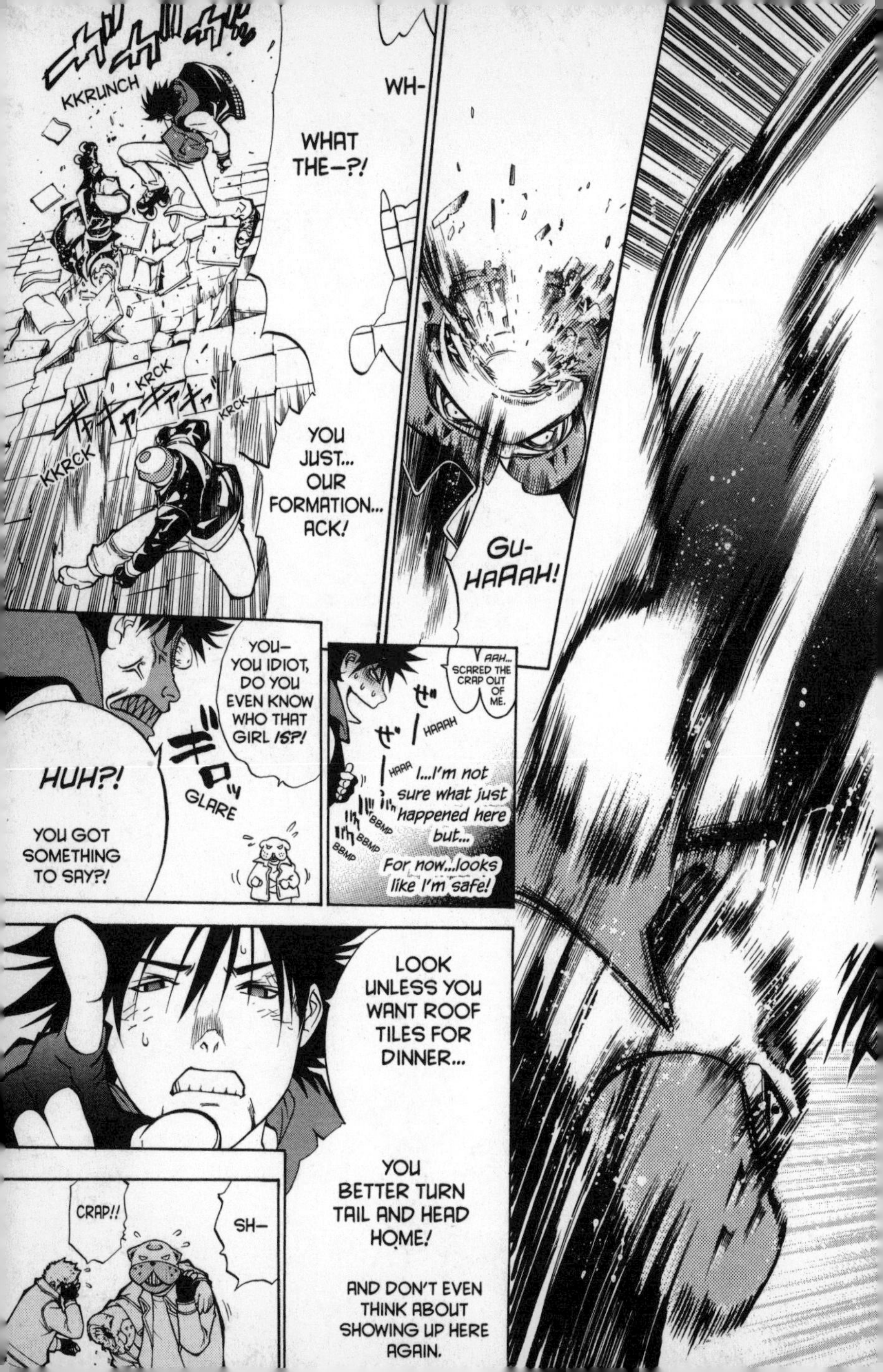

WH-
WHAT THE–?!
GU-HAAAH!
KKRUNCH
KRCK
KRCK
KKRCK
YOU JUST... OUR FORMATION... ACK!
AAH... SCARED THE CRAP OUT OF ME.
HAAAH
HAAA
BBMP
BBMP
BBMP
I...I'm not sure what just happened here but...
For now...looks like I'm safe!
YOU— YOU IDIOT, DO YOU EVEN KNOW WHO THAT GIRL IS?!
GLARE
HUH?!
YOU GOT SOMETHING TO SAY?!
LOOK UNLESS YOU WANT ROOF TILES FOR DINNER...
YOU BETTER TURN TAIL AND HEAD HOME!
AND DON'T EVEN THINK ABOUT SHOWING UP HERE AGAIN.
SH–
CRAP!!

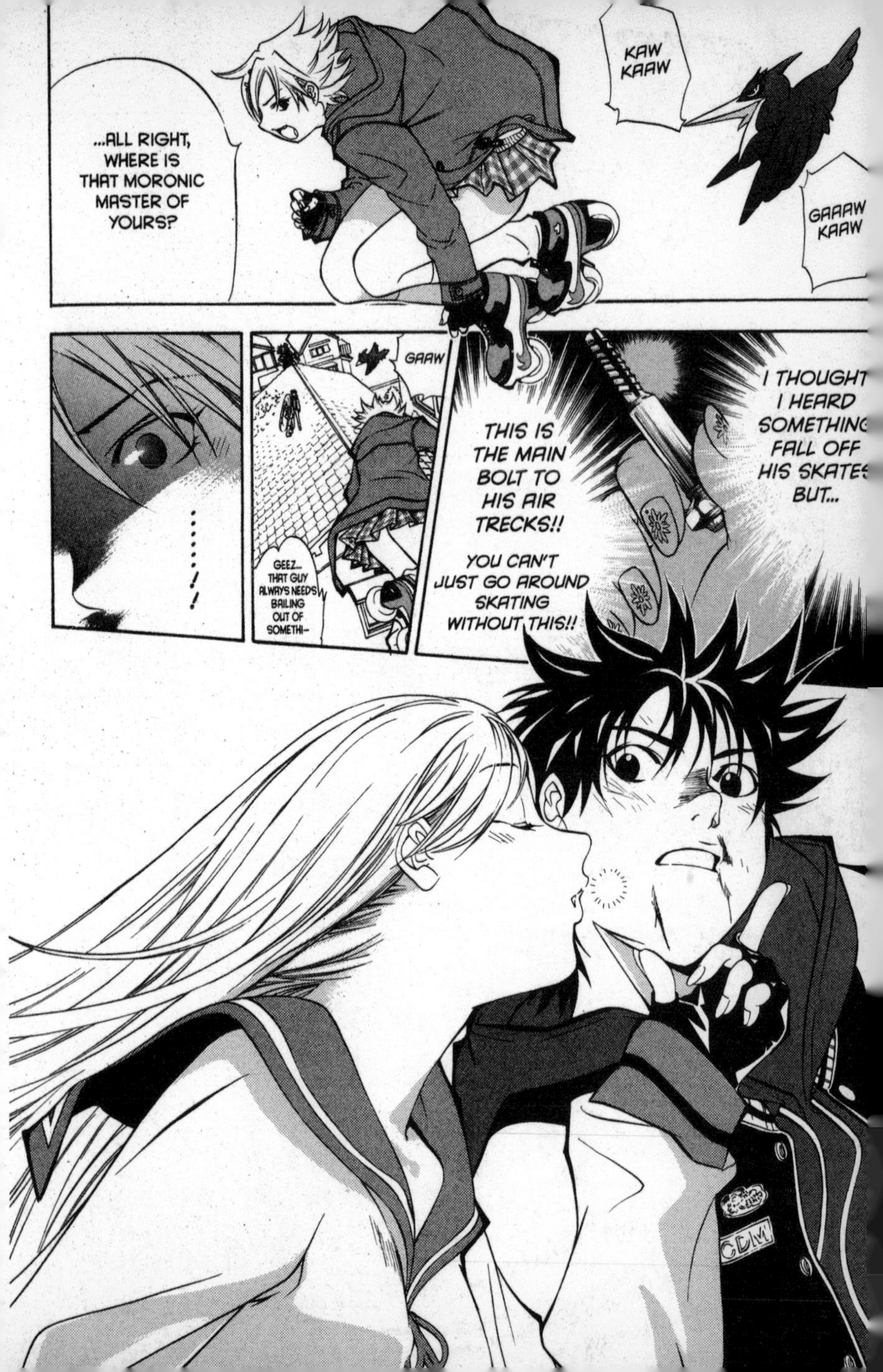
KAW KAAW
GAAAW KAAW
...ALL RIGHT, WHERE IS THAT MORONIC MASTER OF YOURS?
I THOUGHT I HEARD SOMETHING FALL OFF HIS SKATES BUT...
THIS IS THE MAIN BOLT TO HIS AIR TRECKS!!
YOU CAN'T JUST GO AROUND SKATING WITHOUT THIS!!
GAAW
GEEZ... THAT GUY ALWAYS NEEDS BAILING OUT OF SOMETHI–
......!!
CDM

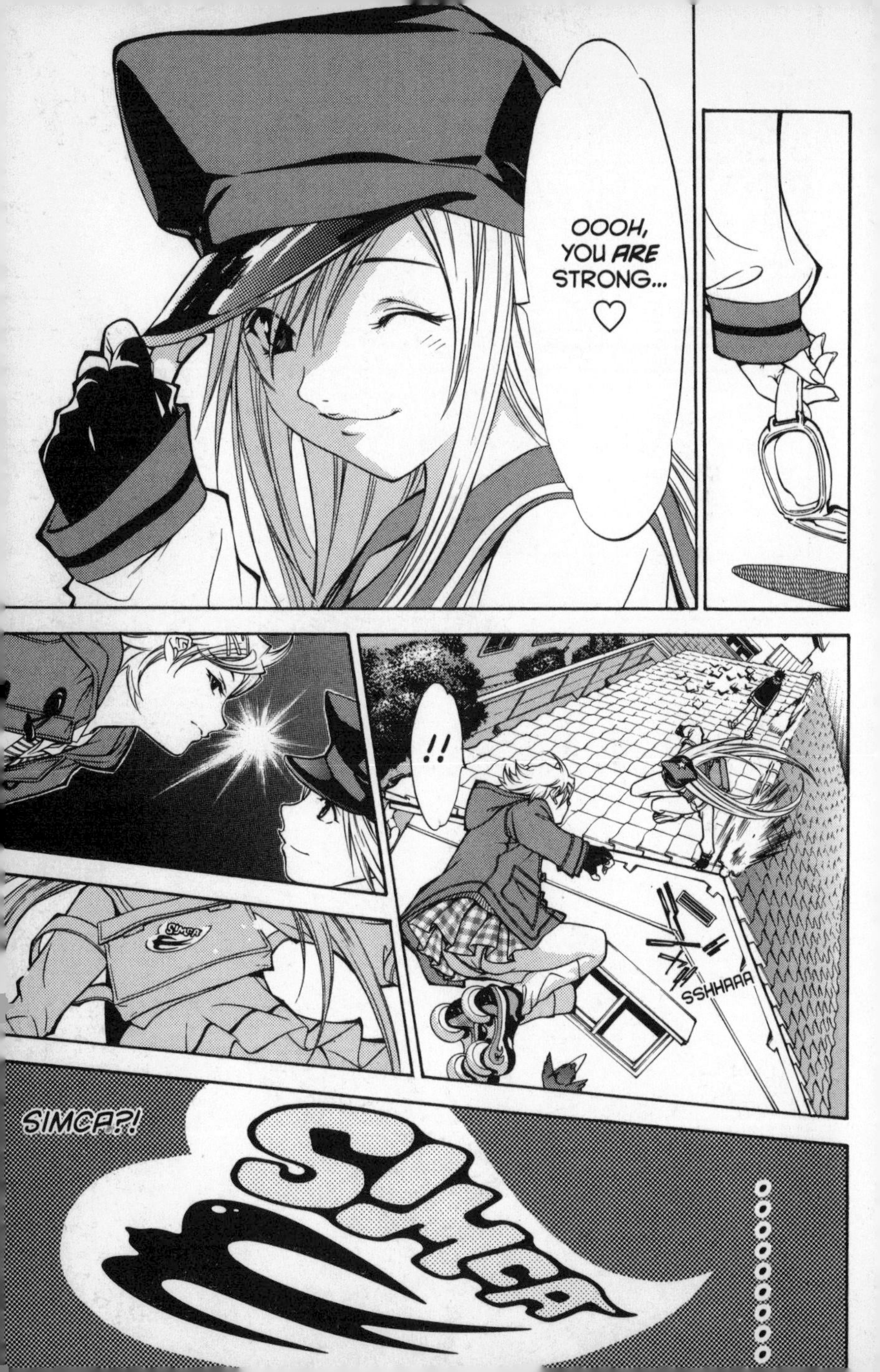

OOOH, YOU ARE STRONG... ♡
!!
SSHHAAA
SIMCA?!
SIMCA
OOOOOOOOOO

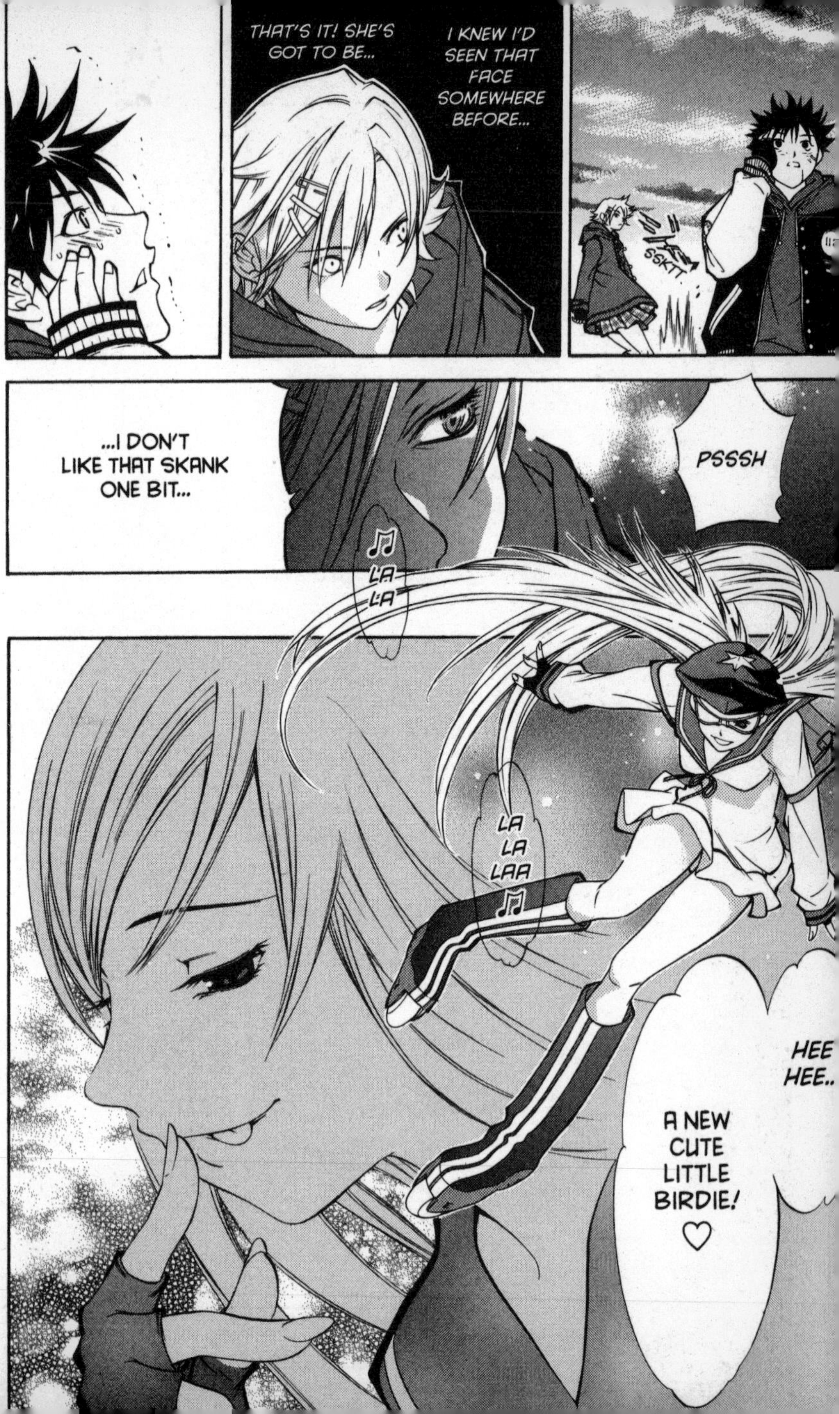
SSKIT
I KNEW I'D SEEN THAT FACE SOMEWHERE BEFORE...
THAT'S IT! SHE'S GOT TO BE...
PSSSH
...I DON'T LIKE THAT SKANK ONE BIT...
HEE HEE..
A NEW CUTE LITTLE BIRDIE! ♡
LA LA LAA ♫
♫ LA LA

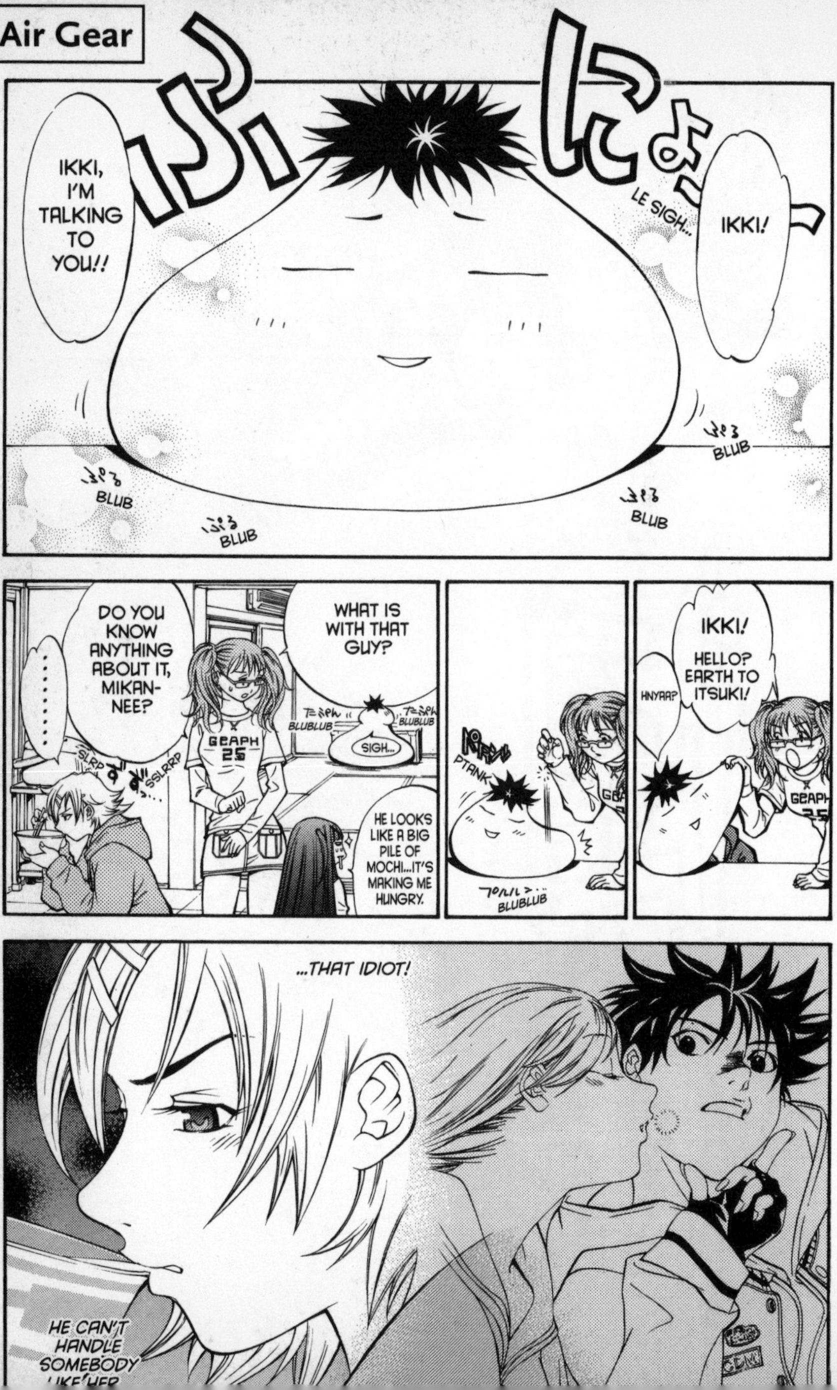
IKKI!
LE SIGH...
IKKI, I'M TALKING TO YOU!!
BLUB
BLUB
BLUB
BLUB
IKKI!
HELLO? EARTH TO ITSUKI!
HNYAA?
PTANK
BLUBLUB
WHAT IS WITH THAT GUY?
DO YOU KNOW ANYTHING ABOUT IT, MIKAN-NEE?
......
SIGH...
BLUBLUB
BLUBLUB
SLRP
SSLRRP
HE LOOKS LIKE A BIG PILE OF MOCHI...IT'S MAKING ME HUNGRY.
...THAT IDIOT!
HE CAN'T HANDLE SOMEBODY

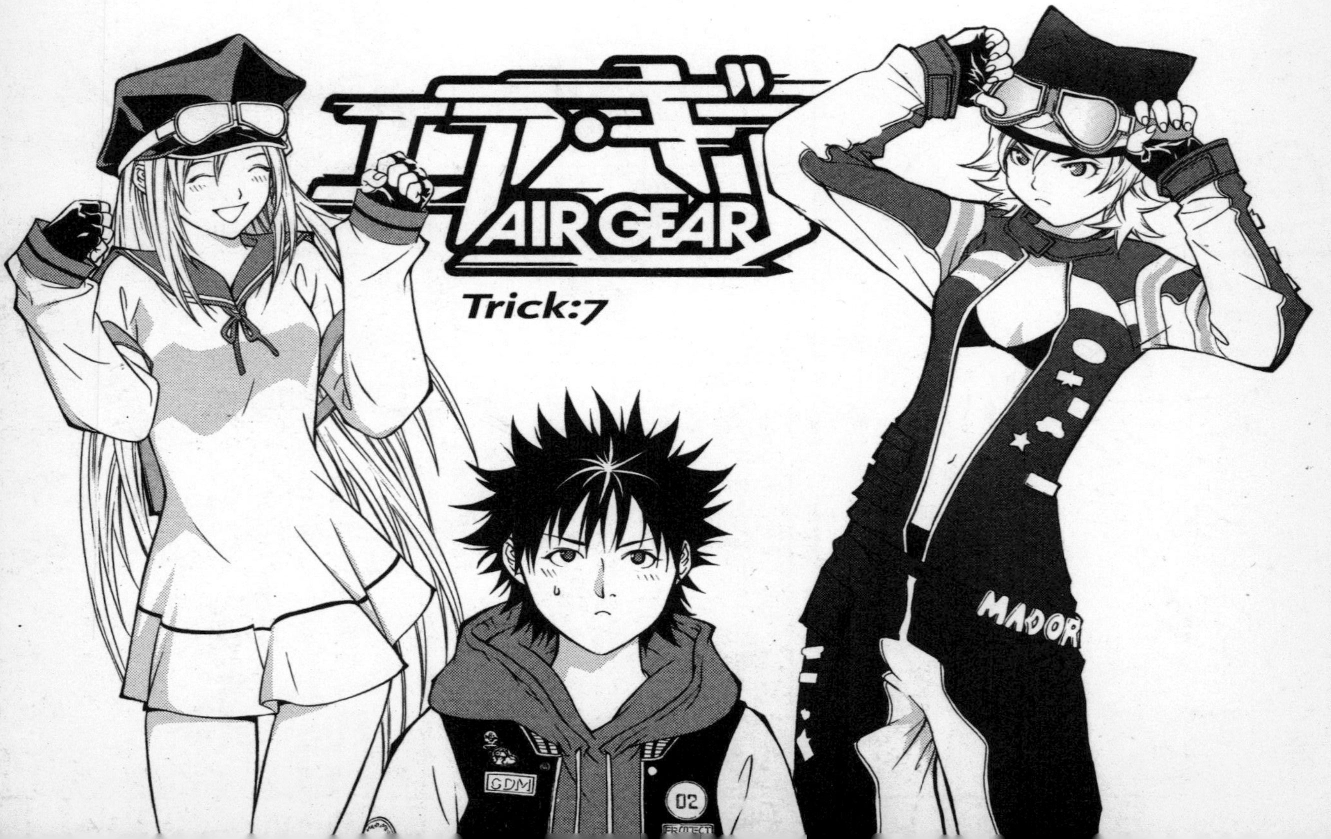
AIR GEAR
Trick:7
MADOR
GDM
02

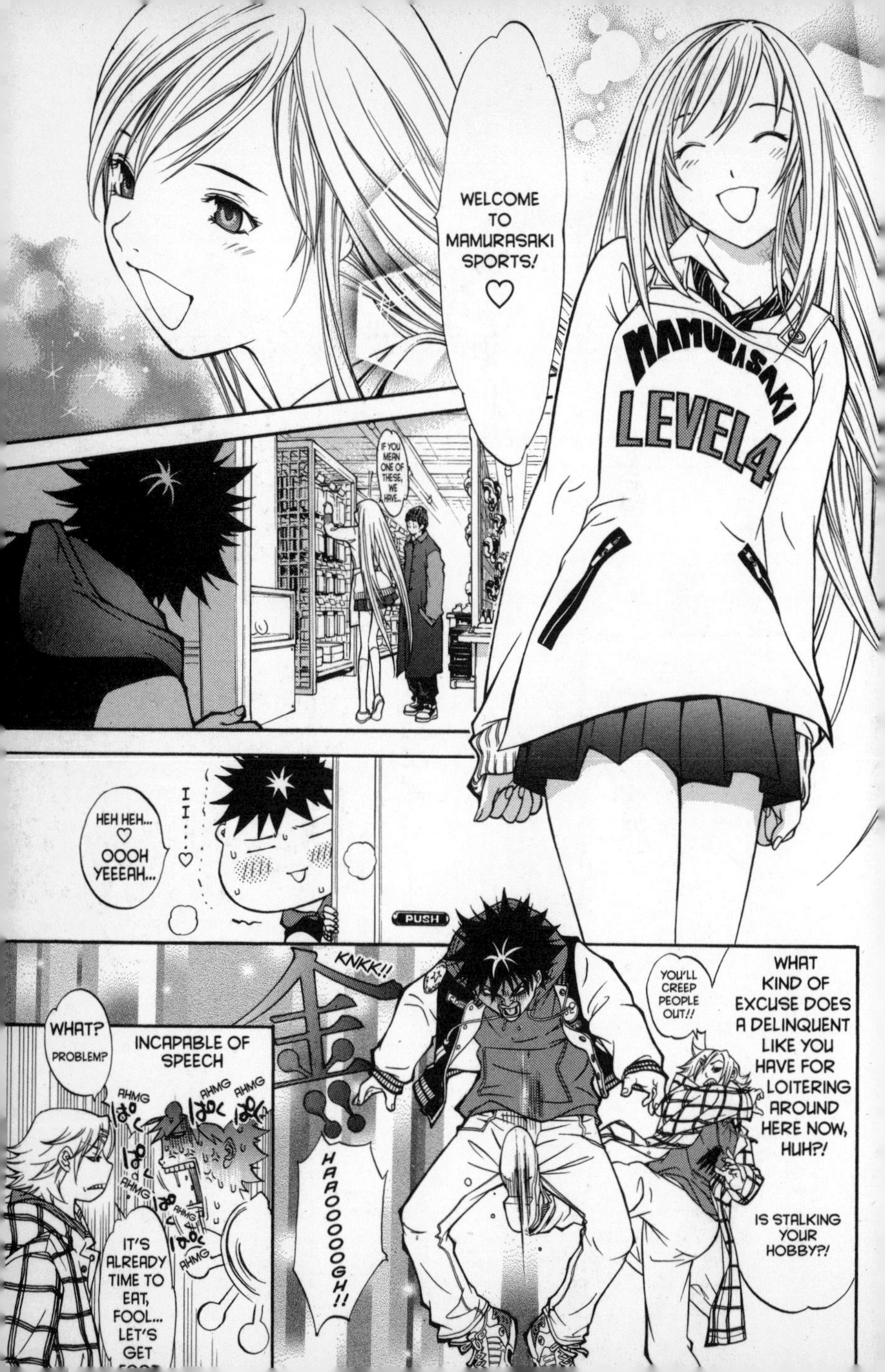
WELCOME TO MAMURASAKI SPORTS! ♡
MAMURASAKI LEVEL4
IF YOU MEAN ONE OF THESE, WE HAVE...
I I... ♡
HEH HEH... ♡ OOOH YEEEAH...
PUSH
WHAT KIND OF EXCUSE DOES A DELINQUENT LIKE YOU HAVE FOR LOITERING AROUND HERE NOW, HUH?!
YOU'LL CREEP PEOPLE OUT!!
KNKK!!
IS STALKING YOUR HOBBY?!
HAROOOOOGH!!
INCAPABLE OF SPEECH
WHAT? PROBLEM?
AHMG AHMG AHMG AHMG AHMG AHMG
IT'S ALREADY TIME TO EAT, FOOL... LET'S GET

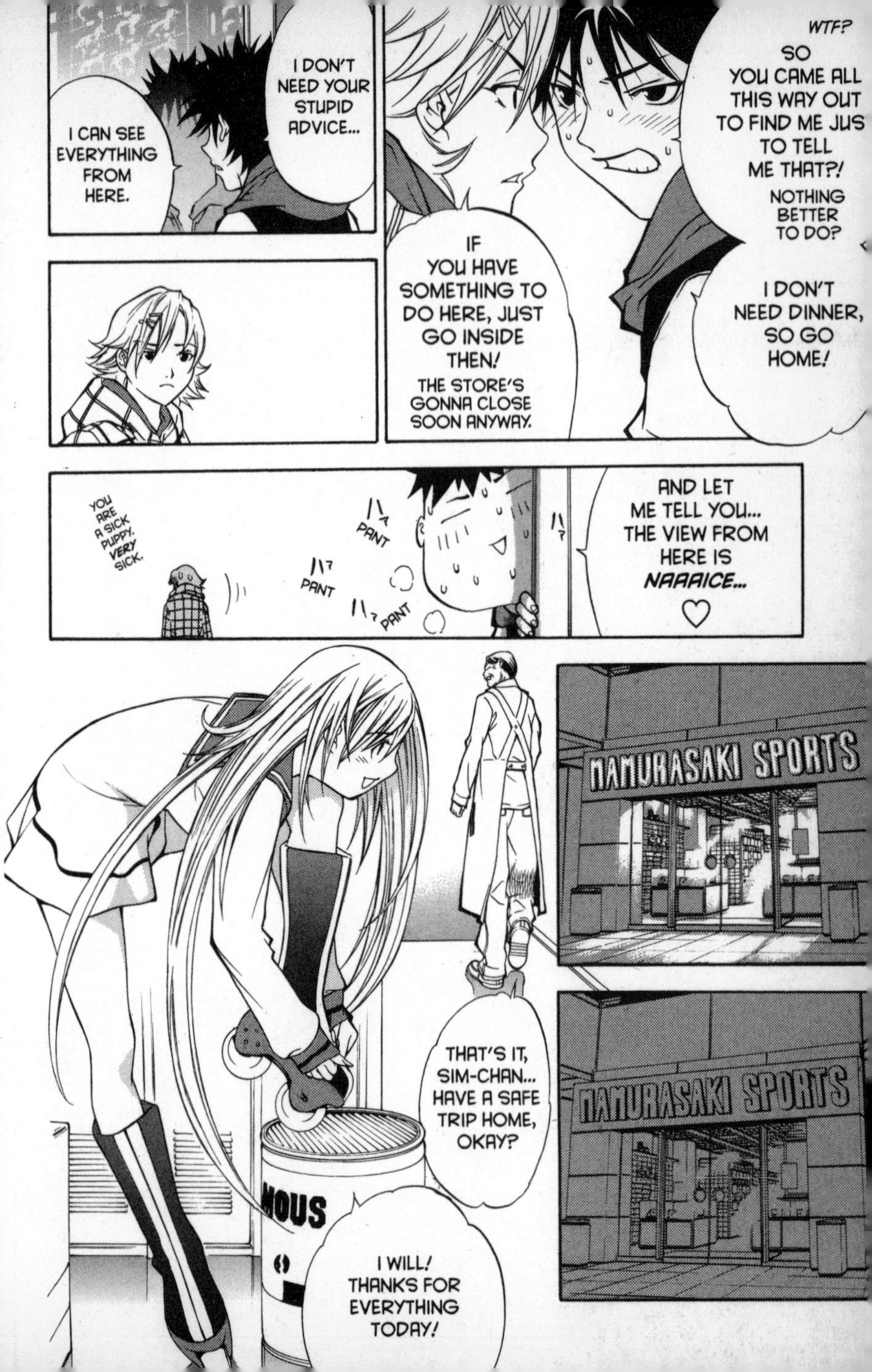
WTF?
SO YOU CAME ALL THIS WAY OUT TO FIND ME JUS TO TELL ME THAT?!
NOTHING BETTER TO DO?
I DON'T NEED DINNER, SO GO HOME!
IF YOU HAVE SOMETHING TO DO HERE, JUST GO INSIDE THEN!
THE STORE'S GONNA CLOSE SOON ANYWAY.
I DON'T NEED YOUR STUPID ADVICE...
I CAN SEE EVERYTHING FROM HERE.
AND LET ME TELL YOU... THE VIEW FROM HERE IS NAAAICE... ♡
ハァ
ハァ PANT
ハァ PANT
ハァ PANT
YOU ARE A SICK PUPPY. VERY SICK.
NAMURASAKI SPORTS
NAMURASAKI SPORTS
THAT'S IT, SIM-CHAN... HAVE A SAFE TRIP HOME, OKAY?
MOUS
I WILL! THANKS FOR EVERYTHING TODAY!

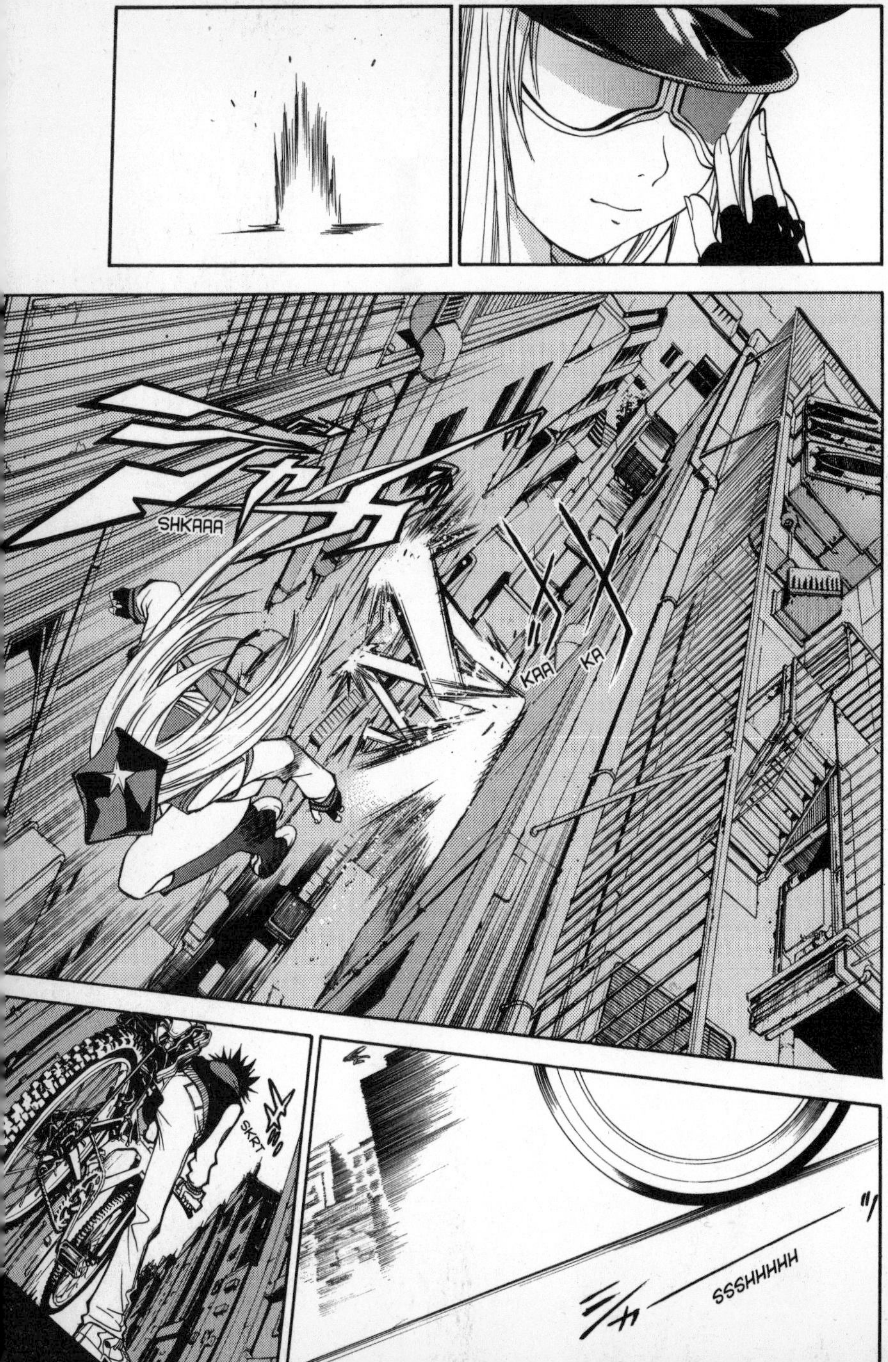
SHKAAA
KAA
KA
SSSHHHHH
SKRT

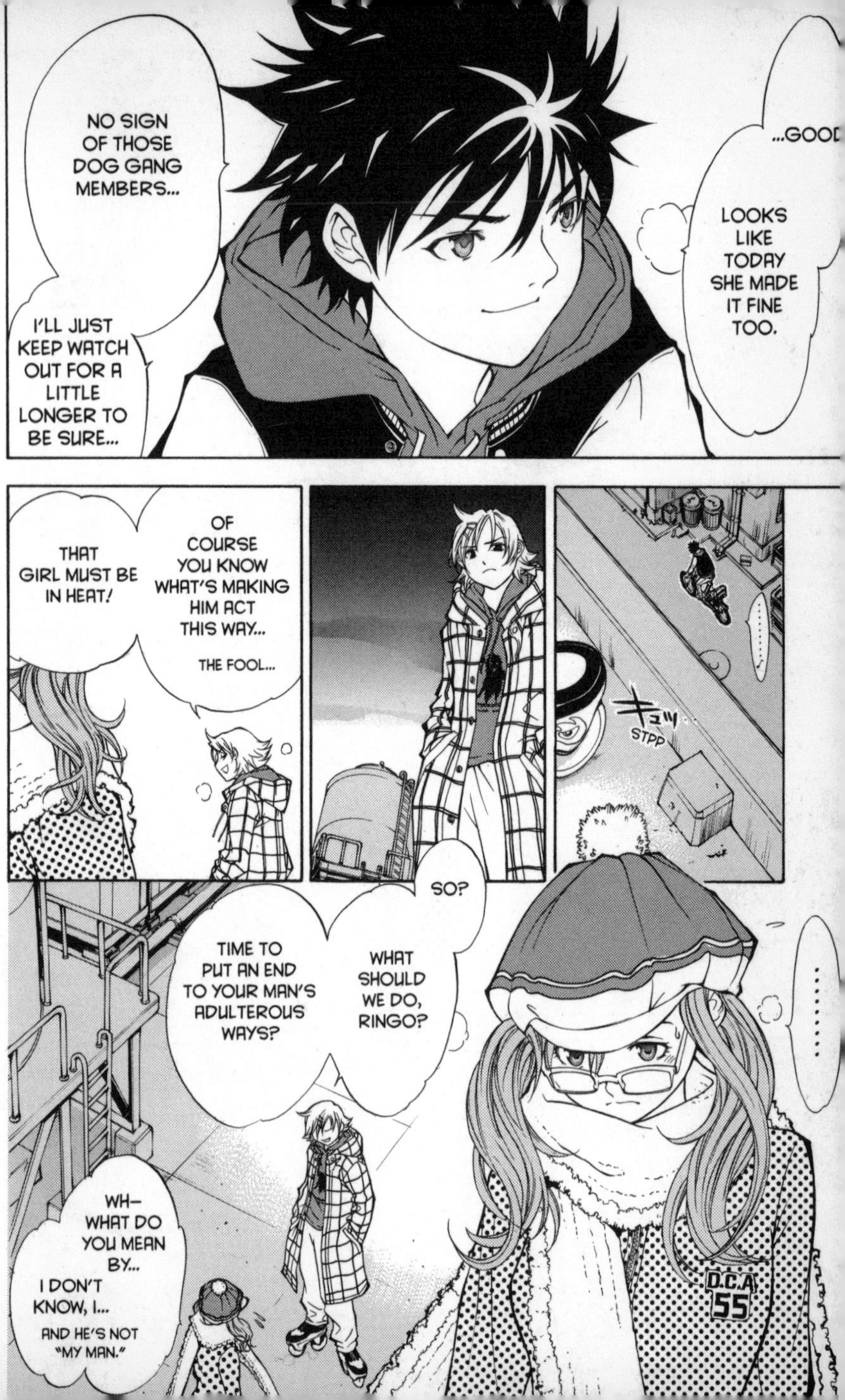
...GOOD
LOOKS LIKE TODAY SHE MADE IT FINE TOO.
NO SIGN OF THOSE DOG GANG MEMBERS...
I'LL JUST KEEP WATCH OUT FOR A LITTLE LONGER TO BE SURE...
...
STPP
OF COURSE YOU KNOW WHAT'S MAKING HIM ACT THIS WAY...
THE FOOL...
THAT GIRL MUST BE IN HEAT!
......
SO?
WHAT SHOULD WE DO, RINGO?
TIME TO PUT AN END TO YOUR MAN'S ADULTEROUS WAYS?
D.C.A 55
WH— WHAT DO YOU MEAN BY...
I DON'T KNOW, I...
AND HE'S NOT "MY MAN."

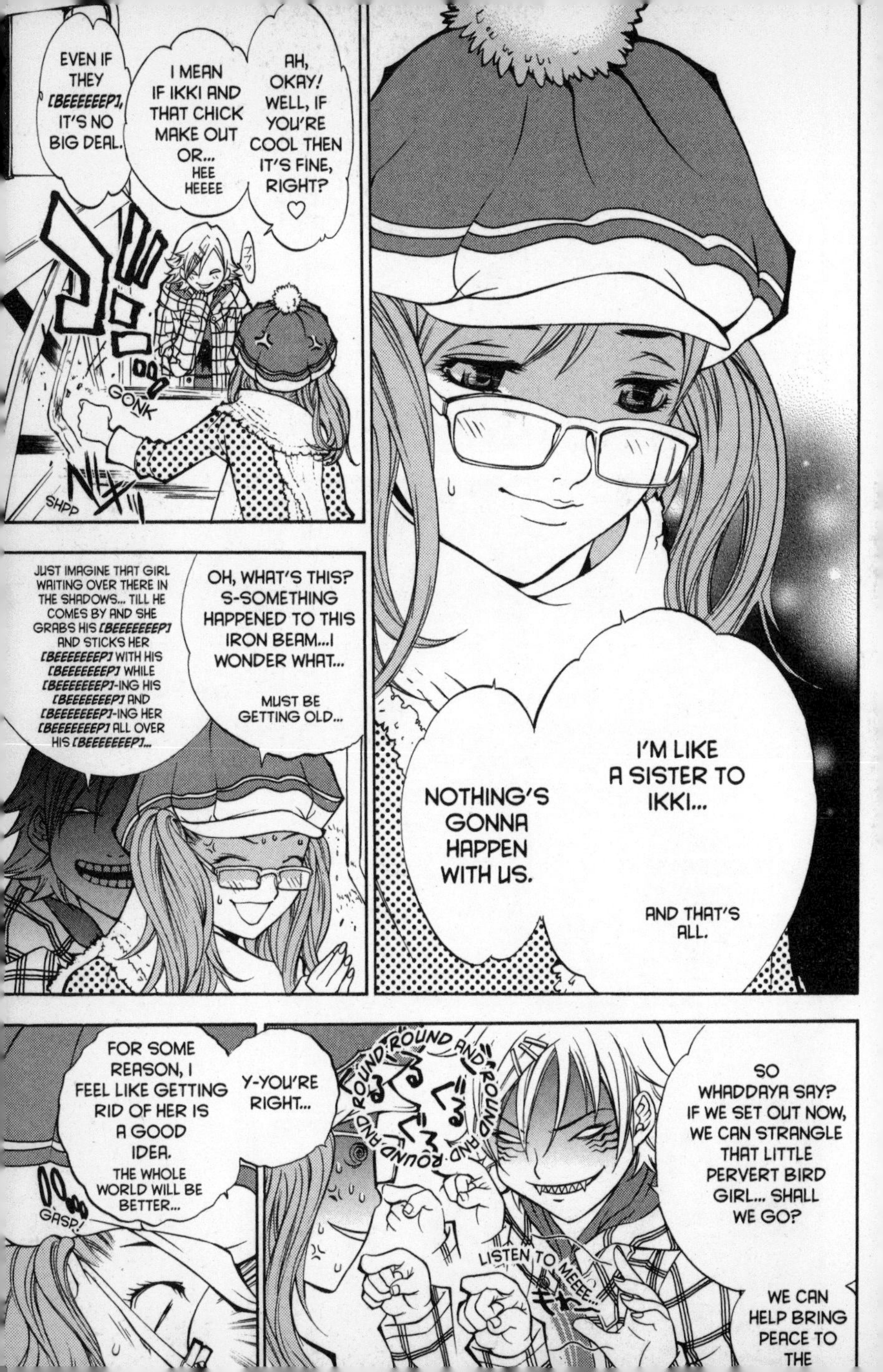
I'M LIKE A SISTER TO IKKI...
NOTHING'S GONNA HAPPEN WITH US.
AND THAT'S ALL.
AH, OKAY! WELL, IF YOU'RE COOL THEN IT'S FINE, RIGHT? ♡
I MEAN IF IKKI AND THAT CHICK MAKE OUT OR... HEE HEEEE
EVEN IF THEY [BEEEEEEP], IT'S NO BIG DEAL.
GONK
SHPP
OH, WHAT'S THIS? S-SOMETHING HAPPENED TO THIS IRON BEAM...I WONDER WHAT...
MUST BE GETTING OLD...
JUST IMAGINE THAT GIRL WAITING OVER THERE IN THE SHADOWS... TILL HE COMES BY AND SHE GRABS HIS [BEEEEEEEP] AND STICKS HER [BEEEEEEEP] WITH HIS [BEEEEEEEP] WHILE [BEEEEEEEP]-ING HIS [BEEEEEEEP] AND [BEEEEEEEP]-ING HER [BEEEEEEEP] ALL OVER HIS [BEEEEEEEP]...
SO WHADDAYA SAY? IF WE SET OUT NOW, WE CAN STRANGLE THAT LITTLE PERVERT BIRD GIRL... SHALL WE GO?
WE CAN HELP BRING PEACE TO THE
LISTEN TO MEEEE...!
ROUND AND ROUND AND ROUND AND ROUND
Y-YOU'RE RIGHT...
FOR SOME REASON, I FEEL LIKE GETTING RID OF HER IS A GOOD IDEA.
THE WHOLE WORLD WILL BE BETTER...
GASP!

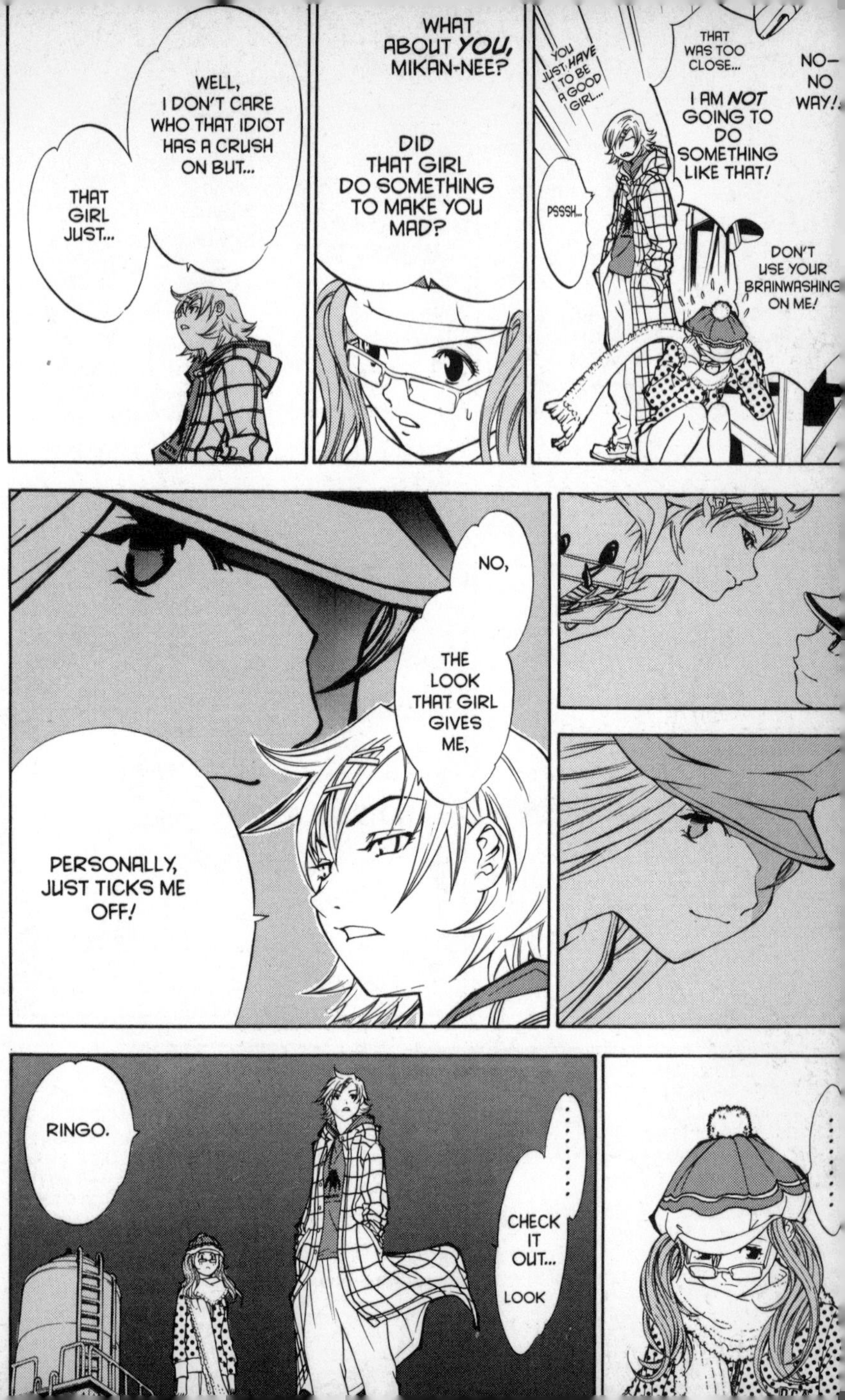
NO— NO WAY!
THAT WAS TOO CLOSE...
I AM *NOT* GOING TO DO SOMETHING LIKE THAT!
YOU JUST *HAVE* TO BE A GOOD GIRL...
DON'T USE YOUR BRAINWASHING ON ME!
PSSSH...
WHAT ABOUT *YOU*, MIKAN-NEE?
DID THAT GIRL DO SOMETHING TO MAKE YOU MAD?
WELL, I DON'T CARE WHO THAT IDIOT HAS A CRUSH ON BUT...
THAT GIRL JUST...
NO,
THE LOOK THAT GIRL GIVES ME,
PERSONALLY, JUST TICKS ME OFF!
......
CHECK IT OUT... LOOK
RINGO.

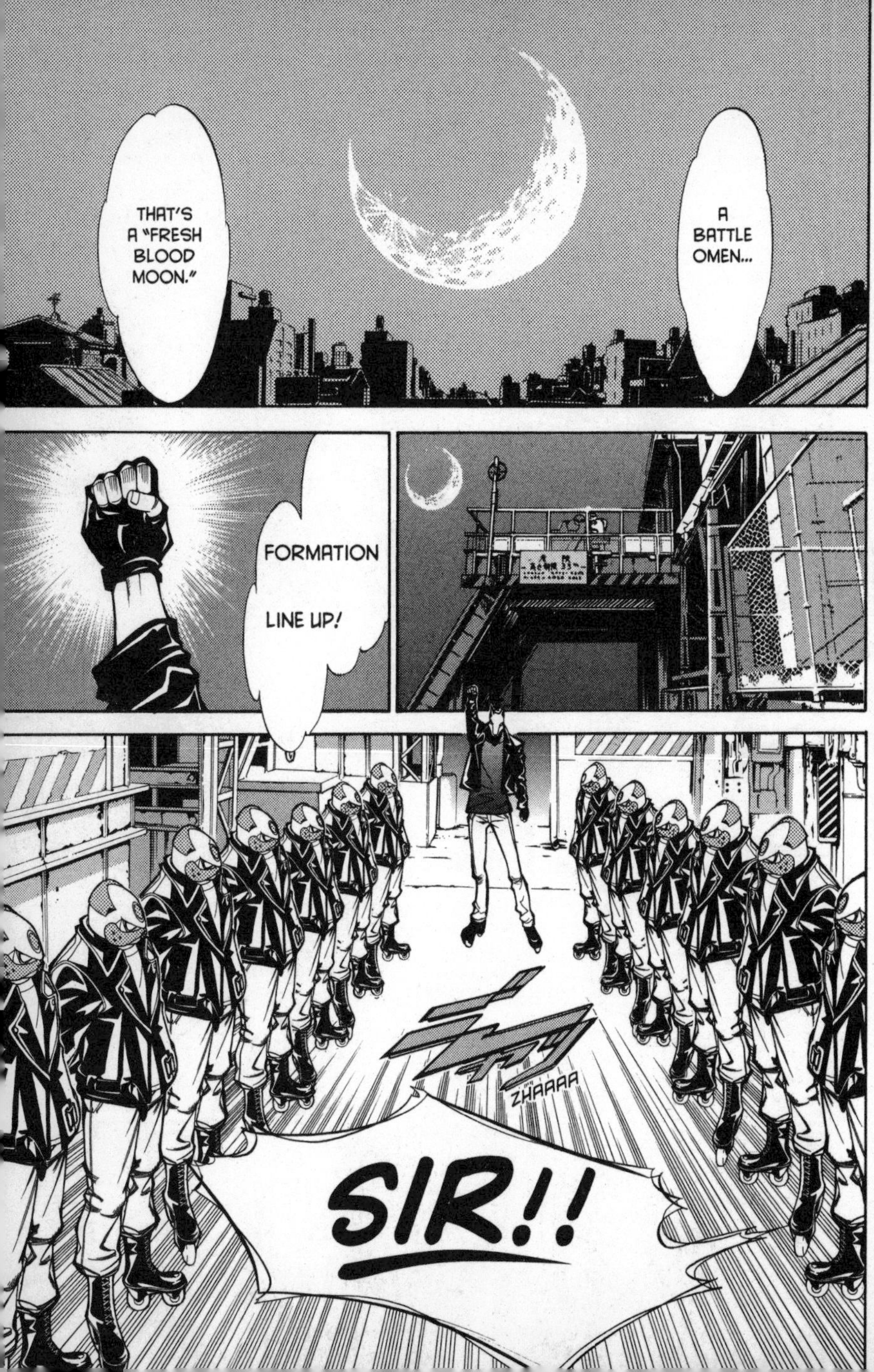
A BATTLE OMEN...
THAT'S A "FRESH BLOOD MOON."
FORMATION LINE UP!
ZHAAAA
SIR!!

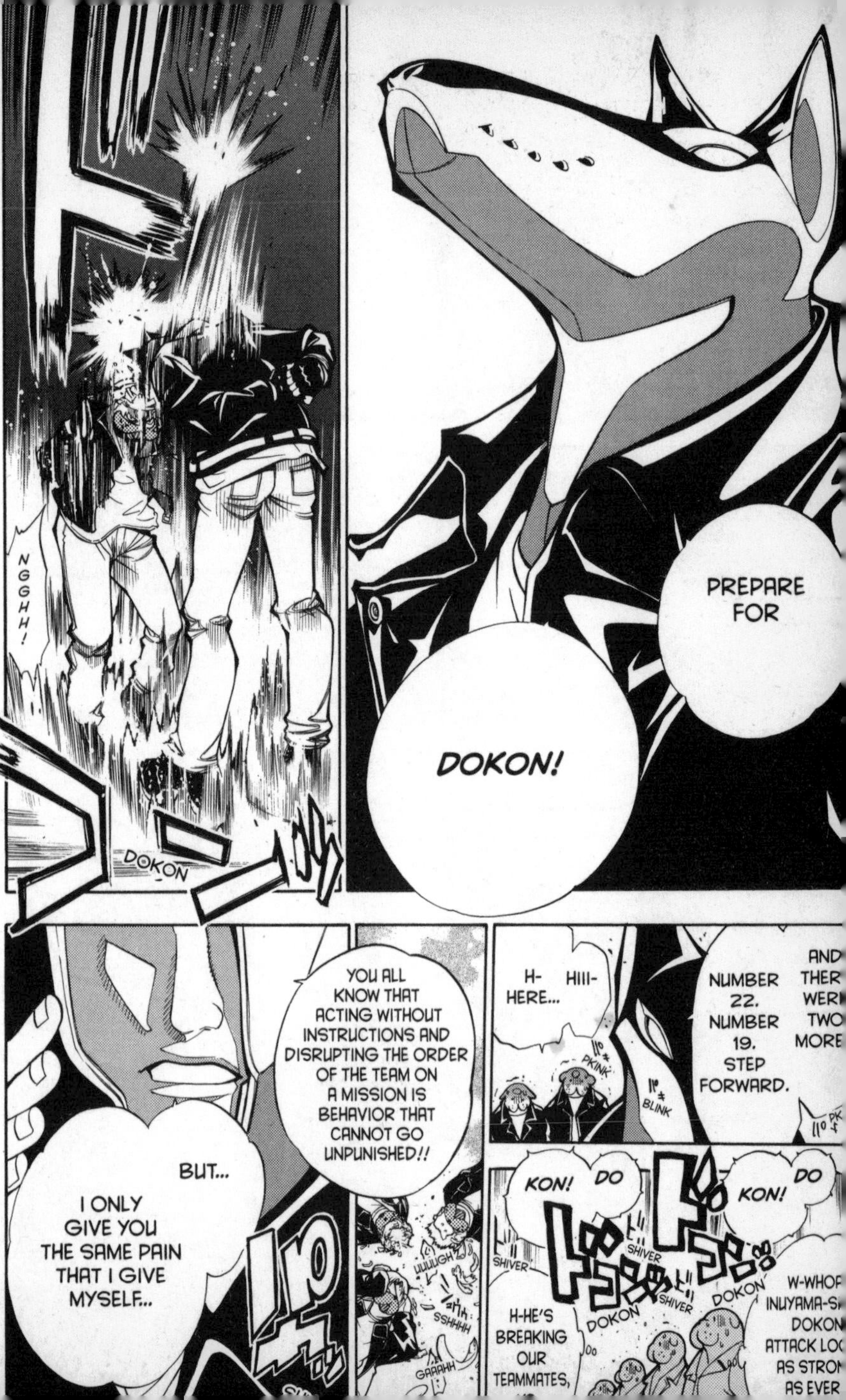
PREPARE FOR
DOKON!
NGGHH!
DOKON
AND THER WER TWO MORE
NUMBER 22. NUMBER 19. STEP FORWARD.
PK
H- HIII- HERE...
PKINK
BLINK
DO KON!
DO KON!
W-WHO INUYAMA-S DOKON ATTACK LO AS STRO AS EVER
DOKON
SHIVER
DOKON
SHIVER
SHIVER
H-HE'S BREAKING OUR TEAMMATES,
YOU ALL KNOW THAT ACTING WITHOUT INSTRUCTIONS AND DISRUPTING THE ORDER OF THE TEAM ON A MISSION IS BEHAVIOR THAT CANNOT GO UNPUNISHED!!
UUUUGH
SSHHHH
GAAAHH
BUT...
I ONLY GIVE YOU THE SAME PAIN THAT I GIVE MYSELF...

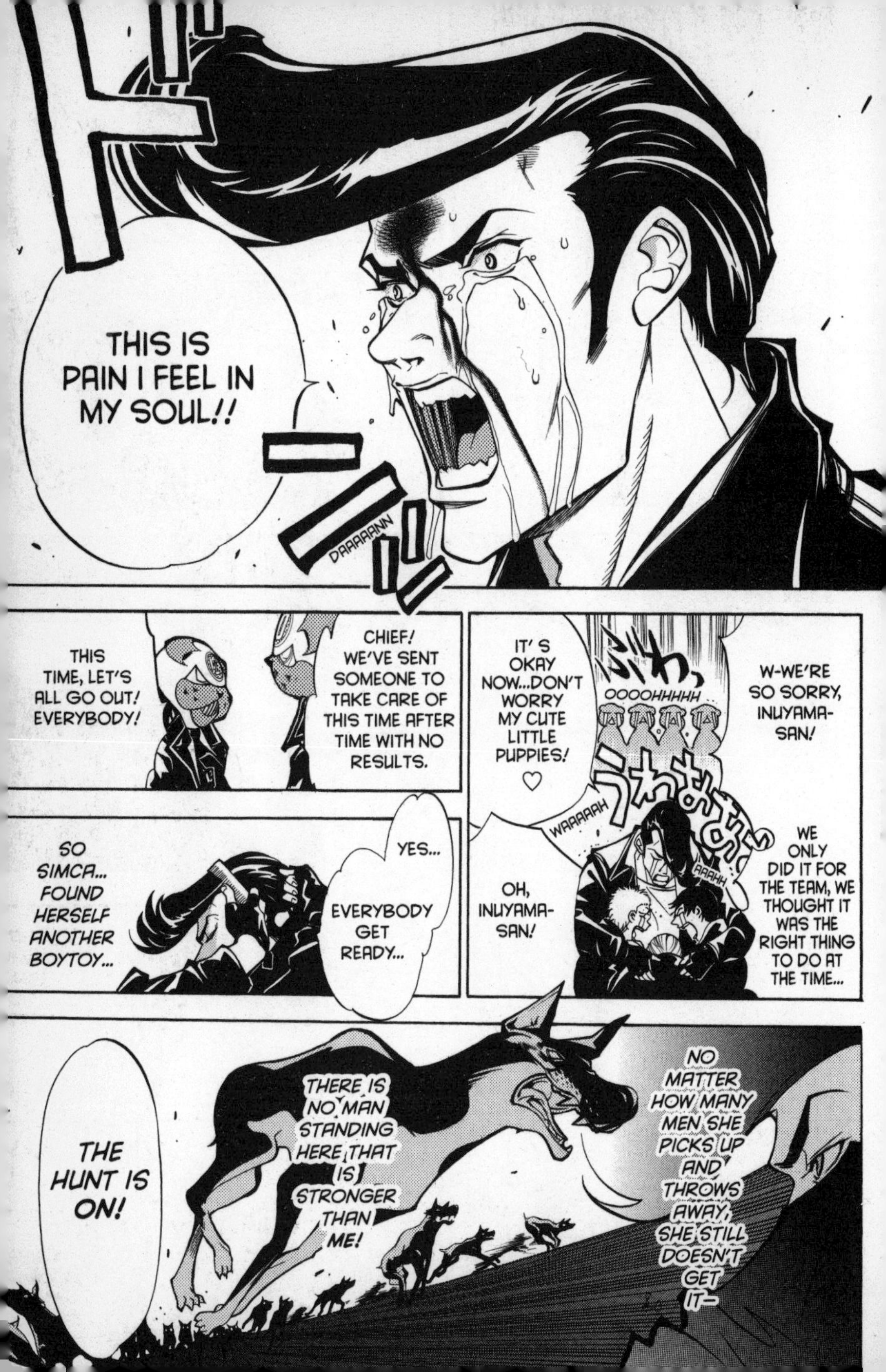
THIS IS PAIN I FEEL IN MY SOUL!!
DAAAAAANN
W-WE'RE SO SORRY, INUYAMA-SAN!
IT'S OKAY NOW...DON'T WORRY MY CUTE LITTLE PUPPIES! ♡
OOOOHHHHH...
WE ONLY DID IT FOR THE TEAM, WE THOUGHT IT WAS THE RIGHT THING TO DO AT THE TIME...
WAAAAAH
AAAHH
OH, INUYAMA-SAN!
CHIEF! WE'VE SENT SOMEONE TO TAKE CARE OF THIS TIME AFTER TIME WITH NO RESULTS.
THIS TIME, LET'S ALL GO OUT! EVERYBODY!
YES... EVERYBODY GET READY...
SO SIMCA... FOUND HERSELF ANOTHER BOYTOY...
NO MATTER HOW MANY MEN SHE PICKS UP AND THROWS AWAY, SHE STILL DOESN'T GET IT—
THERE IS NO MAN STANDING HERE THAT IS STRONGER THAN ME!
THE HUNT IS ON!

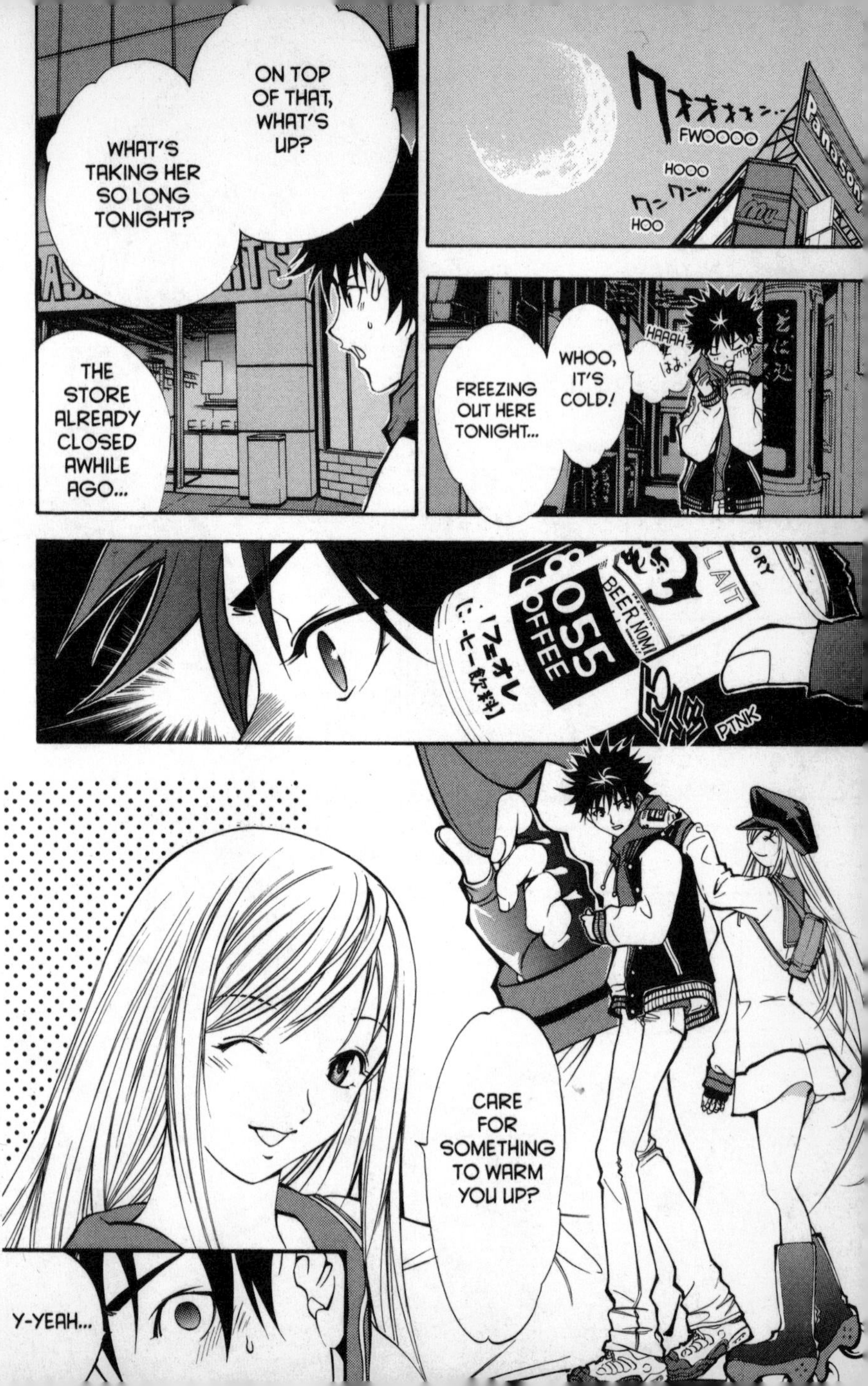
FWOOOO
HOOO
HOO
ON TOP OF THAT, WHAT'S UP?
WHAT'S TAKING HER SO LONG TONIGHT?
HAAAH
WHOO, IT'S COLD!
FREEZING OUT HERE TONIGHT...
THE STORE ALREADY CLOSED AWHILE AGO...
PTNK
CARE FOR SOMETHING TO WARM YOU UP?
Y-YEAH...

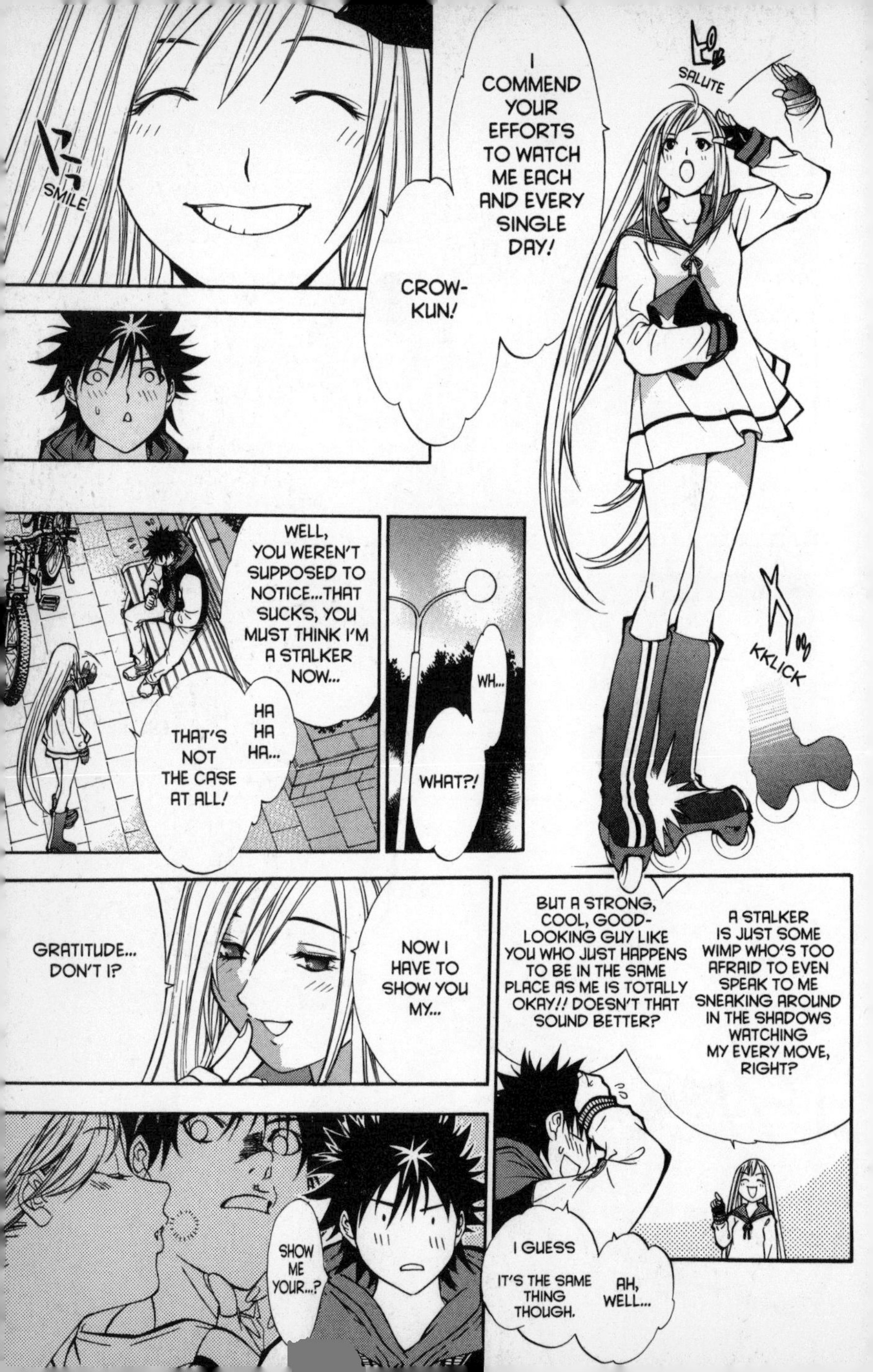
SALUTE
I COMMEND YOUR EFFORTS TO WATCH ME EACH AND EVERY SINGLE DAY!
CROW-KUN!
KKLICK
SMILE
WH...
WHAT?!
WELL, YOU WEREN'T SUPPOSED TO NOTICE...THAT SUCKS, YOU MUST THINK I'M A STALKER NOW...
HA HA HA...
THAT'S NOT THE CASE AT ALL!
A STALKER IS JUST SOME WIMP WHO'S TOO AFRAID TO EVEN SPEAK TO ME SNEAKING AROUND IN THE SHADOWS WATCHING MY EVERY MOVE, RIGHT?
BUT A STRONG, COOL, GOOD-LOOKING GUY LIKE YOU WHO JUST HAPPENS TO BE IN THE SAME PLACE AS ME IS TOTALLY OKAY!! DOESN'T THAT SOUND BETTER?
AH, WELL...
I GUESS
IT'S THE SAME THING THOUGH.
NOW I HAVE TO SHOW YOU MY...
GRATITUDE... DON'T I?
SHOW ME YOUR...?

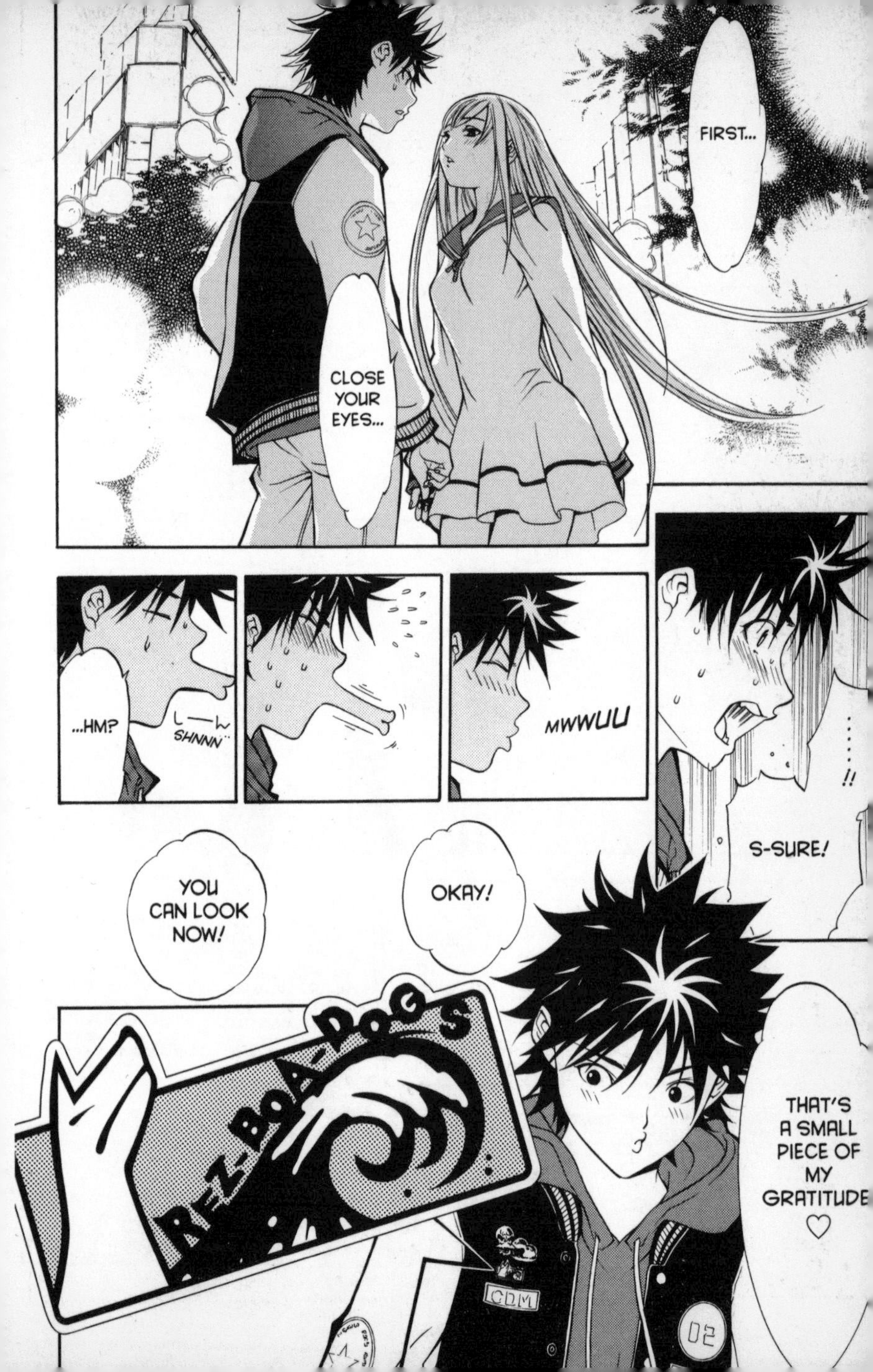
FIRST...
CLOSE YOUR EYES...
......!!
S-SURE!
MWWUU
...HM?
SHNNN
OKAY!
YOU CAN LOOK NOW!
THAT'S A SMALL PIECE OF MY GRATITUDE ♡
REZ-BOA-DOGS
CDM
02

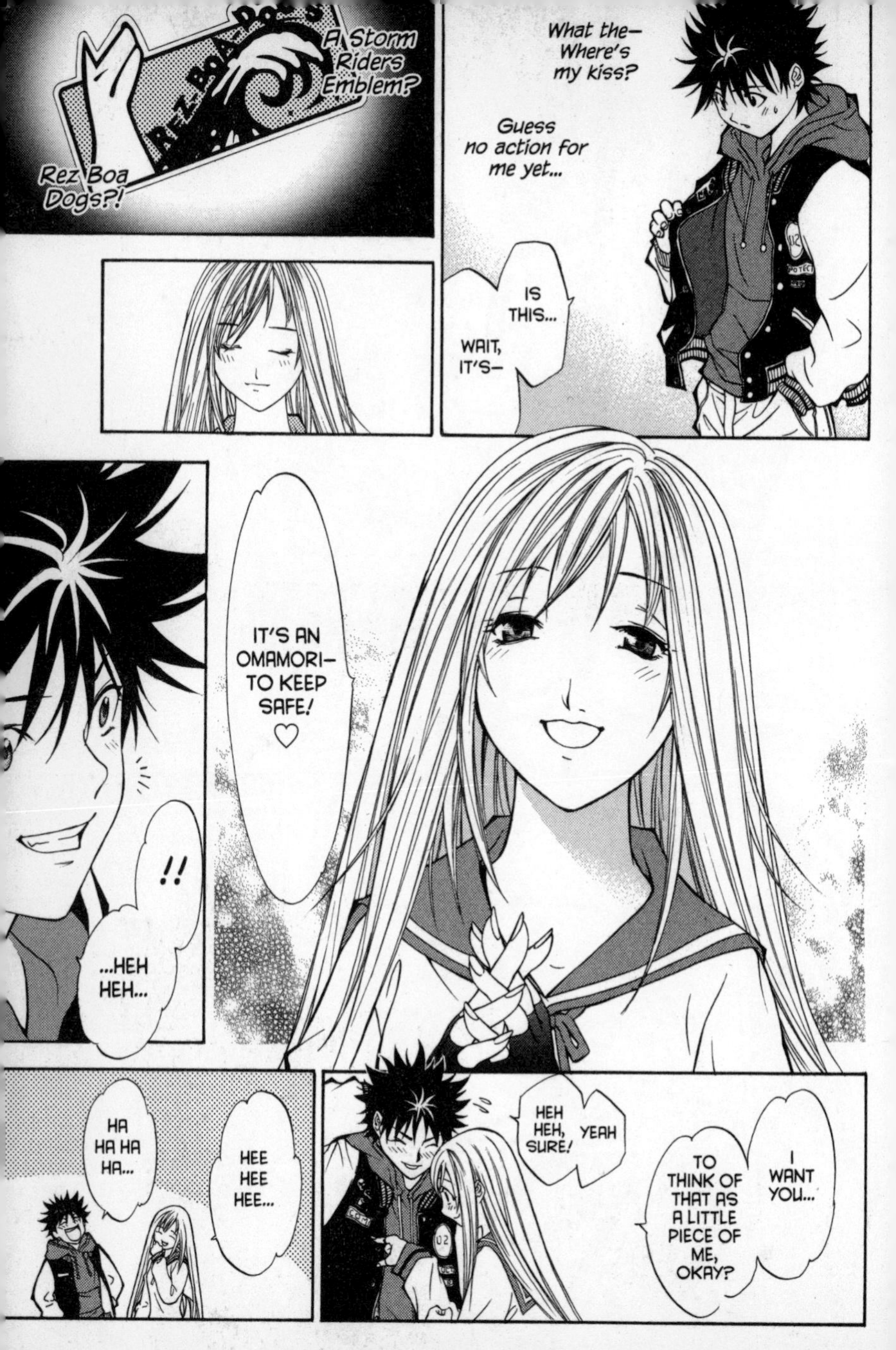
What the— Where's my kiss?
Guess no action for me yet...
IS THIS...
WAIT, IT'S—
A Storm Riders Emblem?
REZ-BOA DOGS
Rez Boa Dogs?!
IT'S AN OMAMORI— TO KEEP SAFE! ♡
!!
...HEH HEH...
I WANT YOU...
TO THINK OF THAT AS A LITTLE PIECE OF ME, OKAY?
YEAH
HEH HEH, SURE!
HEE HEE HEE...
HA HA HA HA...

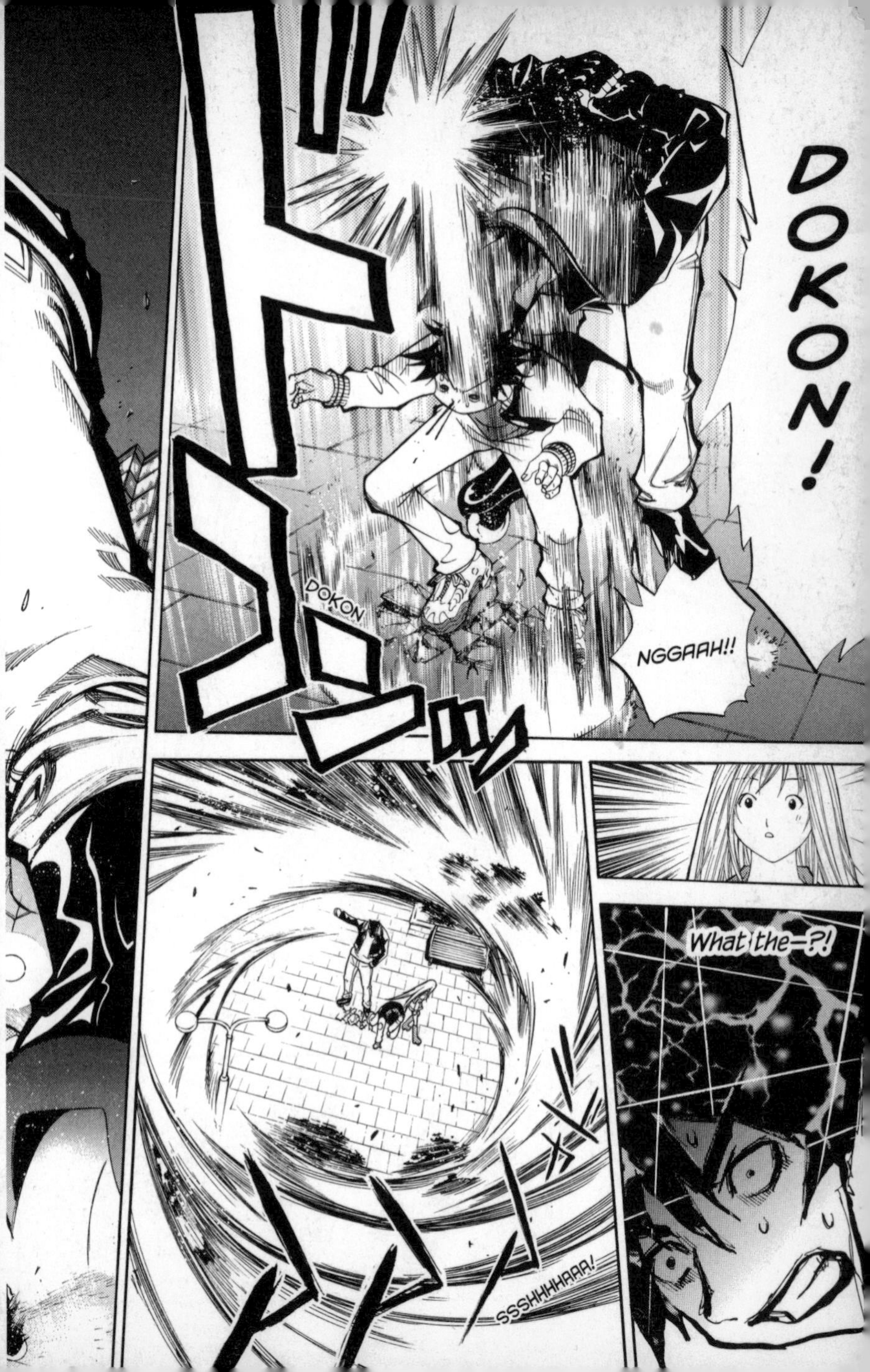
DOKON!
NGGAAH!!
DOKON
What the—?!
SSSHHHHAAA!

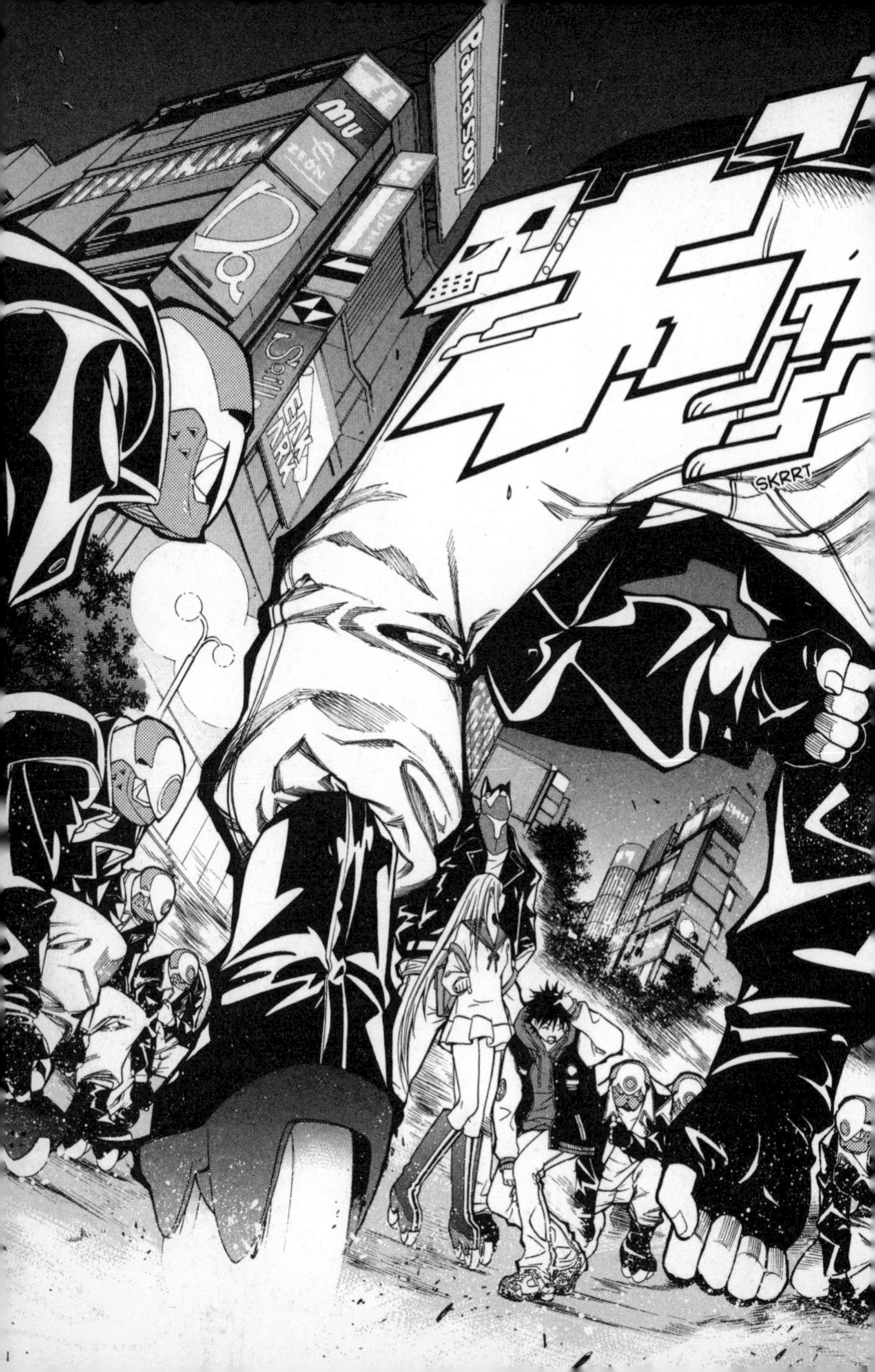
SKRRT

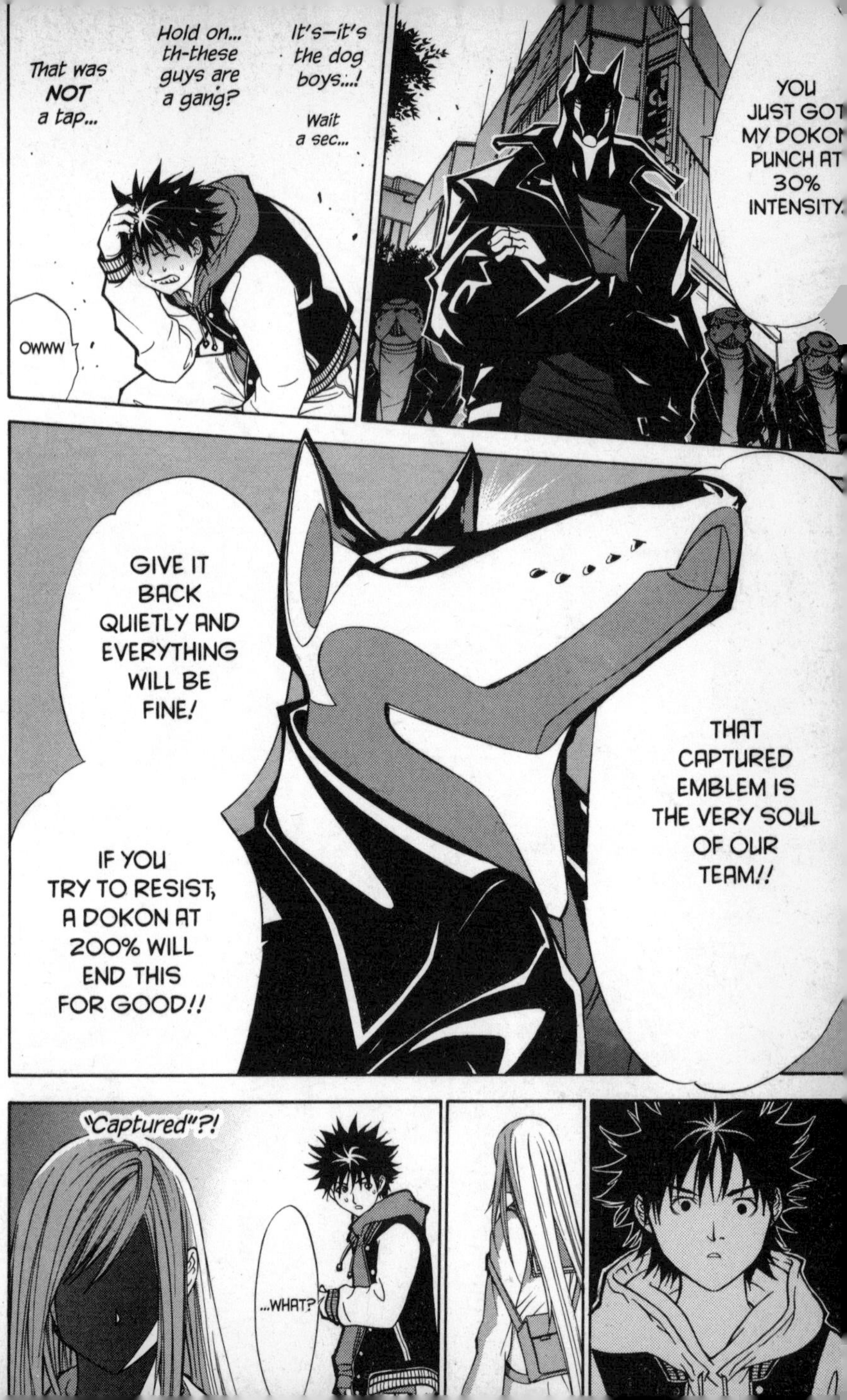
YOU JUST GOT MY DOKON PUNCH AT 30% INTENSITY.
It's—it's the dog boys...!
Wait a sec...
Hold on... th-these guys are a gang?
That was **NOT** a tap...
OWWW
THAT CAPTURED EMBLEM IS THE VERY SOUL OF OUR TEAM!!
GIVE IT BACK QUIETLY AND EVERYTHING WILL BE FINE!
IF YOU TRY TO RESIST, A DOKON AT 200% WILL END THIS FOR GOOD!!
"Captured"?!
...WHAT?

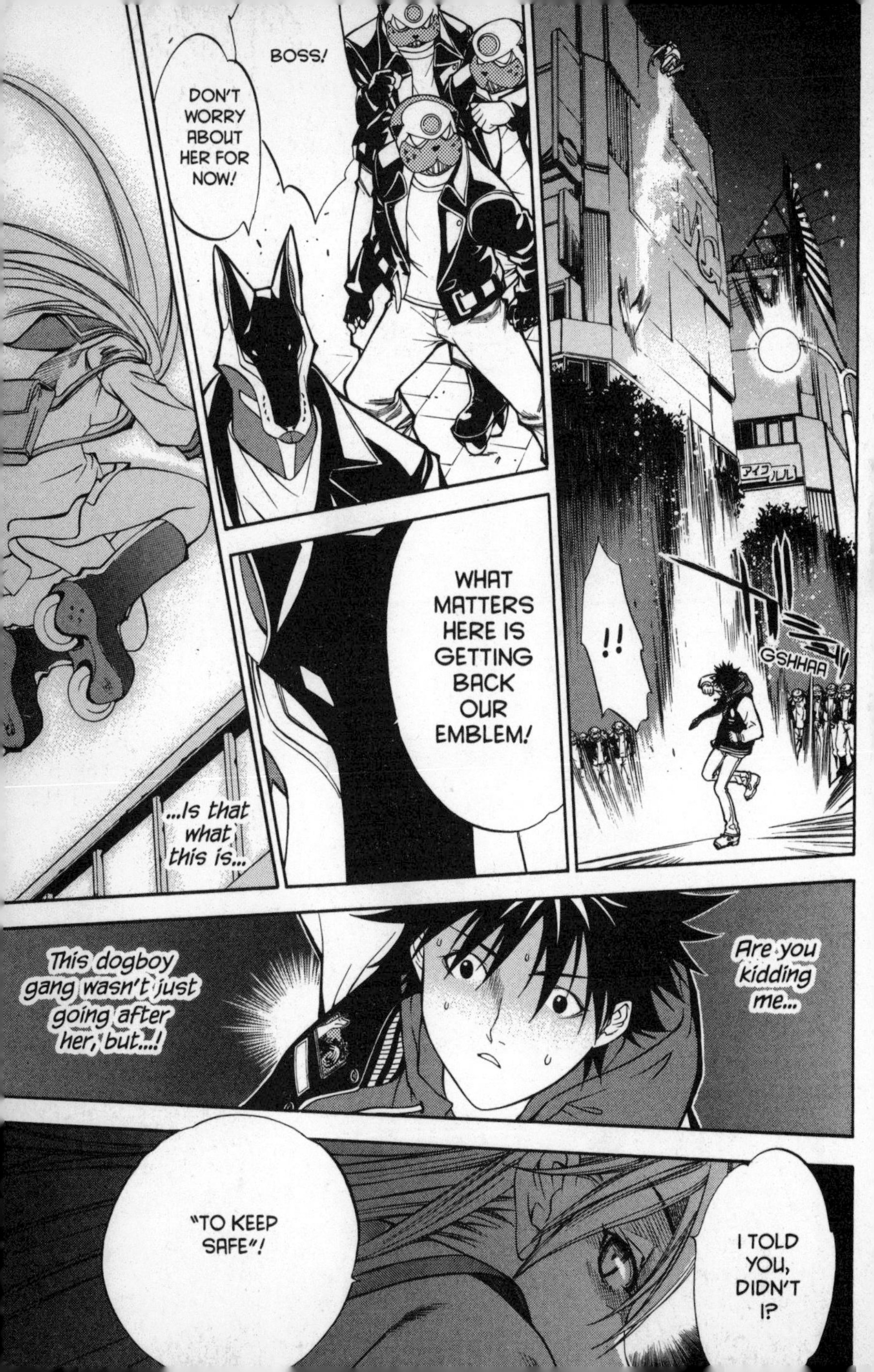
!!
GSHHAA
BOSS!
DON'T WORRY ABOUT HER FOR NOW!
WHAT MATTERS HERE IS GETTING BACK OUR EMBLEM!
...Is that what this is...
Are you kidding me...
This dogboy gang wasn't just going after her, but...!
I TOLD YOU, DIDN'T I?
"TO KEEP SAFE"!

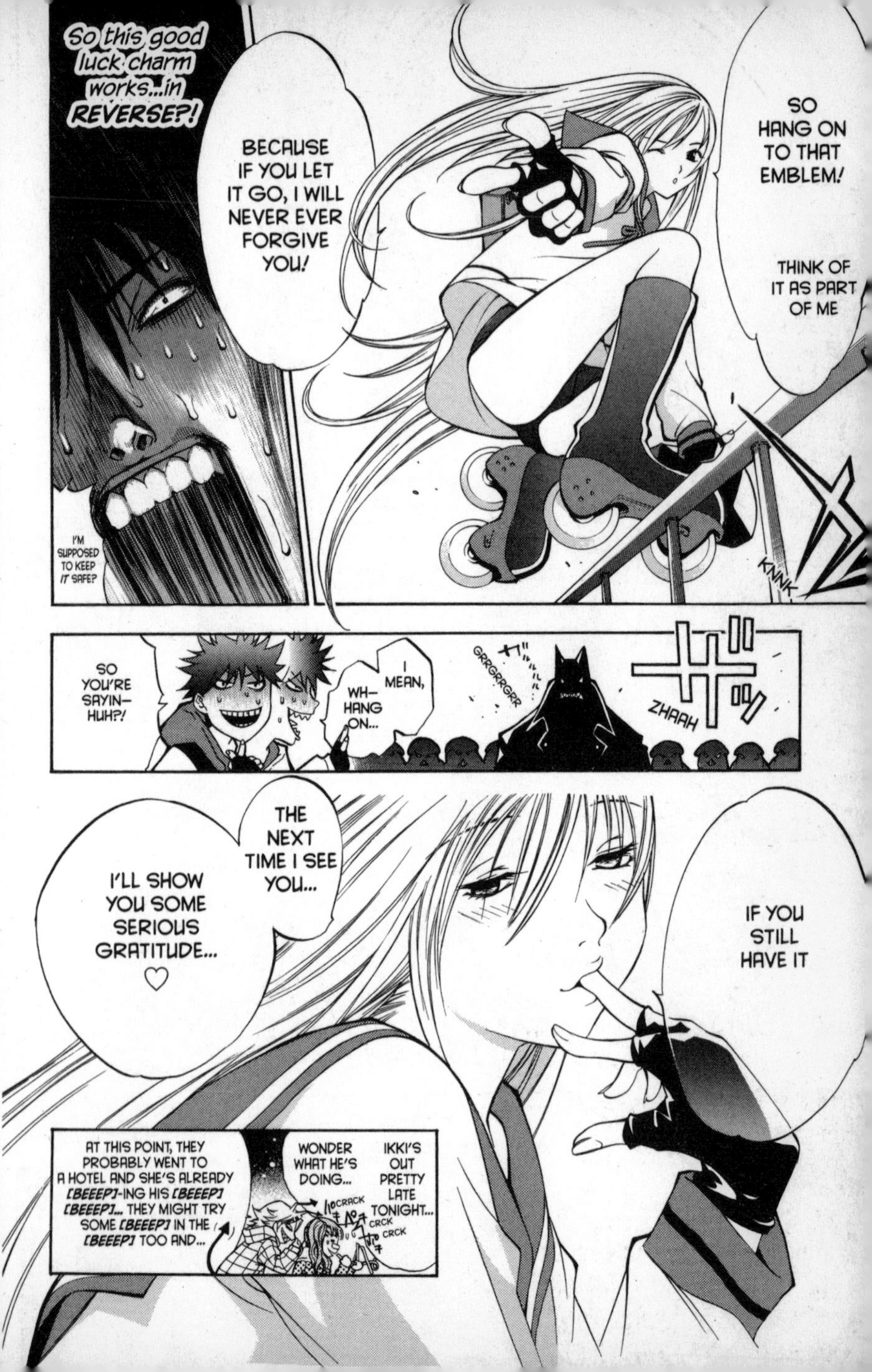
SO HANG ON TO THAT EMBLEM!
THINK OF IT AS PART OF ME
BECAUSE IF YOU LET IT GO, I WILL NEVER EVER FORGIVE YOU!
KNNK
So this good luck charm works...in REVERSE?!
I'M SUPPOSED TO KEEP IT SAFE?
ZHAAH
GRRGRRGRR
I MEAN, WH-HANG ON...
SO YOU'RE SAYIN— HUH?!
IF YOU STILL HAVE IT
THE NEXT TIME I SEE YOU...
I'LL SHOW YOU SOME SERIOUS GRATITUDE... ♡
IKKI'S OUT PRETTY LATE TONIGHT...
WONDER WHAT HE'S DOING...
AT THIS POINT, THEY PROBABLY WENT TO A HOTEL AND SHE'S ALREADY [BEEEP]-ING HIS [BEEEP] [BEEEP]... THEY MIGHT TRY SOME [BEEEP] IN THE [BEEEP] TOO AND...
CRACK
CRCK
CRCK

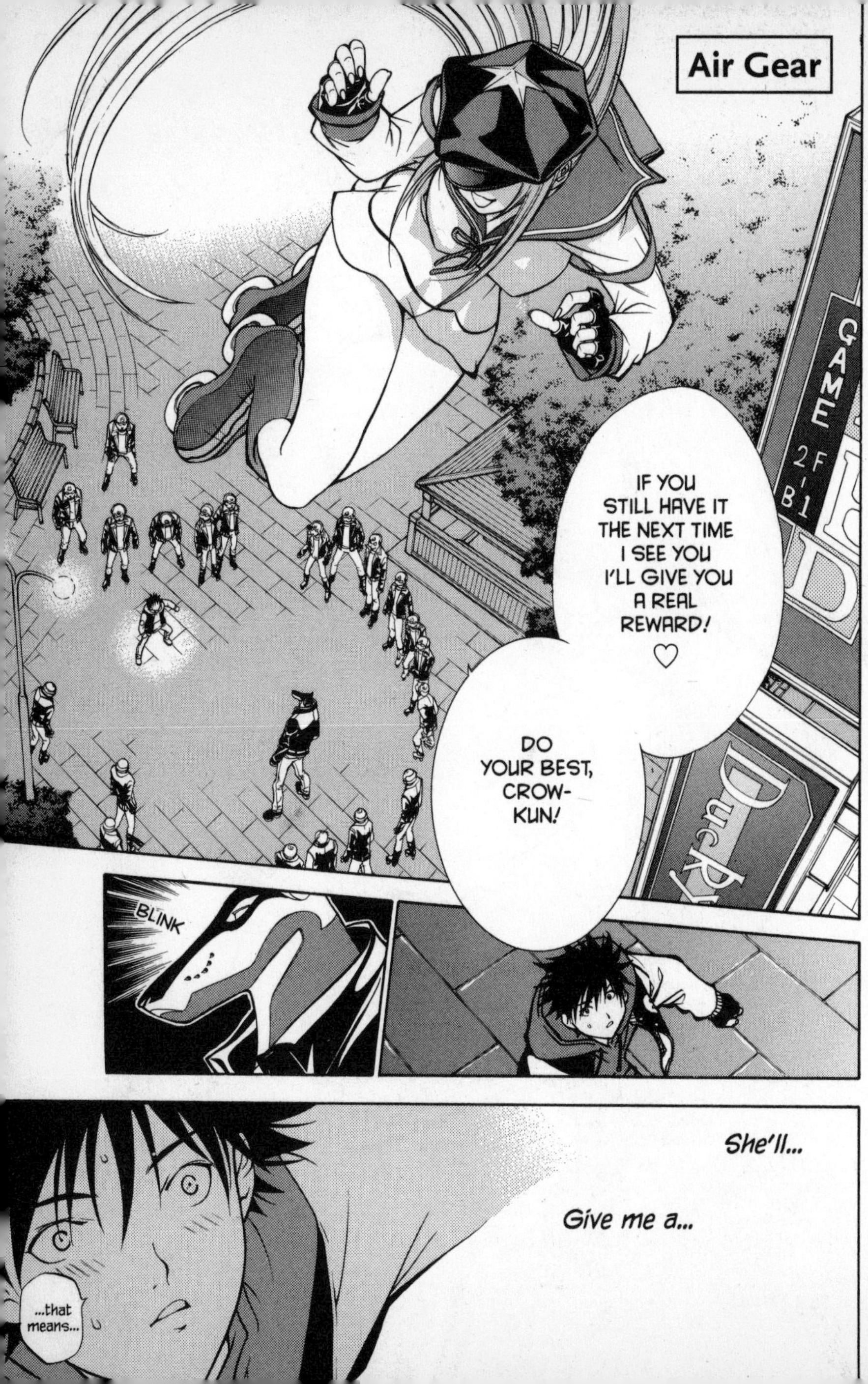
GAME
2F-B1
IF YOU STILL HAVE IT THE NEXT TIME I SEE YOU I'LL GIVE YOU A REAL REWARD! ♡
DO YOUR BEST, CROW-KUN!
BLINK
She'll...
Give me a...
...that means...

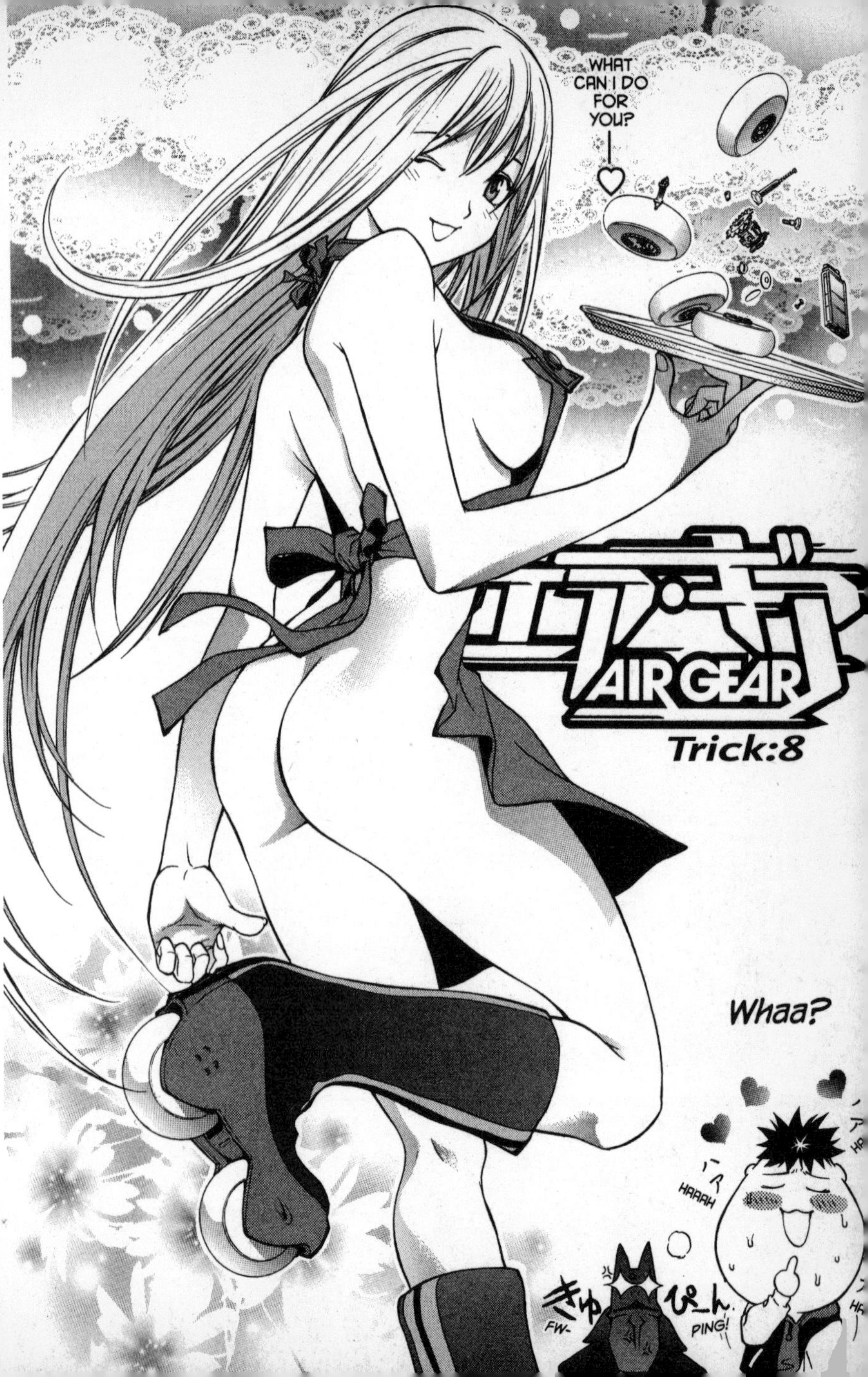
WHAT CAN I DO FOR YOU?
AIR GEAR
Trick:8
Whaa?
ハァ
HAAAH
ぴーん
PING!
きゅ
FW-

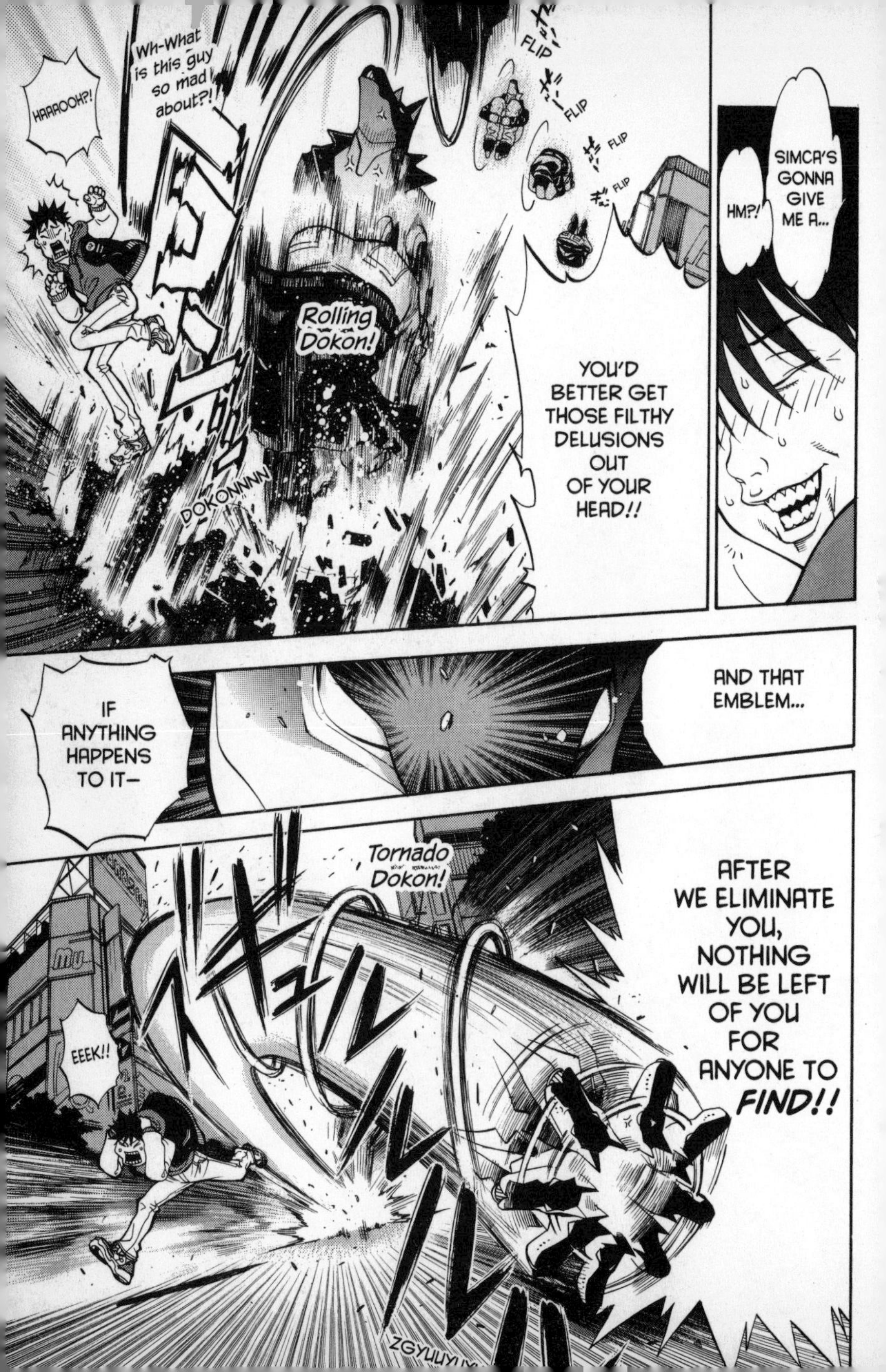
SIMCA'S GONNA GIVE ME A...
HM?!
FLIP
FLIP
FLIP
FLIP
YOU'D BETTER GET THOSE FILTHY DELUSIONS OUT OF YOUR HEAD!!
Rolling Dokon!
DOKONNNN
Wh-What is this guy so mad about?!
HAAAOOH?!
AND THAT EMBLEM...
IF ANYTHING HAPPENS TO IT—
AFTER WE ELIMINATE YOU, NOTHING WILL BE LEFT OF YOU FOR ANYONE TO *FIND!!*
Tornado Dokon!
EEEK!!
ZGYUUUYUY

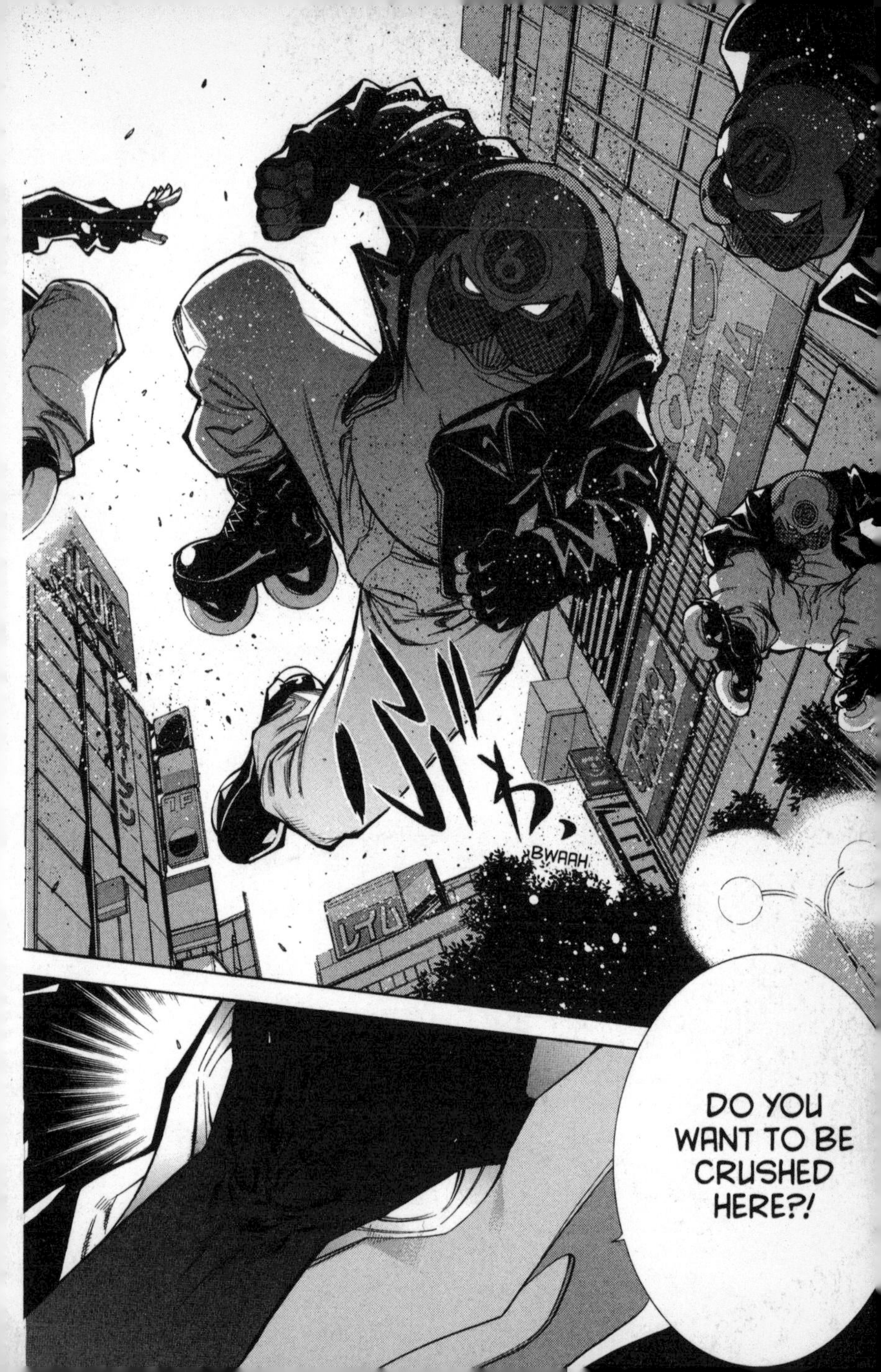
BWAAH
DO YOU WANT TO BE CRUSHED HERE?!

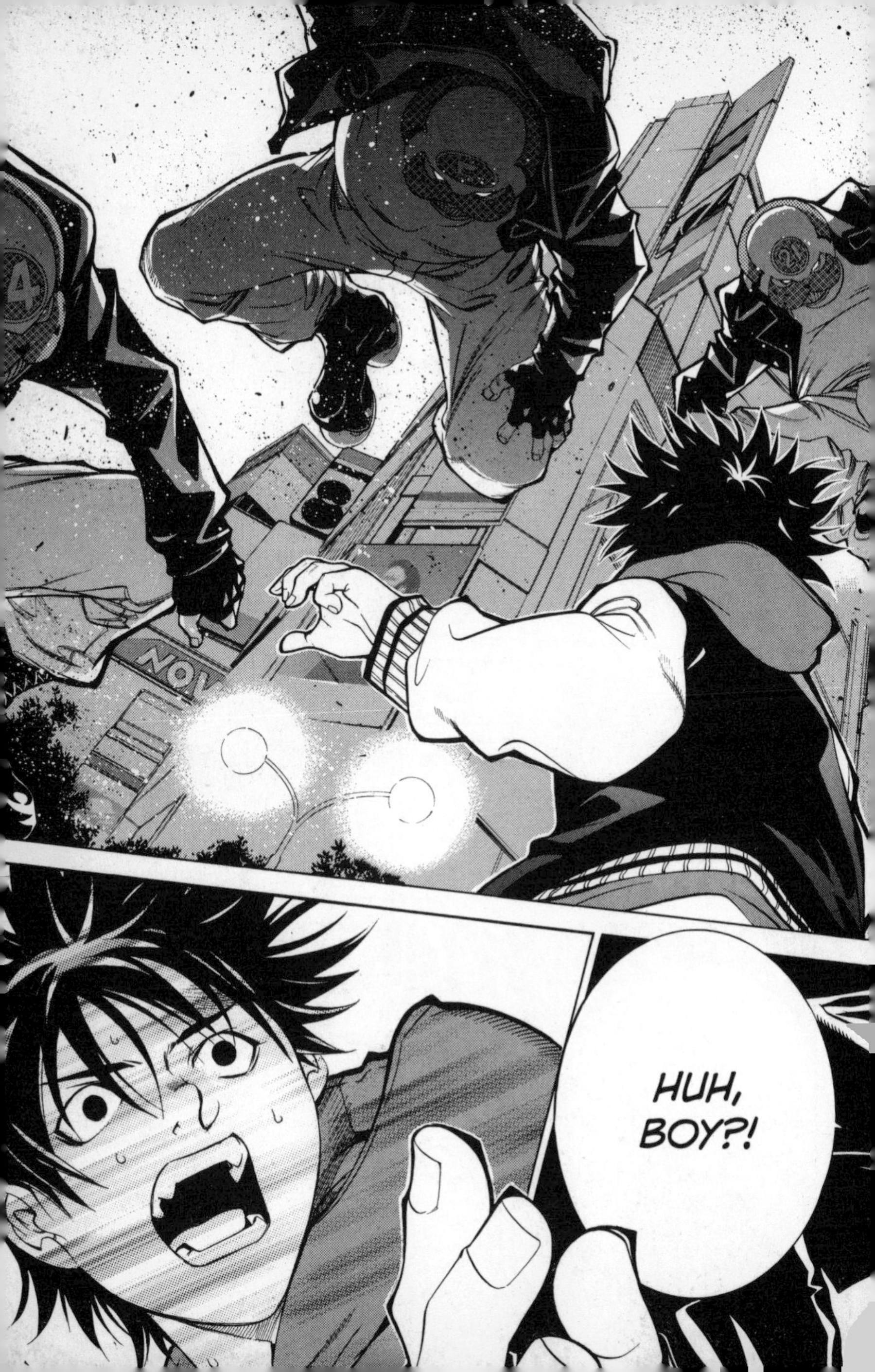
HUH, BOY?!

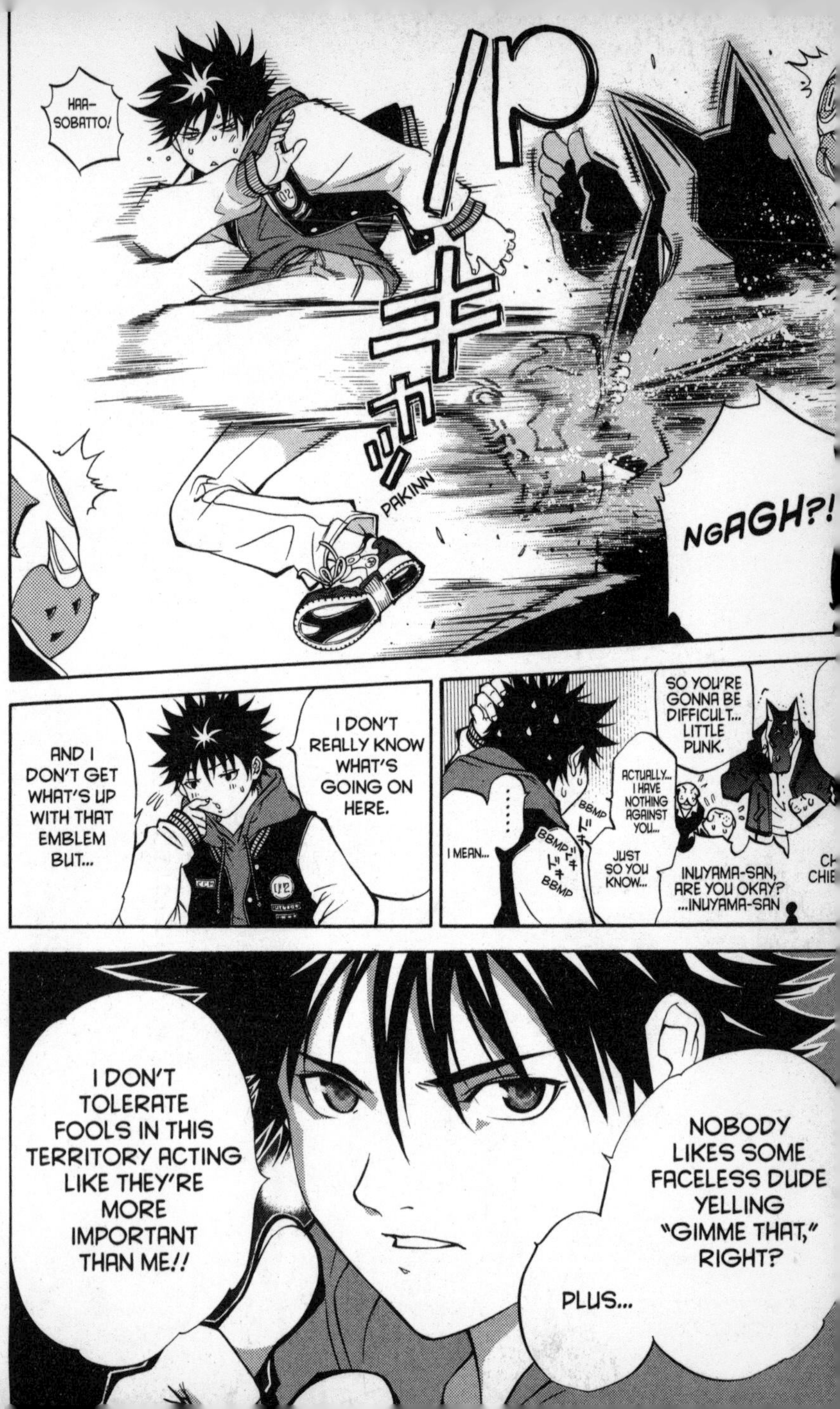
HAA-SOBATTO!
PAKINN
NGAGH?!
SO YOU'RE GONNA BE DIFFICULT... LITTLE PUNK.
ACTUALLY... I HAVE NOTHING AGAINST YOU...
JUST SO YOU KNOW...
INUYAMA-SAN, ARE YOU OKAY? ...INUYAMA-SAN
BBMP
BBMP
BBMP
......
I MEAN...
I DON'T REALLY KNOW WHAT'S GOING ON HERE.
AND I DON'T GET WHAT'S UP WITH THAT EMBLEM BUT...
NOBODY LIKES SOME FACELESS DUDE YELLING "GIMME THAT," RIGHT?
PLUS...
I DON'T TOLERATE FOOLS IN THIS TERRITORY ACTING LIKE THEY'RE MORE IMPORTANT THAN ME!!

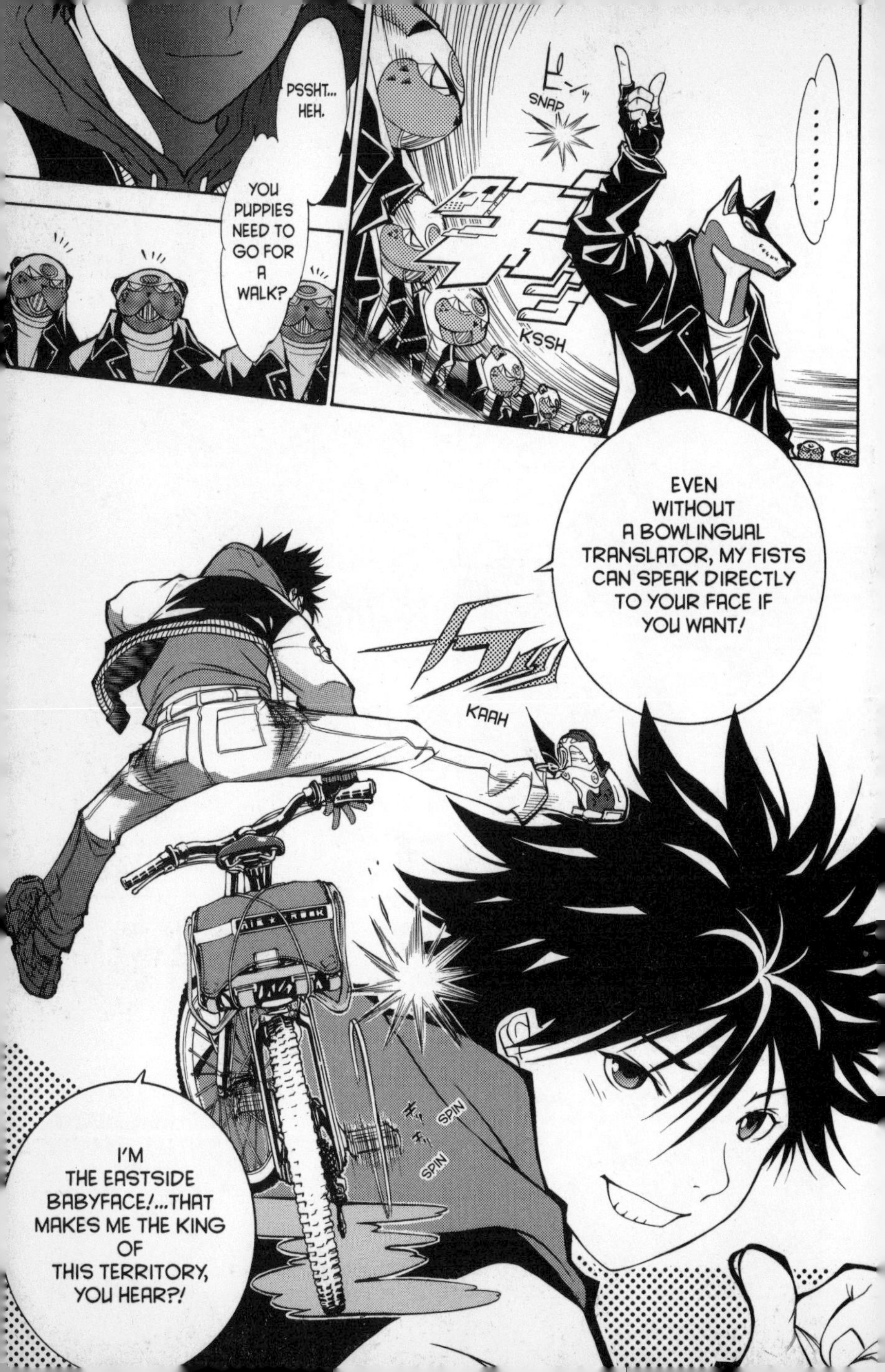

......
SNAP
KSSH
PSSHT... HEH.
YOU PUPPIES NEED TO GO FOR A WALK?
EVEN WITHOUT A BOWLINGUAL TRANSLATOR, MY FISTS CAN SPEAK DIRECTLY TO YOUR FACE IF YOU WANT!
KAAH
SPIN
SPIN
I'M THE EASTSIDE BABYFACE!...THAT MAKES ME THE KING OF THIS TERRITORY, YOU HEAR?!

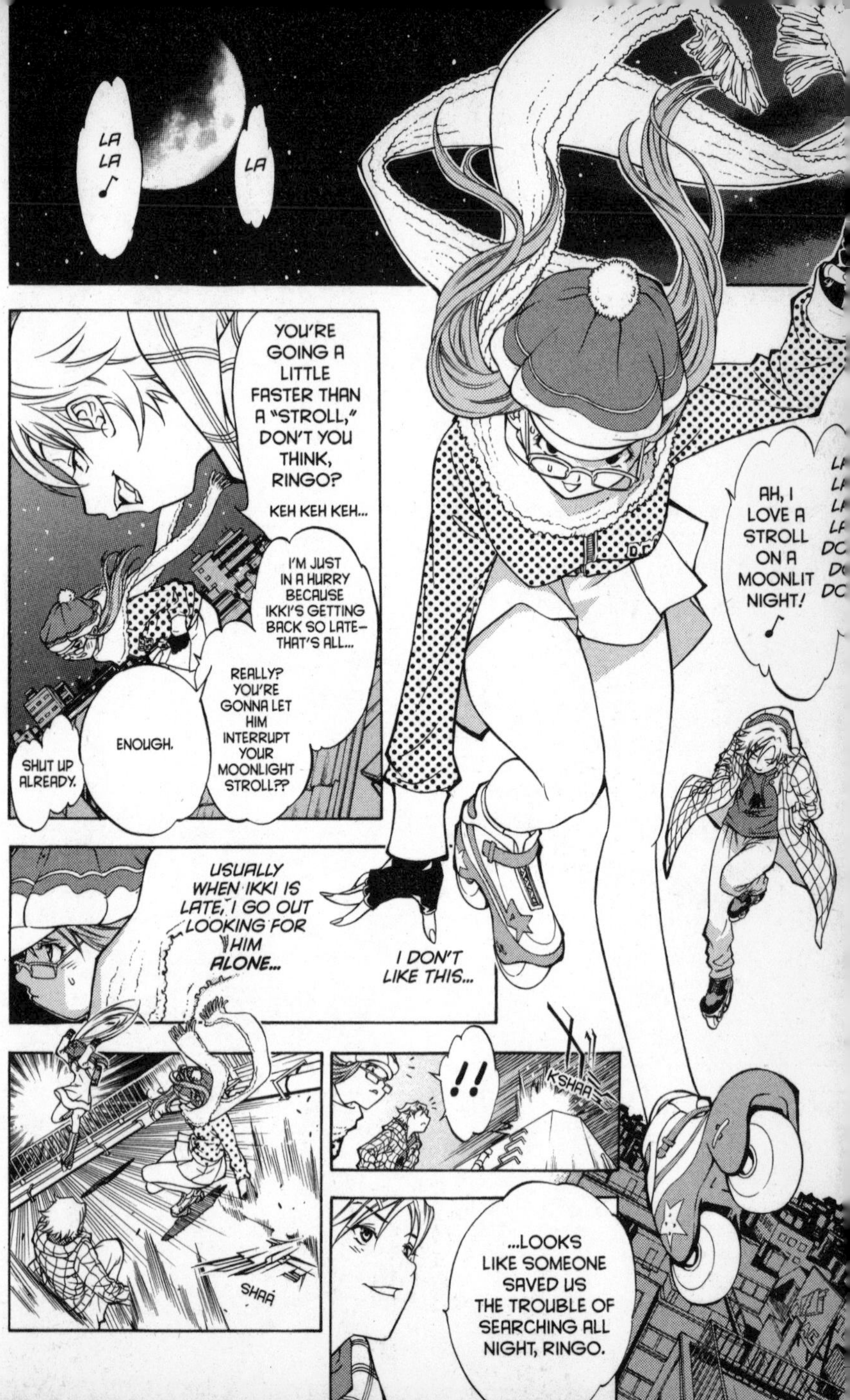
AH, I LOVE A STROLL ON A MOONLIT NIGHT! ♪
LA
LA LA ♪
YOU'RE GOING A LITTLE FASTER THAN A "STROLL," DON'T YOU THINK, RINGO?
KEH KEH KEH...
I'M JUST IN A HURRY BECAUSE IKKI'S GETTING BACK SO LATE—THAT'S ALL...
REALLY? YOU'RE GONNA LET HIM INTERRUPT YOUR MOONLIGHT STROLL??
ENOUGH.
SHUT UP ALREADY.
USUALLY WHEN IKKI IS LATE, I GO OUT LOOKING FOR HIM ALONE...
I DON'T LIKE THIS...
!!
KSHAA
...LOOKS LIKE SOMEONE SAVED US THE TROUBLE OF SEARCHING ALL NIGHT, RINGO.
SHAA

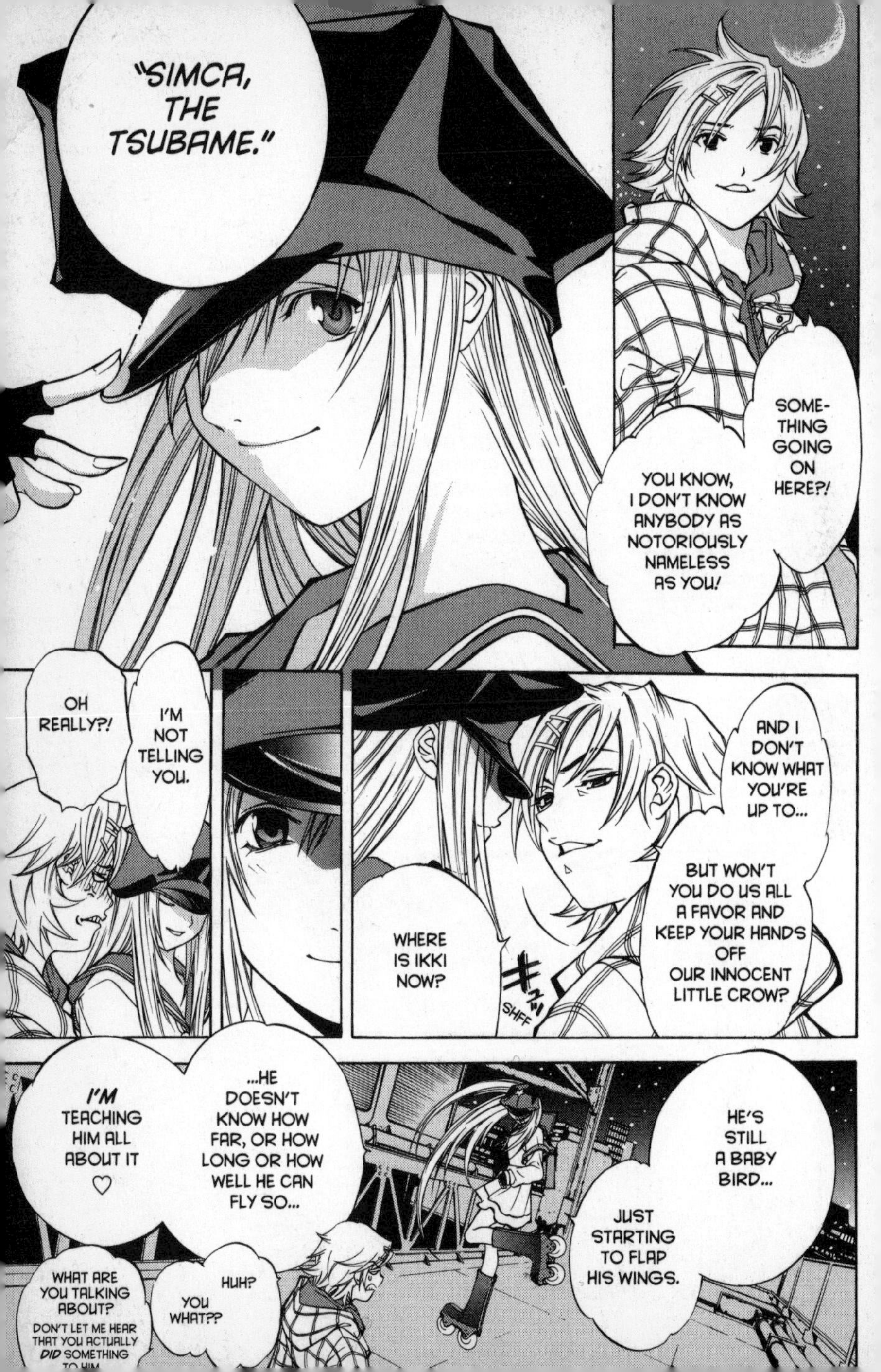
SOME-THING GOING ON HERE?!
YOU KNOW, I DON'T KNOW ANYBODY AS NOTORIOUSLY NAMELESS AS YOU!
"SIMCA, THE TSUBAME."
AND I DON'T KNOW WHAT YOU'RE UP TO...
BUT WON'T YOU DO US ALL A FAVOR AND KEEP YOUR HANDS OFF OUR INNOCENT LITTLE CROW?
SHFF
WHERE IS IKKI NOW?
I'M NOT TELLING YOU.
OH REALLY?!
HE'S STILL A BABY BIRD...
JUST STARTING TO FLAP HIS WINGS.
...HE DOESN'T KNOW HOW FAR, OR HOW LONG OR HOW WELL HE CAN FLY SO...
I'M TEACHING HIM ALL ABOUT IT ♡
HUH? YOU WHAT??
WHAT ARE YOU TALKING ABOUT? DON'T LET ME HEAR THAT YOU ACTUALLY *DID* SOMETHING

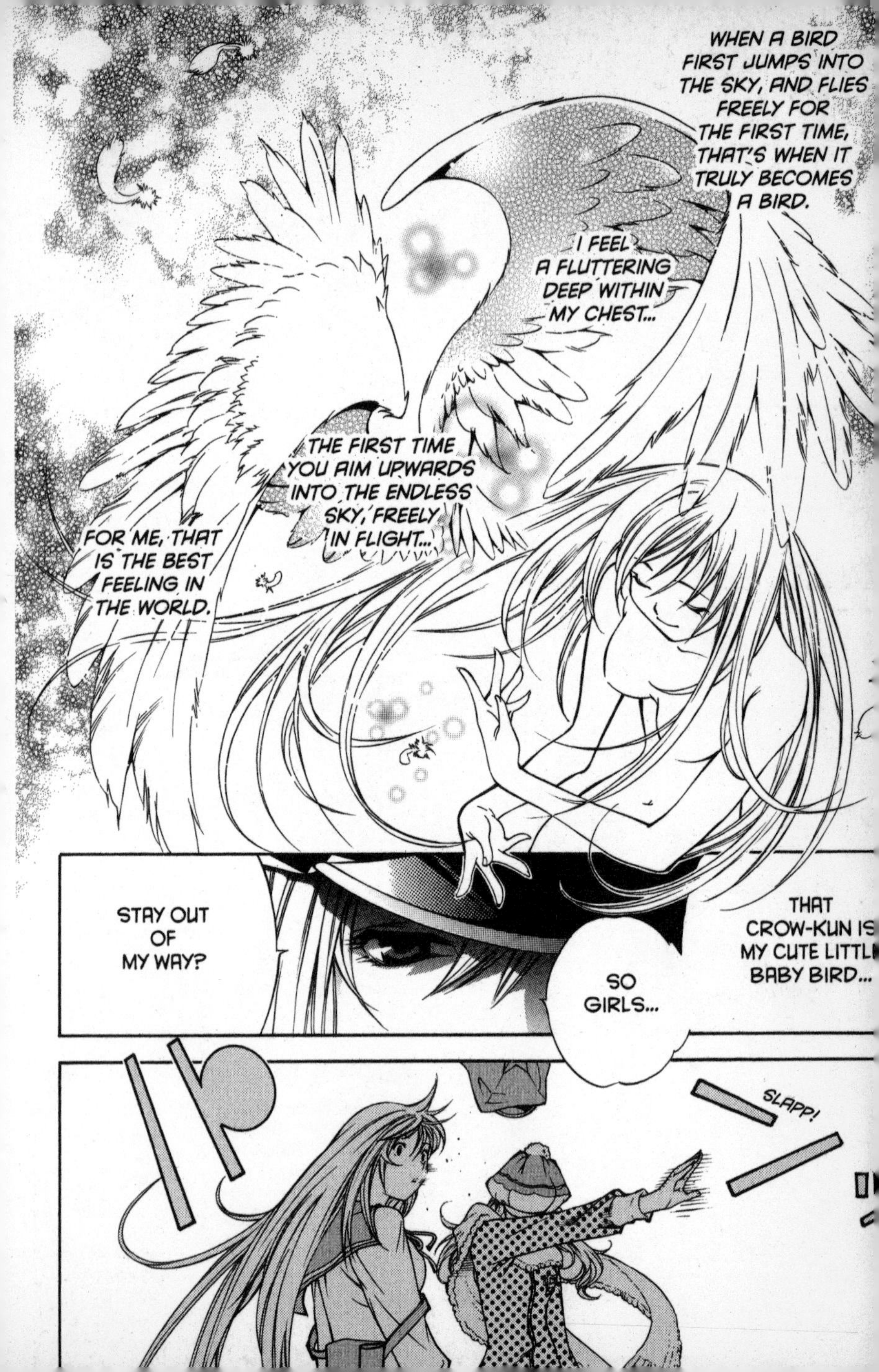
WHEN A BIRD FIRST JUMPS INTO THE SKY, AND FLIES FREELY FOR THE FIRST TIME, THAT'S WHEN IT TRULY BECOMES A BIRD.
I FEEL A FLUTTERING DEEP WITHIN MY CHEST...
THE FIRST TIME YOU AIM UPWARDS INTO THE ENDLESS SKY, FREELY IN FLIGHT...
FOR ME, THAT IS THE BEST FEELING IN THE WORLD.
THAT CROW-KUN IS MY CUTE LITTL BABY BIRD...
SO GIRLS...
STAY OUT OF MY WAY?
SLAPP!

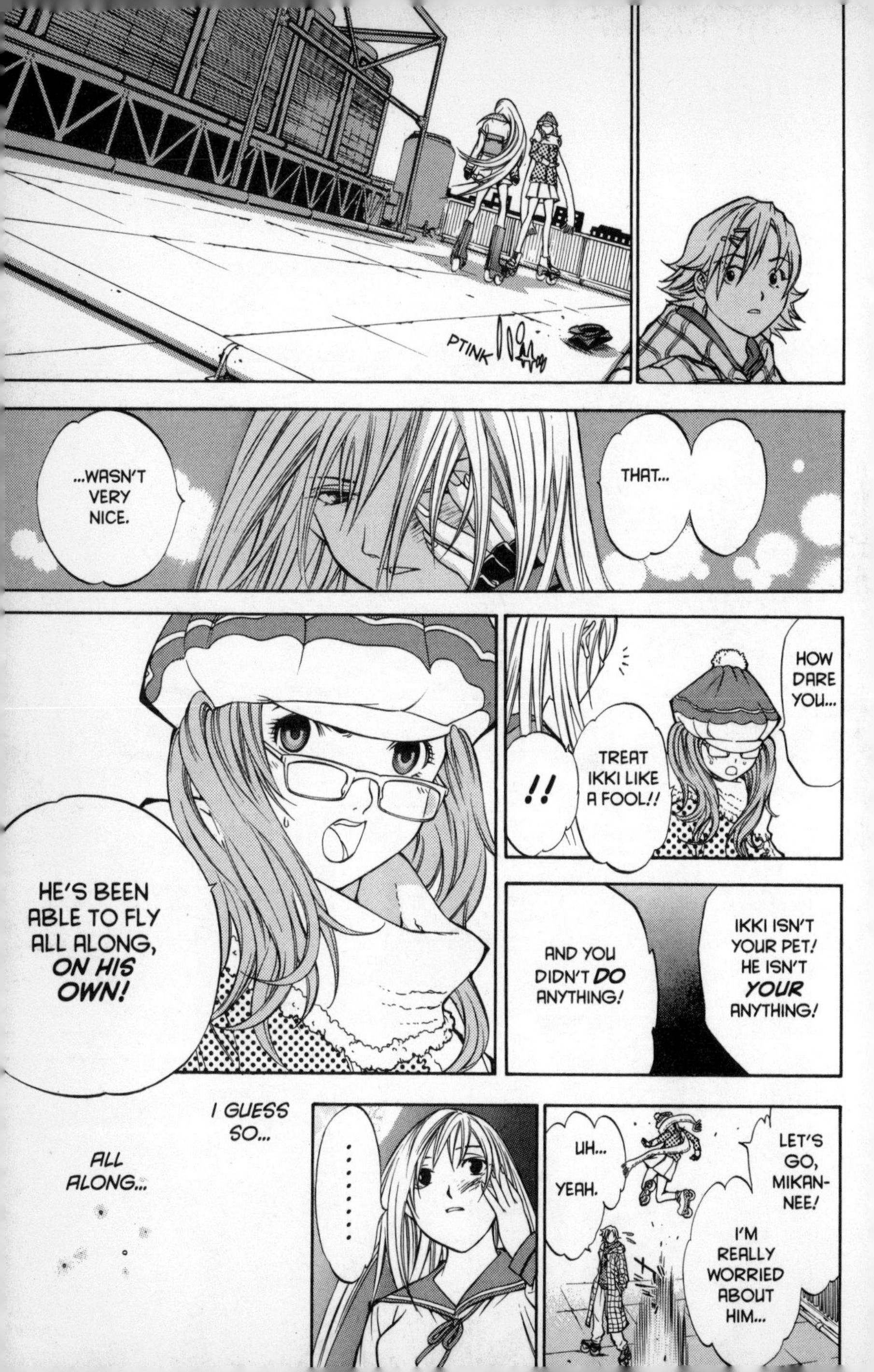
PTINK
THAT...
...WASN'T VERY NICE.
HOW DARE YOU...
TREAT IKKI LIKE A FOOL!!
!!
IKKI ISN'T YOUR PET! HE ISN'T *YOUR* ANYTHING!
AND YOU DIDN'T *DO* ANYTHING!
HE'S BEEN ABLE TO FLY ALL ALONG, *ON HIS OWN!*
LET'S GO, MIKAN-NEE!
I'M REALLY WORRIED ABOUT HIM...
UH...
YEAH.
......
I GUESS SO...
ALL ALONG...

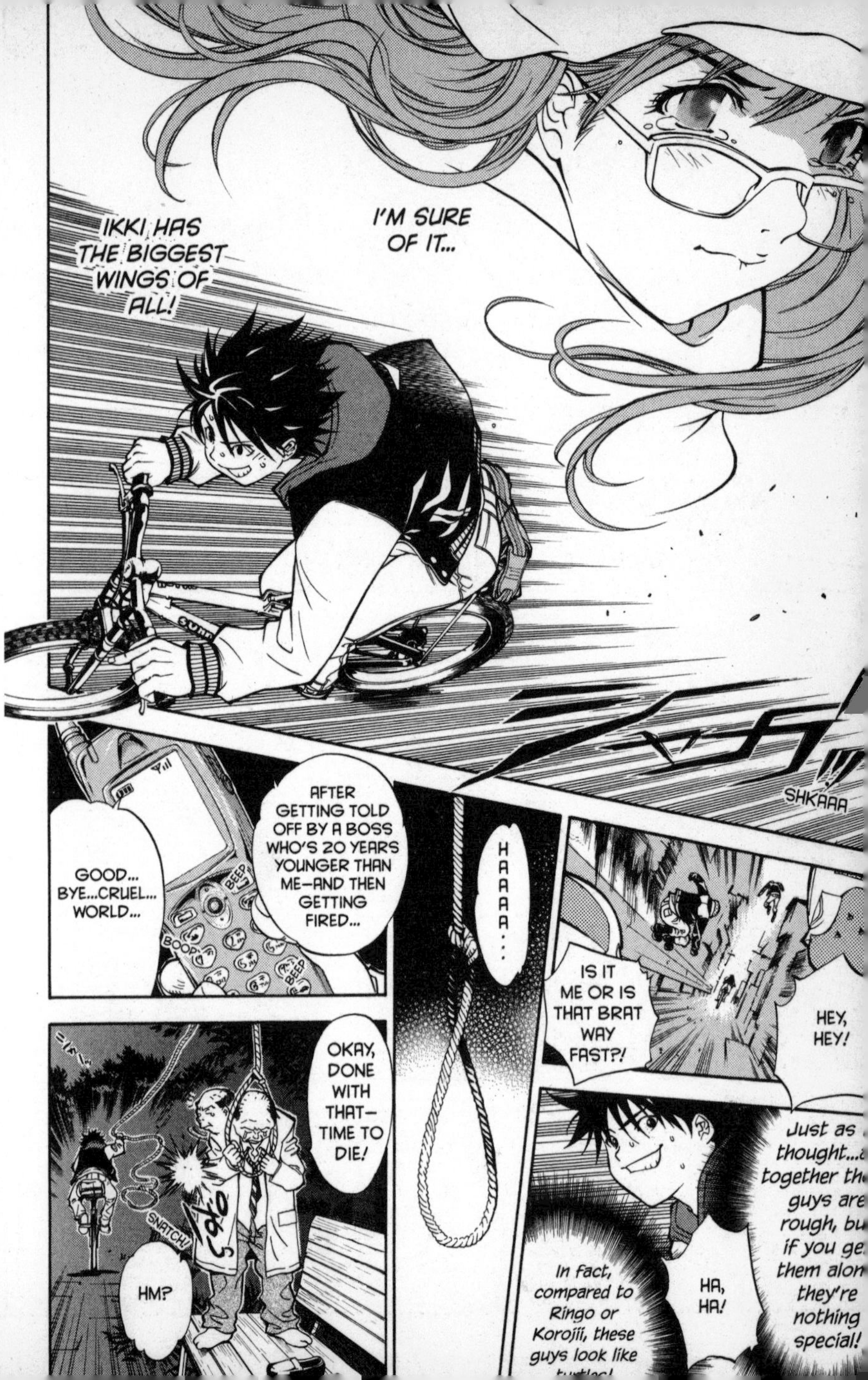
I'M SURE OF IT...
IKKI HAS THE BIGGEST WINGS OF ALL!
SHKAAA
HEY, HEY!
IS IT ME OR IS THAT BRAT WAY FAST?!
Just as thought... together th guys are rough, bu if you ge them alon they're nothing special!
HA, HA!
In fact, compared to Ringo or Korojii, these guys look like
HAAAAA...
AFTER GETTING TOLD OFF BY A BOSS WHO'S 20 YEARS YOUNGER THAN ME—AND THEN GETTING FIRED...
BEEP
BOOP
BEEP
GOOD... BYE...CRUEL... WORLD...
OKAY, DONE WITH THAT— TIME TO DIE!
SNATCH!
HM?

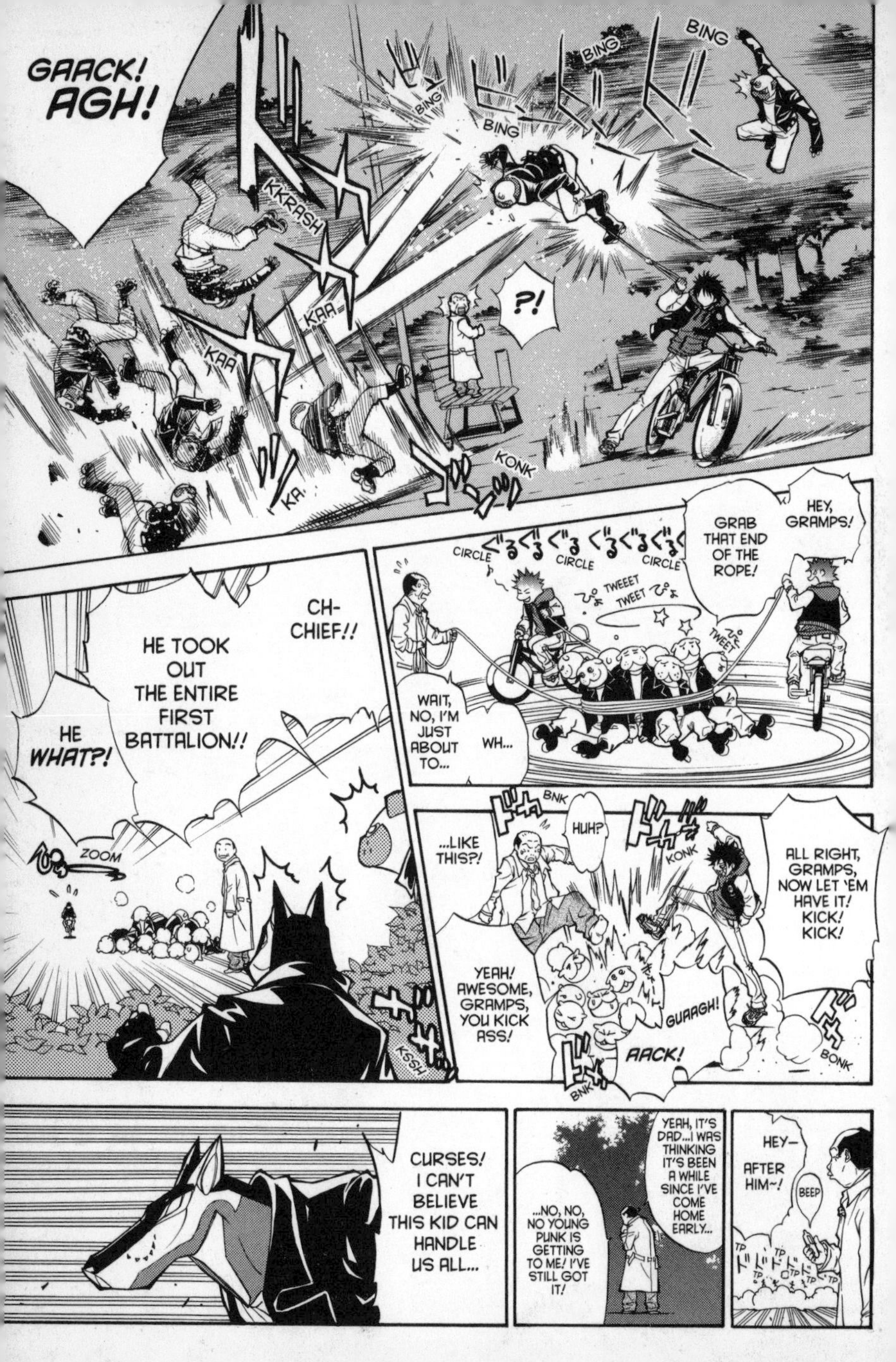

BING
BING
BING
BING
GAACK! AGH!
KKRASH
?!
KAA
KAA
KONK
KA
HEY, GRAMPS!
GRAB THAT END OF THE ROPE!
ぐるぐるぐる ぐるぐるぐる
CIRCLE
CIRCLE
CIRCLE
TWEEET
TWEET
TWEET
WH...
WAIT, NO, I'M JUST ABOUT TO...
ALL RIGHT, GRAMPS, NOW LET 'EM HAVE IT! KICK! KICK!
KONK
HUH?
BNK
...LIKE THIS?!
BONK
GUAAGH!
AACK!
YEAH! AWESOME, GRAMPS, YOU KICK ASS!
BNK
CH-CHIEF!!
HE TOOK OUT THE ENTIRE FIRST BATTALION!!
HE WHAT?!
ZOOM
KSSH
HEY—
AFTER HIM~!
BEEP
TP TP TP TP TP TP
YEAH, IT'S DAD...I WAS THINKING IT'S BEEN A WHILE SINCE I'VE COME HOME EARLY...
...NO, NO, NO YOUNG PUNK IS GETTING TO ME! I'VE STILL GOT IT!
CURSES! I CAN'T BELIEVE THIS KID CAN HANDLE US ALL...

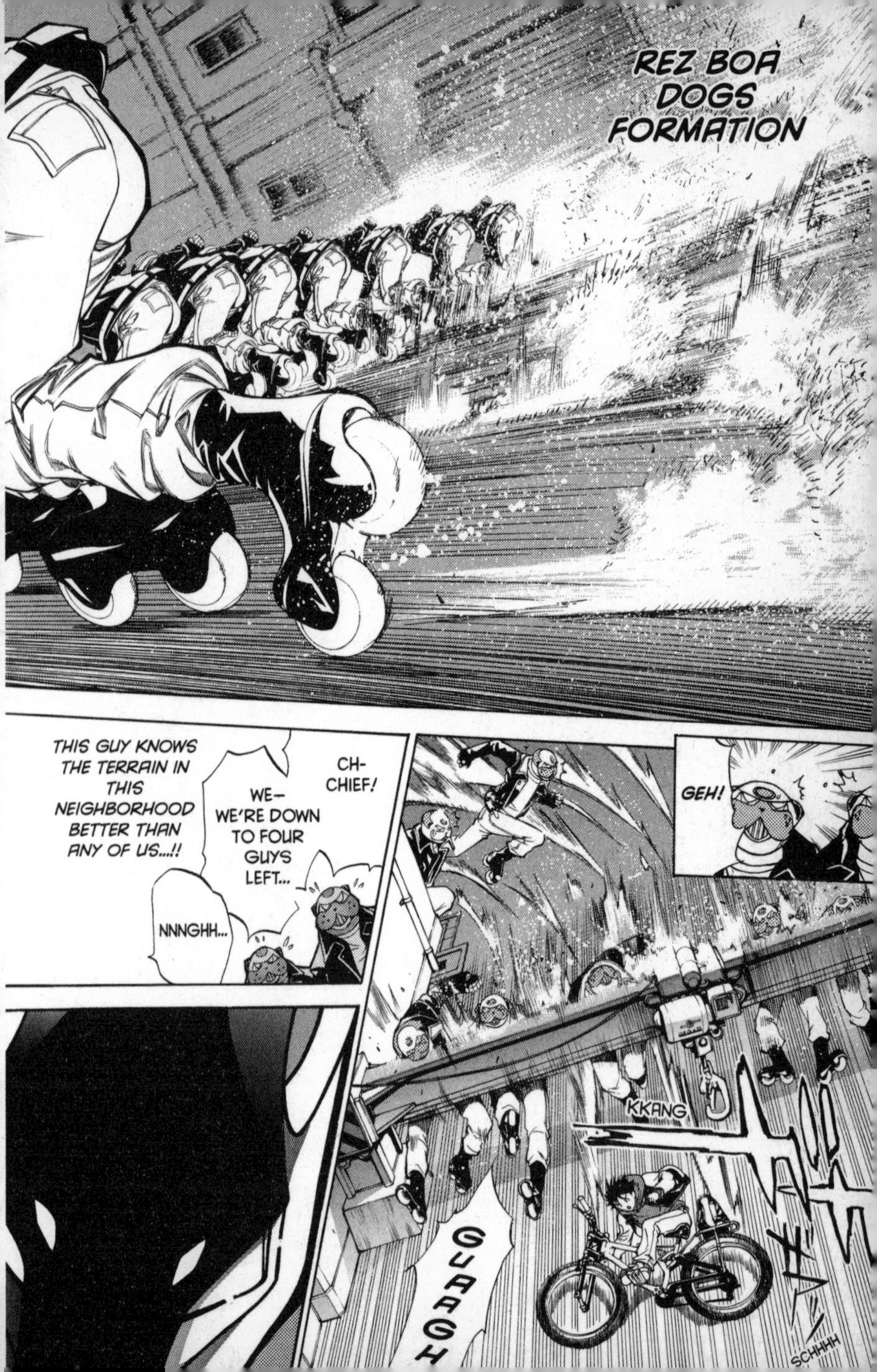
REZ BOA DOGS FORMATION
GEH!
KKANG
GUAAGH
SCHHHH
CH-CHIEF!
WE—WE'RE DOWN TO FOUR GUYS LEFT...
THIS GUY KNOWS THE TERRAIN IN THIS NEIGHBORHOOD BETTER THAN ANY OF US...!!
NNNGHH...

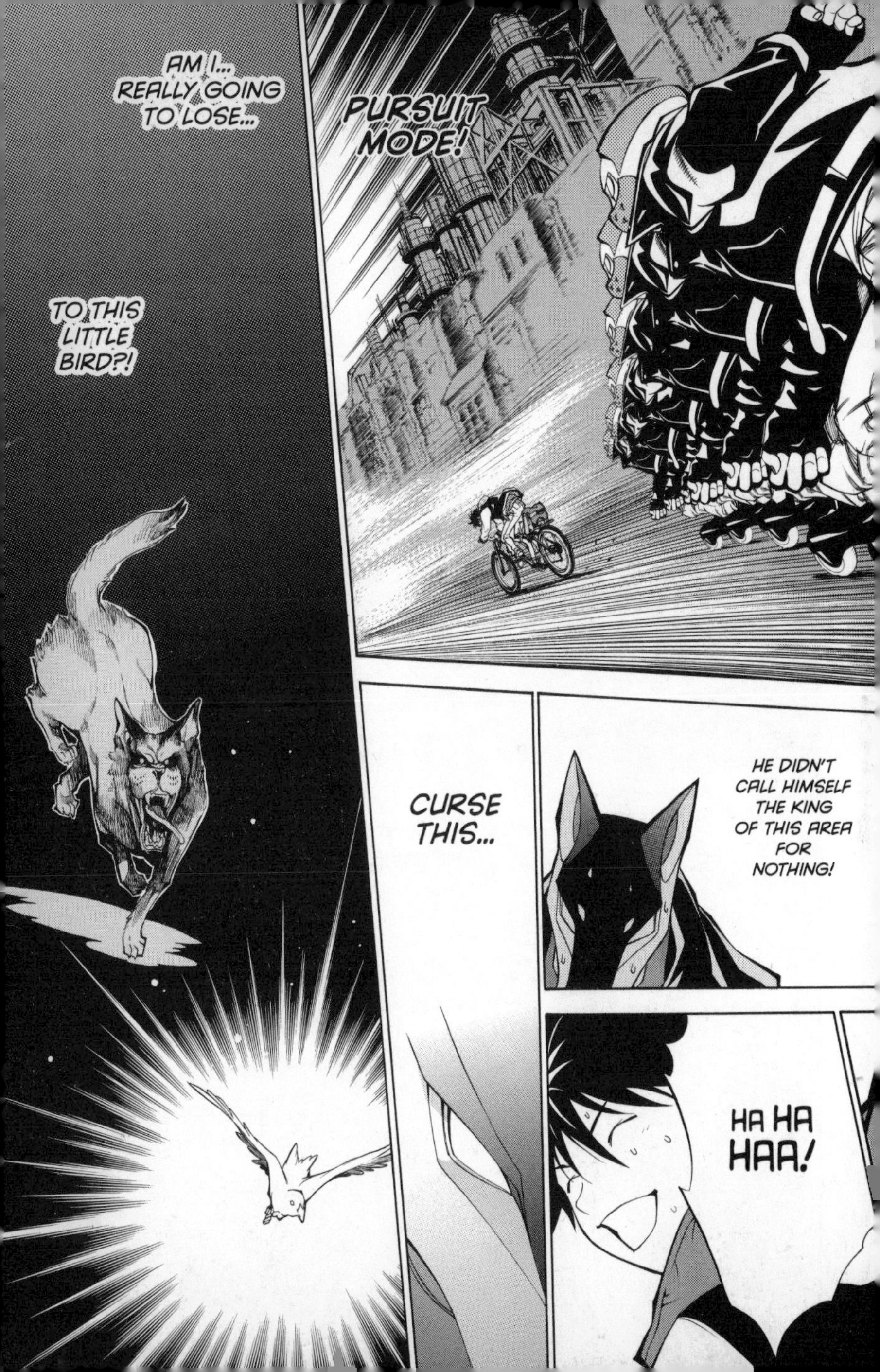
PURSUIT MODE!
HE DIDN'T CALL HIMSELF THE KING OF THIS AREA FOR NOTHING!
CURSE THIS...
HA HA HAA!
AM I... REALLY GOING TO LOSE...
TO THIS LITTLE BIRD?!

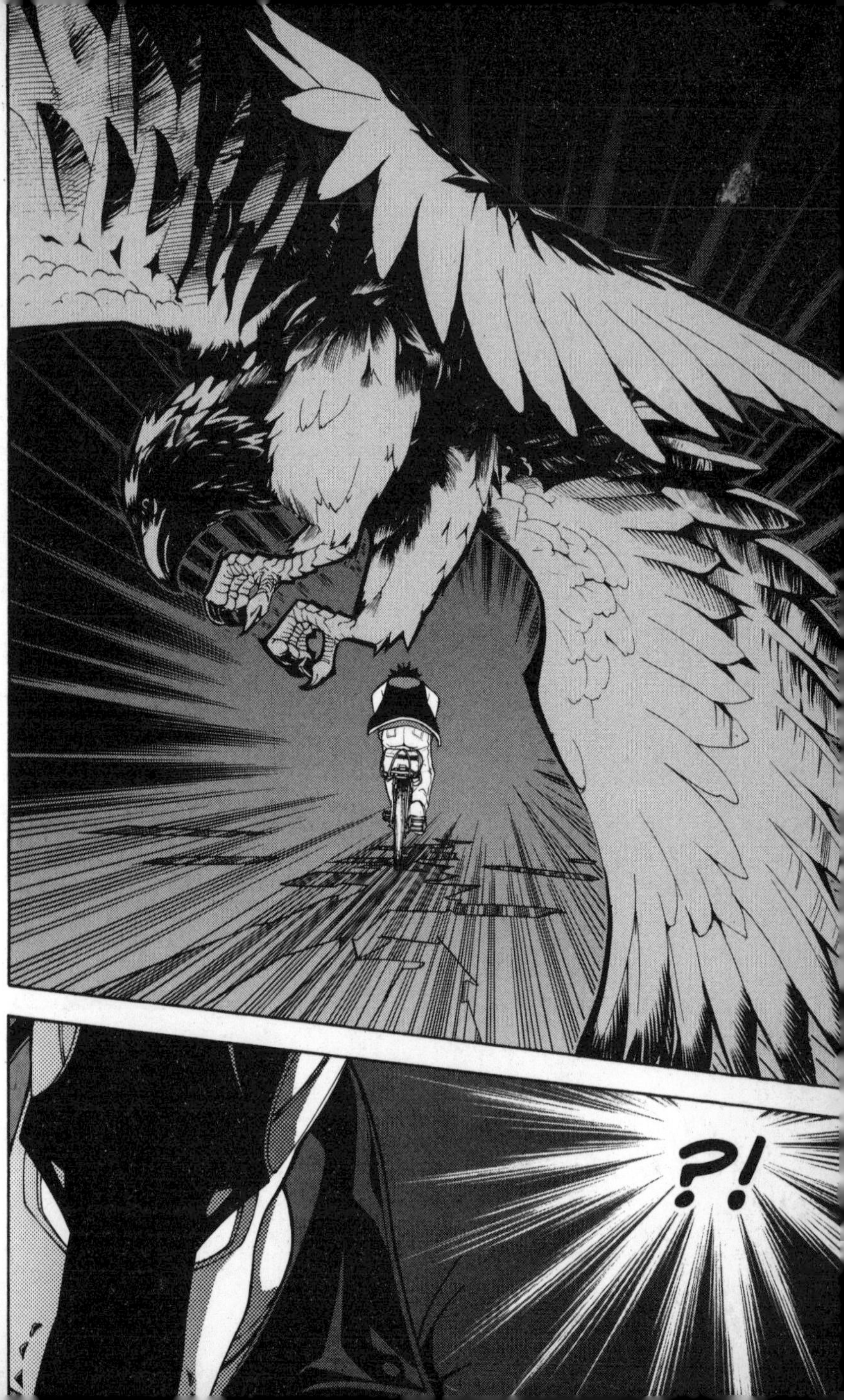
?!

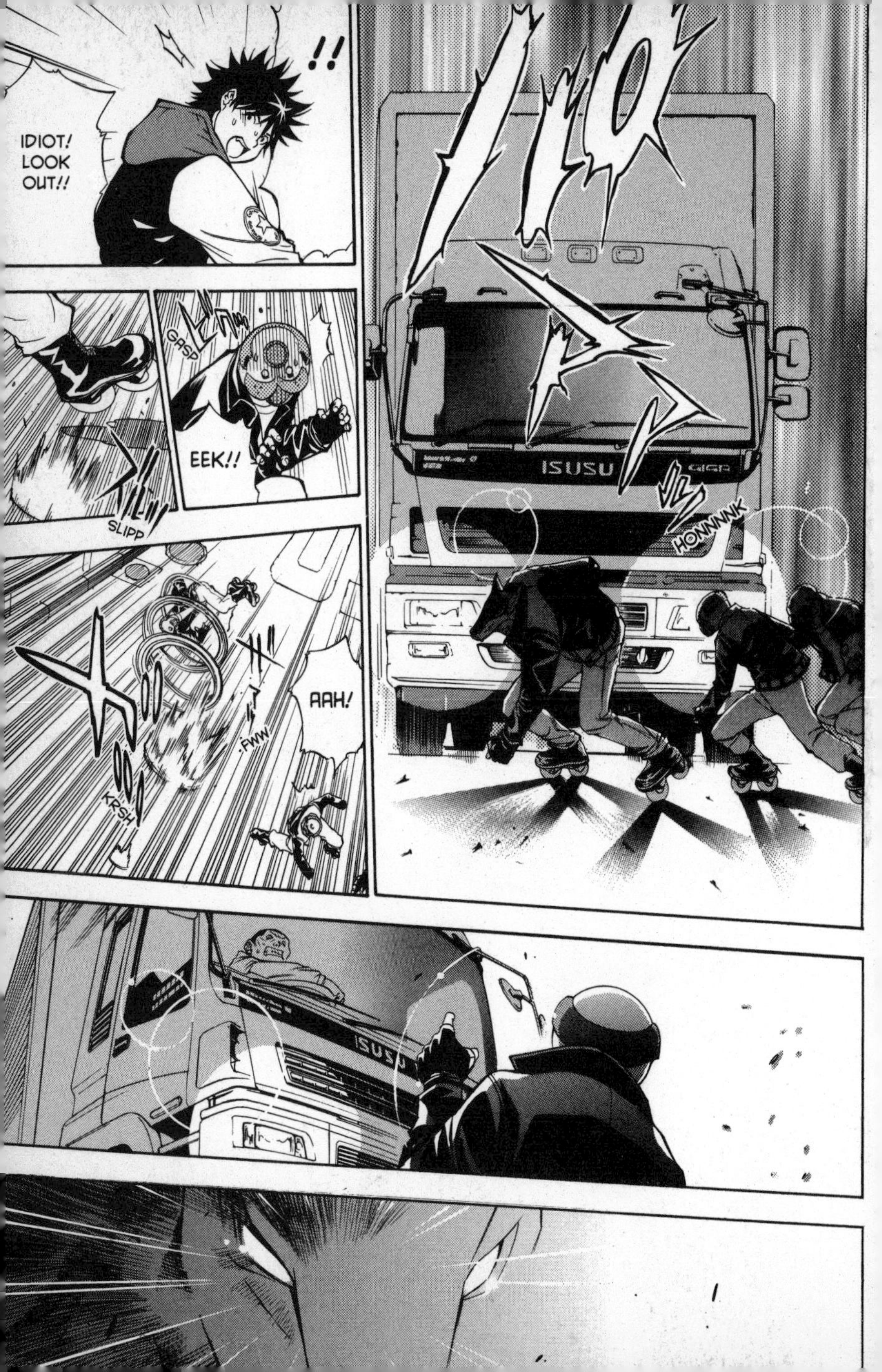
HONNNNK
!!
IDIOT! LOOK OUT!!
GASP
EEK!!
SLIPP
AAH!
FWW
KRSH

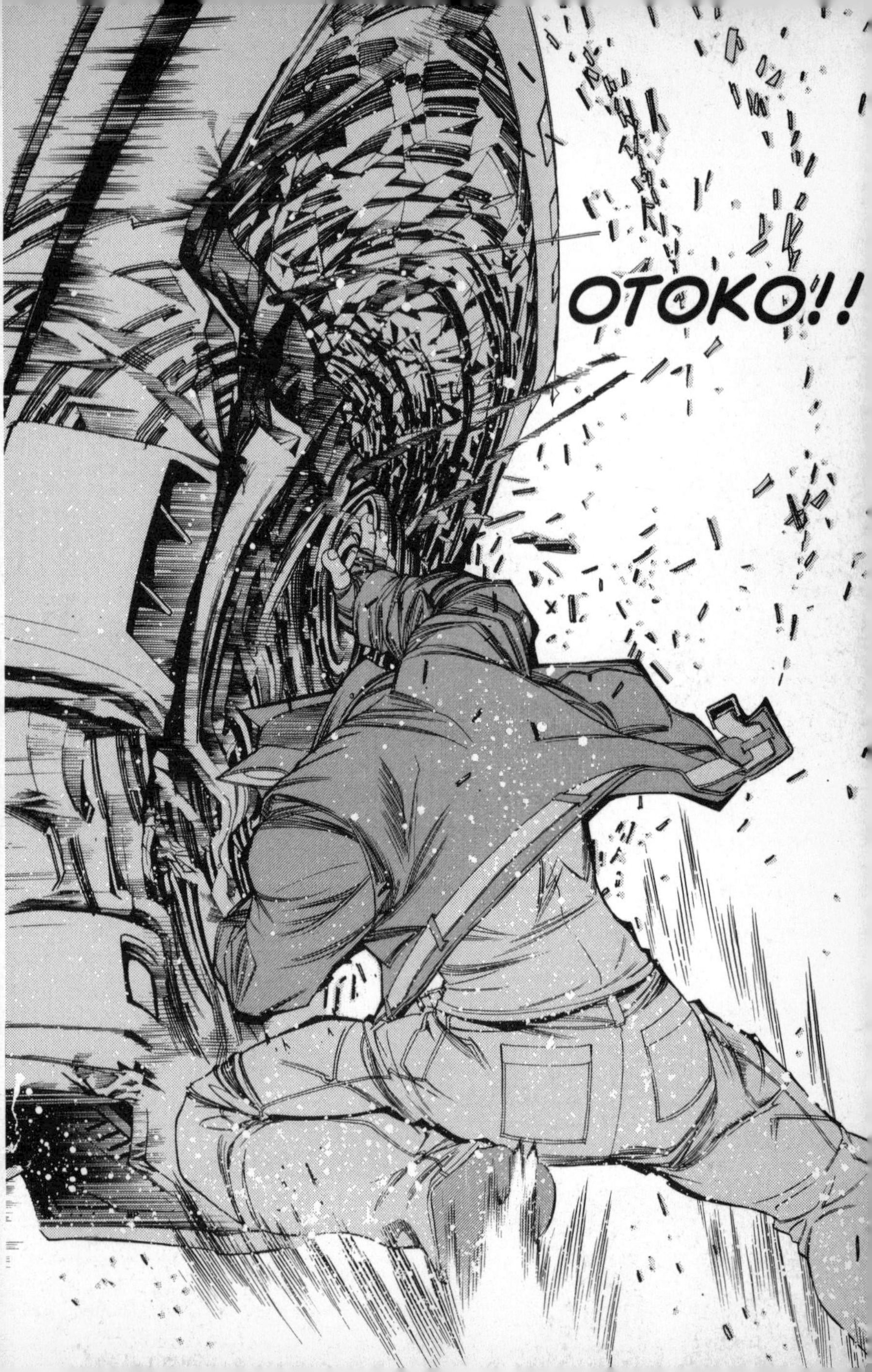
OTOKO!!

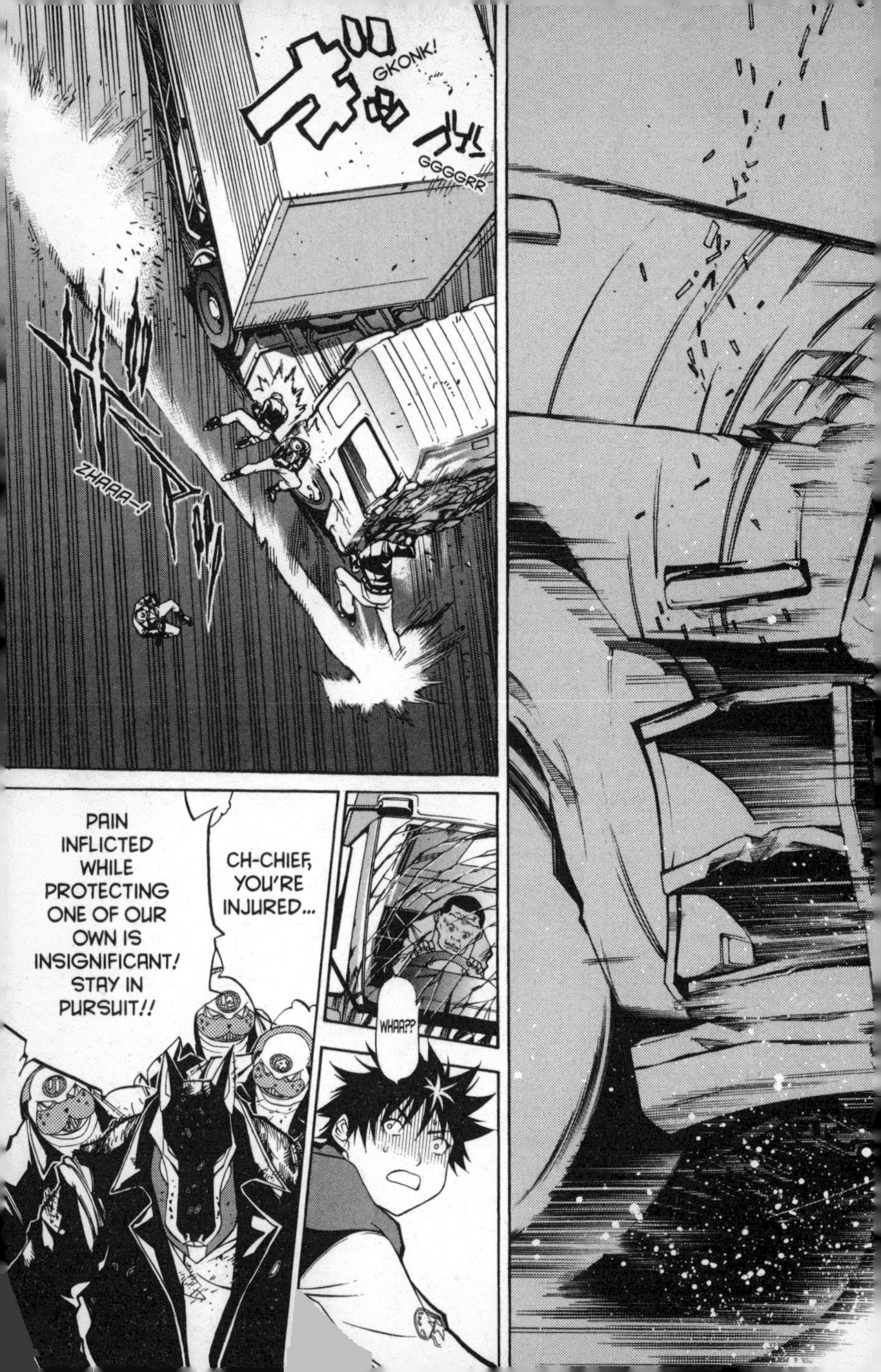
GKONK!
GGGGRR
ZHAAA-!
WHAA??
CH-CHIEF, YOU'RE INJURED...
PAIN INFLICTED WHILE PROTECTING ONE OF OUR OWN IS INSIGNIFICANT! STAY IN PURSUIT!!

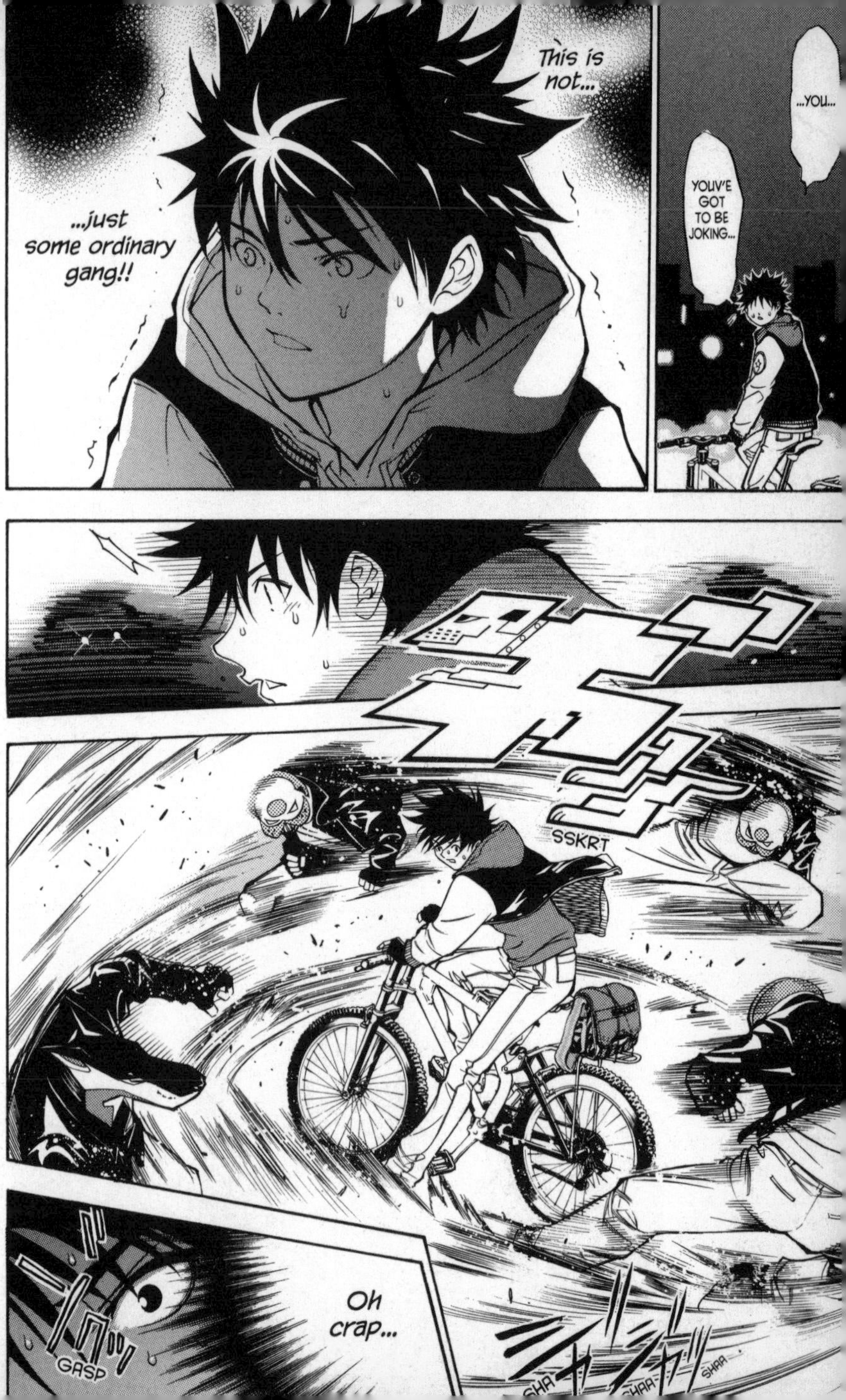
...YOU...
YOU'VE GOT TO BE JOKING...
This is not...
...just some ordinary gang!!
SSKRT
Oh crap...
GASP
SHAA
SHAA
SHAA

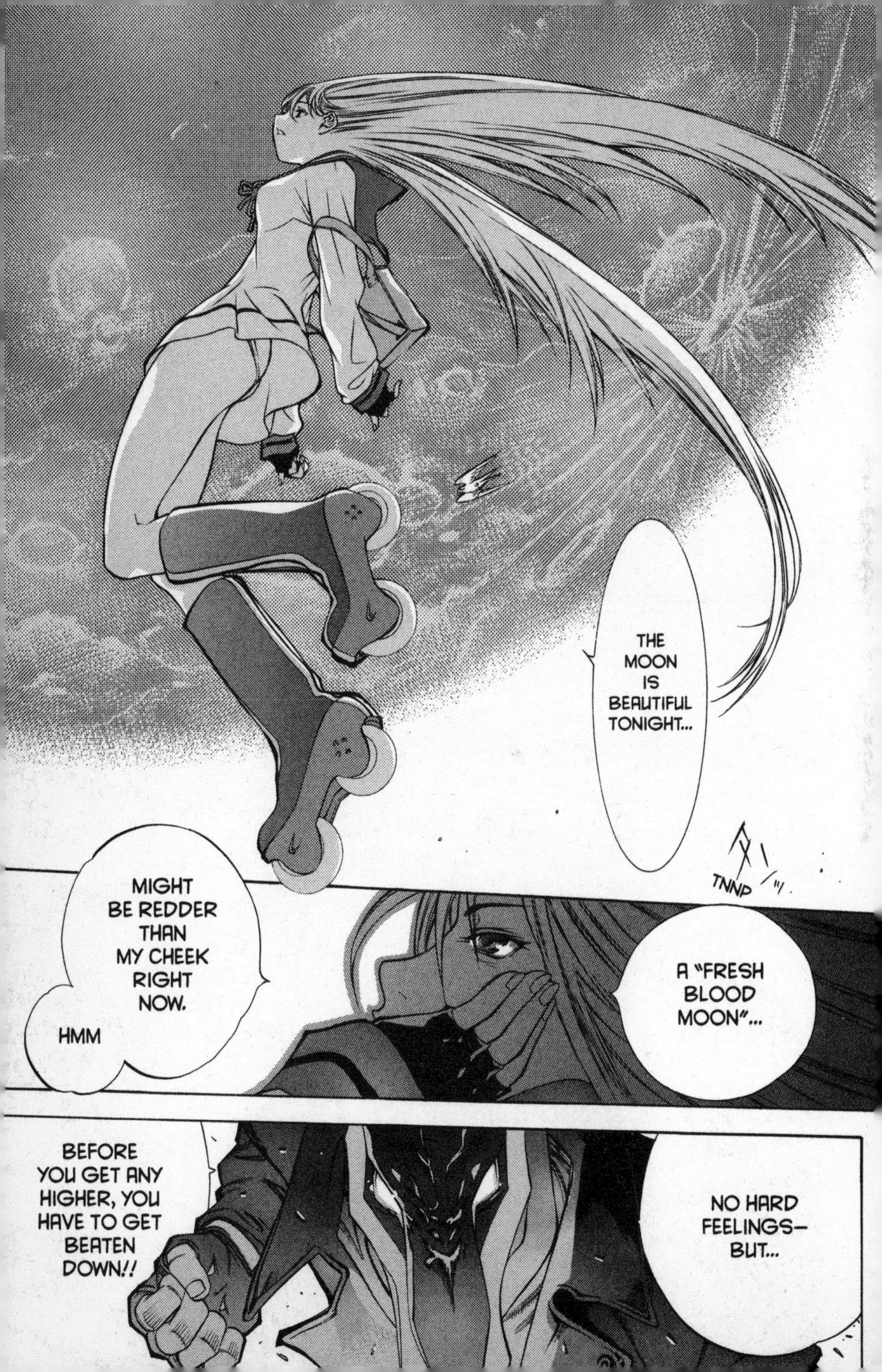
THE MOON IS BEAUTIFUL TONIGHT...
TNNP
A "FRESH BLOOD MOON"...
MIGHT BE REDDER THAN MY CHEEK RIGHT NOW.
HMM
NO HARD FEELINGS— BUT...
BEFORE YOU GET ANY HIGHER, YOU HAVE TO GET BEATEN DOWN!!

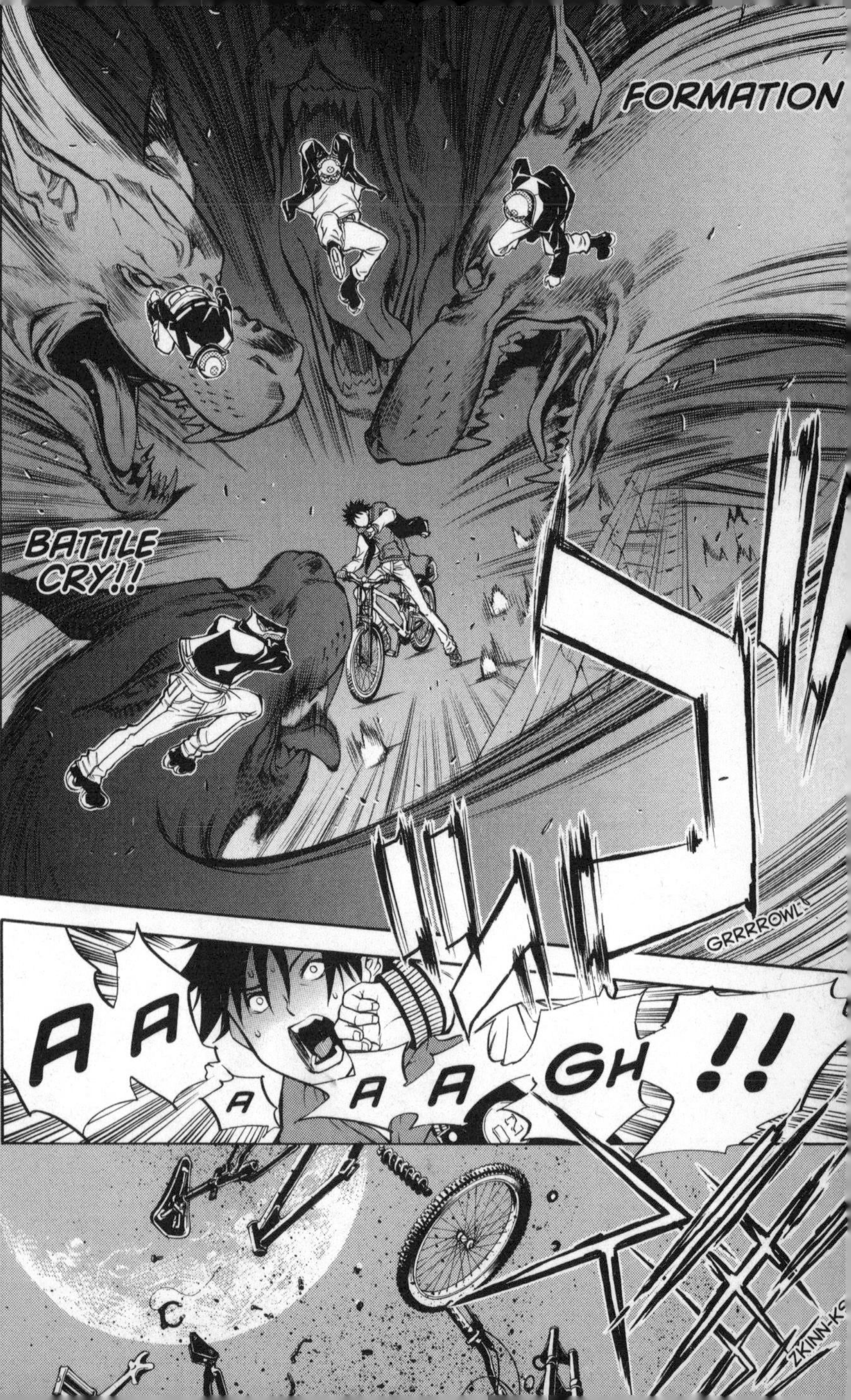
FORMATION
BATTLE CRY!!
GRRRROWL
A A A A A GH !!
ZKINN-K

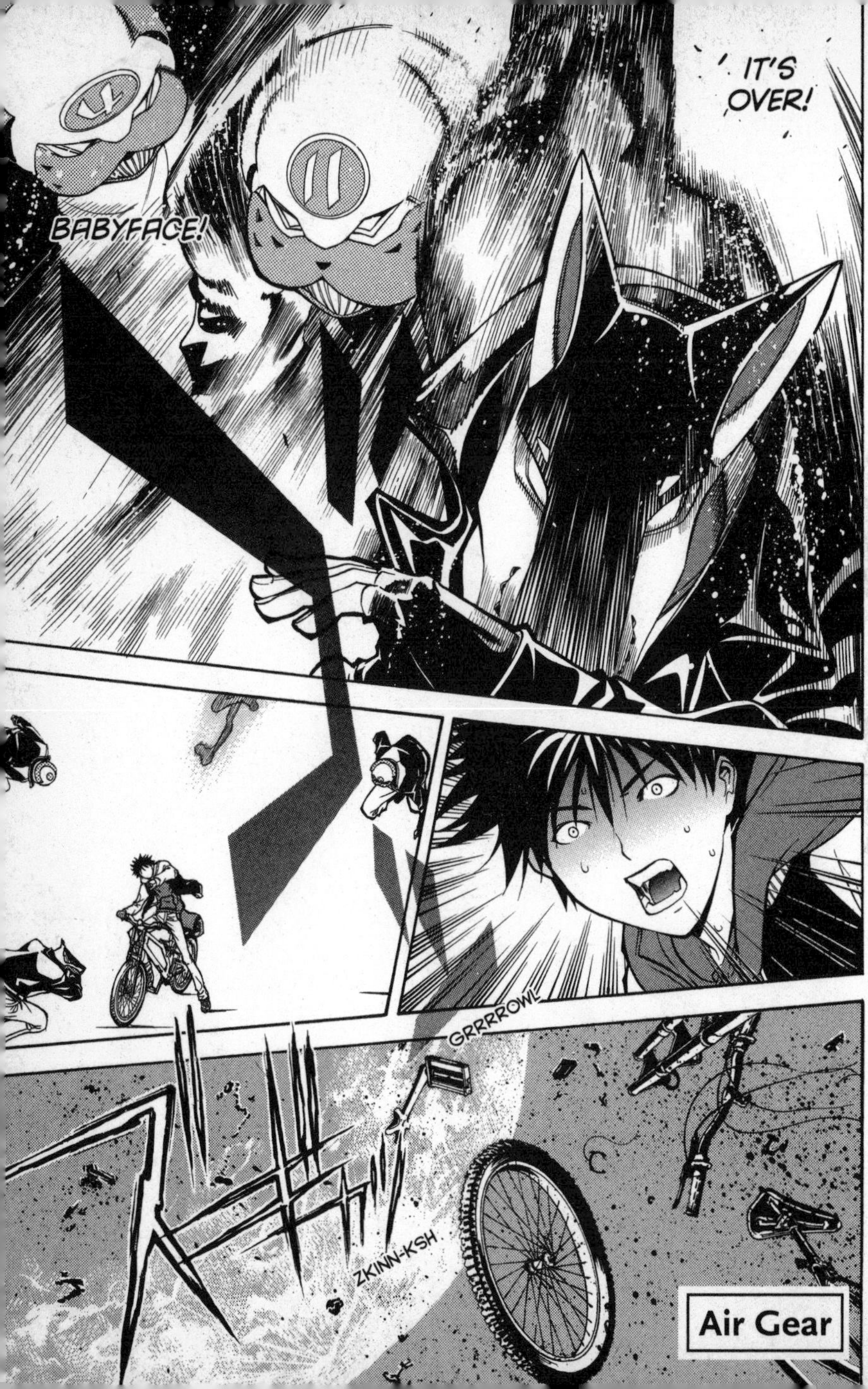
IT'S OVER!
BABYFACE!
GRRRROWL
ZKINN-KSH
Air Gear

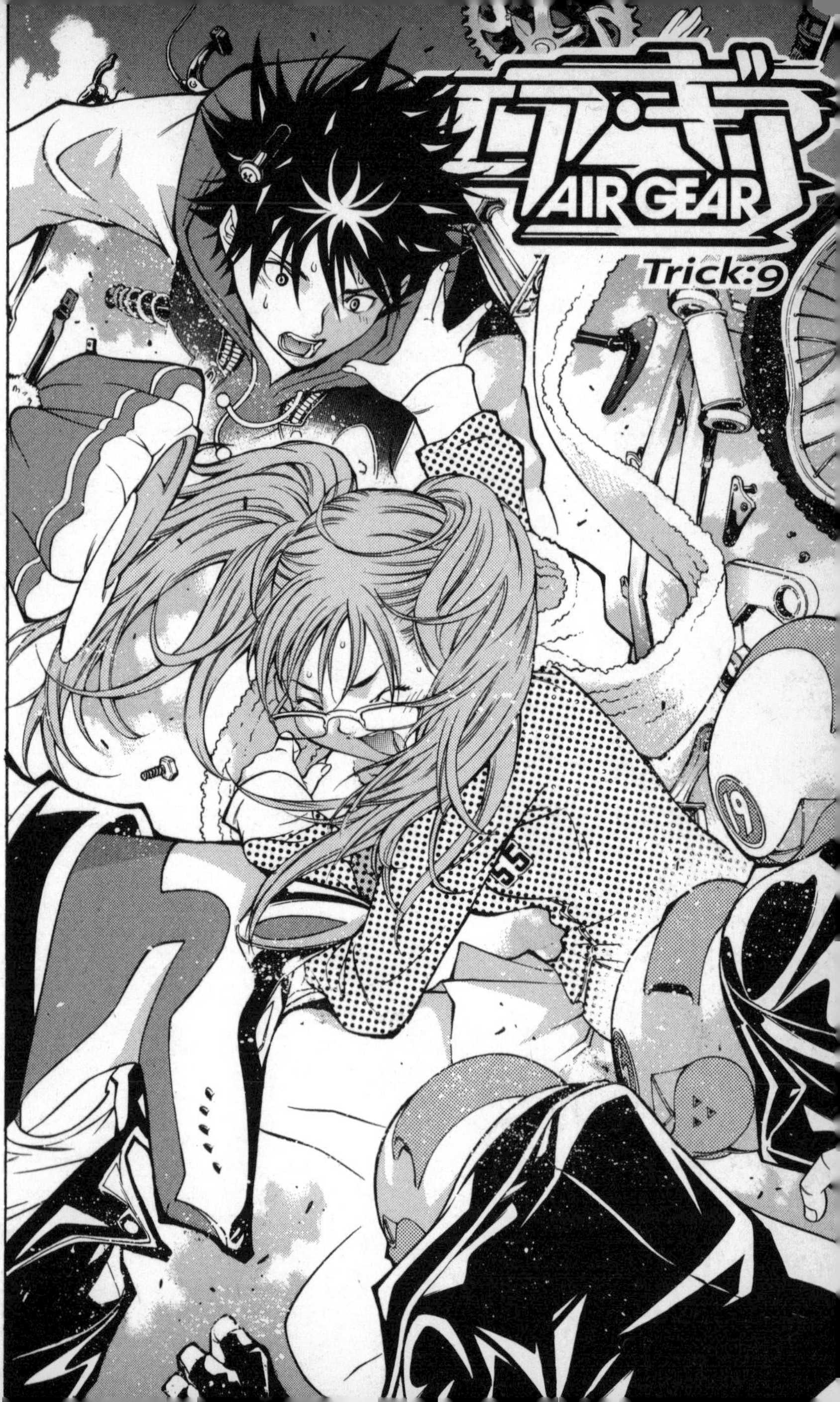
エア・ギア
AIR GEAR
Trick:9

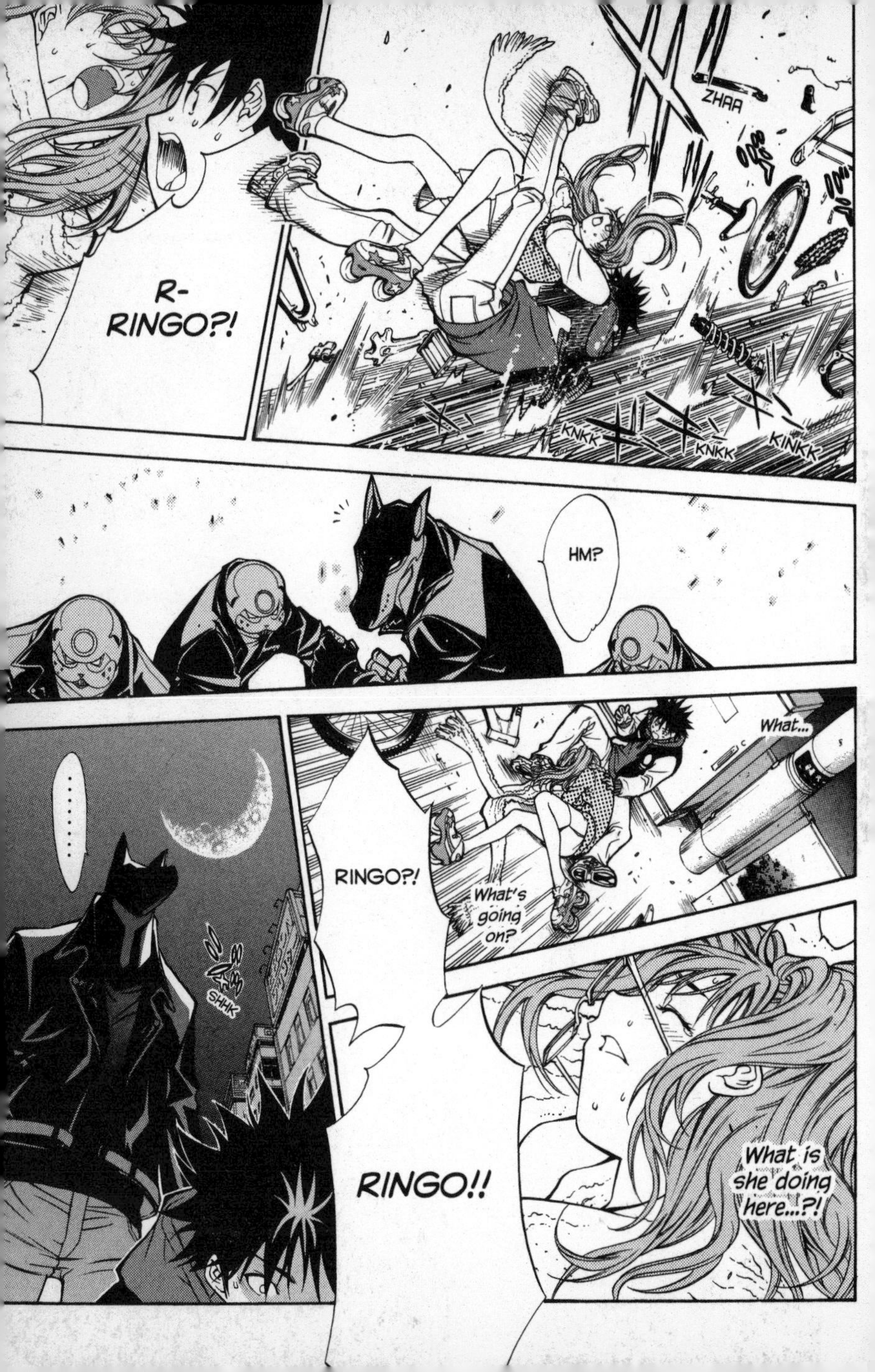
ZHAA
KNKK
KNKK
KINKK
R- RINGO?!
HM?
What...
RINGO?!
What's going on?
What is she doing here...?!
RINGO!!
......
SHHK

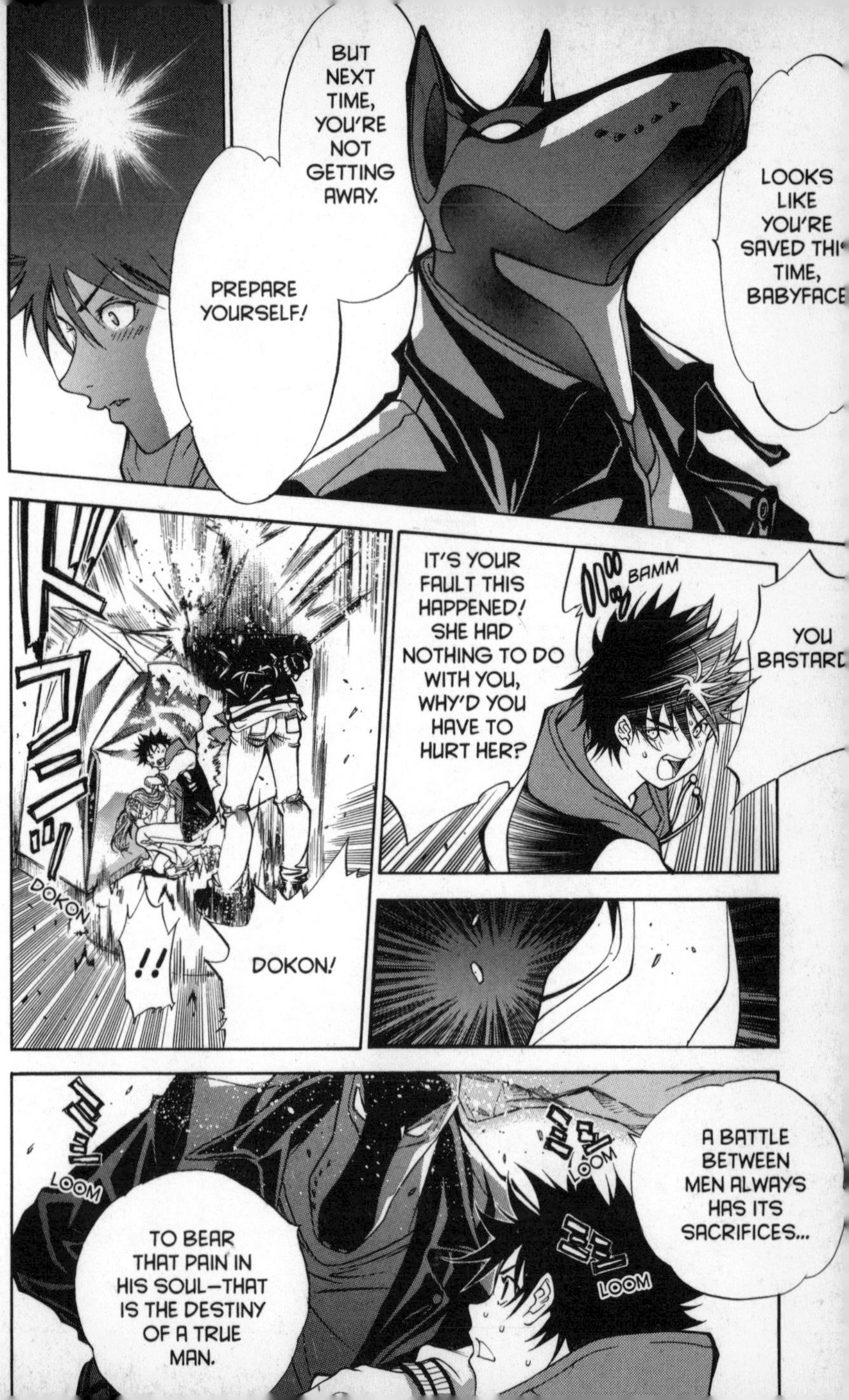
LOOKS LIKE YOU'RE SAVED THI TIME, BABYFACE
BUT NEXT TIME, YOU'RE NOT GETTING AWAY.
PREPARE YOURSELF!
YOU BASTARD
BAMM
IT'S YOUR FAULT THIS HAPPENED! SHE HAD NOTHING TO DO WITH YOU, WHY'D YOU HAVE TO HURT HER?
DOKON
!!
DOKON!
A BATTLE BETWEEN MEN ALWAYS HAS ITS SACRIFICES...
LOOM
LOOM
LOOM
TO BEAR THAT PAIN IN HIS SOUL—THAT IS THE DESTINY OF A TRUE MAN.

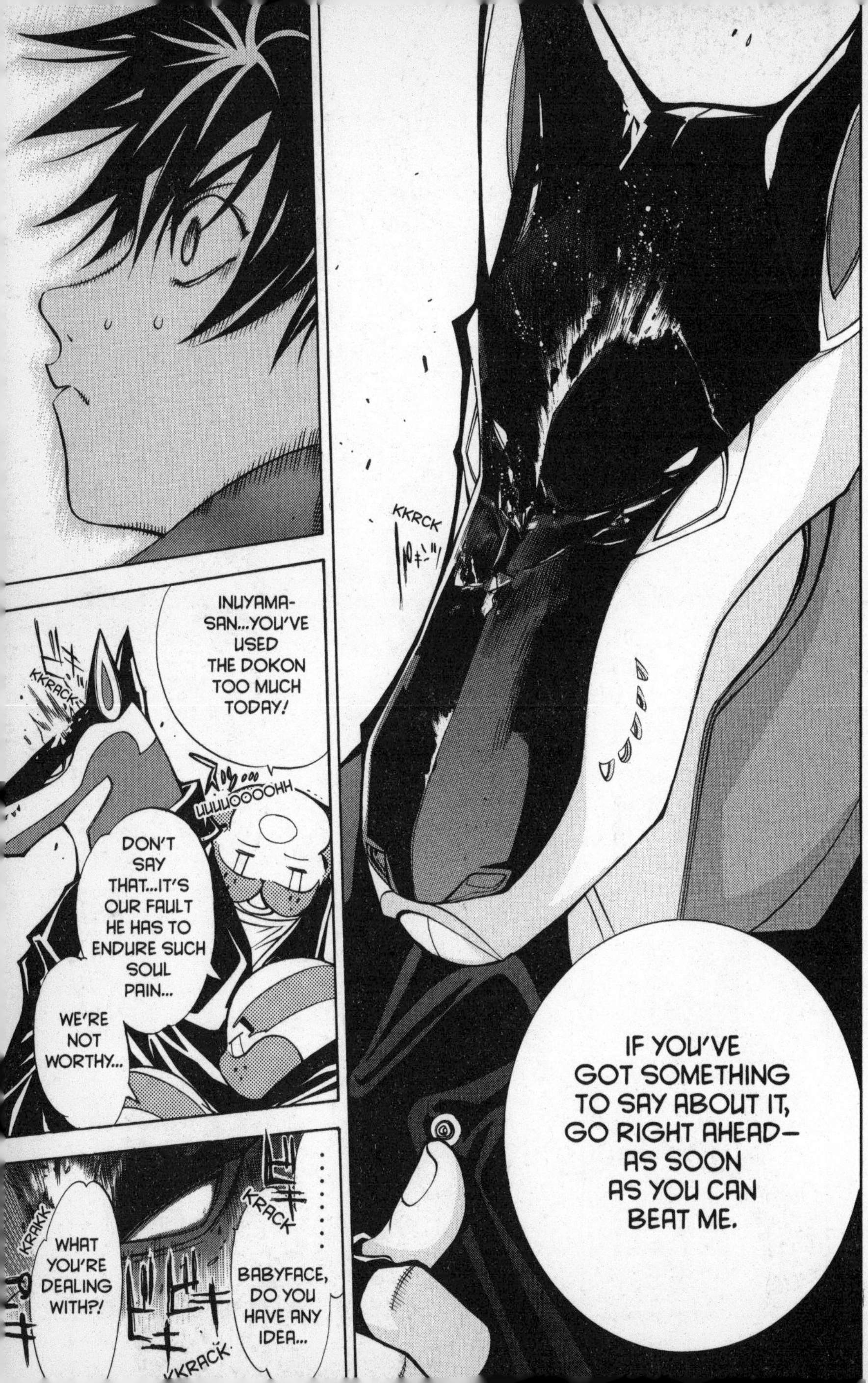
KKRCK
INUYAMA-SAN...YOU'VE USED THE DOKON TOO MUCH TODAY!
KKRACK
UUUUOOOOHH
DON'T SAY THAT...IT'S OUR FAULT HE HAS TO ENDURE SUCH SOUL PAIN...
WE'RE NOT WORTHY...
IF YOU'VE GOT SOMETHING TO SAY ABOUT IT, GO RIGHT AHEAD—AS SOON AS YOU CAN BEAT ME.
KRACK
BABYFACE, DO YOU HAVE ANY IDEA...
KRAKK
WHAT YOU'RE DEALING WITH?!
KRACK

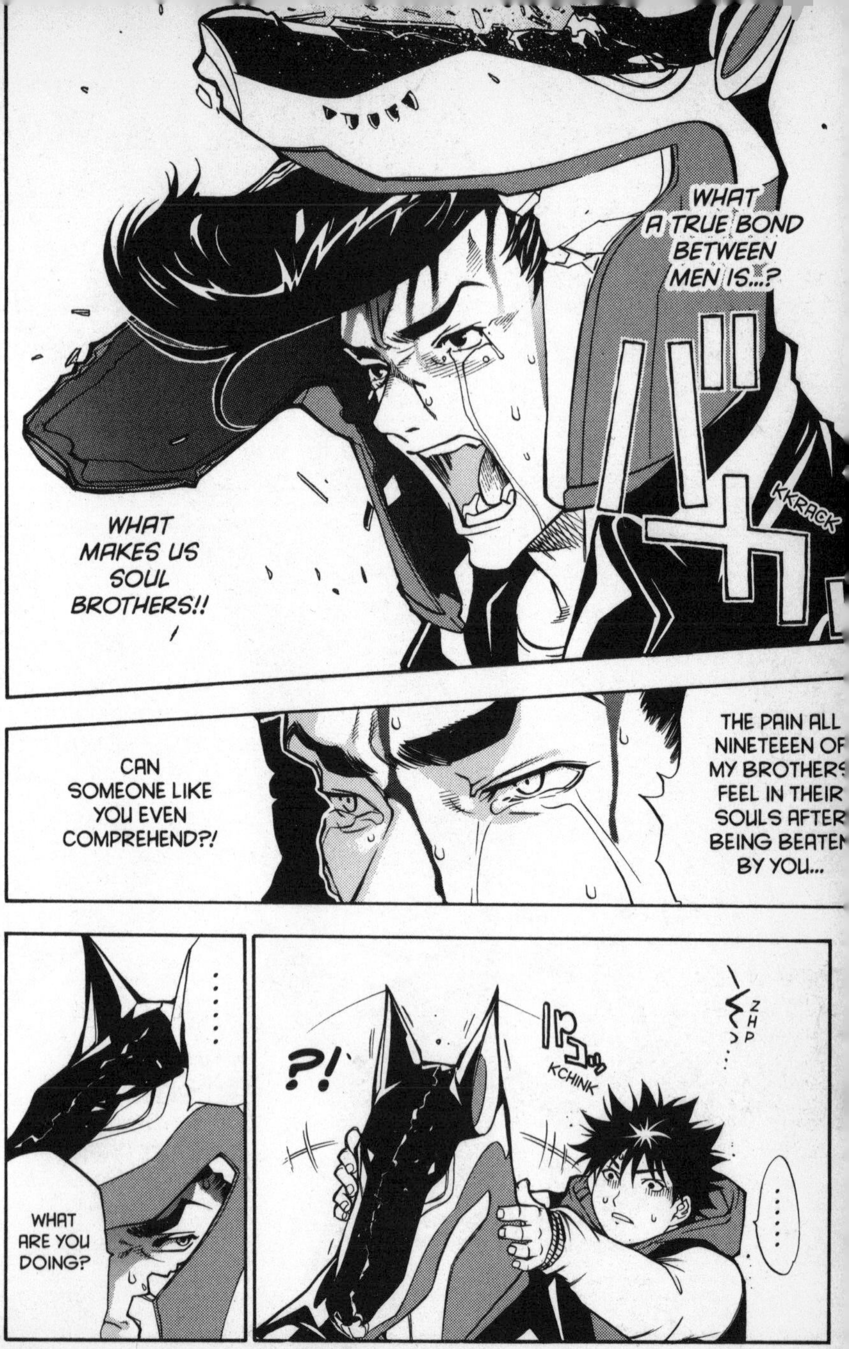
WHAT A TRUE BOND BETWEEN MEN IS...?
KKRACK
WHAT MAKES US SOUL BROTHERS!!
THE PAIN ALL NINETEEEN OF MY BROTHERS FEEL IN THEIR SOULS AFTER BEING BEATEN BY YOU...
CAN SOMEONE LIKE YOU EVEN COMPREHEND?!
ZHP
......
KCHINK
?!
......
WHAT ARE YOU DOING?

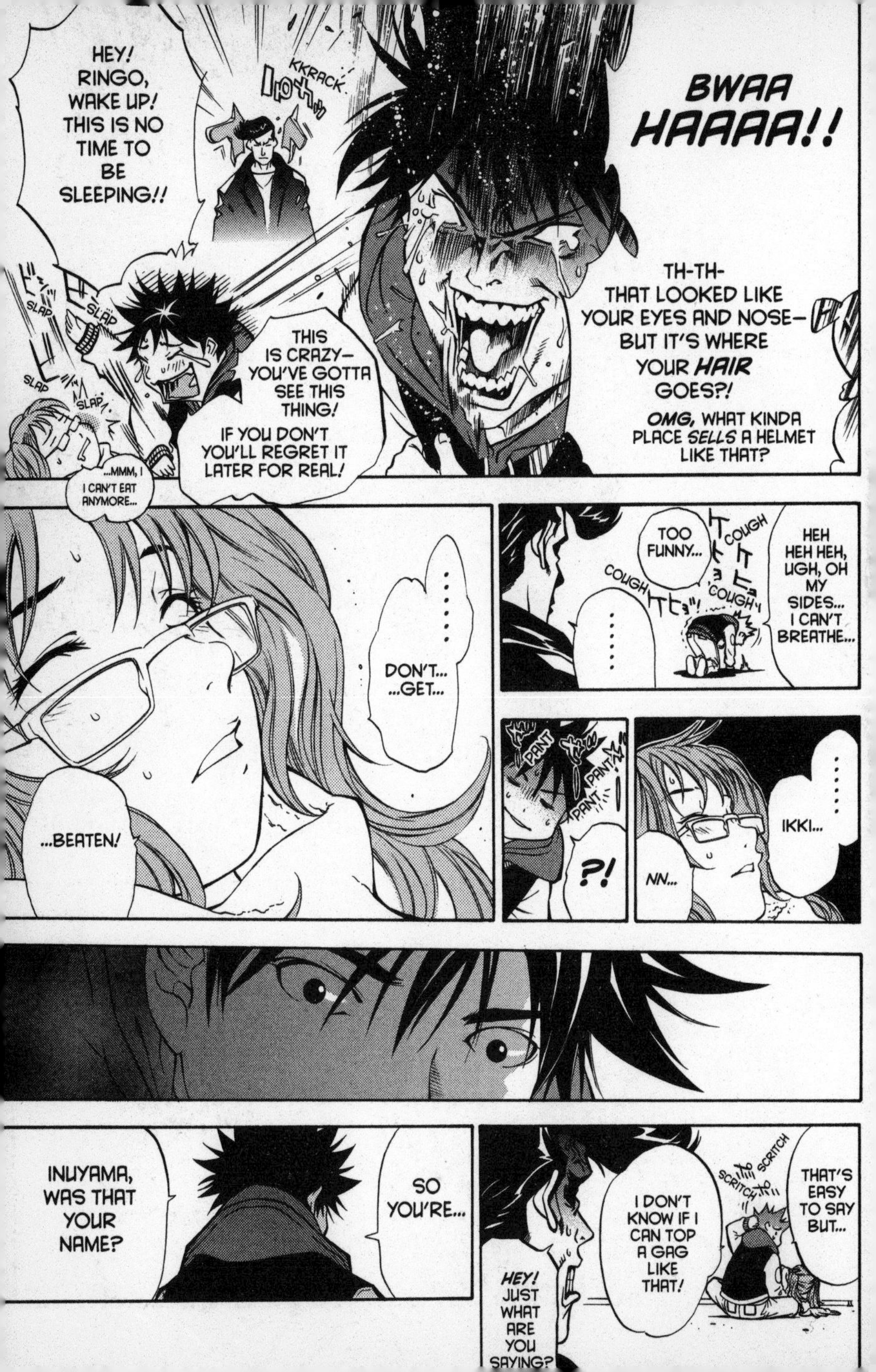
BWAA HAAAAA!!
KKRACK
HEY! RINGO, WAKE UP! THIS IS NO TIME TO BE SLEEPING!!
TH-TH- THAT LOOKED LIKE YOUR EYES AND NOSE— BUT IT'S WHERE YOUR HAIR GOES?!
OMG, WHAT KINDA PLACE SELLS A HELMET LIKE THAT?
THIS IS CRAZY— YOU'VE GOTTA SEE THIS THING!
IF YOU DON'T YOU'LL REGRET IT LATER FOR REAL!
SLAP SLAP SLAP SLAP
...MMM, I I CAN'T EAT ANYMORE...
HEH HEH HEH, UGH, OH MY SIDES... I CAN'T BREATHE...
COUGH
TOO FUNNY...
COUGH COUGH
......
......
IKKI...
NN...
PANT PANT PANT
?!
......
DON'T... ...GET...
...BEATEN!
THAT'S EASY TO SAY BUT...
SCRITCH SCRITCH
I DON'T KNOW IF I CAN TOP A GAG LIKE THAT!
HEY! JUST WHAT ARE YOU SAYING?
SO YOU'RE...
INUYAMA, WAS THAT YOUR NAME?

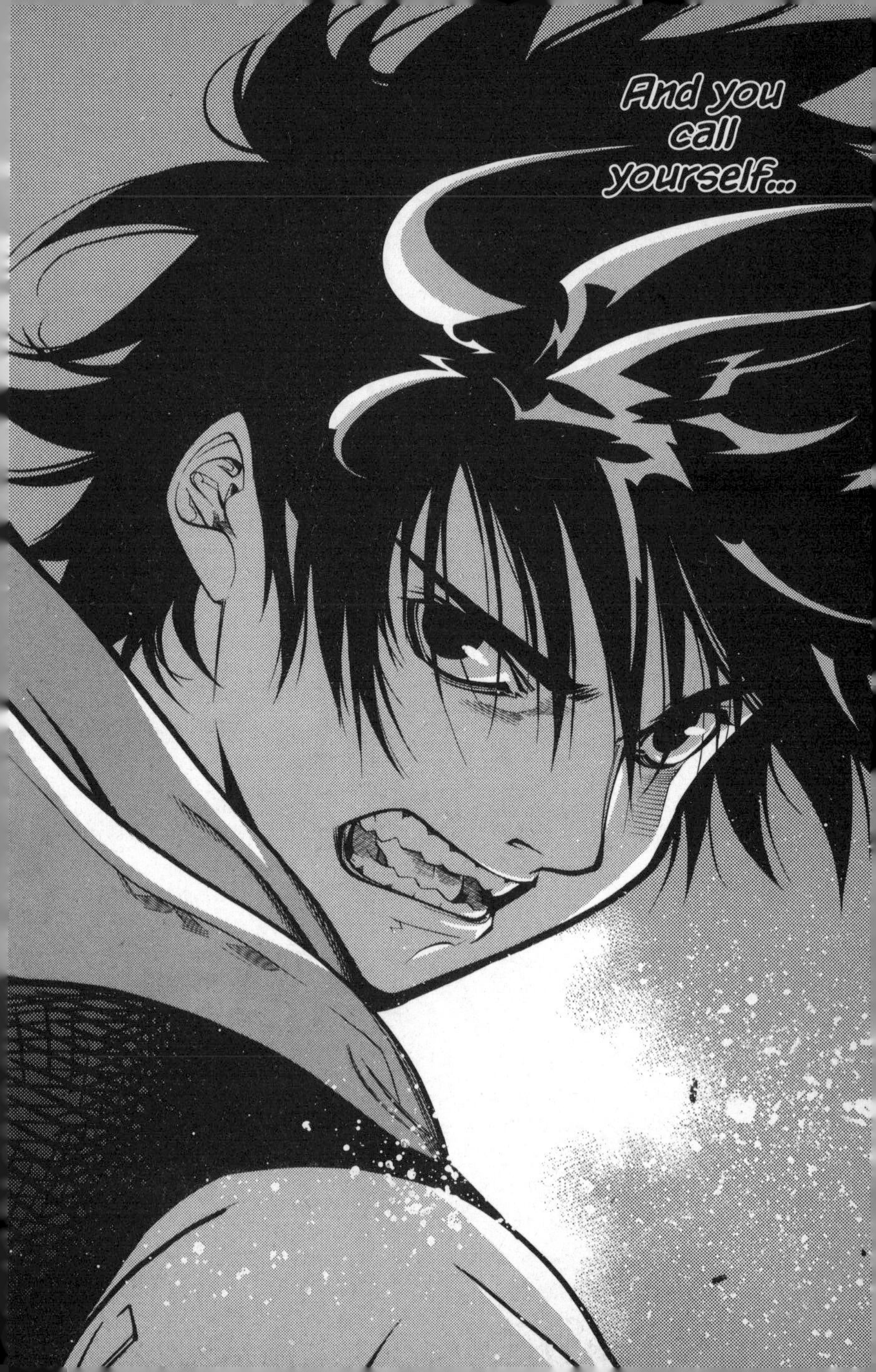
And you call yourself...

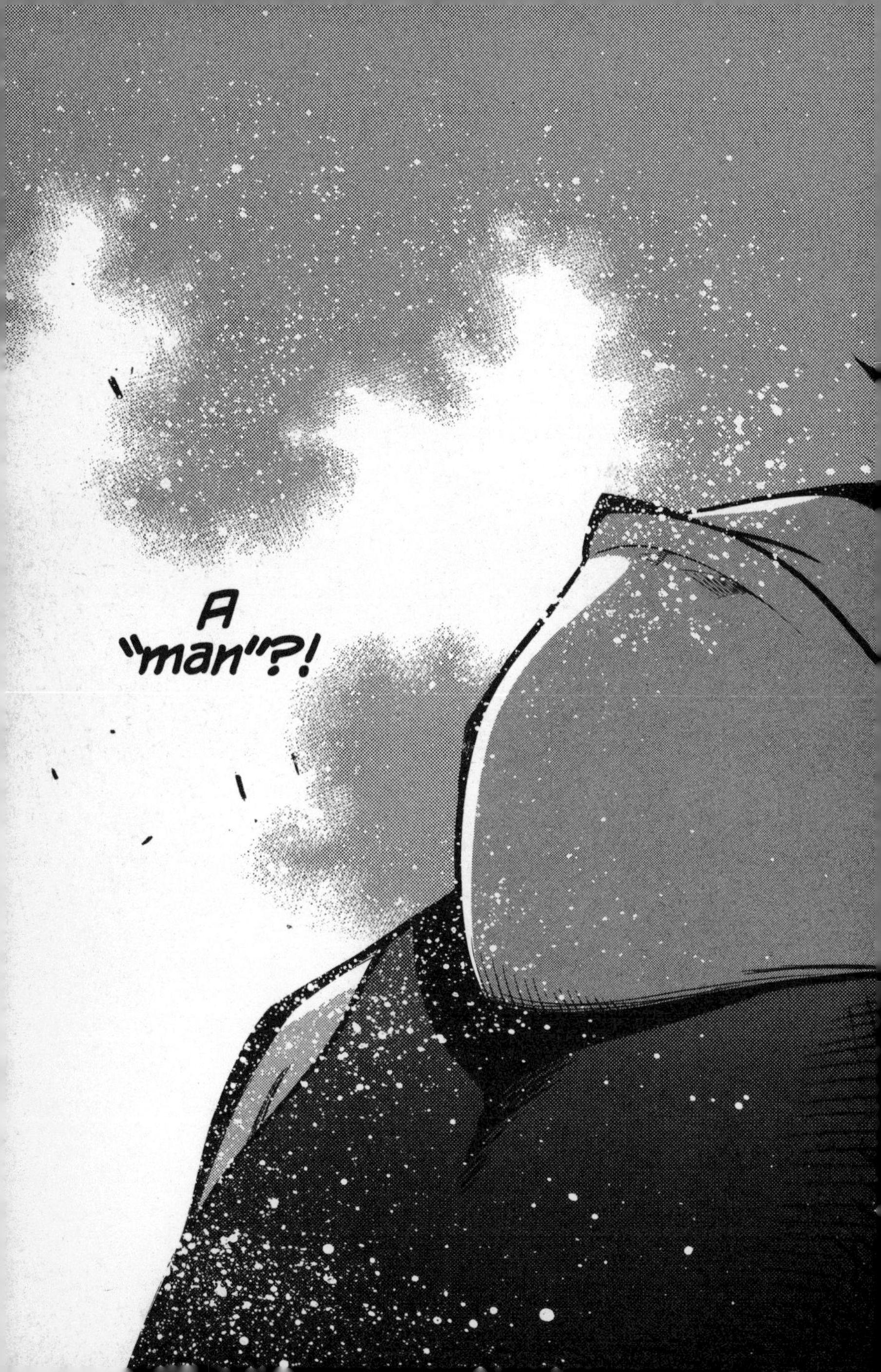
A "man"?!

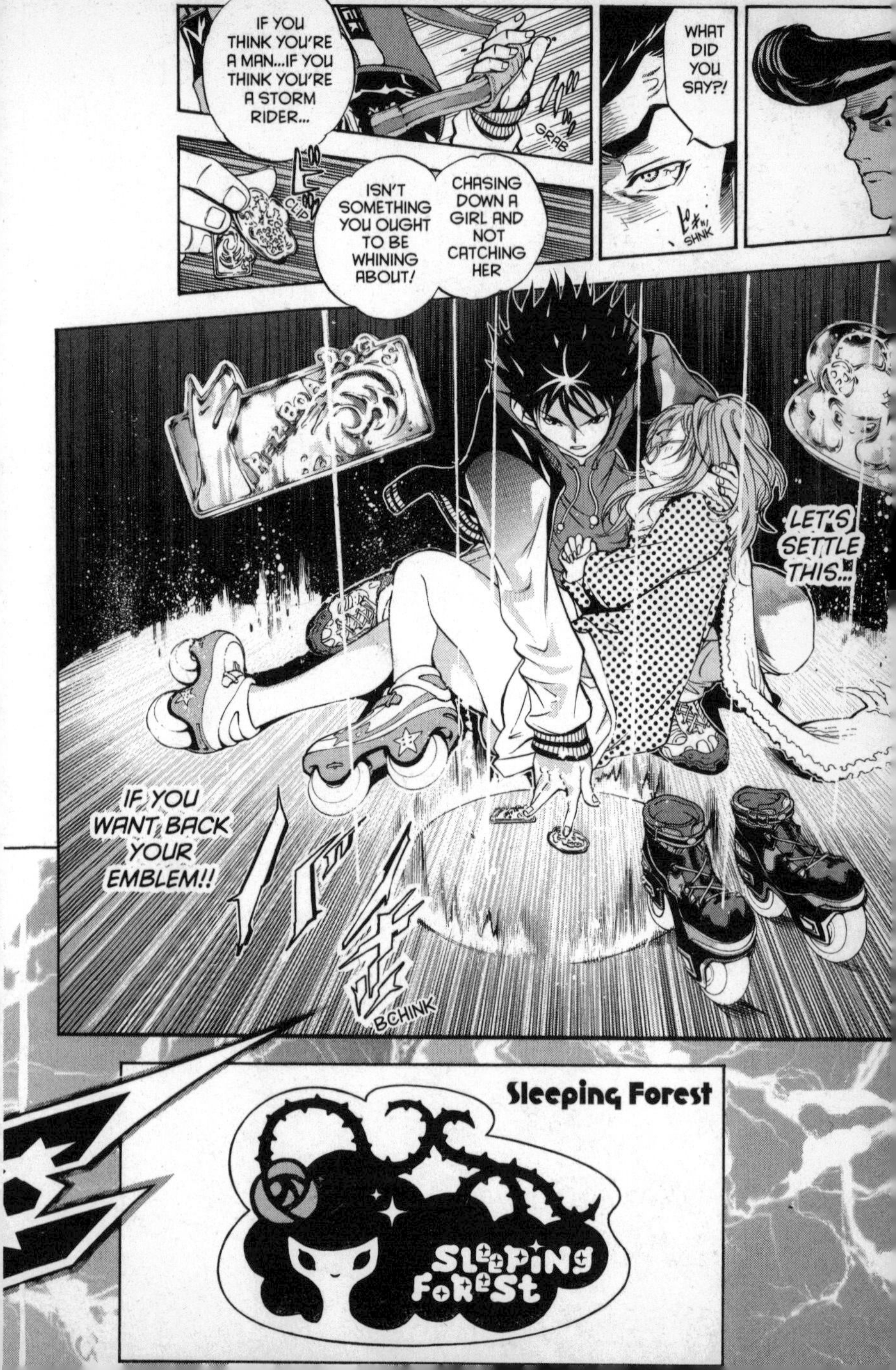
WHAT DID YOU SAY?!
SHNK
IF YOU THINK YOU'RE A MAN...IF YOU THINK YOU'RE A STORM RIDER...
GRAB
CHASING DOWN A GIRL AND NOT CATCHING HER
ISN'T SOMETHING YOU OUGHT TO BE WHINING ABOUT!
CLIP
LET'S SETTLE THIS...
IF YOU WANT BACK YOUR EMBLEM!!
BCHINK
Sleeping Forest
SLEEPING FOREST

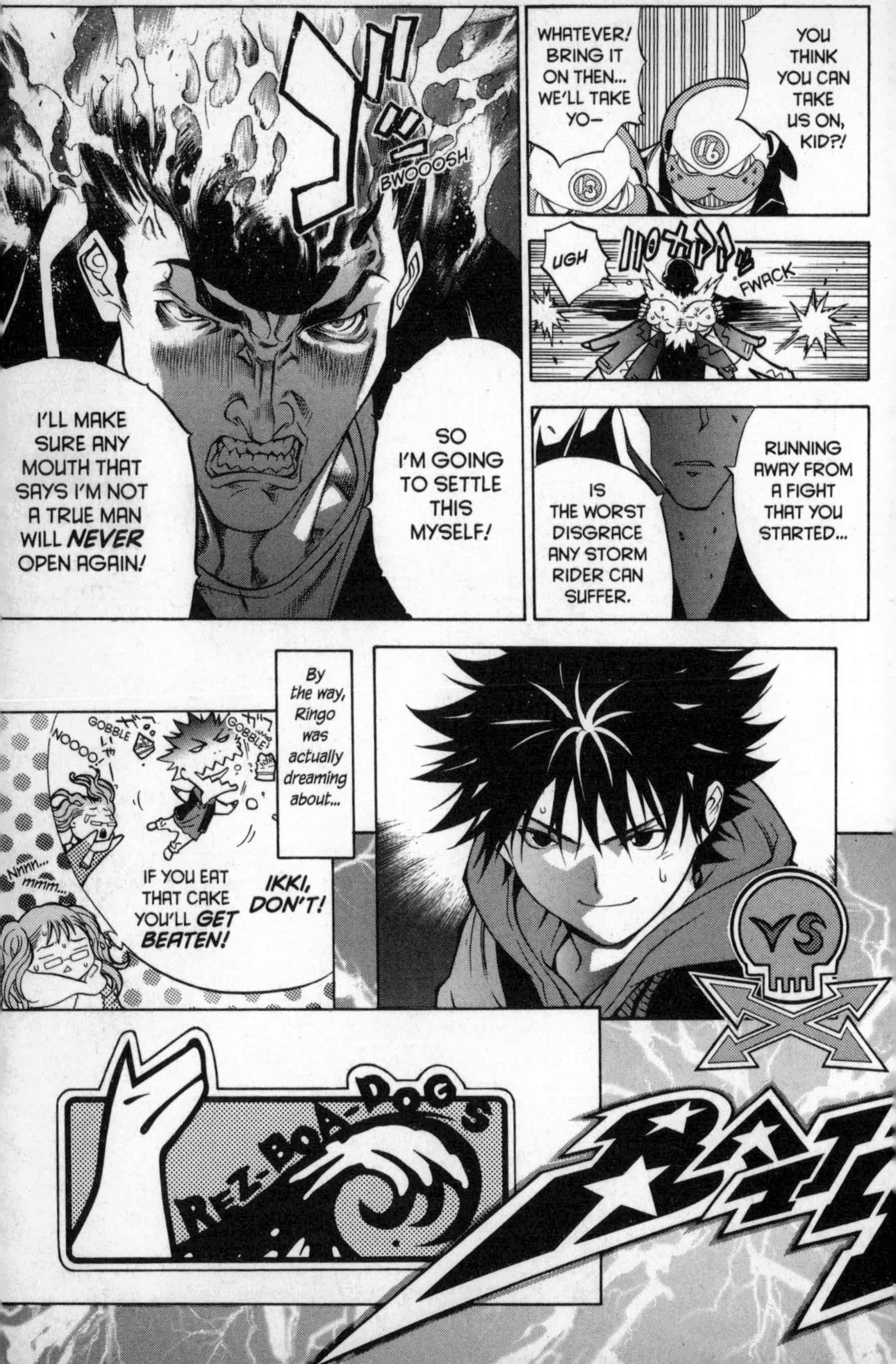
YOU THINK YOU CAN TAKE US ON, KID?!
WHATEVER! BRING IT ON THEN... WE'LL TAKE YO—
UGH
FWACK
RUNNING AWAY FROM A FIGHT THAT YOU STARTED...
IS THE WORST DISGRACE ANY STORM RIDER CAN SUFFER.
BWOOOSH
SO I'M GOING TO SETTLE THIS MYSELF!
I'LL MAKE SURE ANY MOUTH THAT SAYS I'M NOT A TRUE MAN WILL *NEVER* OPEN AGAIN!
By the way, Ringo was actually dreaming about...
GOBBLE
GOBBLE
NOOOO!
IKKI, DON'T!
IF YOU EAT THAT CAKE YOU'LL *GET BEATEN!*
Nnnn... mmm...
VS
REZ-BOA-DOGS

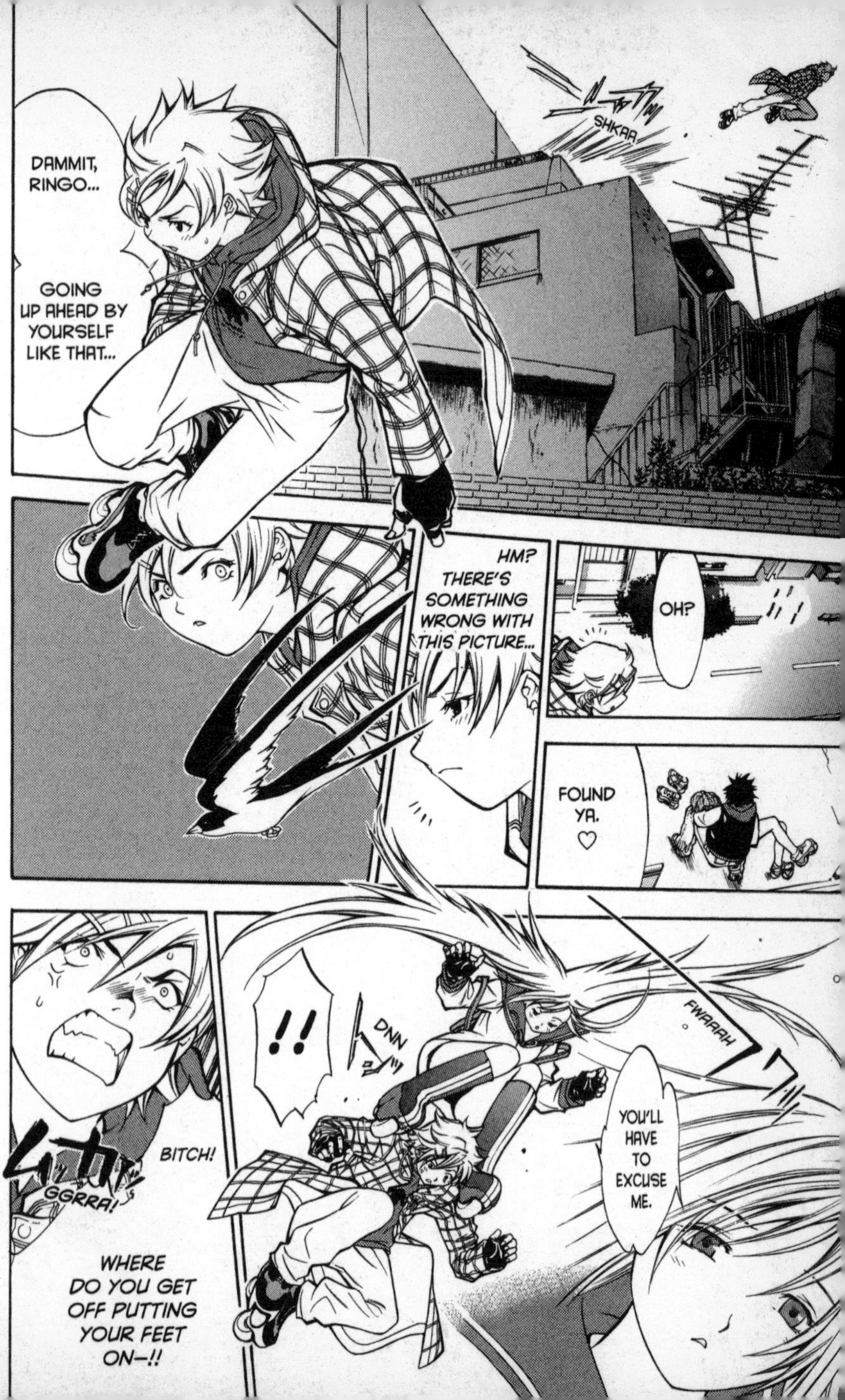
SHKAA
DAMMIT, RINGO...
GOING UP AHEAD BY YOURSELF LIKE THAT...
OH?
FOUND YA. ♡
HM? THERE'S SOMETHING WRONG WITH THIS PICTURE...
FWAAAH
YOU'LL HAVE TO EXCUSE ME.
!!
DNN
BITCH!
GGRRA!
WHERE DO YOU GET OFF PUTTING YOUR FEET ON–!!

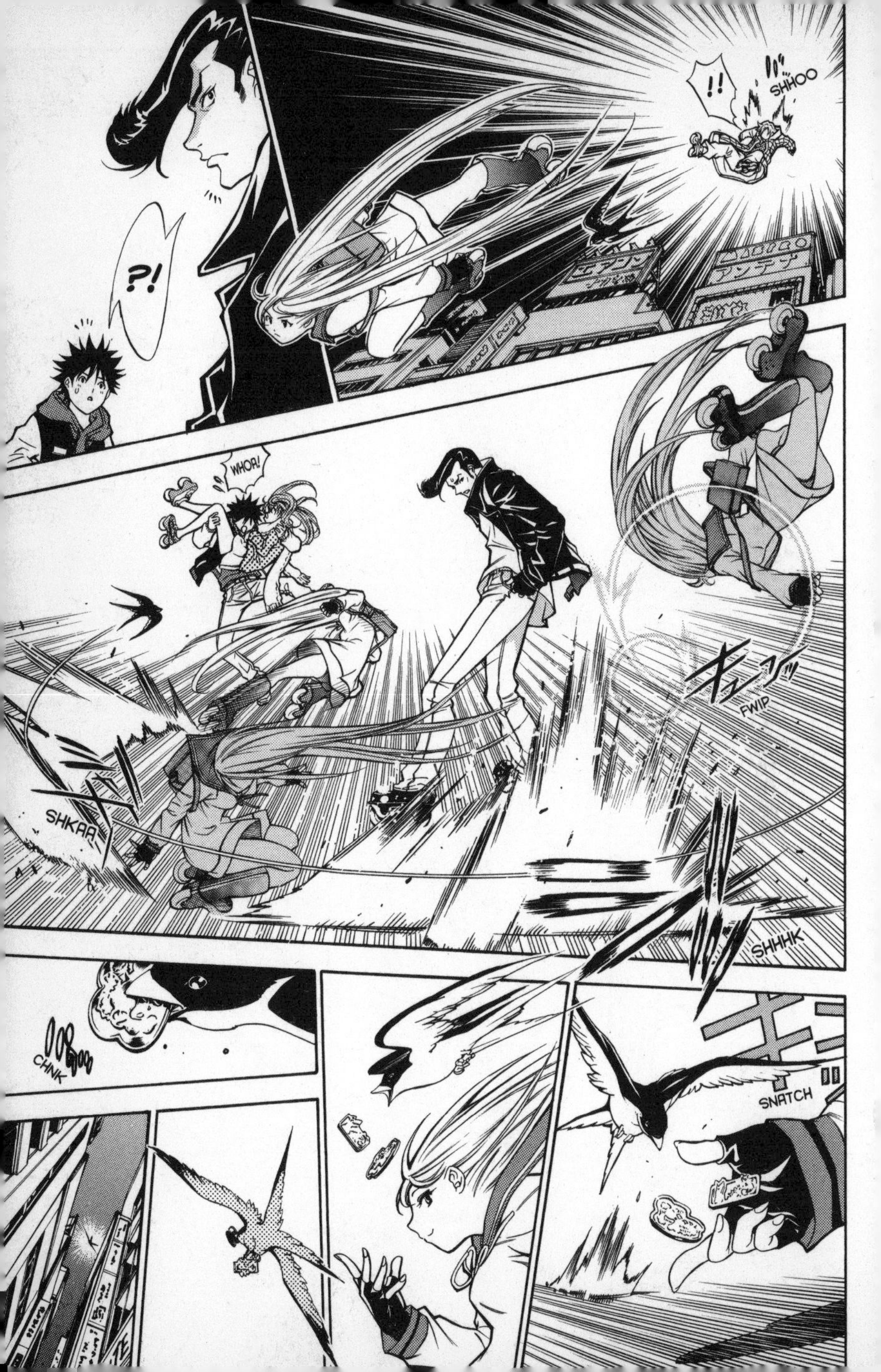
!!
SHHOO
?!
FWIP
WHOA!
SHKAA
SHHHK
SNATCH
CHNK

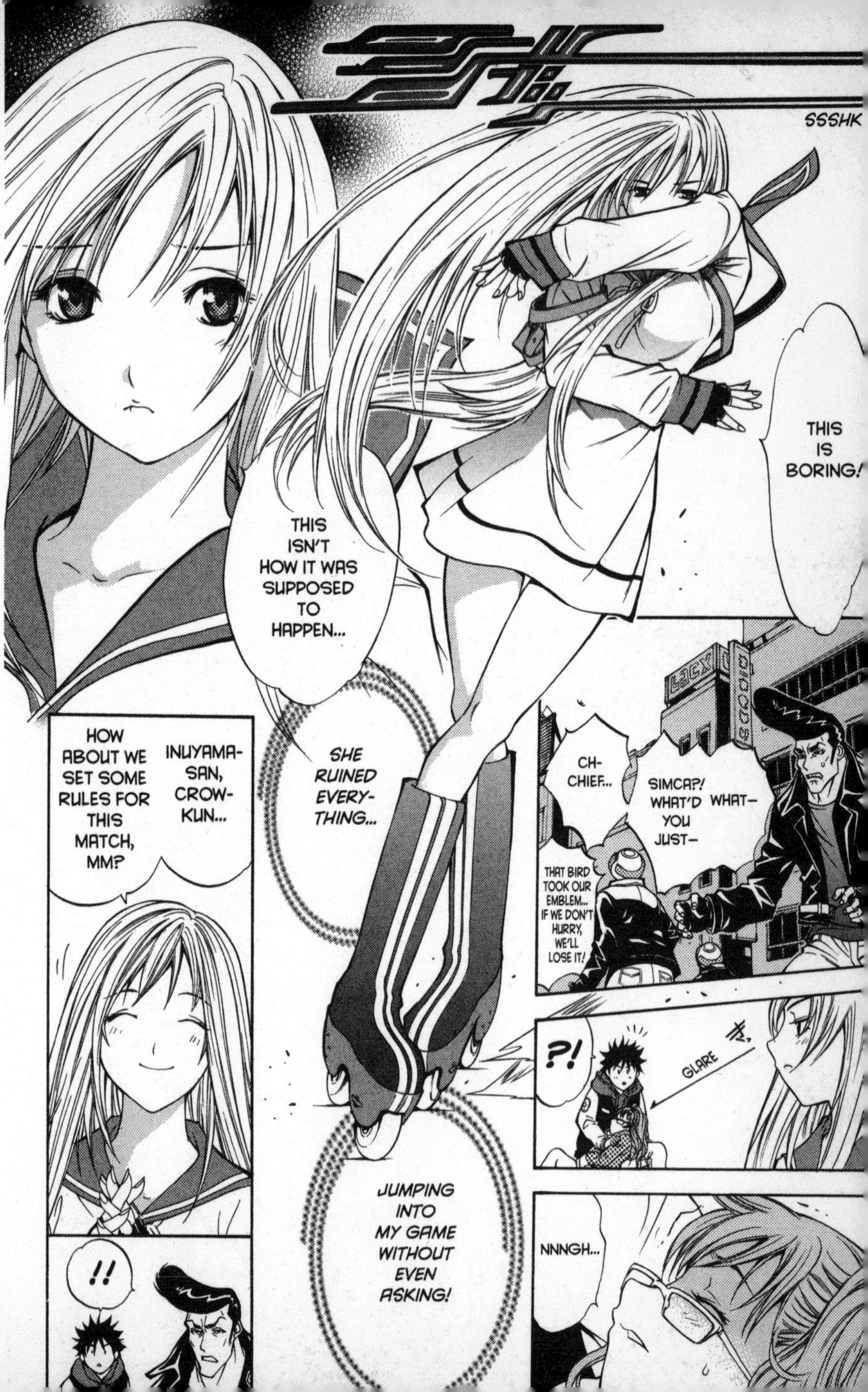
SSSHK
THIS IS BORING!
THIS ISN'T HOW IT WAS SUPPOSED TO HAPPEN...
WHAT—
SIMCA?! WHAT'D YOU JUST—
CH-CHIEF...
THAT BIRD TOOK OUR EMBLEM... IF WE DON'T HURRY, WE'LL LOSE IT!
GLARE
?!
NNNGH...
SHE RUINED EVERY-THING...
JUMPING INTO MY GAME WITHOUT EVEN ASKING!
INUYAMA-SAN, CROW-KUN...
HOW ABOUT WE SET SOME RULES FOR THIS MATCH, MM?
!!

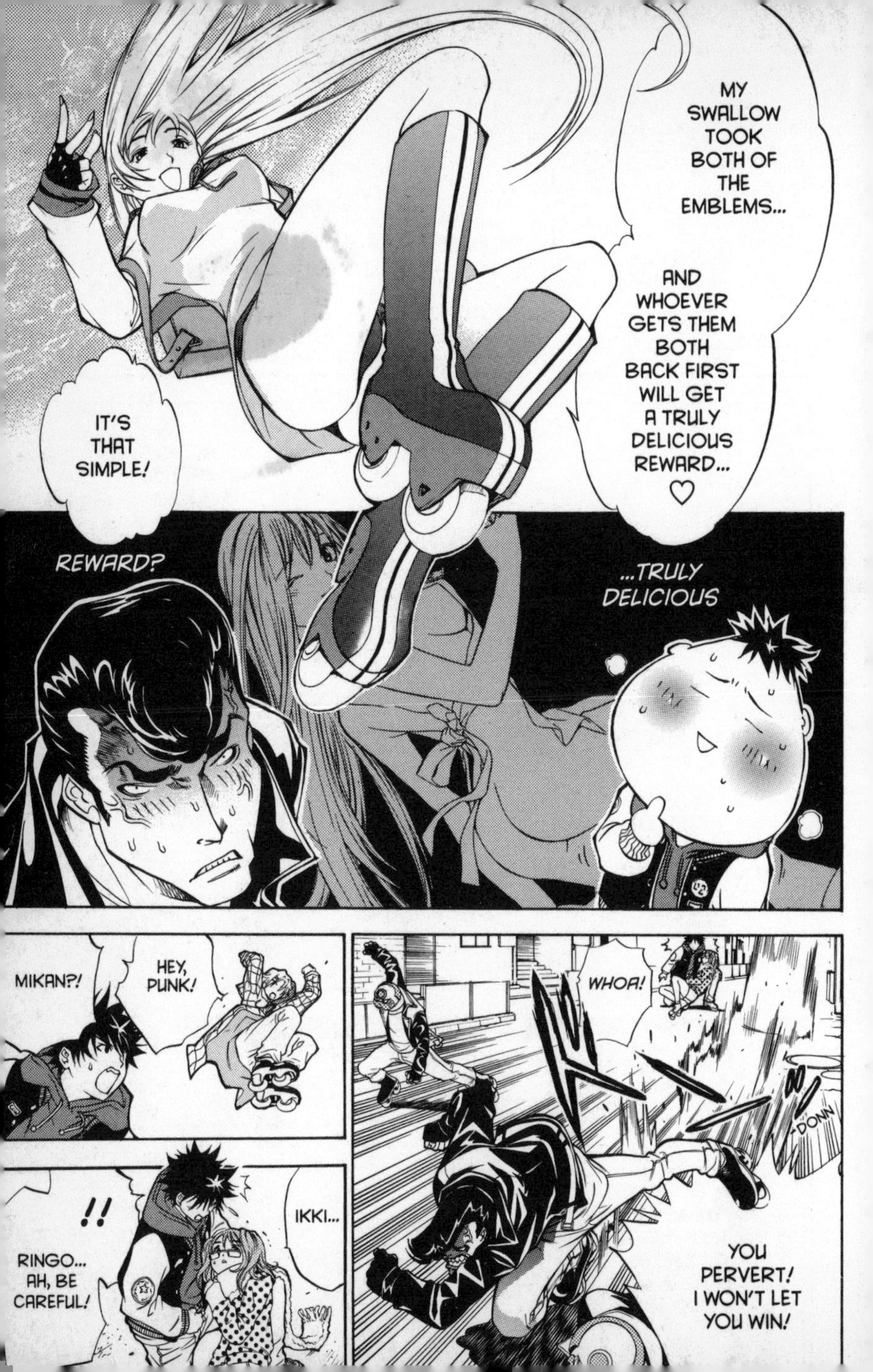
MY SWALLOW TOOK BOTH OF THE EMBLEMS...
AND WHOEVER GETS THEM BOTH BACK FIRST WILL GET A TRULY DELICIOUS REWARD... ♡
IT'S THAT SIMPLE!
...TRULY DELICIOUS
REWARD?
WHOA!
DONN
YOU PERVERT! I WON'T LET YOU WIN!
HEY, PUNK!
MIKAN?!
IKKI...
!!
RINGO... AH, BE CAREFUL!

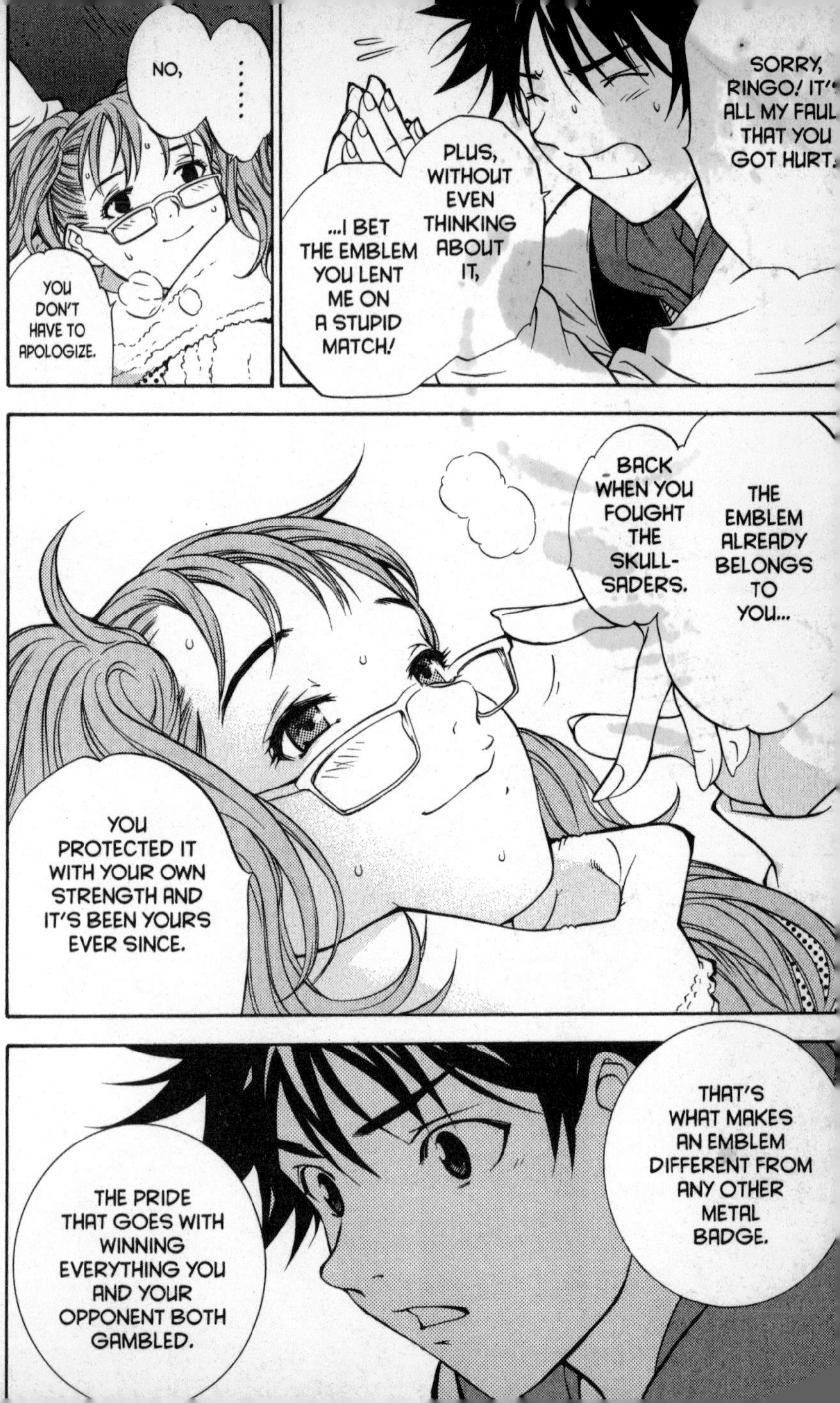
SORRY, RINGO! IT'S ALL MY FAUL THAT YOU GOT HURT.
PLUS, WITHOUT EVEN THINKING ABOUT IT,
...I BET THE EMBLEM YOU LENT ME ON A STUPID MATCH!
NO, ...
YOU DON'T HAVE TO APOLOGIZE.
THE EMBLEM ALREADY BELONGS TO YOU...
BACK WHEN YOU FOUGHT THE SKULL-SADERS.
YOU PROTECTED IT WITH YOUR OWN STRENGTH AND IT'S BEEN YOURS EVER SINCE.
THAT'S WHAT MAKES AN EMBLEM DIFFERENT FROM ANY OTHER METAL BADGE.
THE PRIDE THAT GOES WITH WINNING EVERYTHING YOU AND YOUR OPPONENT BOTH GAMBLED.

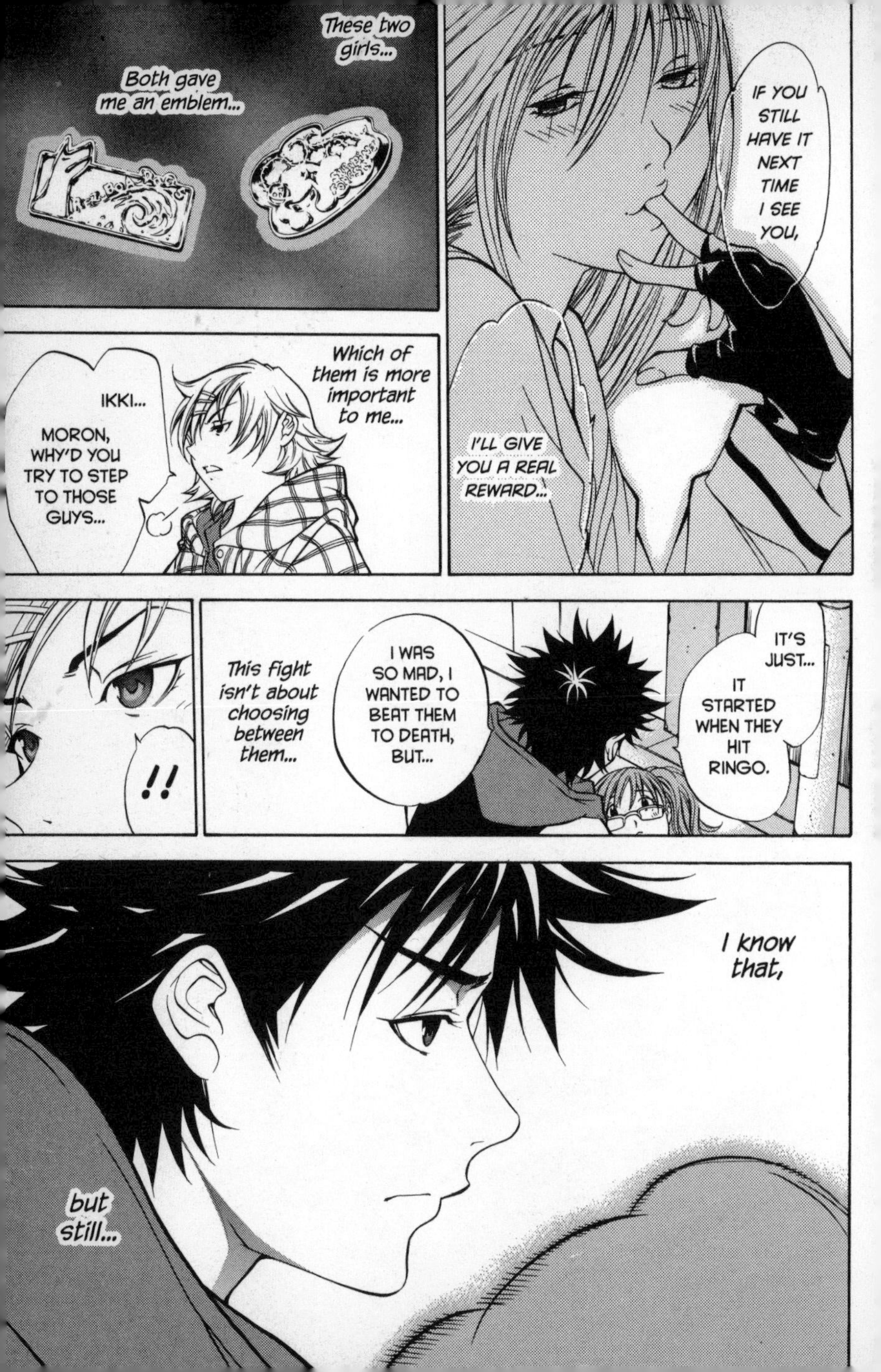
IF YOU STILL HAVE IT NEXT TIME I SEE YOU,
I'LL GIVE YOU A REAL REWARD...
These two girls...
Both gave me an emblem...
Which of them is more important to me...
IKKI...
MORON, WHY'D YOU TRY TO STEP TO THOSE GUYS...
IT'S JUST...
IT STARTED WHEN THEY HIT RINGO.
I WAS SO MAD, I WANTED TO BEAT THEM TO DEATH, BUT...
This fight isn't about choosing between them...
!!
I know that,
but still...

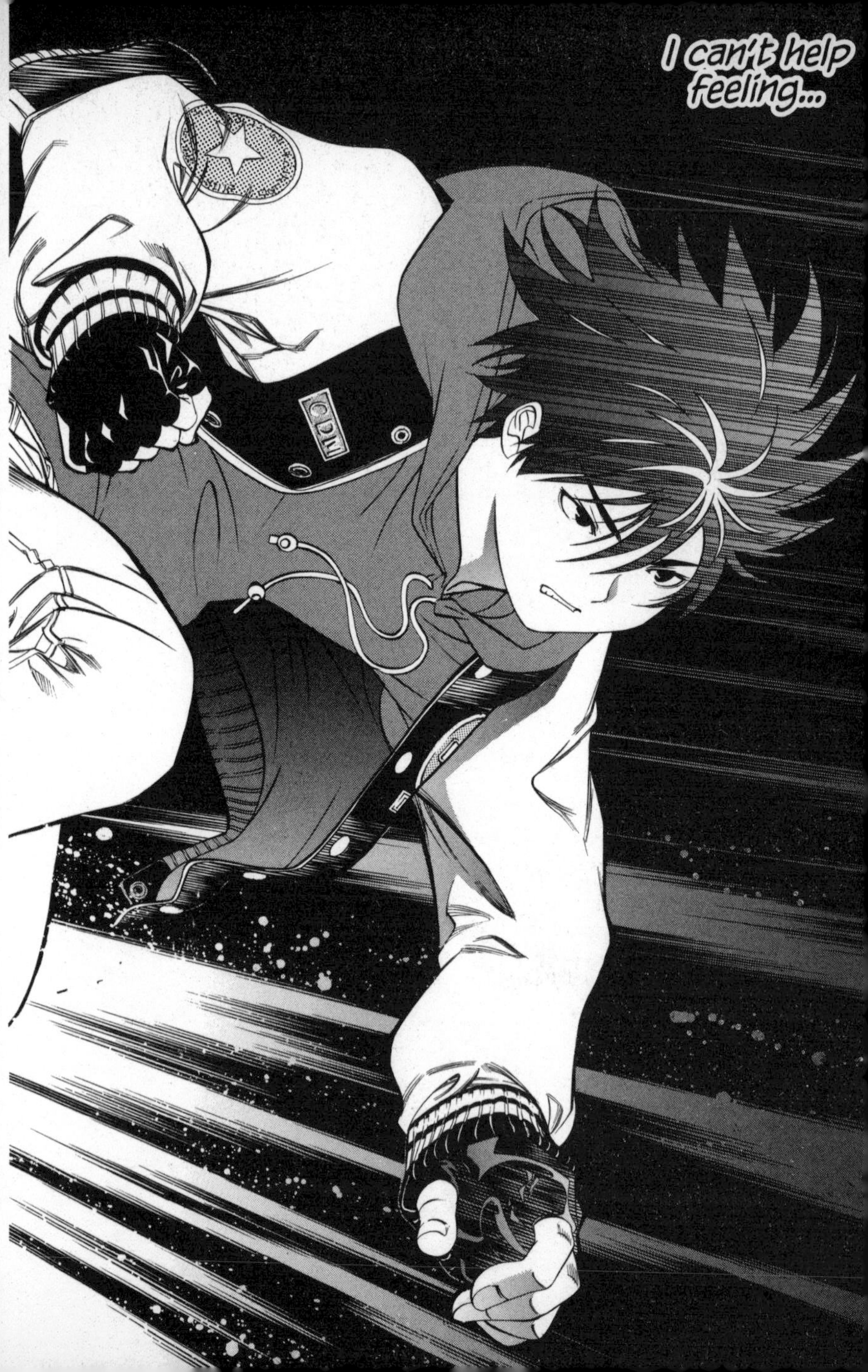
I can't help feeling...

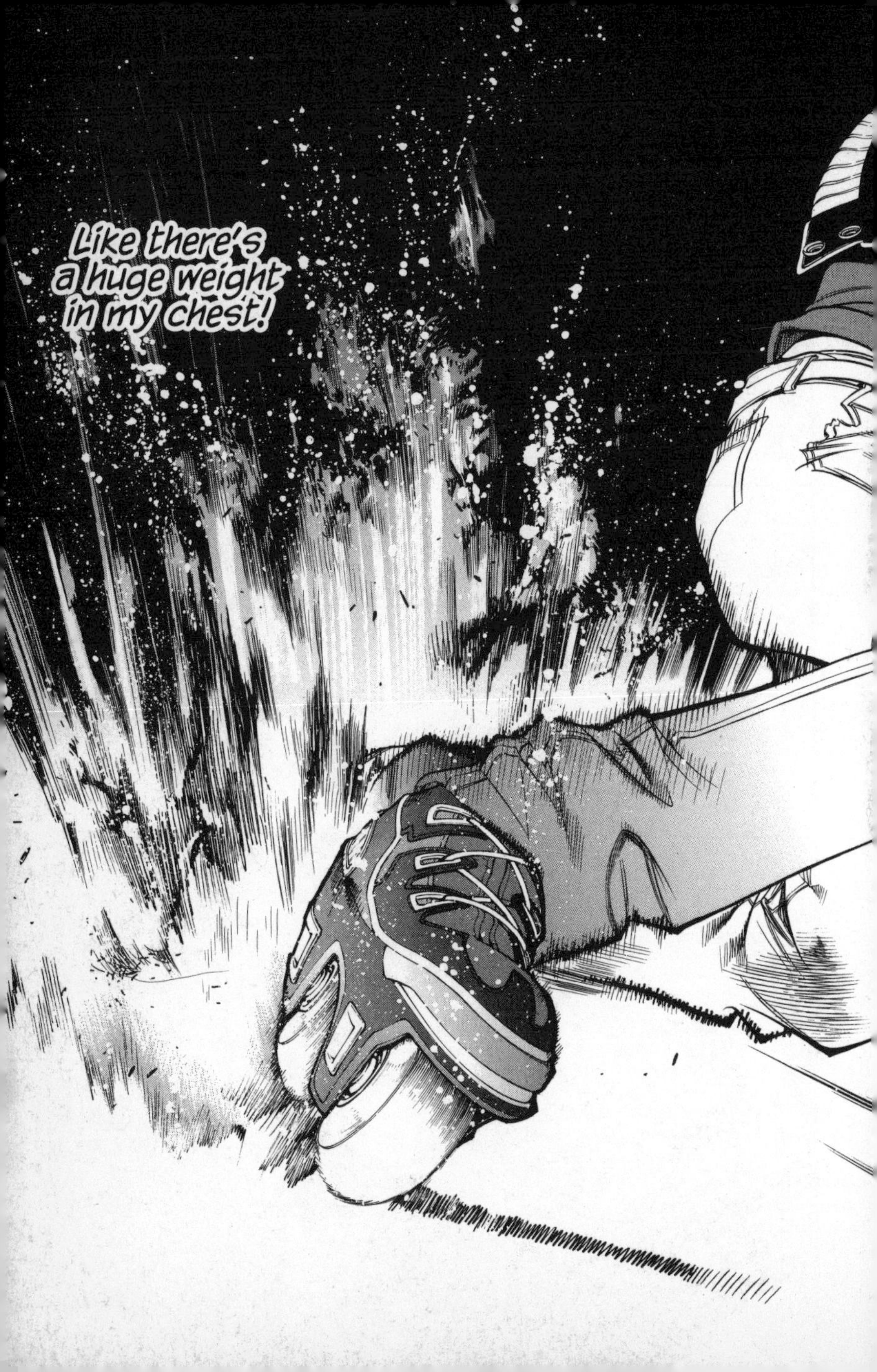
Like there's a huge weight in my chest!

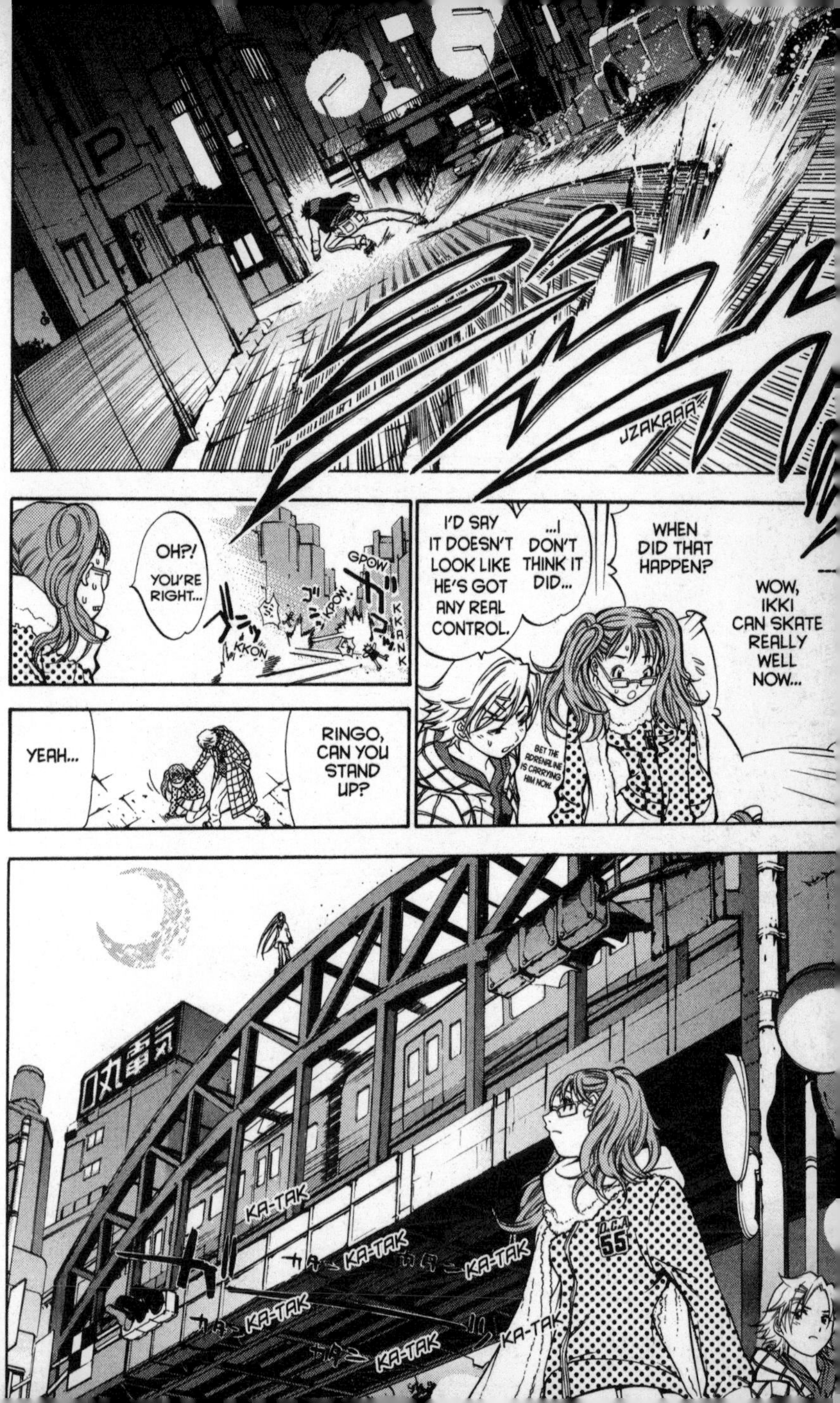
JZAKAAA
WOW, IKKI CAN SKATE REALLY WELL NOW...
WHEN DID THAT HAPPEN?
...I DON'T THINK IT DID...
I'D SAY IT DOESN'T LOOK LIKE HE'S GOT ANY REAL CONTROL.
BET THE ADRENALINE IS CARRYING HIM NOW.
OH?! YOU'RE RIGHT...
GPOW
KPOW
KKANK
KKON
RINGO, CAN YOU STAND UP?
YEAH...
KA-TAK
KA-TAK
KA-TAK
KA-TAK
KA-TAK
KA-TAK
KA-TAK

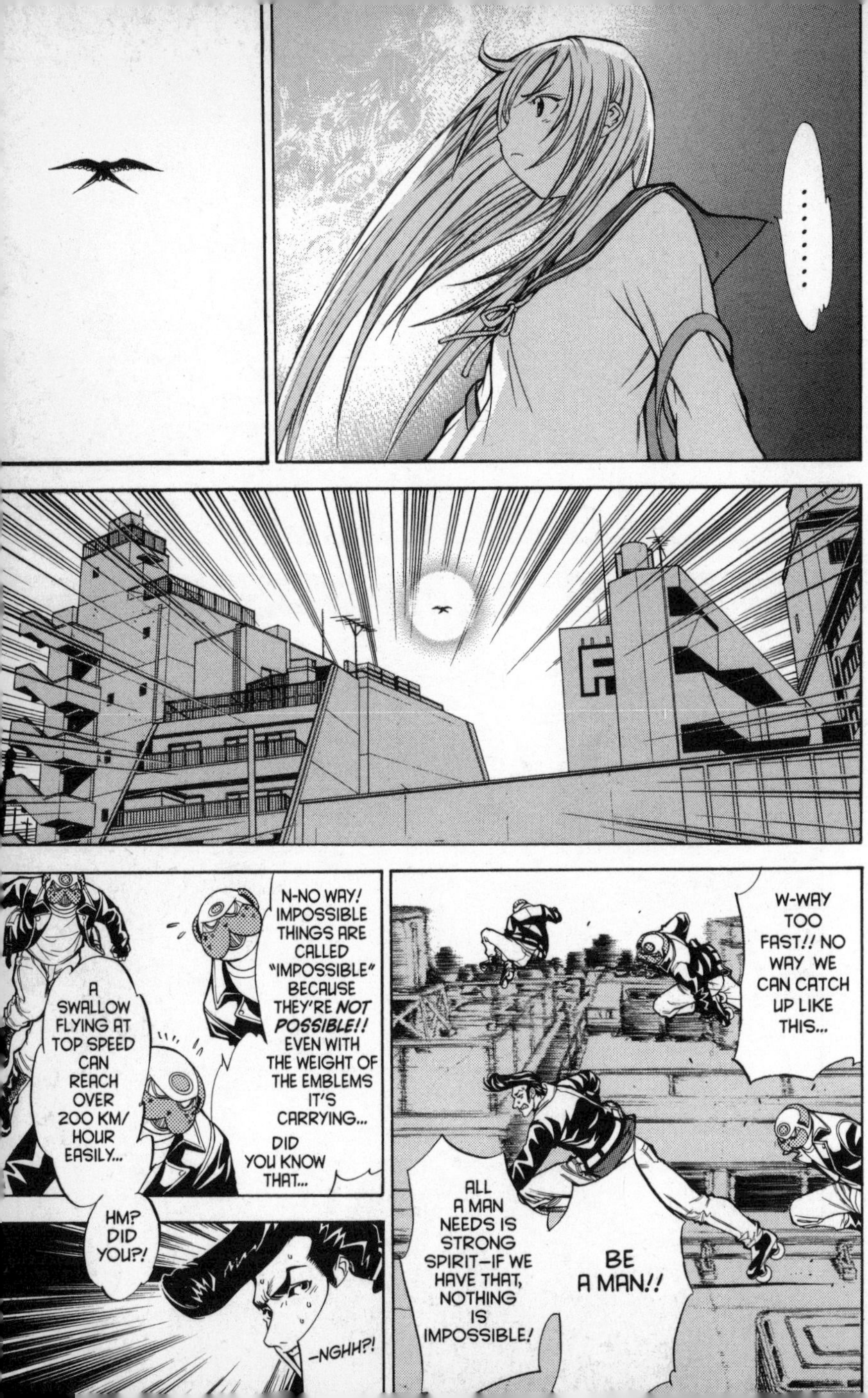
……
W-WAY TOO FAST!! NO WAY WE CAN CATCH UP LIKE THIS...
ALL A MAN NEEDS IS STRONG SPIRIT—IF WE HAVE THAT, NOTHING IS IMPOSSIBLE!
BE A MAN!!
N-NO WAY! IMPOSSIBLE THINGS ARE CALLED "IMPOSSIBLE" BECAUSE THEY'RE *NOT POSSIBLE!!* EVEN WITH THE WEIGHT OF THE EMBLEMS IT'S CARRYING...
A SWALLOW FLYING AT TOP SPEED CAN REACH OVER 200 KM/HOUR EASILY...
DID YOU KNOW THAT...
HM? DID YOU?!
–NGHH?!

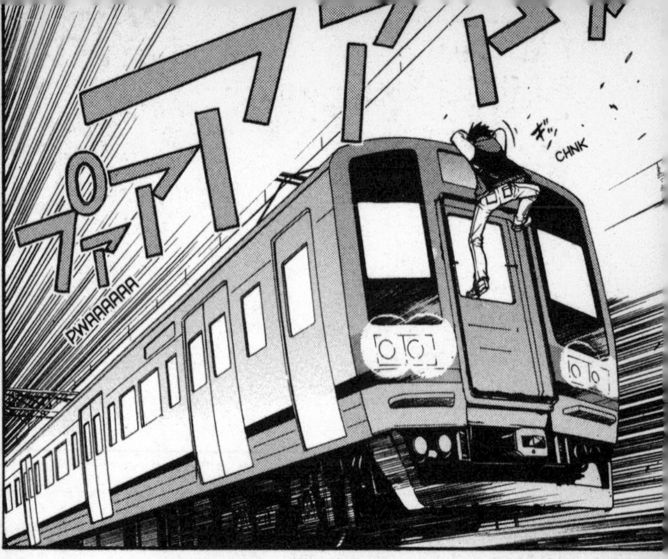
PWAAAAAA
CHNK
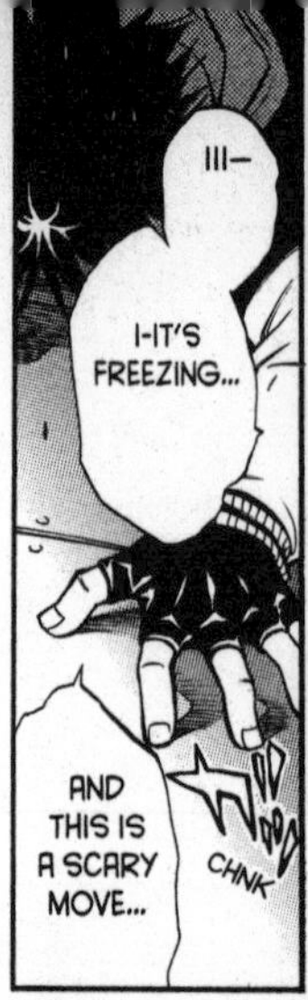
III—
I-IT'S FREEZING...
AND THIS IS A SCARY MOVE...
CHNK
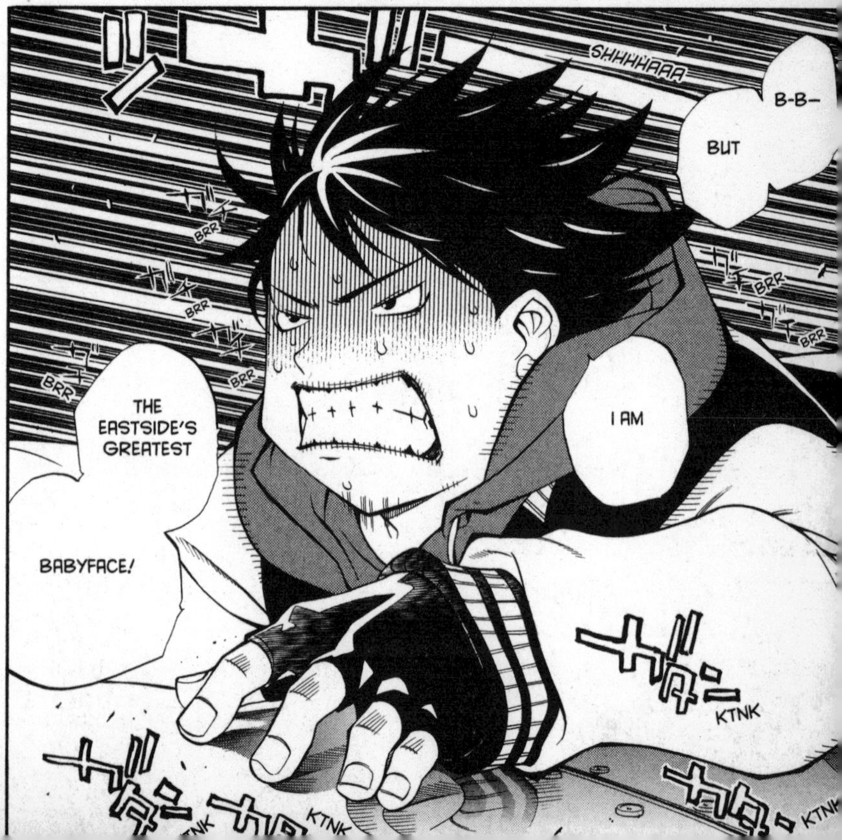
SHHHHAAA
B-B—
BUT
I AM
THE EASTSIDE'S GREATEST
BABYFACE!
BRR
BRR
BRR
BRR
BRR
BRR
KTNK
KTNK
KTNK
KTNK

Air Gear

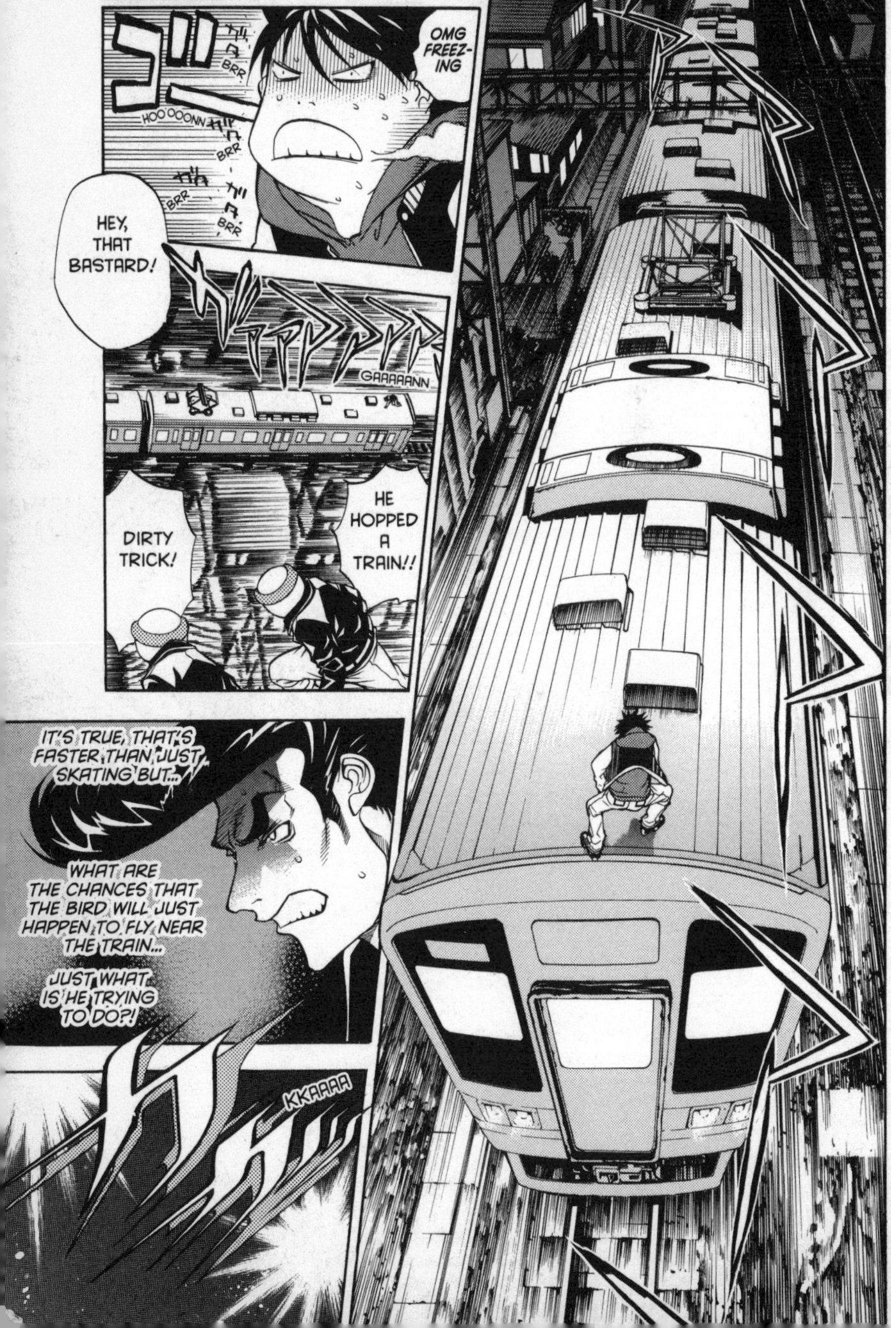
PWAAAAAAA
OMG FREEZ-ING
BRR
HOO'OOONN
BRR
BRR
BRR
HEY, THAT BASTARD!
GAAAAAANN
HE HOPPED A TRAIN!!
DIRTY TRICK!
IT'S TRUE, THAT'S FASTER THAN JUST SKATING BUT...
WHAT ARE THE CHANCES THAT THE BIRD WILL JUST HAPPEN TO FLY NEAR THE TRAIN...
JUST WHAT IS HE TRYING TO DO?!
KKAAAA

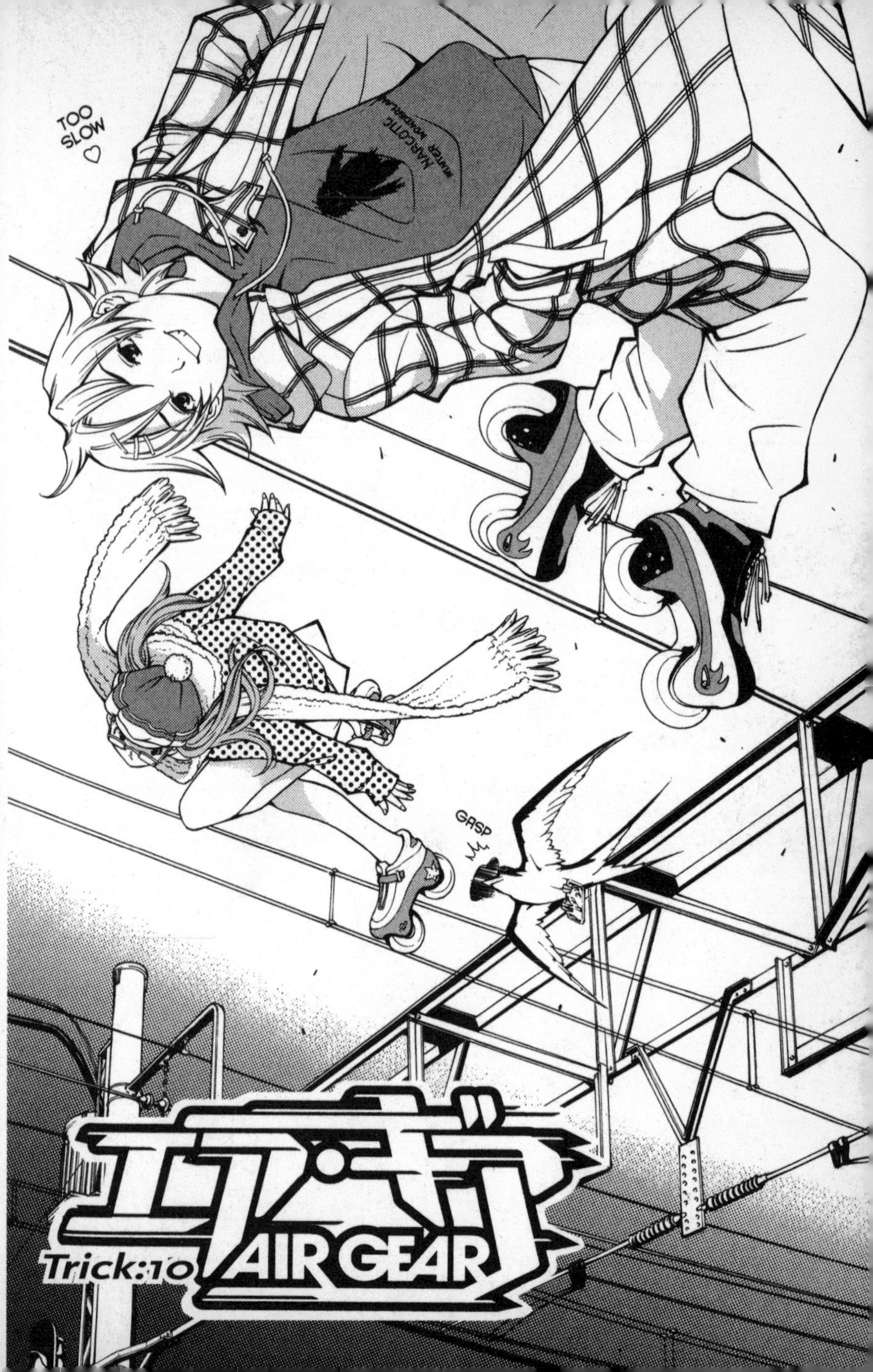
TOO SLOW ♡
GASP
エア・ギア
AIR GEAR
Trick:10

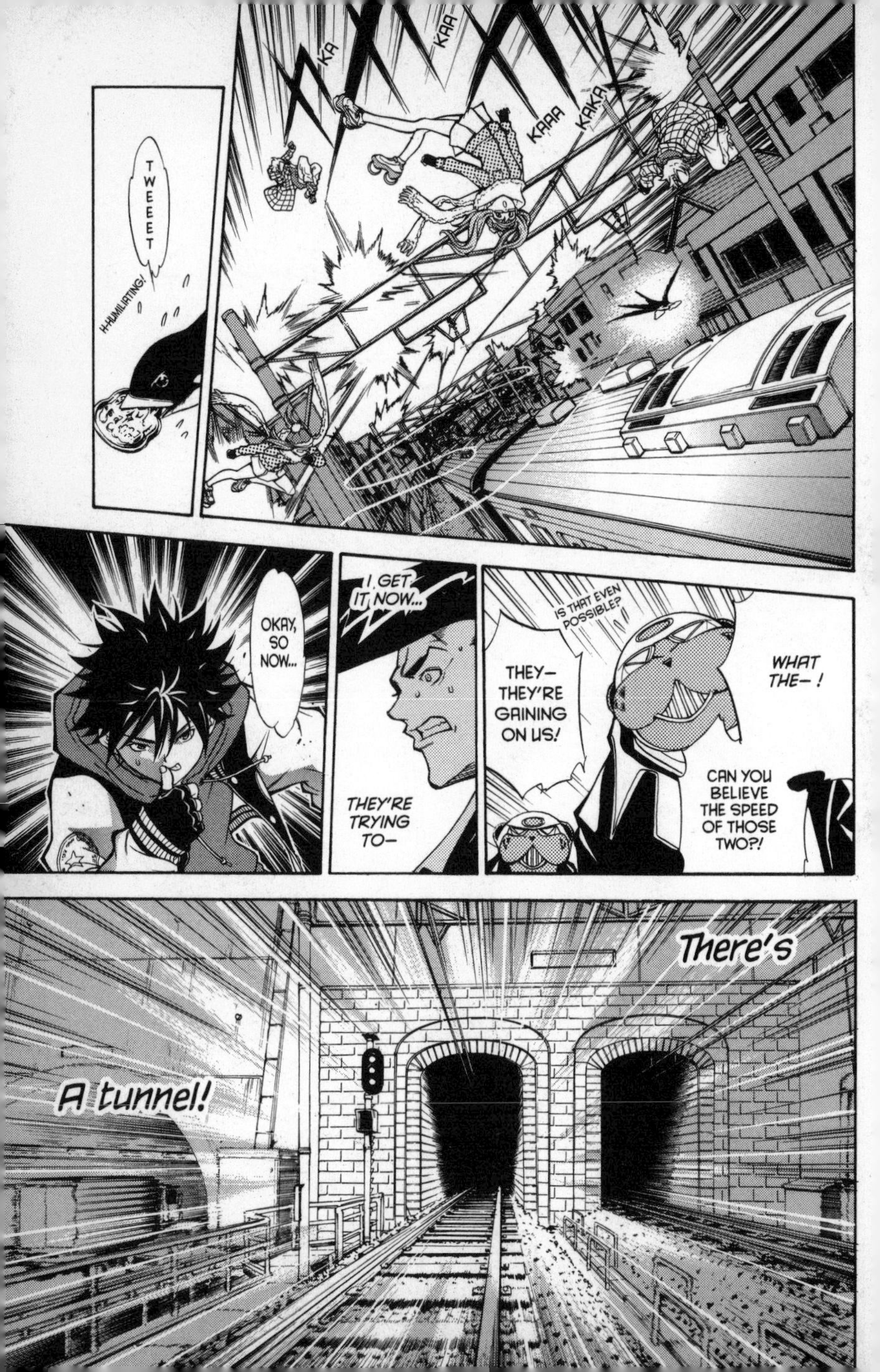
KAKA
KAAA
KAA
KA
TWEEEET
H-HUMILIATING!
WHAT THE—!
CAN YOU BELIEVE THE SPEED OF THOSE TWO?!
THEY— THEY'RE GAINING ON US!
IS THAT EVEN POSSIBLE?
I GET IT NOW...
THEY'RE TRYING TO—
OKAY, SO NOW...
There's
A tunnel!

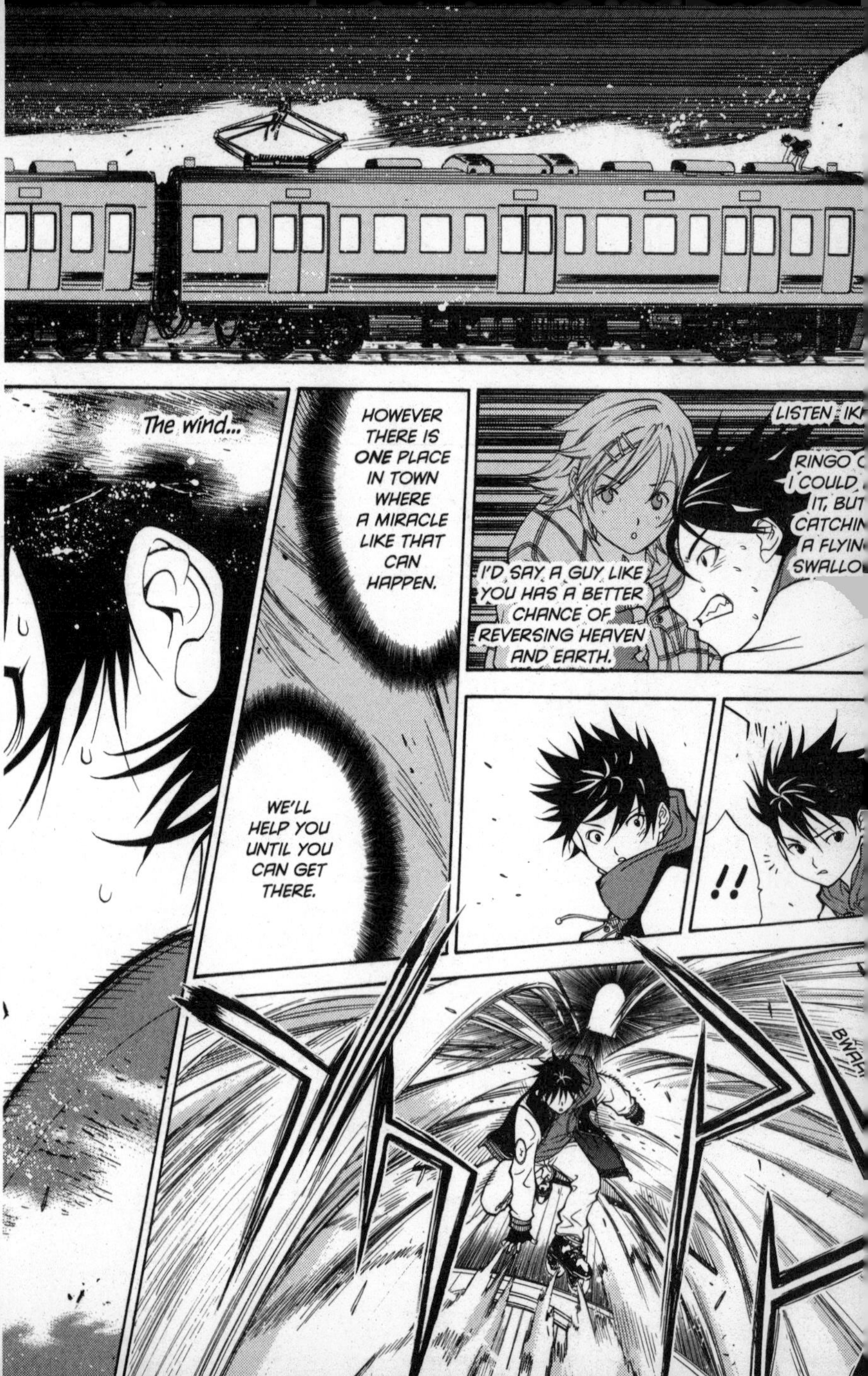
LISTEN IK
RINGO C I COULD IT, BUT CATCHIN A FLYIN SWALLO
I'D SAY A GUY LIKE YOU HAS A BETTER CHANCE OF REVERSING HEAVEN AND EARTH.
HOWEVER THERE IS ONE PLACE IN TOWN WHERE A MIRACLE LIKE THAT CAN HAPPEN.
WE'LL HELP YOU UNTIL YOU CAN GET THERE.
!!
The wind...
BWAH!!

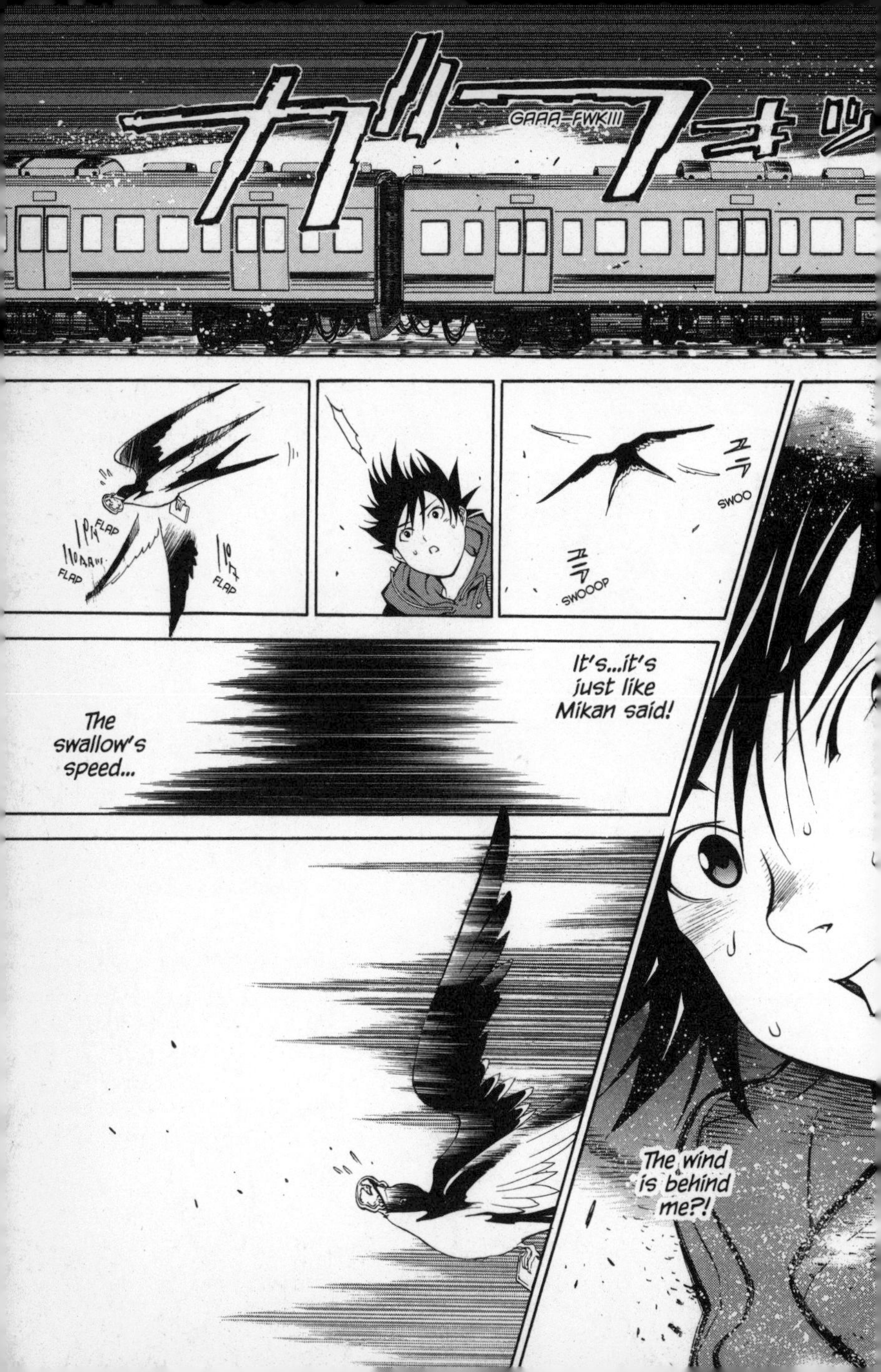
GAAA-FWKIII
SWOO
SWOOOP
FLAP
FLAP
FLAP
The wind is behind me?!
It's...it's just like Mikan said!
The swallow's speed...

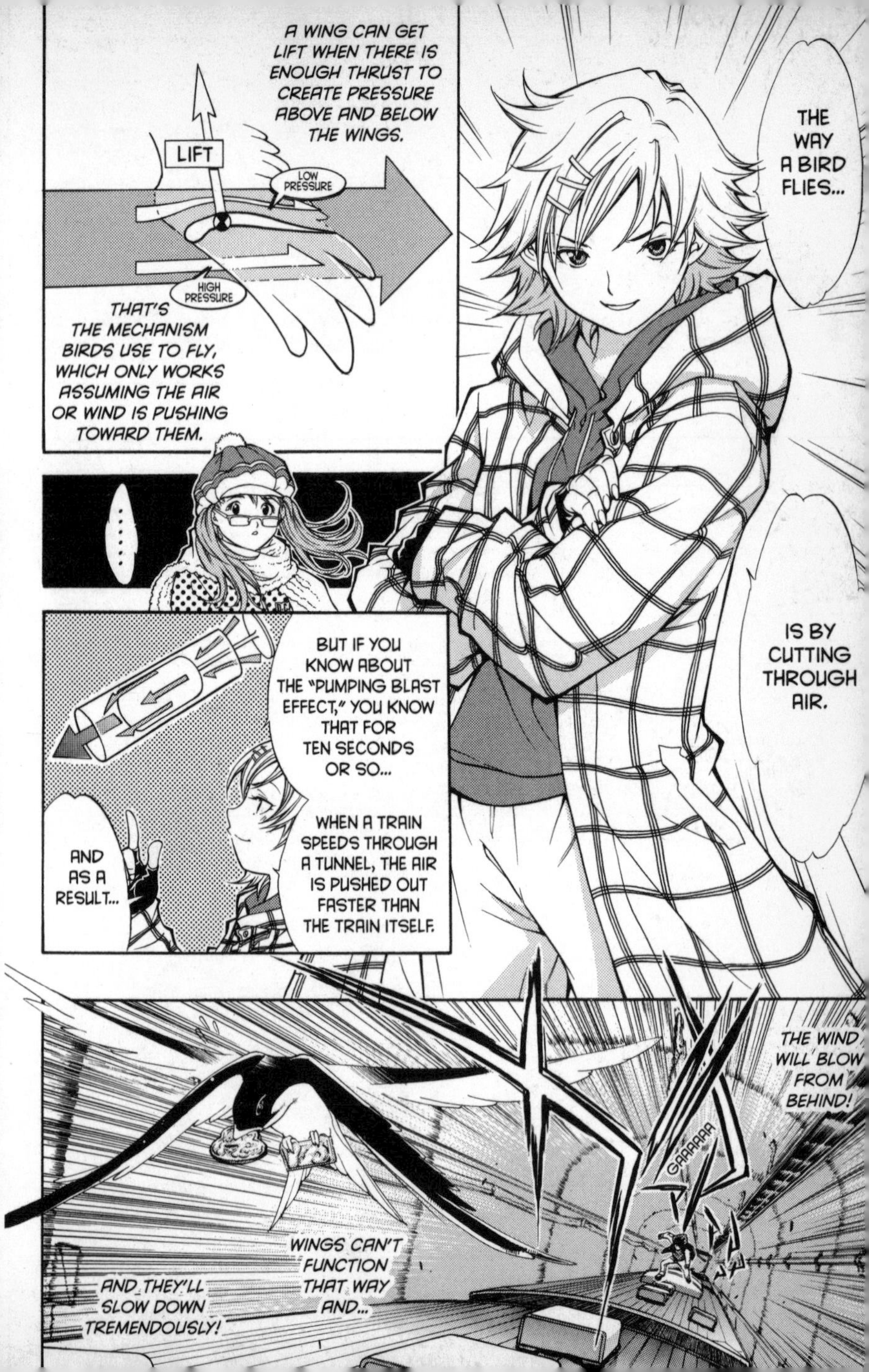
THE WAY A BIRD FLIES...
IS BY CUTTING THROUGH AIR.
A WING CAN GET LIFT WHEN THERE IS ENOUGH THRUST TO CREATE PRESSURE ABOVE AND BELOW THE WINGS.
LIFT
LOW PRESSURE
HIGH PRESSURE
THAT'S THE MECHANISM BIRDS USE TO FLY, WHICH ONLY WORKS ASSUMING THE AIR OR WIND IS PUSHING TOWARD THEM.
......
BUT IF YOU KNOW ABOUT THE "PUMPING BLAST EFFECT," YOU KNOW THAT FOR TEN SECONDS OR SO...
WHEN A TRAIN SPEEDS THROUGH A TUNNEL, THE AIR IS PUSHED OUT FASTER THAN THE TRAIN ITSELF.
AND AS A RESULT...
THE WIND WILL BLOW FROM BEHIND!
WINGS CAN'T FUNCTION THAT WAY AND...
AND THEY'LL SLOW DOWN TREMENDOUSLY!

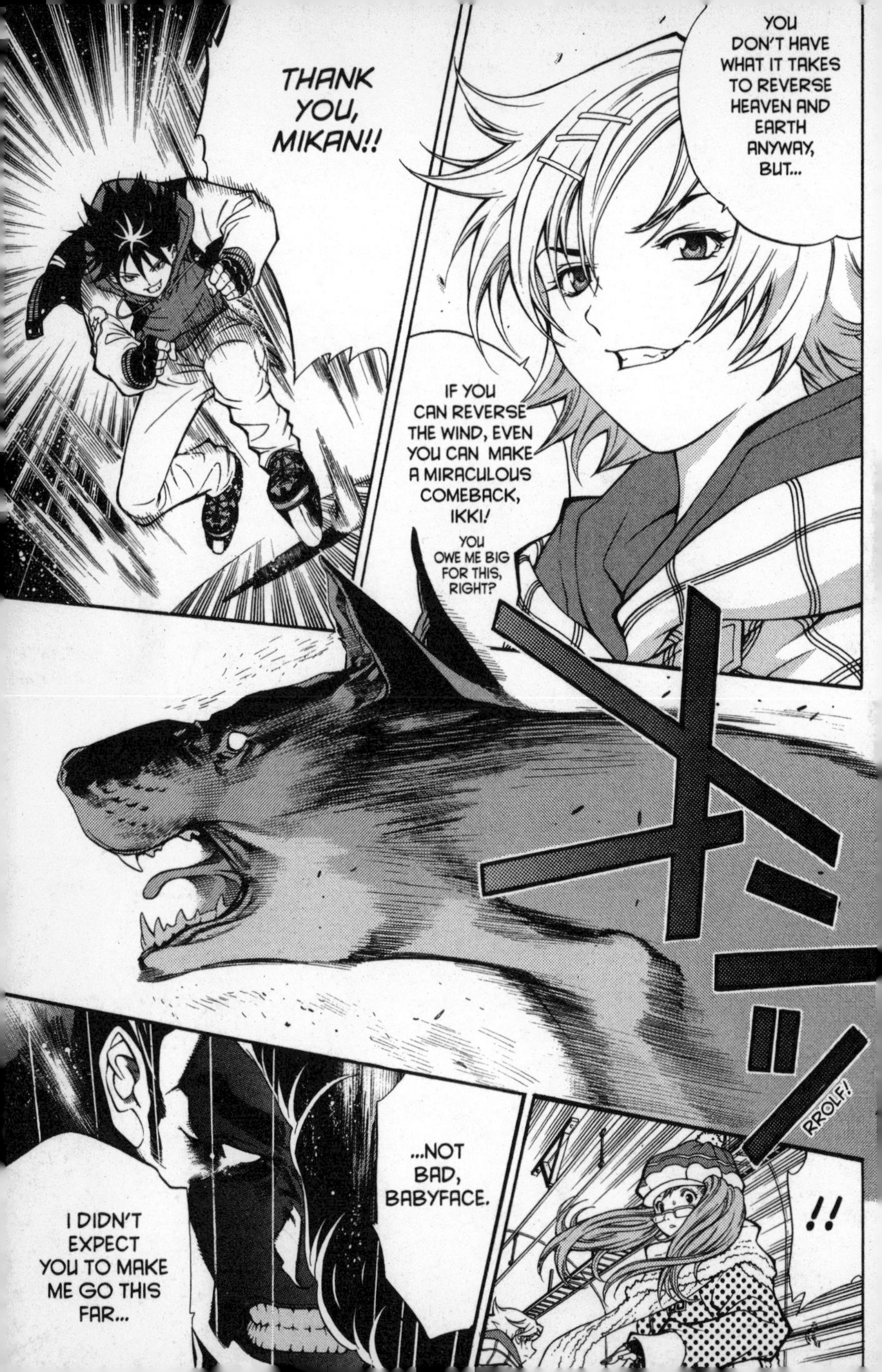
YOU DON'T HAVE WHAT IT TAKES TO REVERSE HEAVEN AND EARTH ANYWAY, BUT...
IF YOU CAN REVERSE THE WIND, EVEN YOU CAN MAKE A MIRACULOUS COMEBACK, IKKI!
YOU OWE ME BIG FOR THIS, RIGHT?
THANK YOU, MIKAN!!
RROLF!
!!
...NOT BAD, BABYFACE.
I DIDN'T EXPECT YOU TO MAKE ME GO THIS FAR...

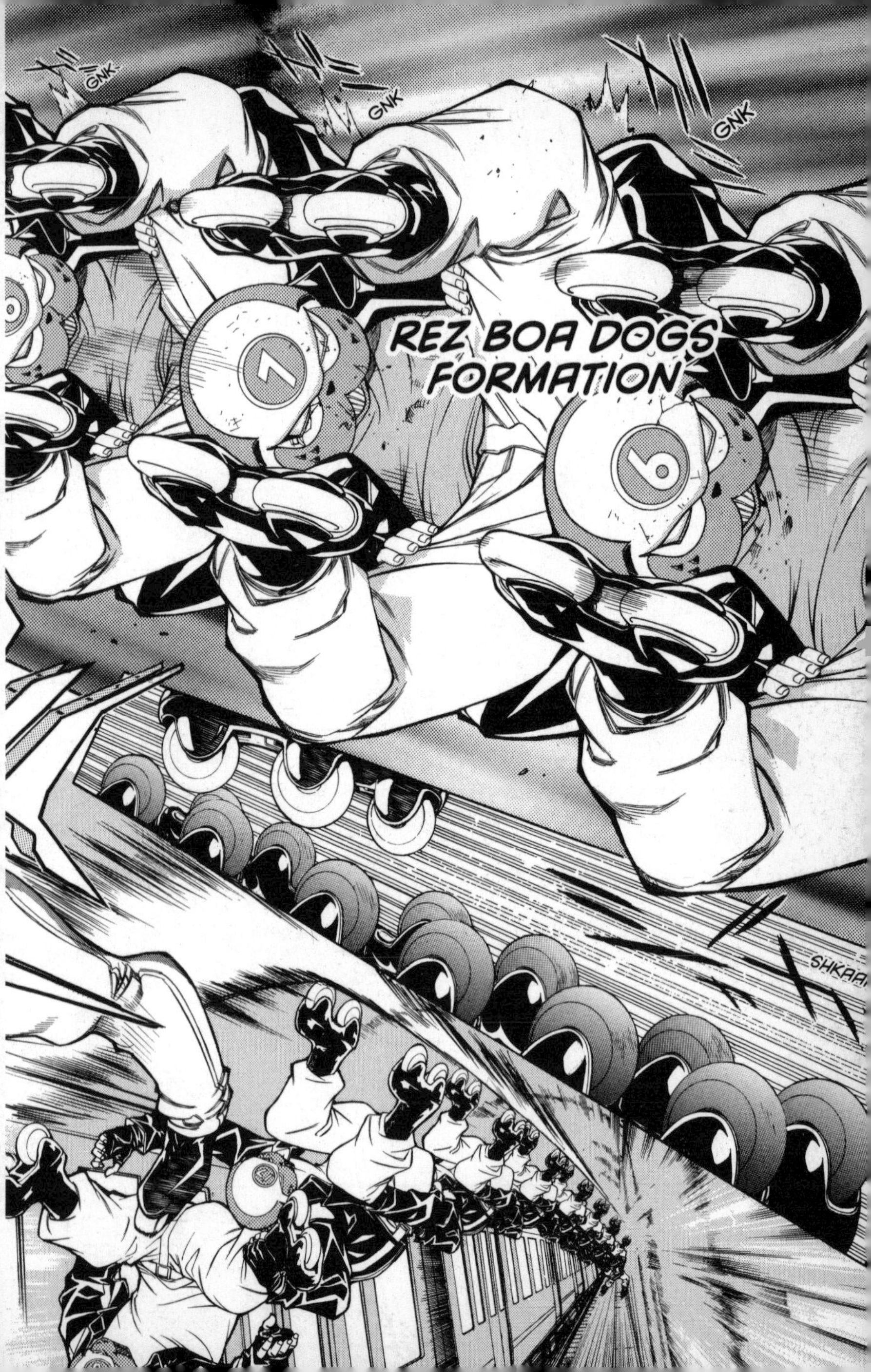
GNK
GNK
GNK
REZ BOA DOGS FORMATION
SHKAA

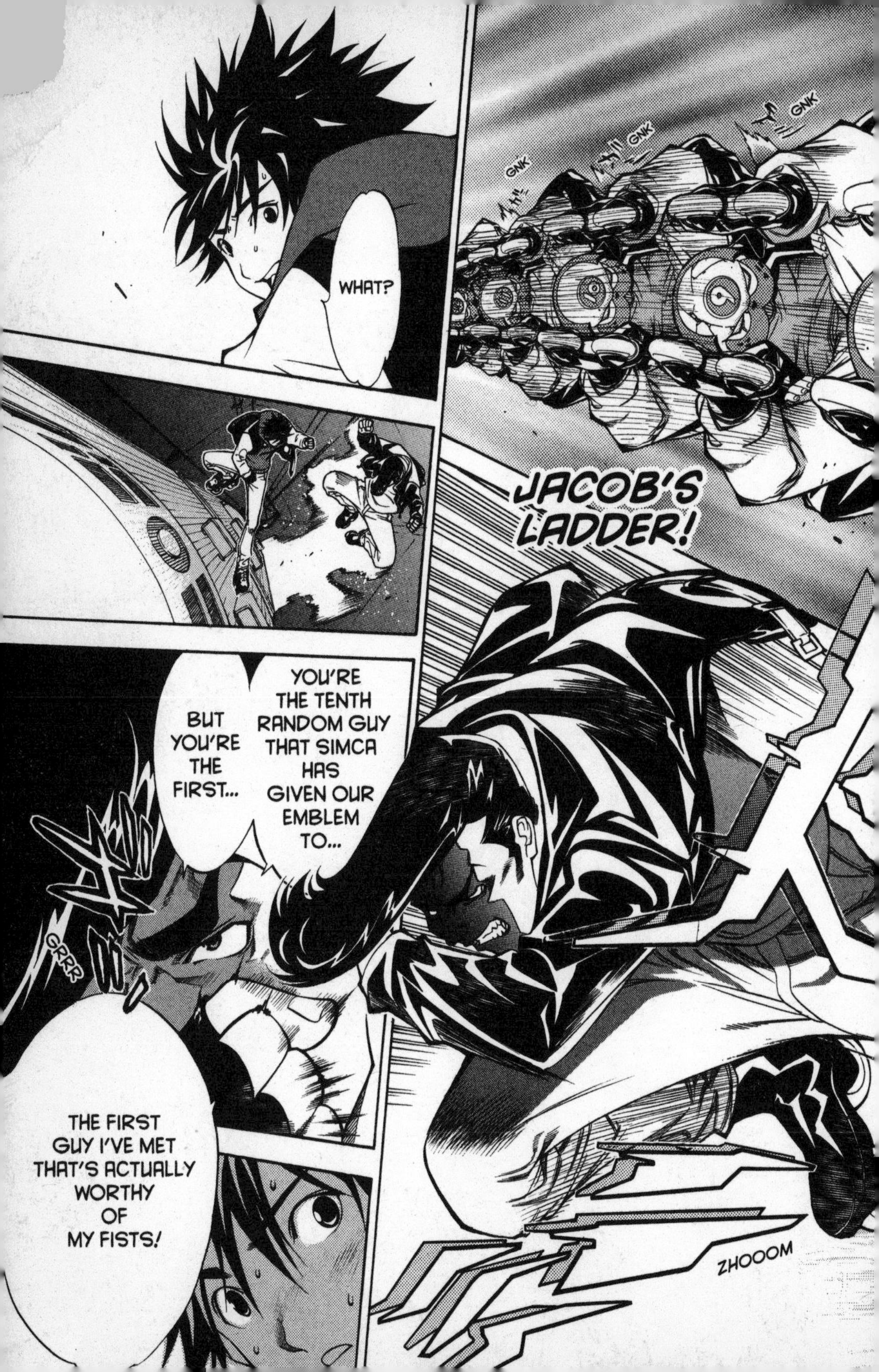
GNK
GNK
GNK
JACOB'S LADDER!
ZHOOOM
WHAT?
YOU'RE THE TENTH RANDOM GUY THAT SIMCA HAS GIVEN OUR EMBLEM TO...
BUT YOU'RE THE FIRST...
GRRR
THE FIRST GUY I'VE MET THAT'S ACTUALLY WORTHY OF MY FISTS!

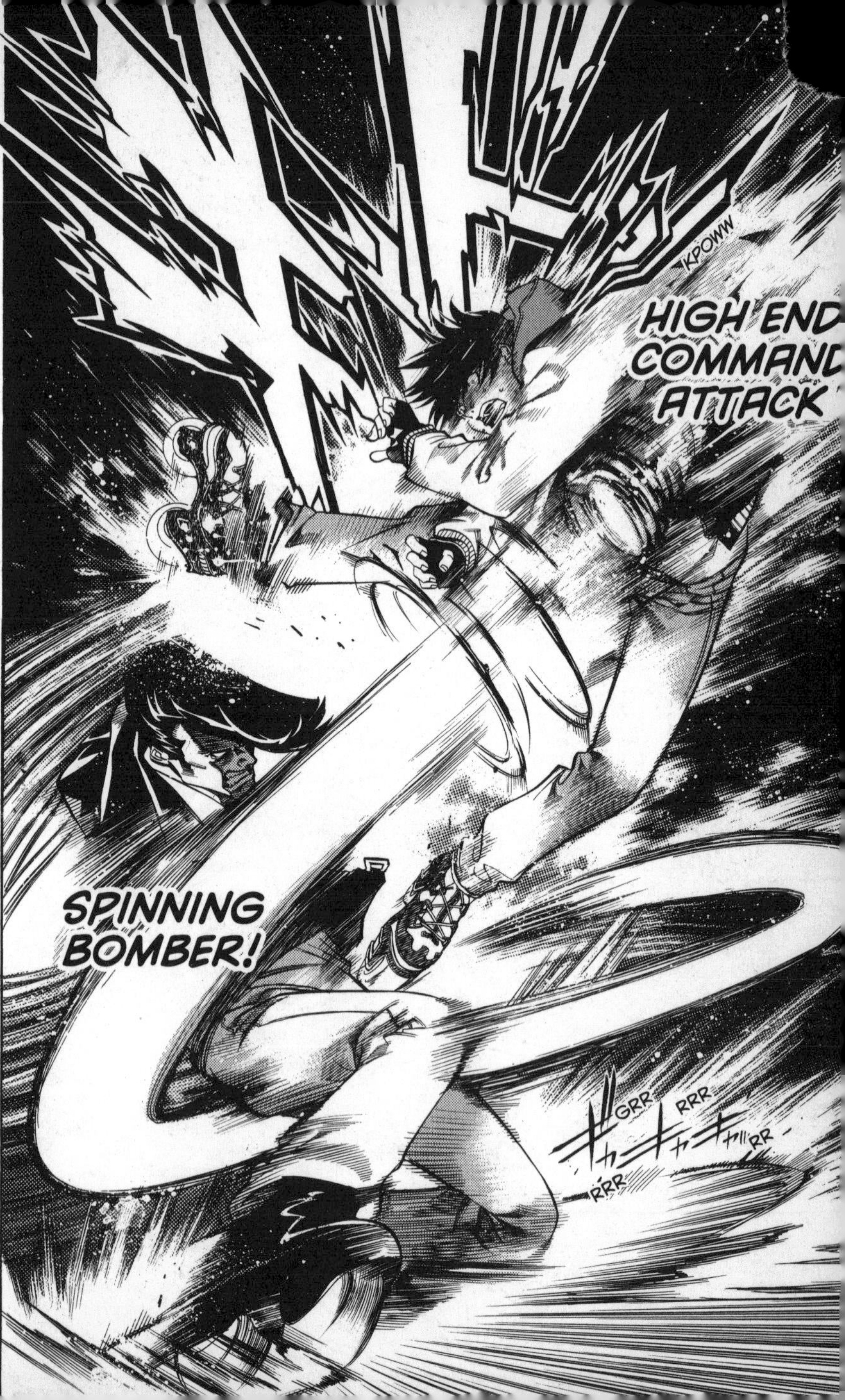
KPOWW
HIGH END COMMAND ATTACK
SPINNING BOMBER!
GRR RRR RR RRR

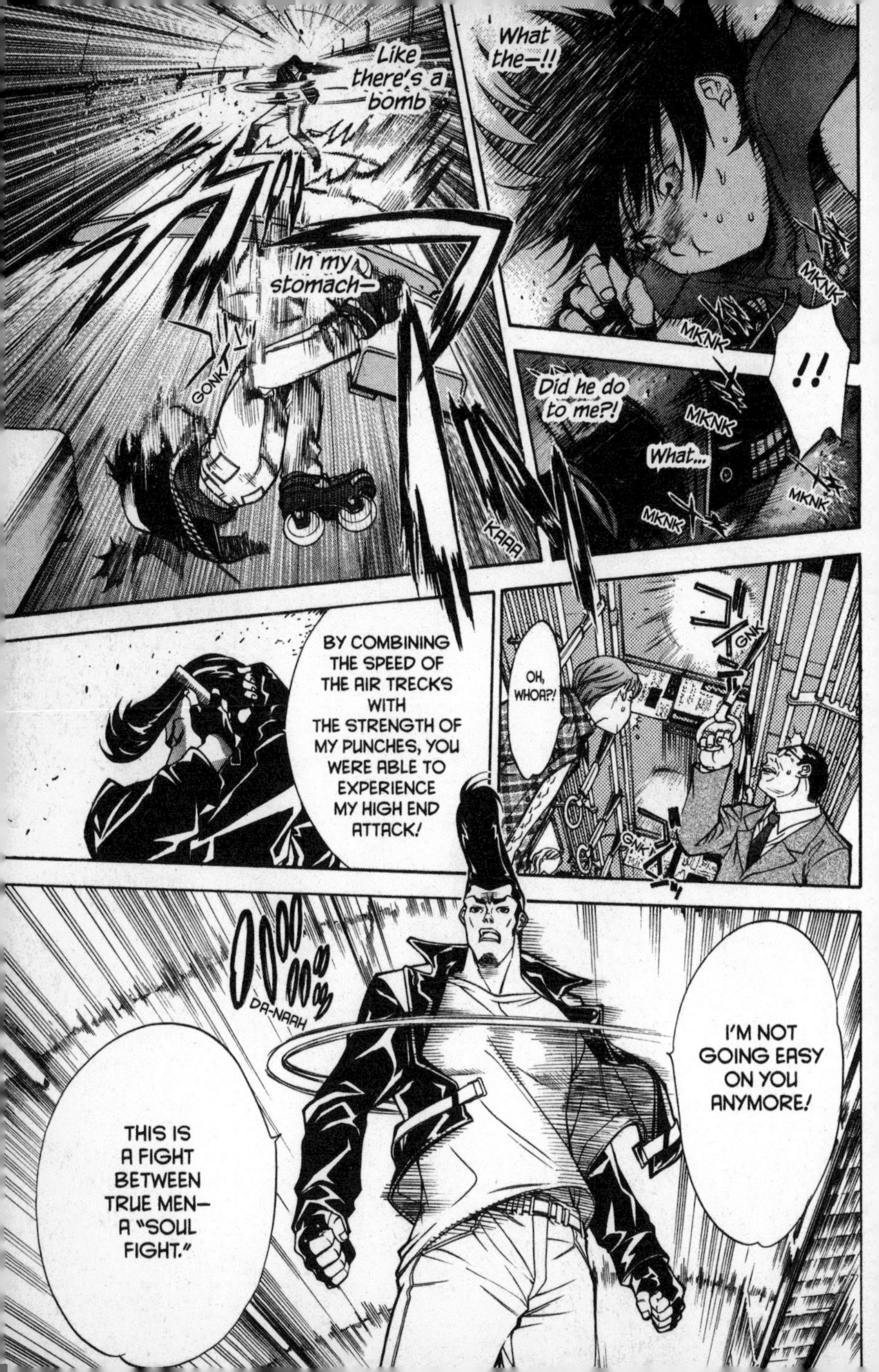
What the—!!
MKNK
MKNK
!!
Did he do to me?!
MKNK
What...
MKNK
MKNK
Like there's a bomb
In my stomach—
GONK
KAAA
GNK
OH, WHOA?!
GNK
BY COMBINING THE SPEED OF THE AIR TRECKS WITH THE STRENGTH OF MY PUNCHES, YOU WERE ABLE TO EXPERIENCE MY HIGH END ATTACK!
I'M NOT GOING EASY ON YOU ANYMORE!
DA-NAAH
THIS IS A FIGHT BETWEEN TRUE MEN—A "SOUL FIGHT."

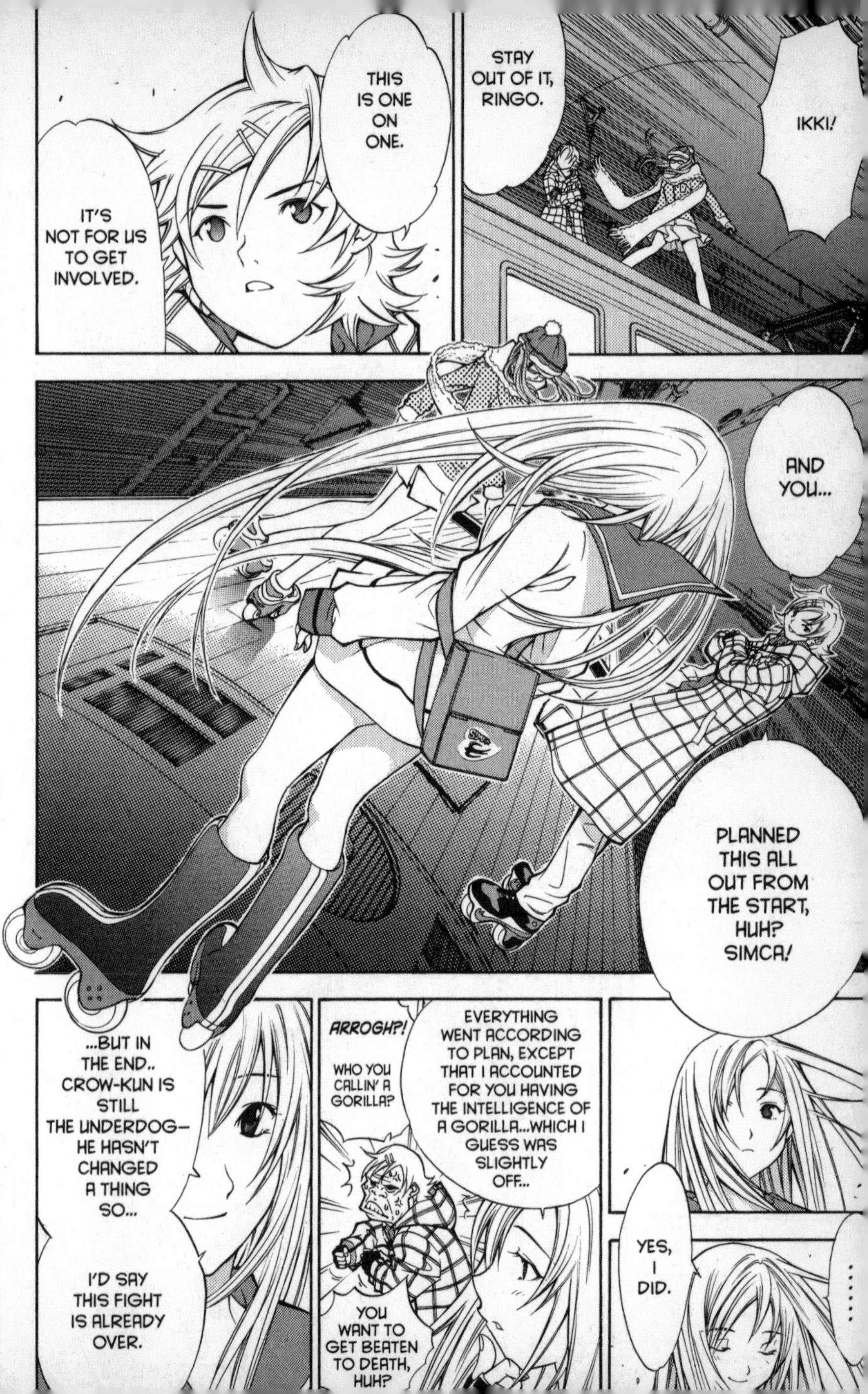
IKKI!
STAY OUT OF IT, RINGO.
THIS IS ONE ON ONE.
IT'S NOT FOR US TO GET INVOLVED.
AND YOU...
PLANNED THIS ALL OUT FROM THE START, HUH? SIMCA!
......
YES, I DID.
EVERYTHING WENT ACCORDING TO PLAN, EXCEPT THAT I ACCOUNTED FOR YOU HAVING THE INTELLIGENCE OF A GORILLA...WHICH I GUESS WAS SLIGHTLY OFF...
ARROGH?!
WHO YOU CALLIN' A GORILLA?
YOU WANT TO GET BEATEN TO DEATH, HUH?
...BUT IN THE END.. CROW-KUN IS STILL THE UNDERDOG— HE HASN'T CHANGED A THING SO...
I'D SAY THIS FIGHT IS ALREADY OVER.

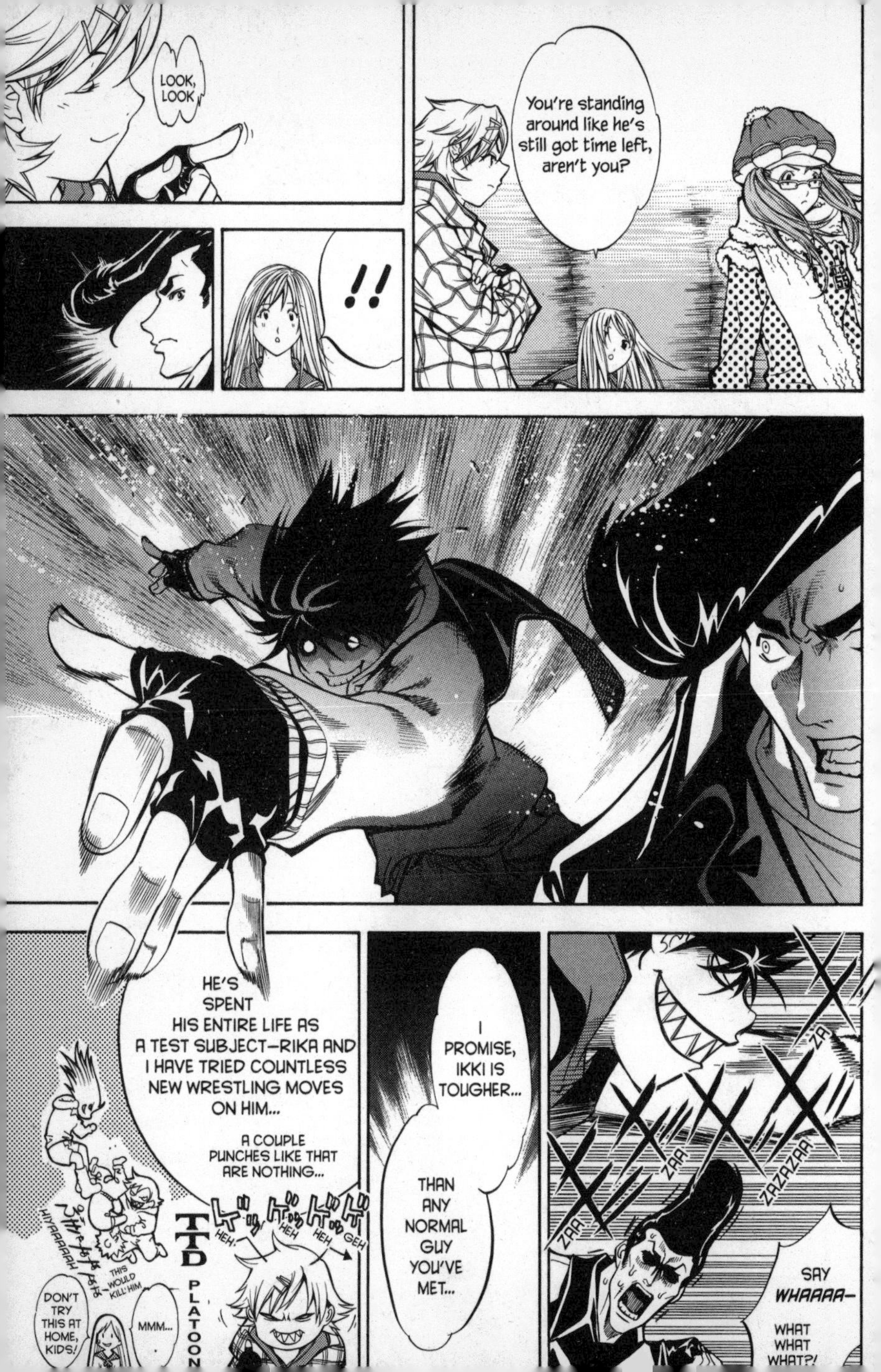
You're standing around like he's still got time left, aren't you?
LOOK, LOOK
!!
SAY WHAAAA—
WHAT WHAT WHAT?!
ZA
ZAA
ZAZAZAA
ZAA
I PROMISE, IKKI IS TOUGHER...
THAN ANY NORMAL GUY YOU'VE MET...
HE'S SPENT HIS ENTIRE LIFE AS A TEST SUBJECT—RIKA AND I HAVE TRIED COUNTLESS NEW WRESTLING MOVES ON HIM...
A COUPLE PUNCHES LIKE THAT ARE NOTHING...
HEH HEH HEH GEH
HIYAAAAAAH
THIS WOULD KILL HIM
DON'T TRY THIS AT HOME, KIDS!
MMM...
TTD PLATOON

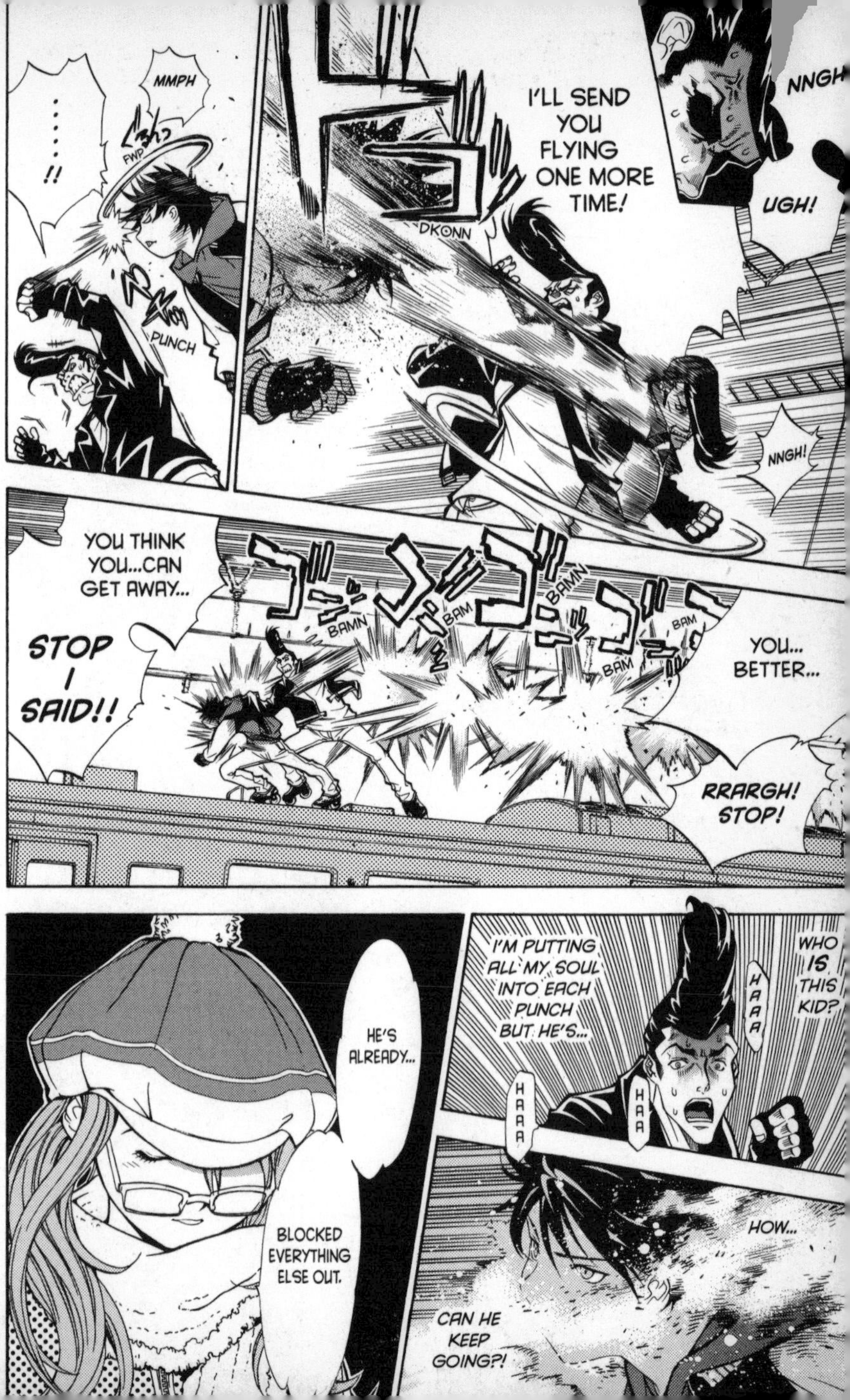

NNGH
UGH!
I'LL SEND YOU FLYING ONE MORE TIME!
DKONN
NNGH!
MMPH
......!!
FWP
PUNCH
YOU... BETTER...
RRARGH! STOP!
BAM
BAM
BAMN
BAM
BAMN
YOU THINK YOU...CAN GET AWAY...
STOP I SAID!!
WHO IS THIS KID?
HAAA
I'M PUTTING ALL MY SOUL INTO EACH PUNCH BUT HE'S...
HAA
HAAA
HOW...
CAN HE KEEP GOING?!
HE'S ALREADY...
BLOCKED EVERYTHING ELSE OUT.

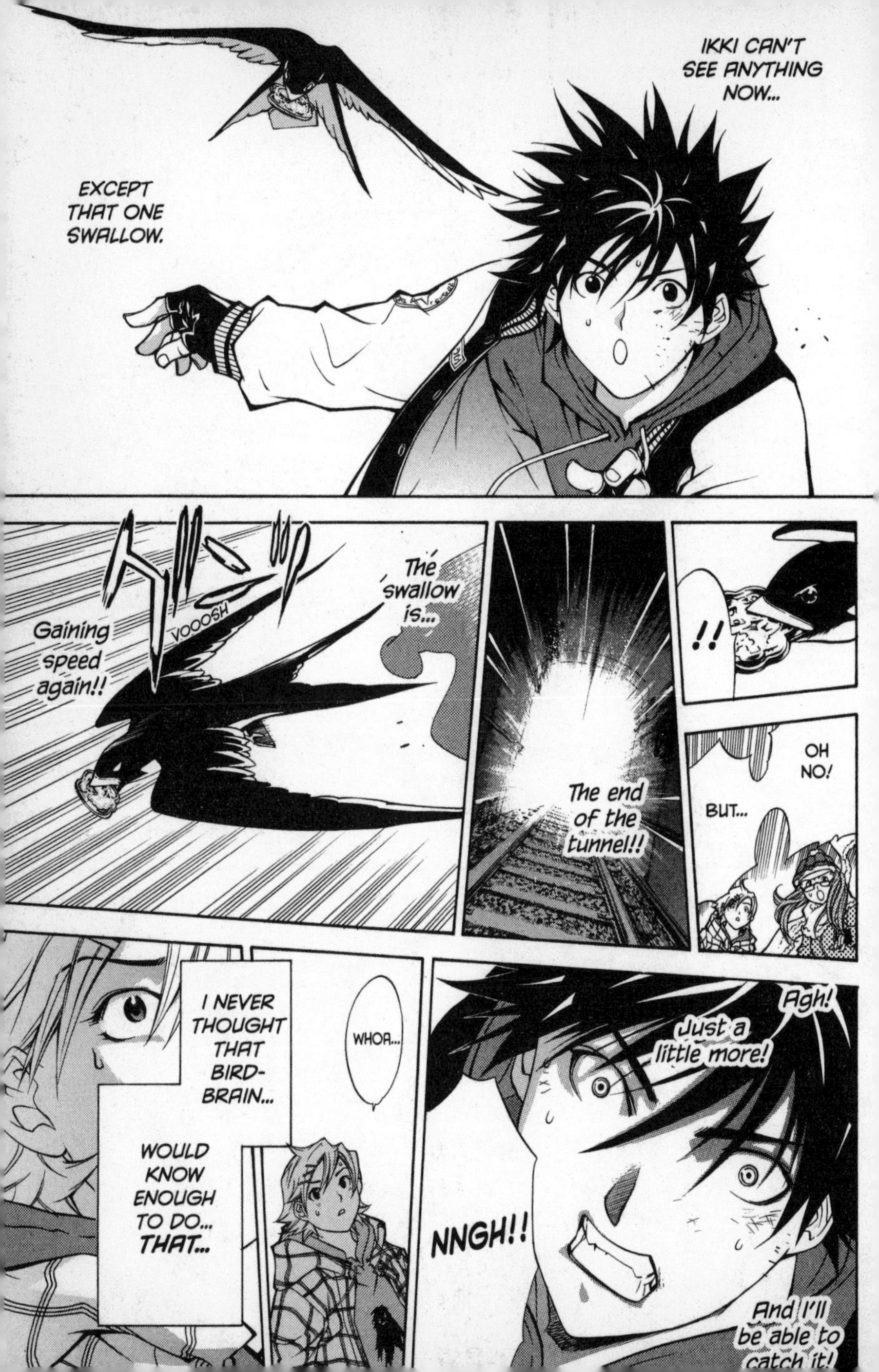
IKKI CAN'T SEE ANYTHING NOW...
EXCEPT THAT ONE SWALLOW.
!!
OH NO!
BUT...
The end of the tunnel!!
The swallow is...
VOOOSH
Gaining speed again!!
Agh!
Just a little more!
NNGH!!
And I'll be able to catch it!
WHOA...
I NEVER THOUGHT THAT BIRD-BRAIN...
WOULD KNOW ENOUGH TO DO... THAT...

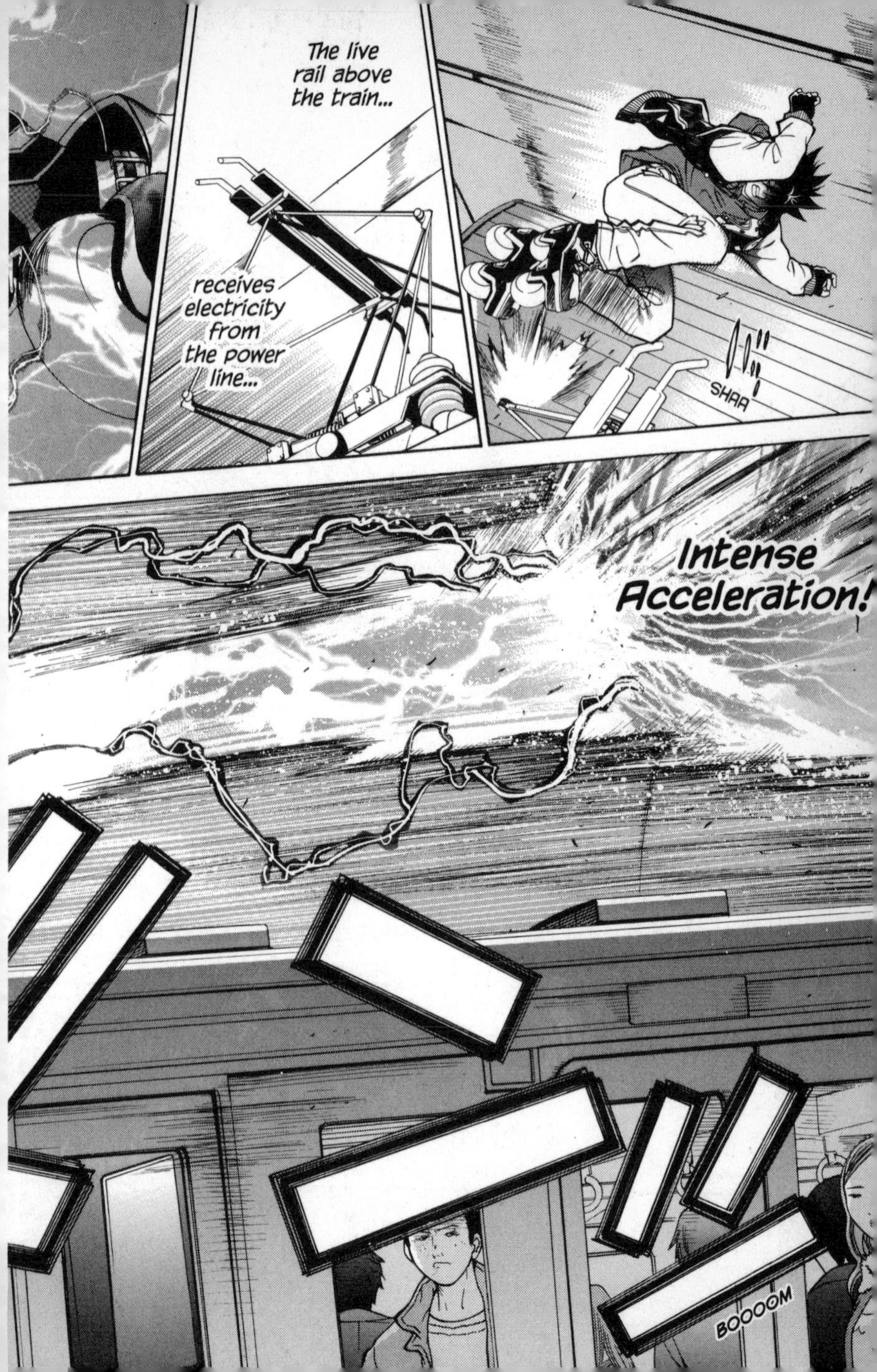
SHAA
The live rail above the train...
receives electricity from the power line...
Intense Acceleration!
BOOOOM

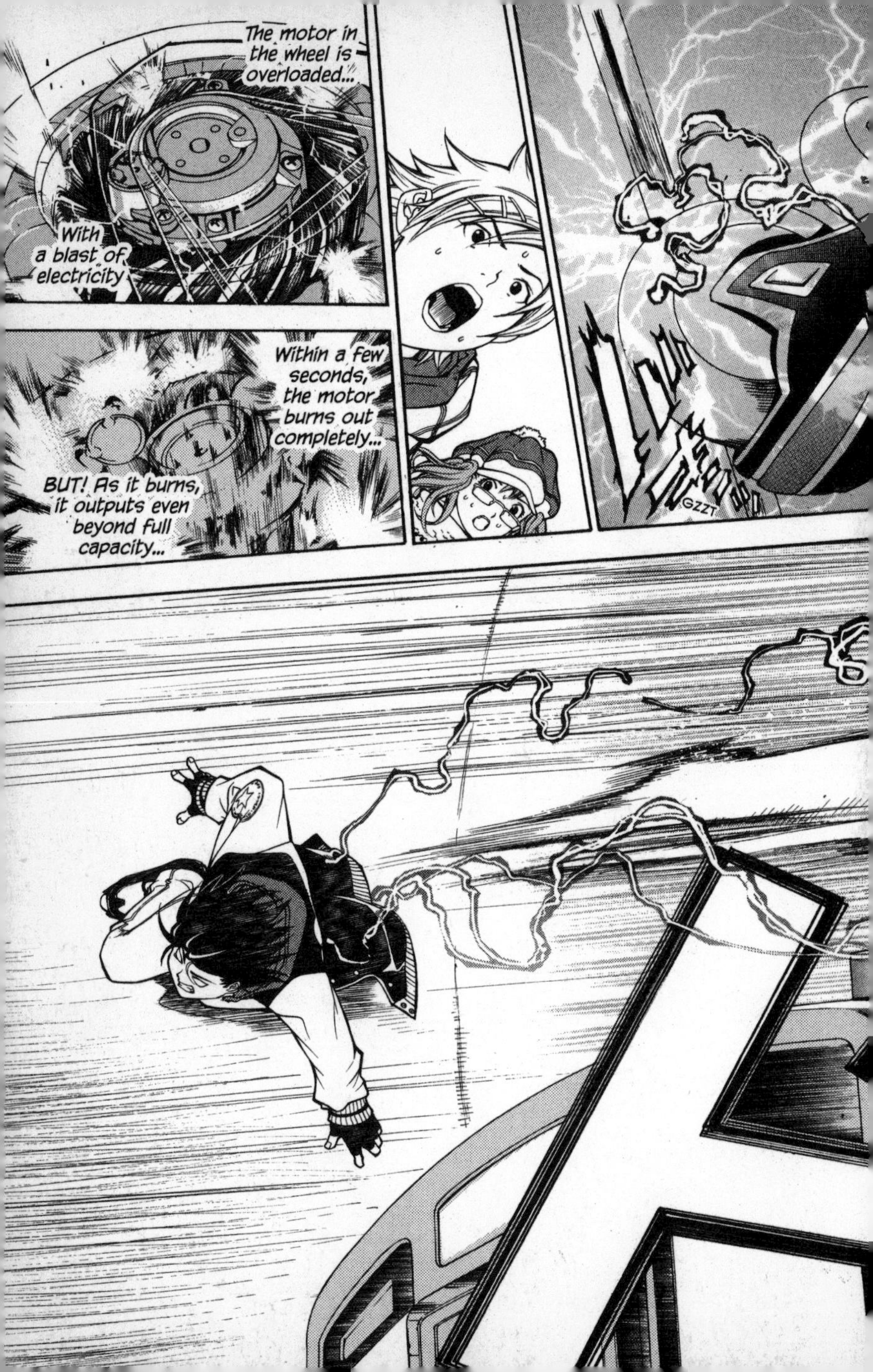
GZZT
The motor in the wheel is overloaded...
With a blast of electricity
Within a few seconds, the motor burns out completely...
BUT! As it burns, it outputs even beyond full capacity...

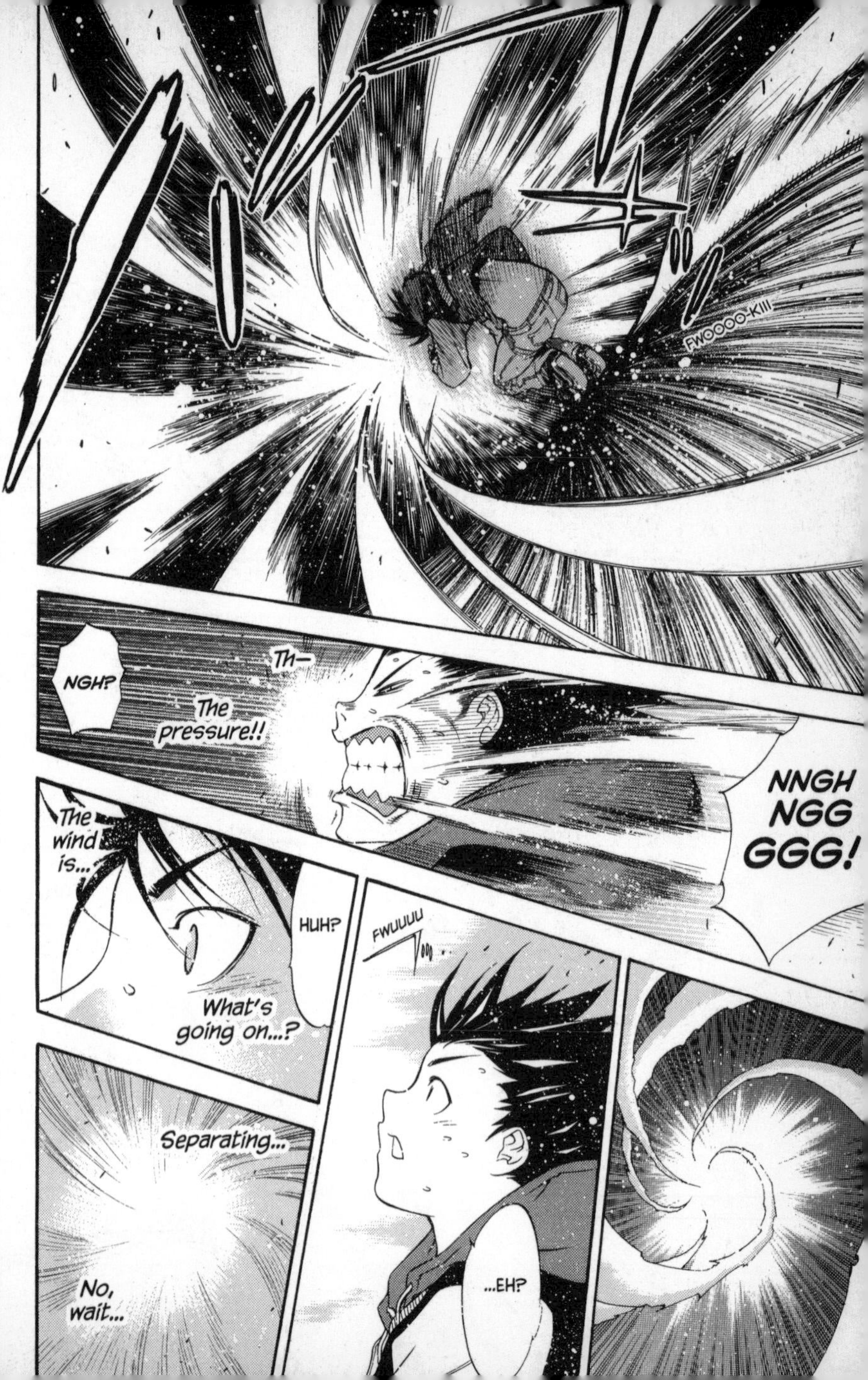
FWOOOO-KIII
NNGH NGG GGG!
Th–
The pressure!!
NGH?
FWUUUU
...EH?
The wind is...
HUH?
What's going on...?
Separating...
No, wait...

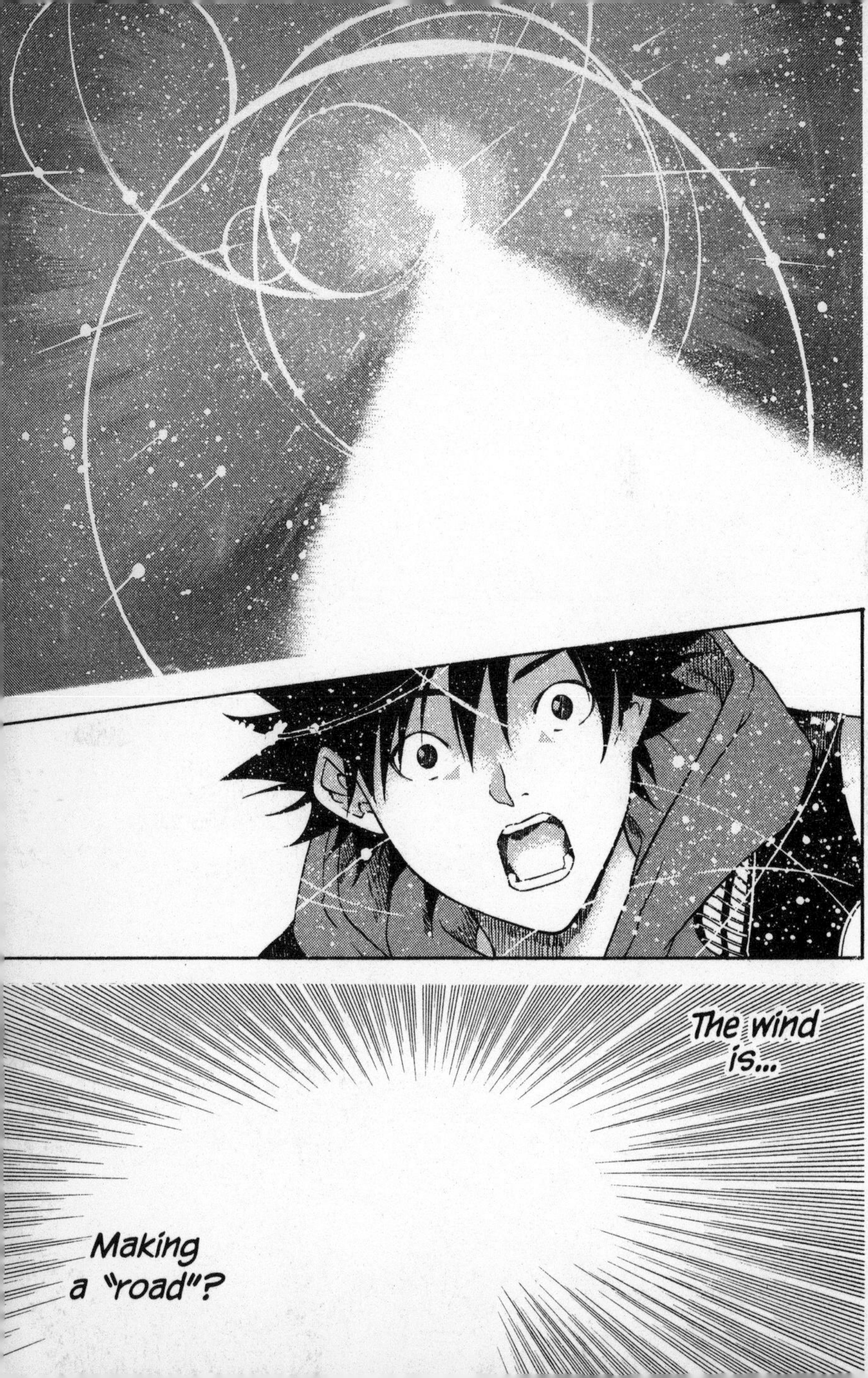
The wind is...
Making a "road"?

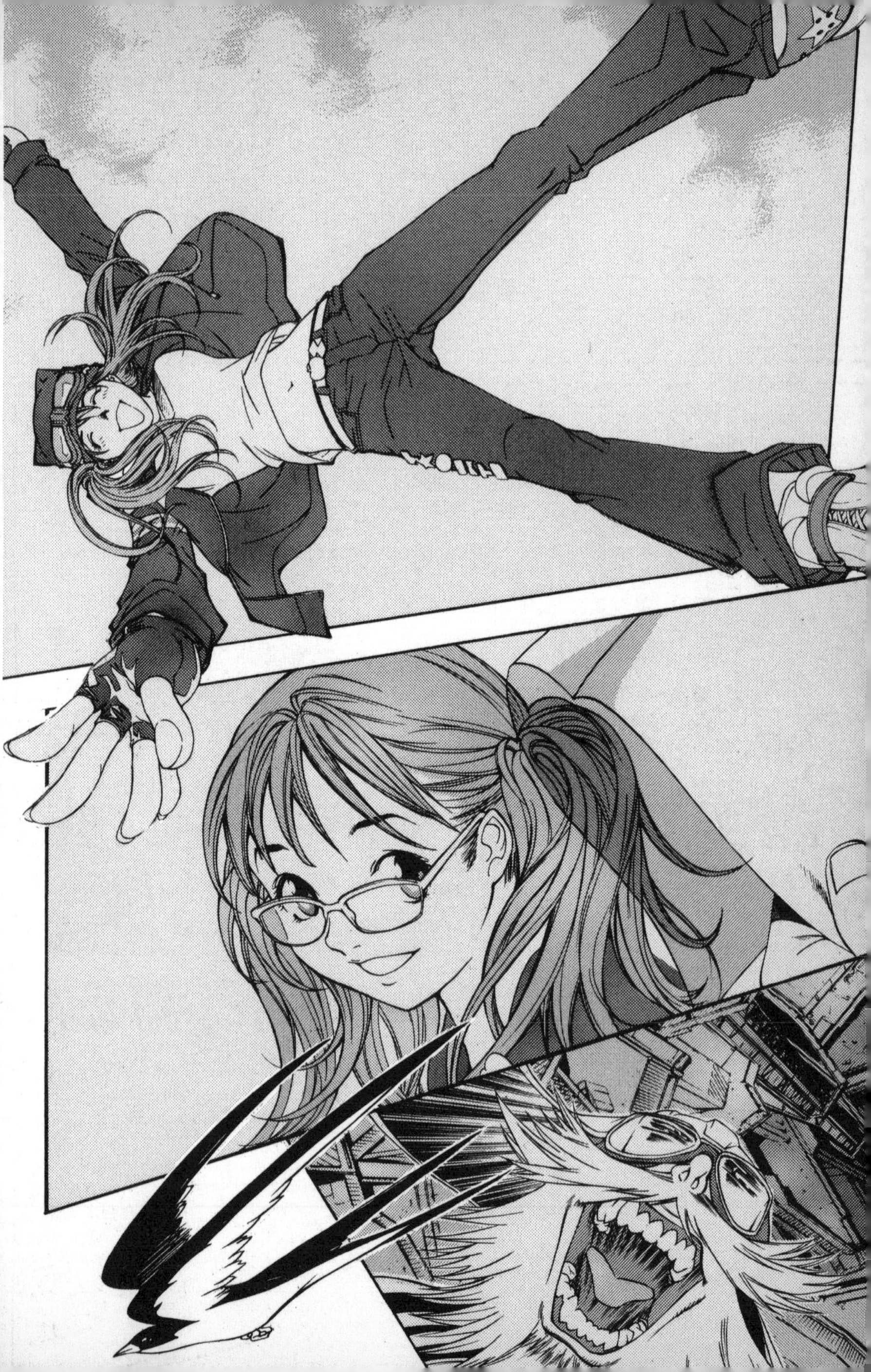

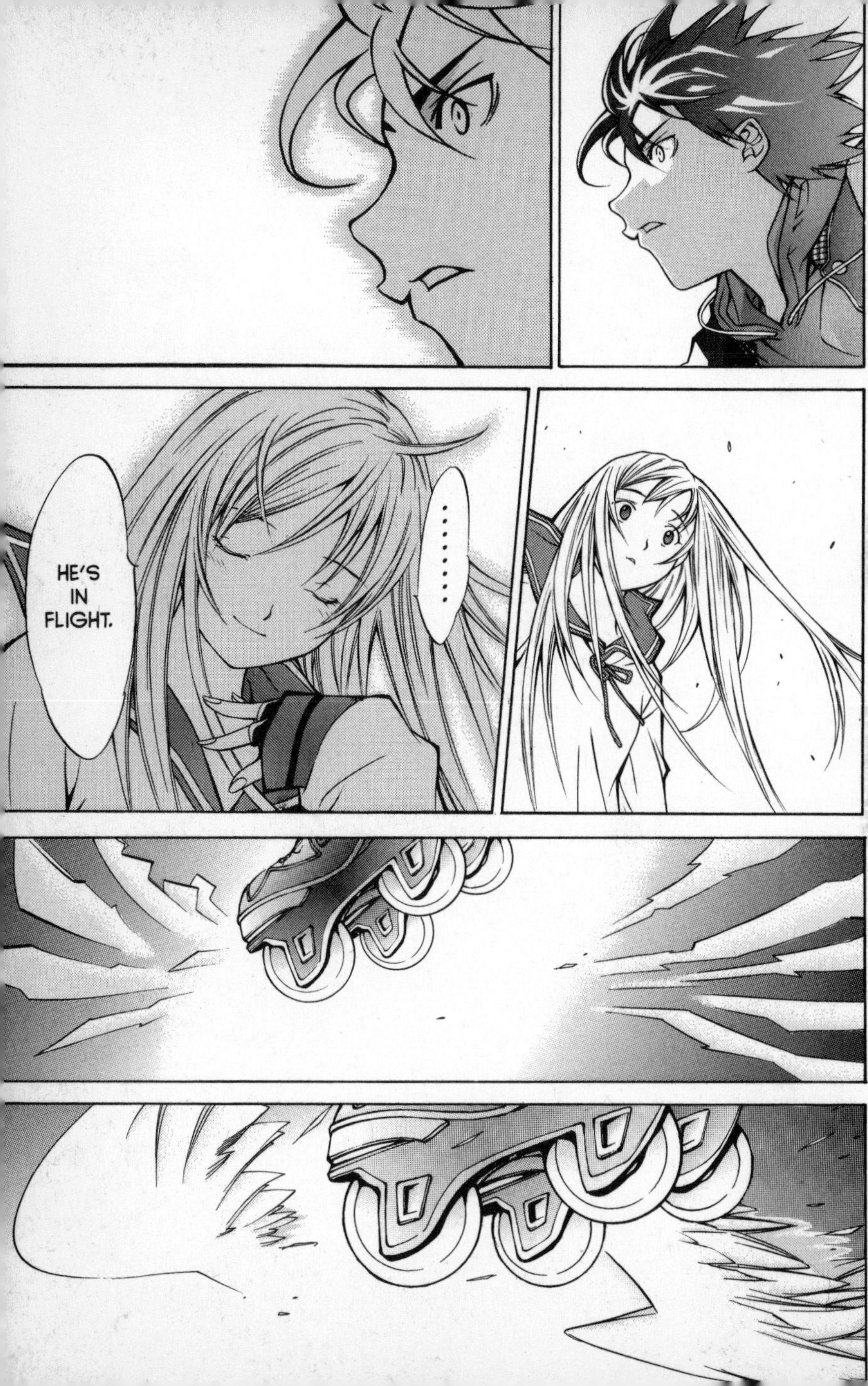
......
HE'S IN FLIGHT.

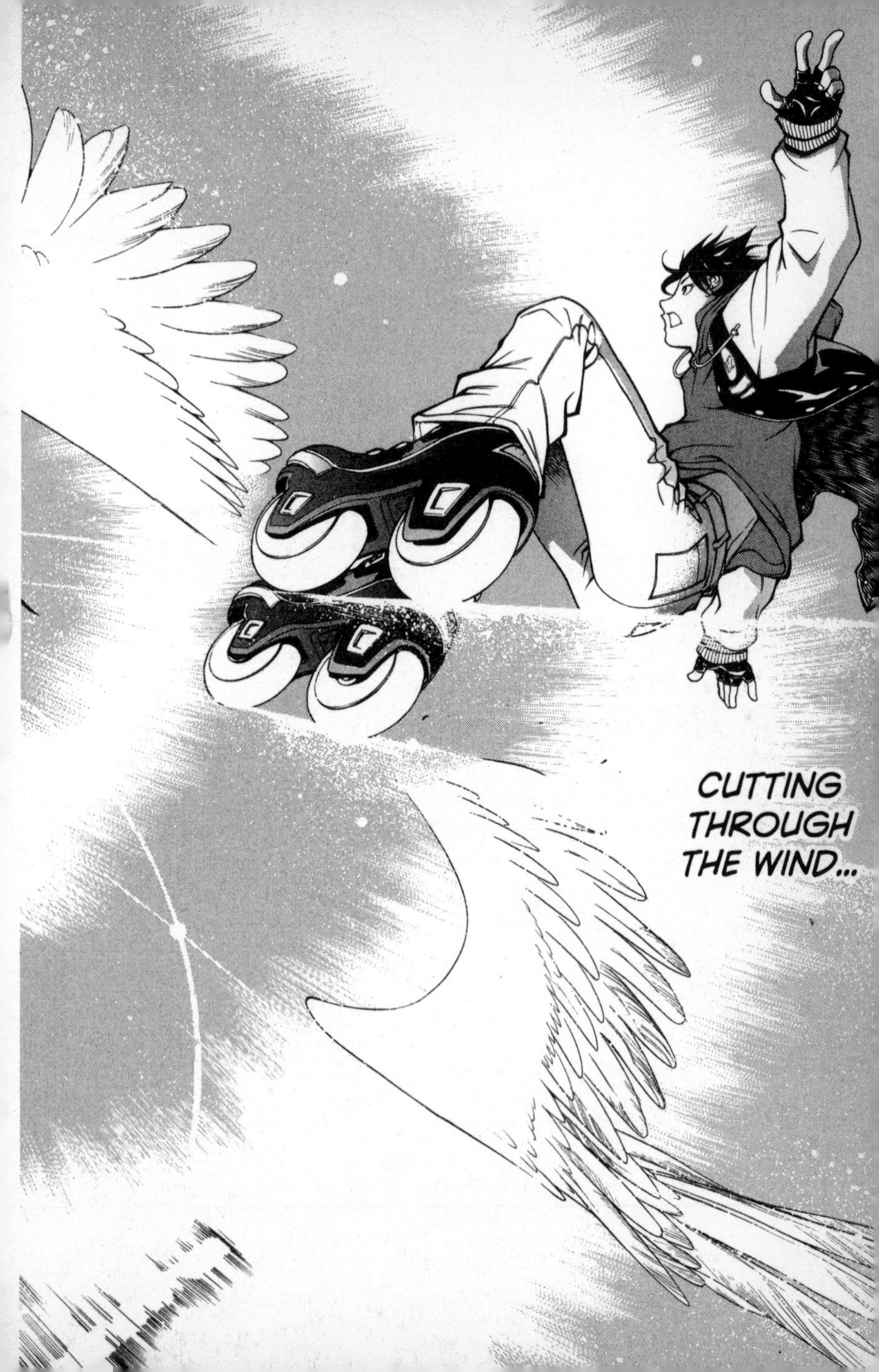
CUTTING THROUGH THE WIND...

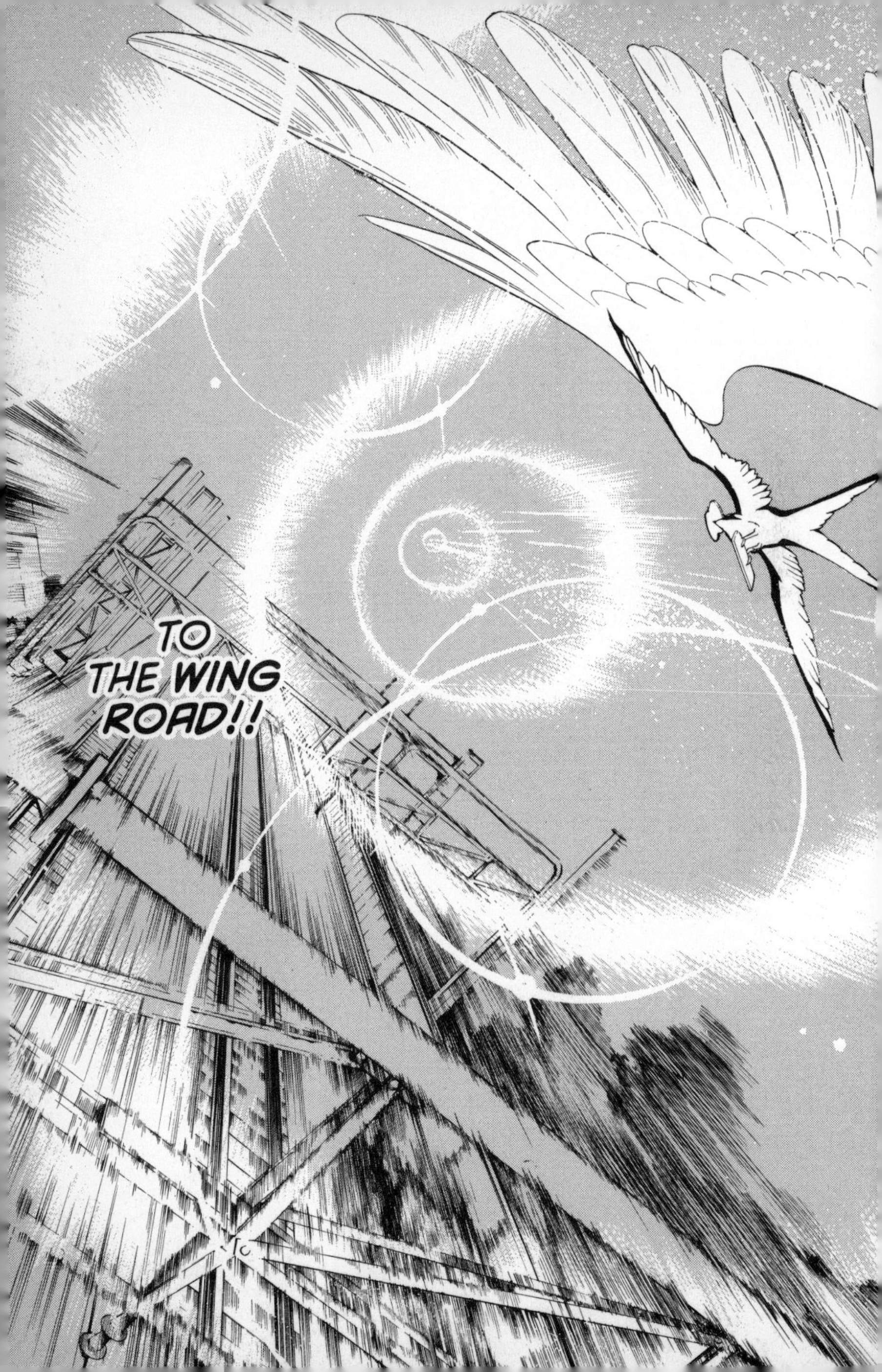
TO THE WING ROAD!!

THE SPARROW IS OH!GREAT'S FAVORITE KIND OF BIRD.

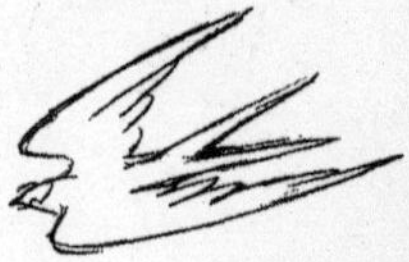

IT'S THE FASTEST OF ALL BIRDS, BUT WITH ONE MAJOR WEAKNESS: SPARROWS CAN'T TAKE FLIGHT DIRECTLY FROM THE GROUND LIKE OTHER SIMILAR SIZED BIRDS.

Trick:11

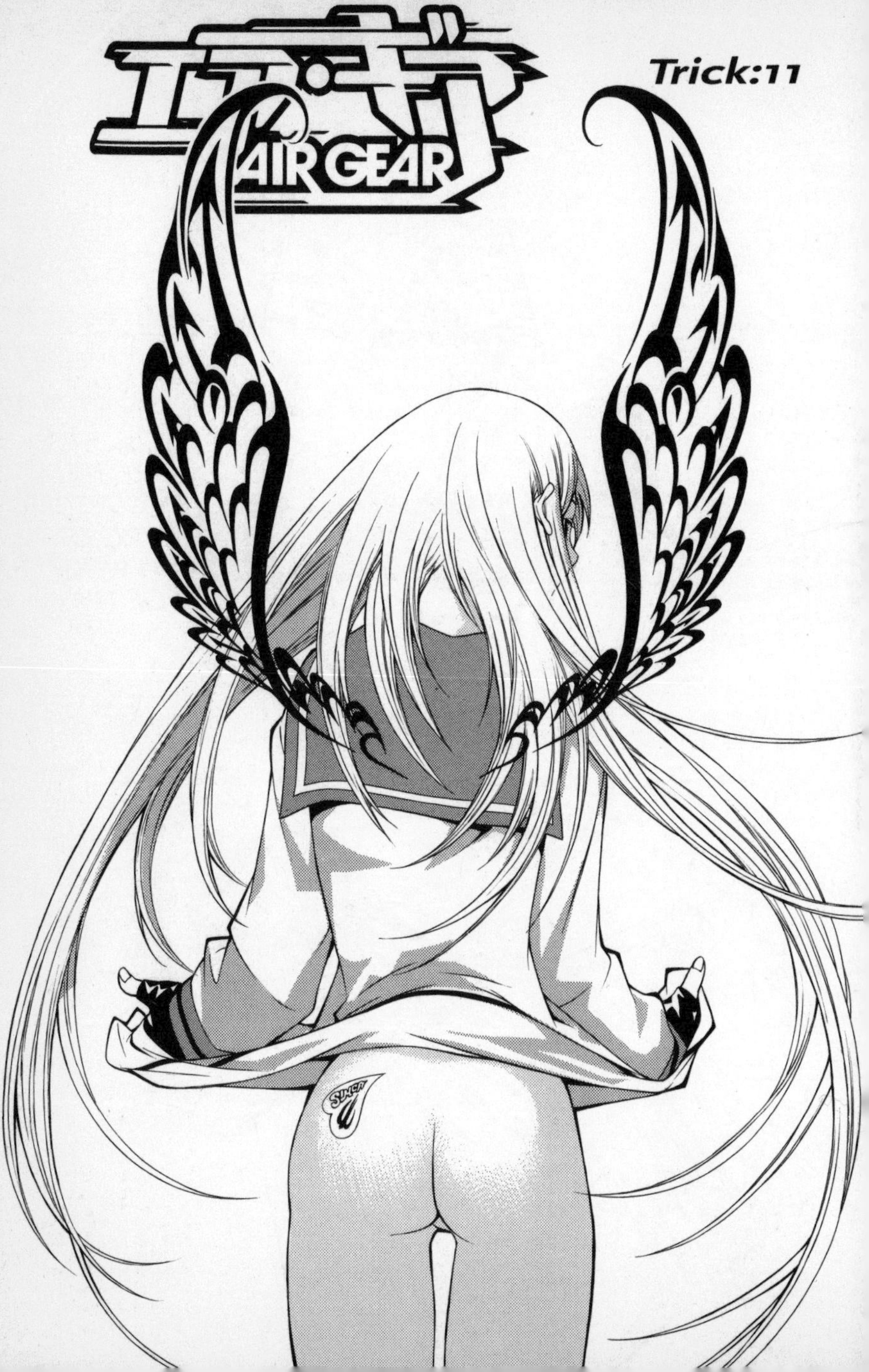
AIR GEAR

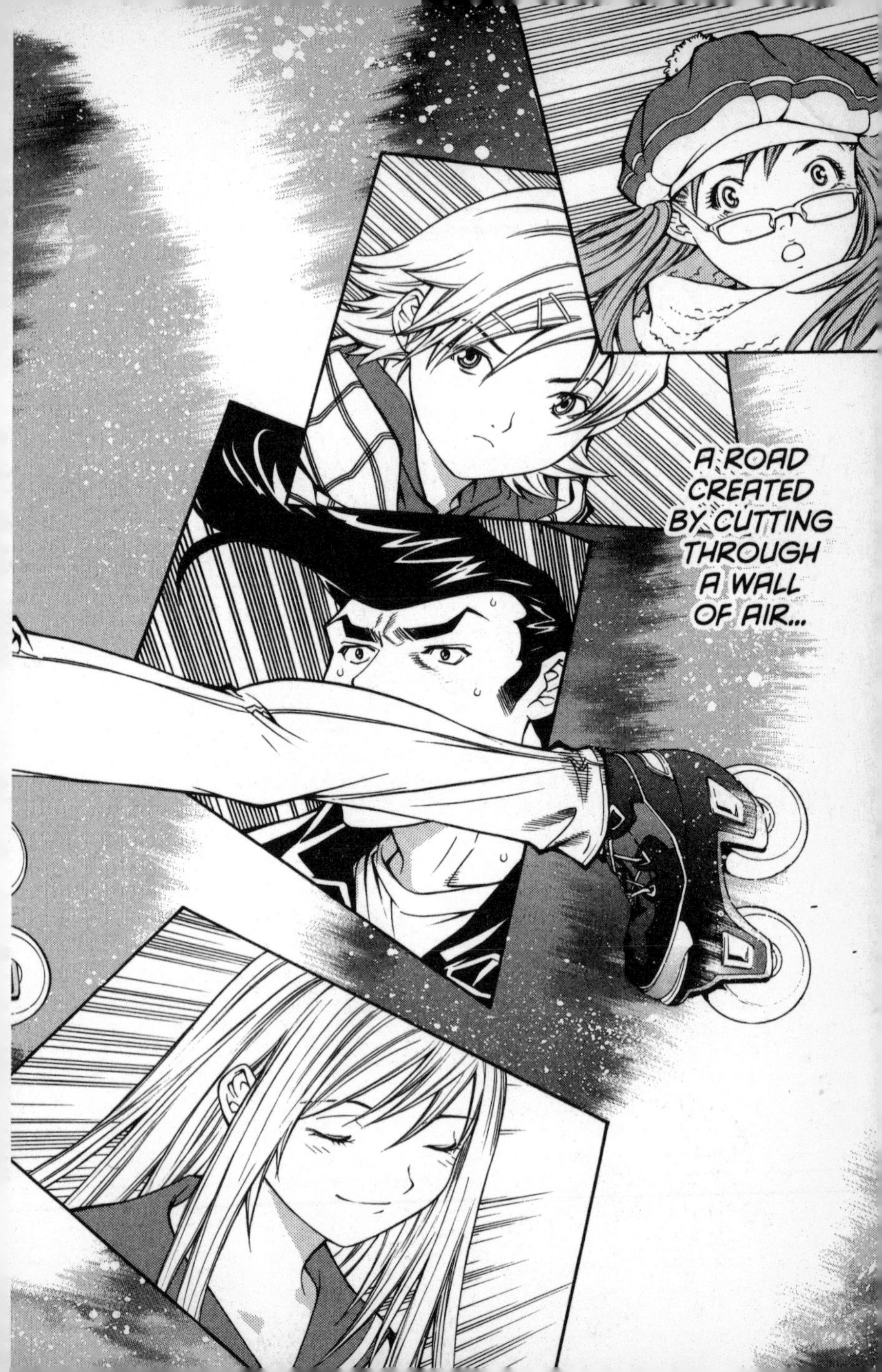
A ROAD CREATED BY CUTTING THROUGH A WALL OF AIR...

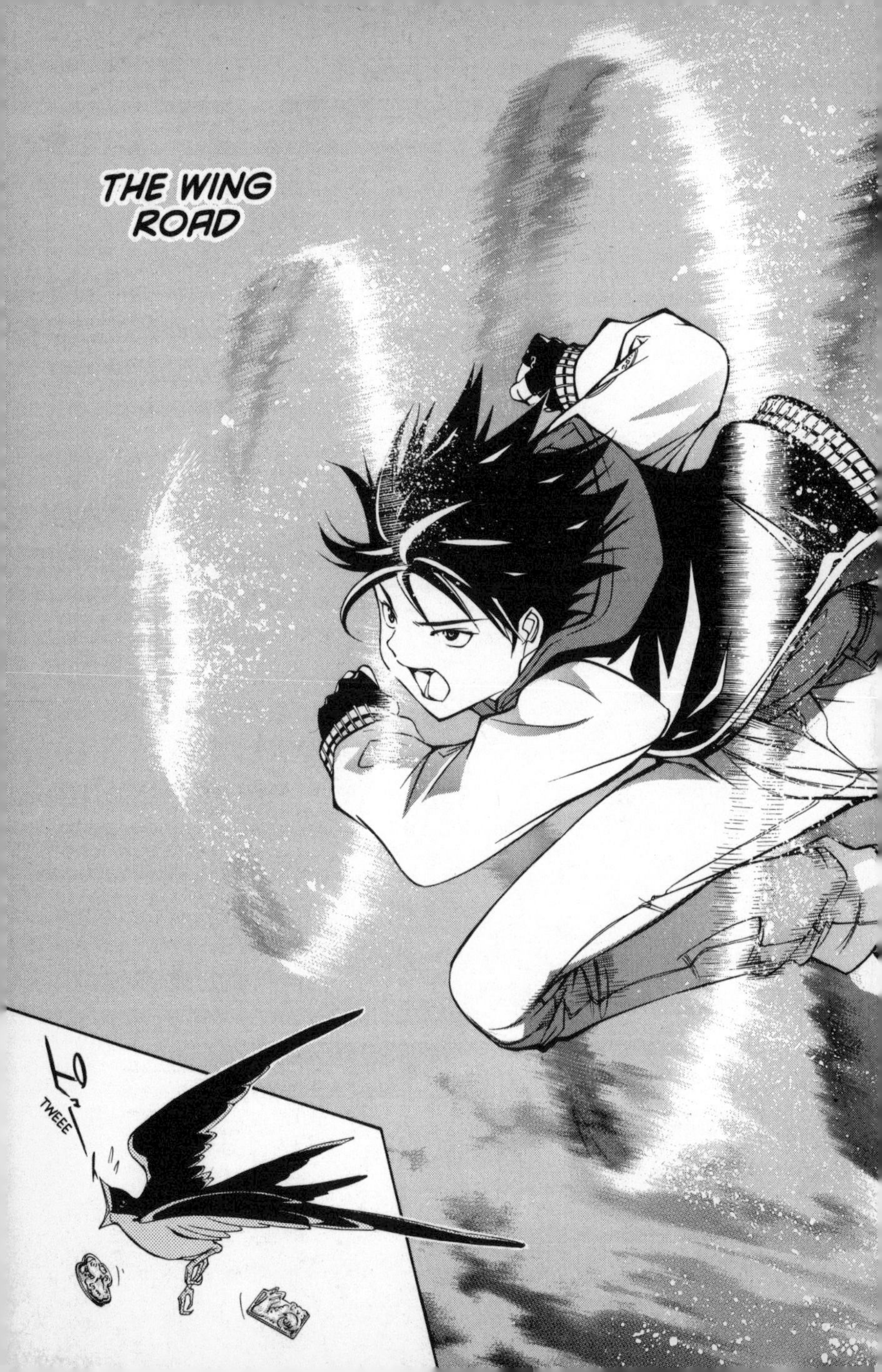
THE WING ROAD
TWEEE

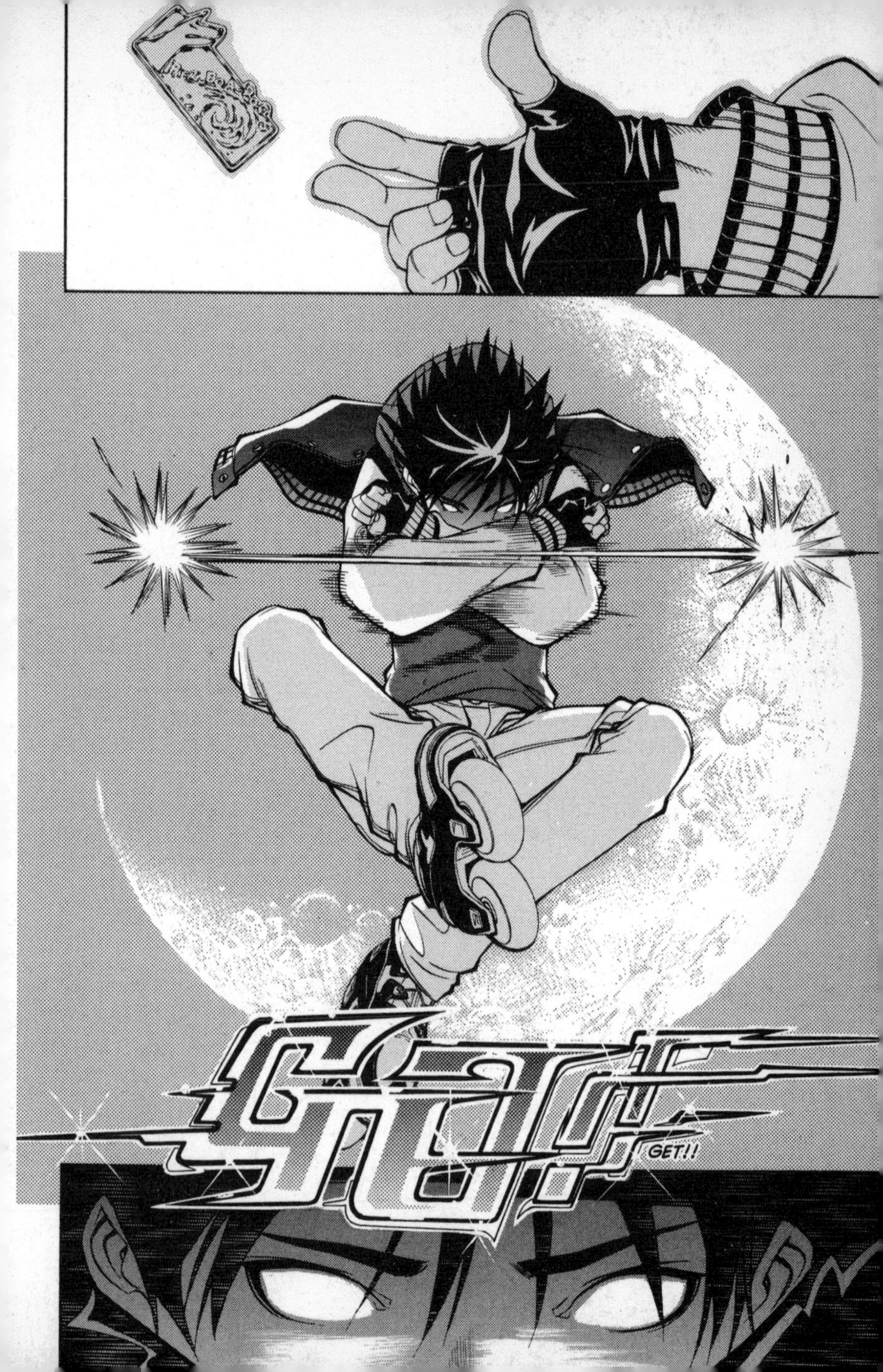
GET!!

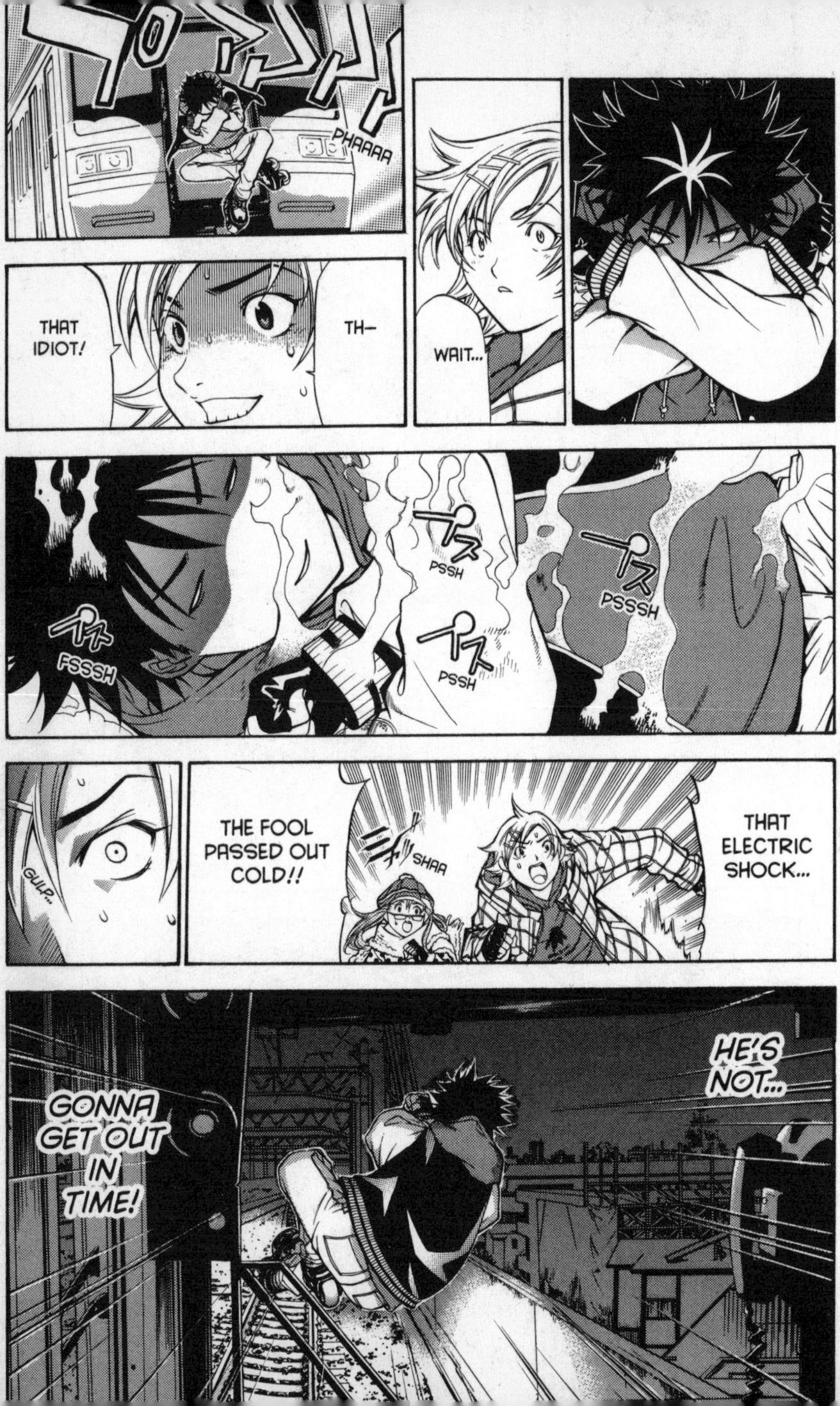
WAIT...
PHAAAA
TH–
THAT IDIOT!
PSSSH
PSSH
PSSH
FSSSH
THAT ELECTRIC SHOCK...
SHAA
THE FOOL PASSED OUT COLD!!
GULP...
HE'S NOT...
GONNA GET OUT IN TIME!

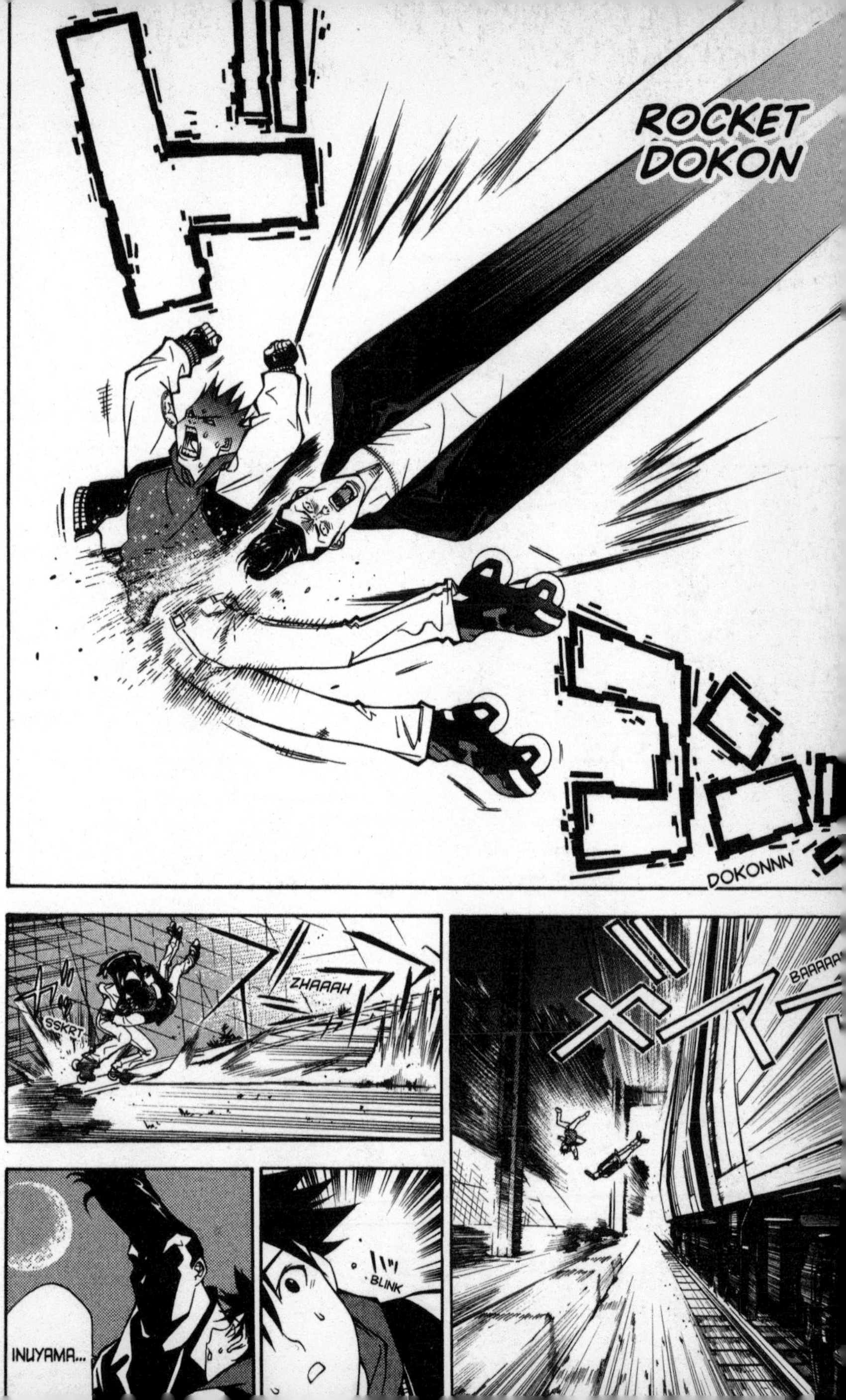
ROCKET DOKON
DOKONNN
BAAAAA
ZHAAAH
SSKRT
BLINK
INUYAMA...

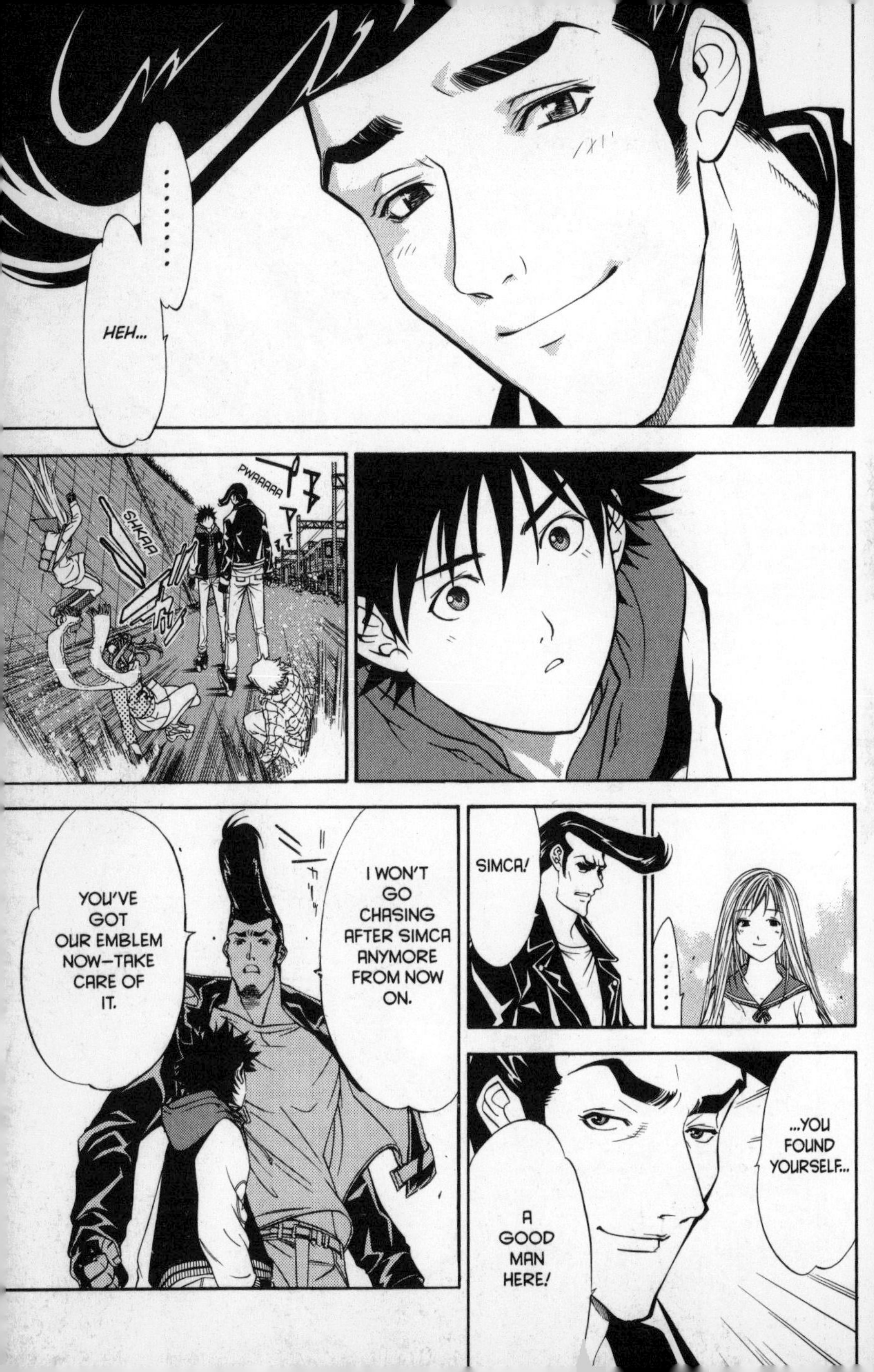
......
HEH...
PWAAAAA
SHKAA
......
SIMCA!
...YOU FOUND YOURSELF...
A GOOD MAN HERE!
I WON'T GO CHASING AFTER SIMCA ANYMORE FROM NOW ON.
YOU'VE GOT OUR EMBLEM NOW—TAKE CARE OF IT.

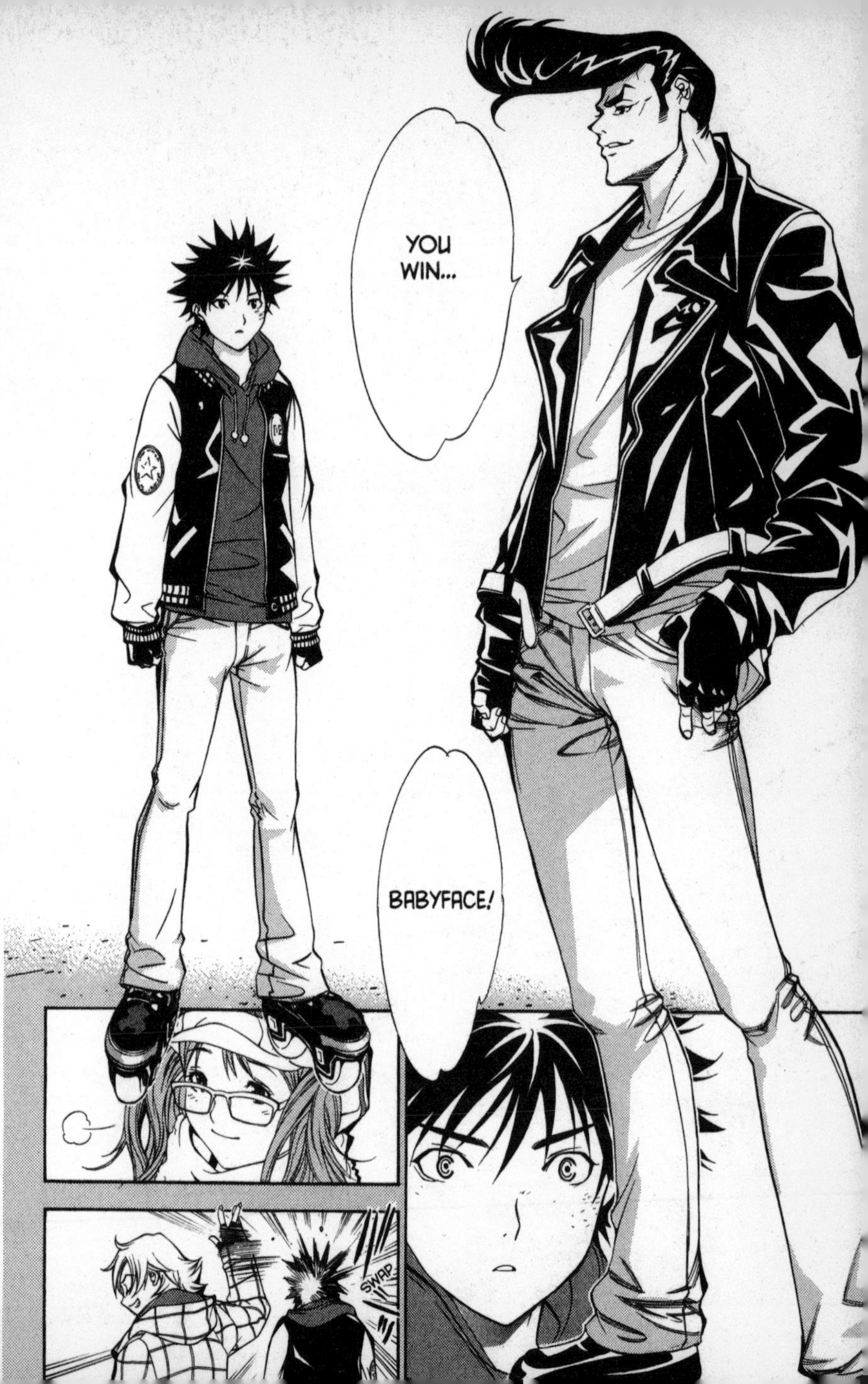
YOU WIN...
BABYFACE!
SWAP

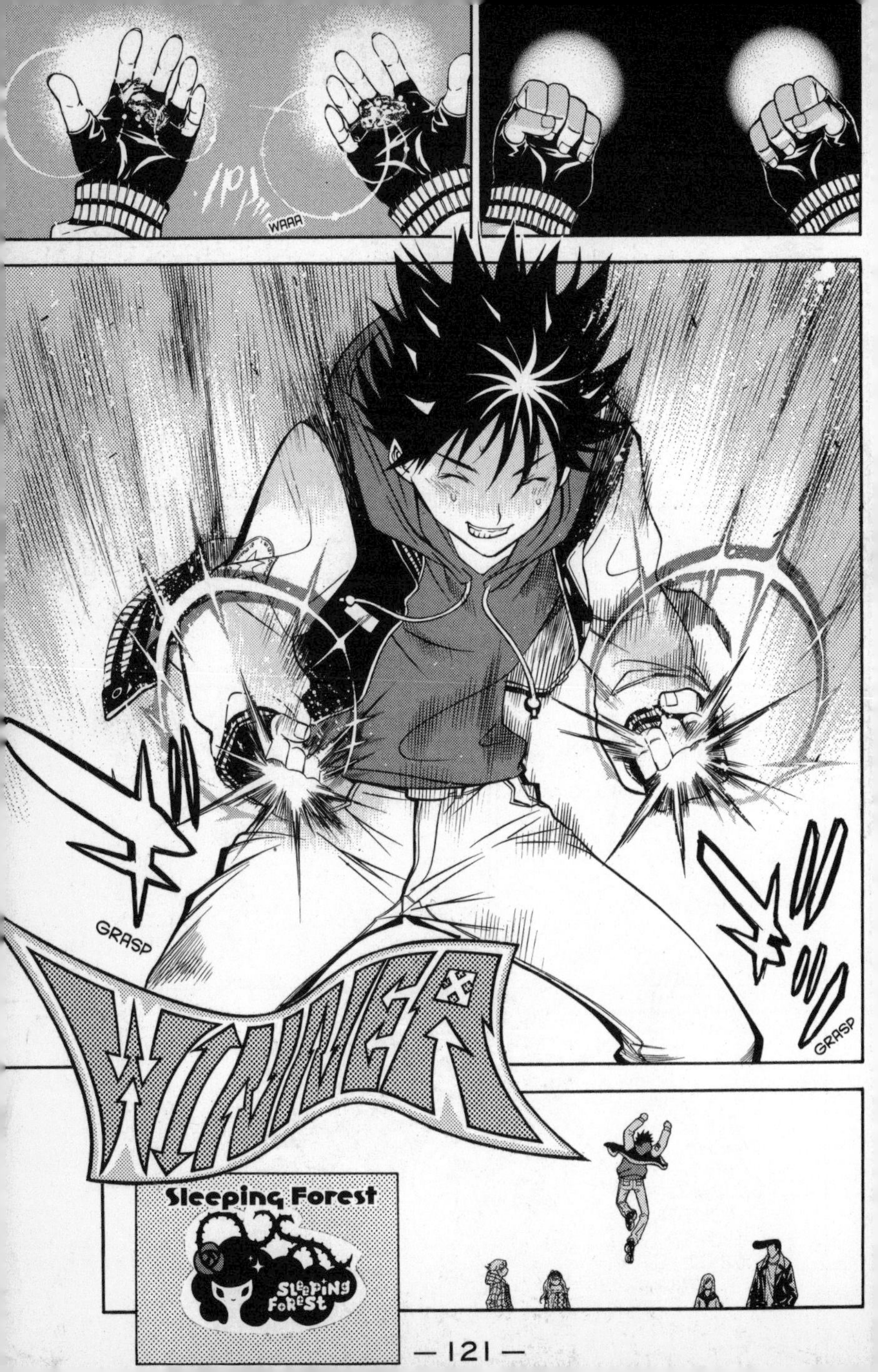
WAAA
GRASP
GRASP
Sleeping Forest
SLEEPING FOREST

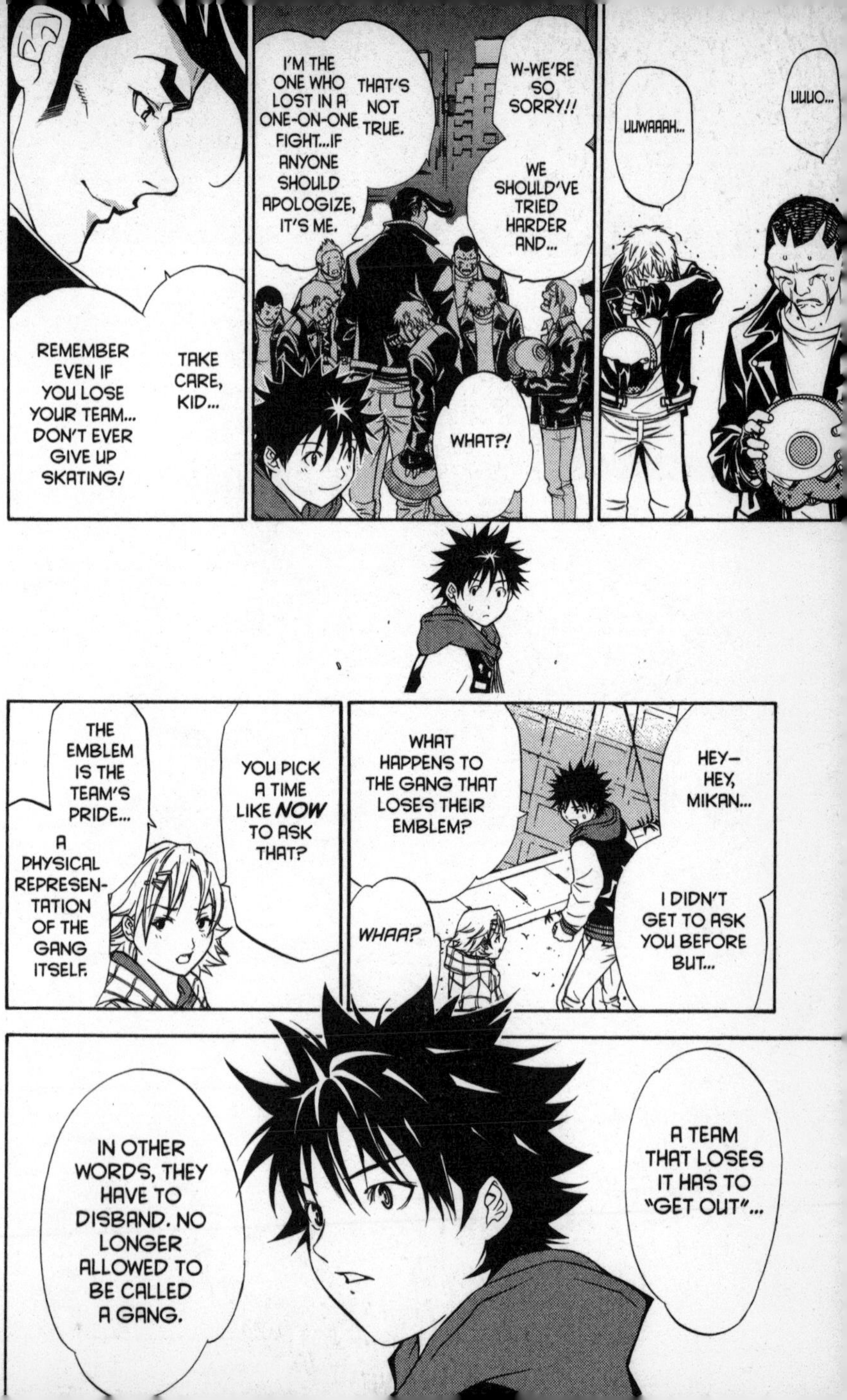
UUUO...
UUWAAAH...
W-WE'RE SO SORRY!!
WE SHOULD'VE TRIED HARDER AND...
THAT'S NOT TRUE.
I'M THE ONE WHO LOST IN A ONE-ON-ONE FIGHT...IF ANYONE SHOULD APOLOGIZE, IT'S ME.
WHAT?!
TAKE CARE, KID...
REMEMBER EVEN IF YOU LOSE YOUR TEAM... DON'T EVER GIVE UP SKATING!
HEY— HEY, MIKAN...
I DIDN'T GET TO ASK YOU BEFORE BUT...
WHAT HAPPENS TO THE GANG THAT LOSES THEIR EMBLEM?
WHAA?
YOU PICK A TIME LIKE *NOW* TO ASK THAT?
THE EMBLEM IS THE TEAM'S PRIDE...
A PHYSICAL REPRESENTATION OF THE GANG ITSELF.
A TEAM THAT LOSES IT HAS TO "GET OUT"...
IN OTHER WORDS, THEY HAVE TO DISBAND. NO LONGER ALLOWED TO BE CALLED A GANG.

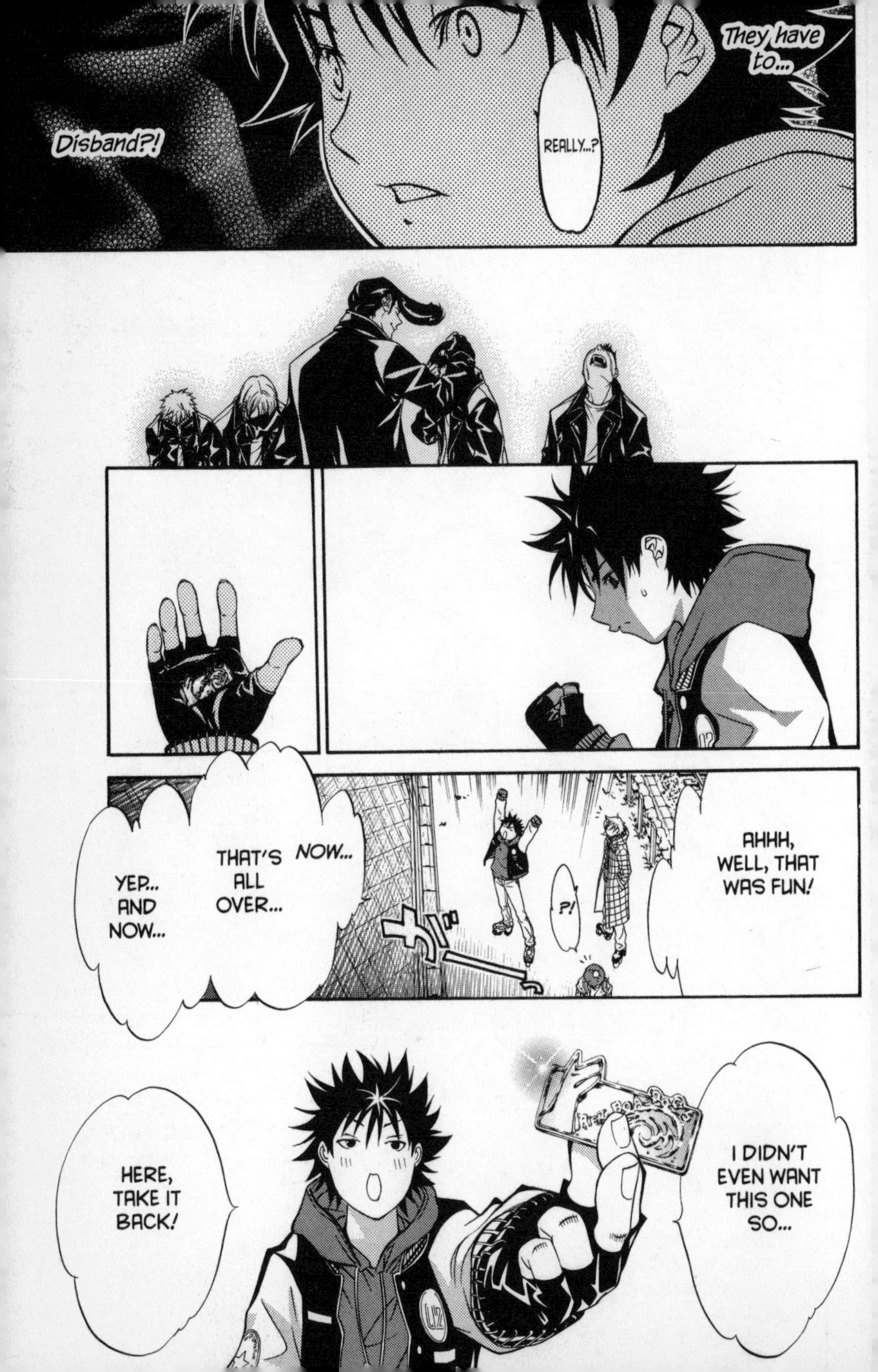

They have to...
REALLY...?
Disband?!
AHHH, WELL, THAT WAS FUN!
?!
NOW... THAT'S ALL OVER...
YEP... AND NOW...
I DIDN'T EVEN WANT THIS ONE SO...
HERE, TAKE IT BACK!

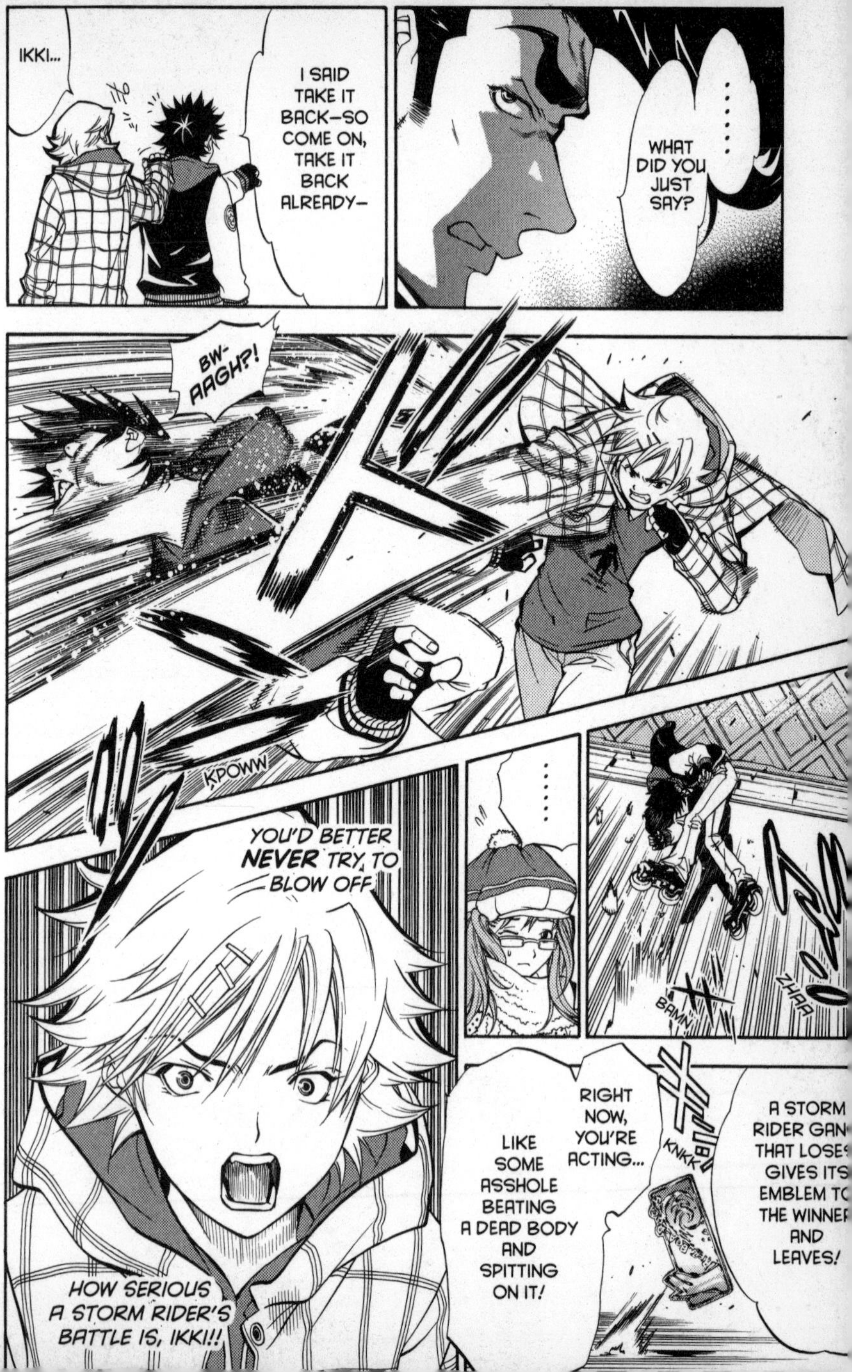

......
WHAT DID YOU JUST SAY?
I SAID TAKE IT BACK—SO COME ON, TAKE IT BACK ALREADY—
IKKI...
BW-AAGH?!
KPOWW
ZHAA
BAMN
......
A STORM RIDER GANG THAT LOSES GIVES ITS EMBLEM TO THE WINNER AND LEAVES!
KNKK
RIGHT NOW, YOU'RE ACTING...
LIKE SOME ASSHOLE BEATING A DEAD BODY AND SPITTING ON IT!
YOU'D BETTER **NEVER** TRY TO BLOW OFF
HOW SERIOUS A STORM RIDER'S BATTLE IS, IKKI!!

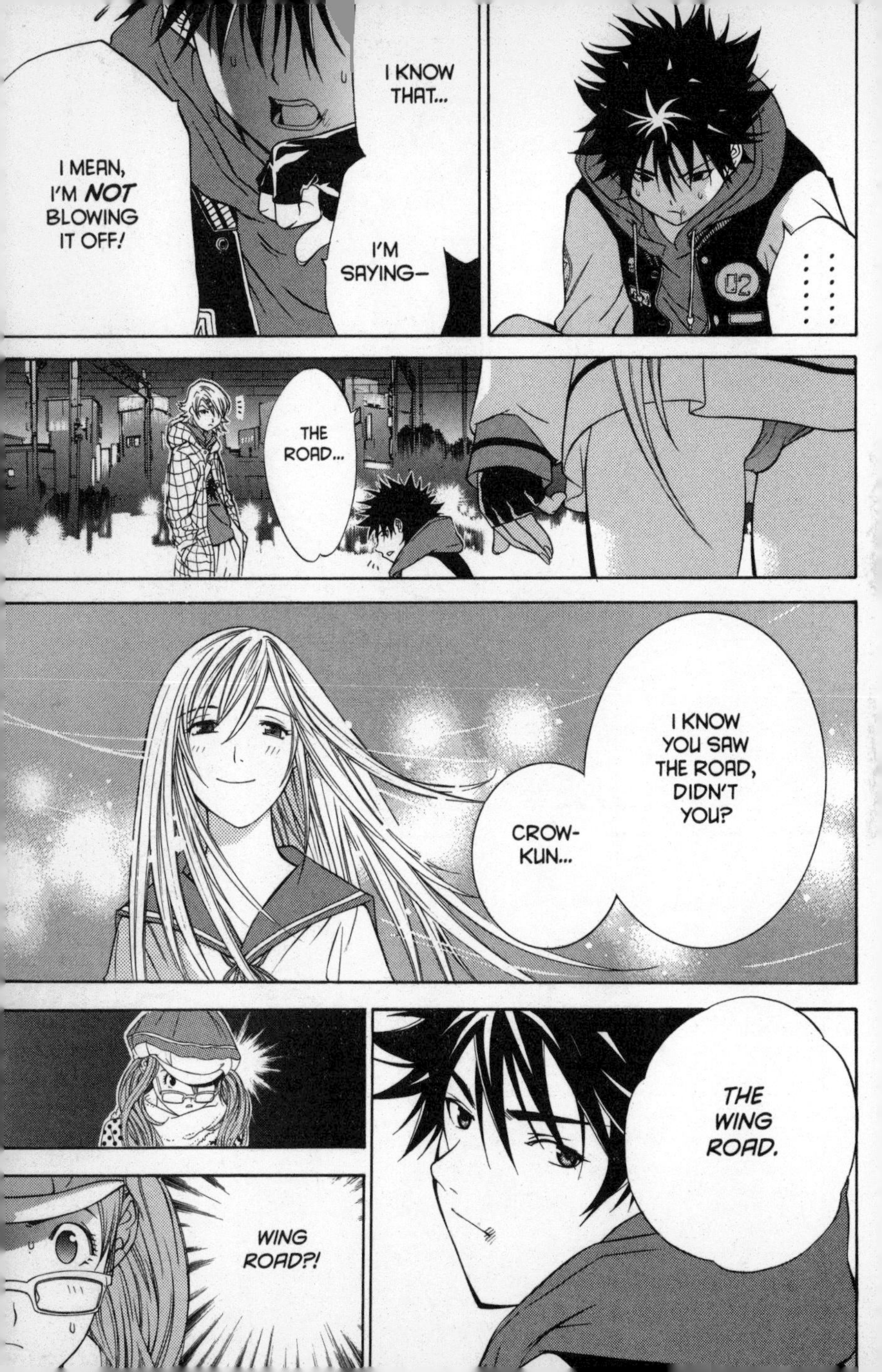
I KNOW THAT...
I MEAN, I'M **NOT** BLOWING IT OFF!
I'M SAYING—
THE ROAD...
I KNOW YOU SAW THE ROAD, DIDN'T YOU?
CROW-KUN...
THE WING ROAD.
WING ROAD?!

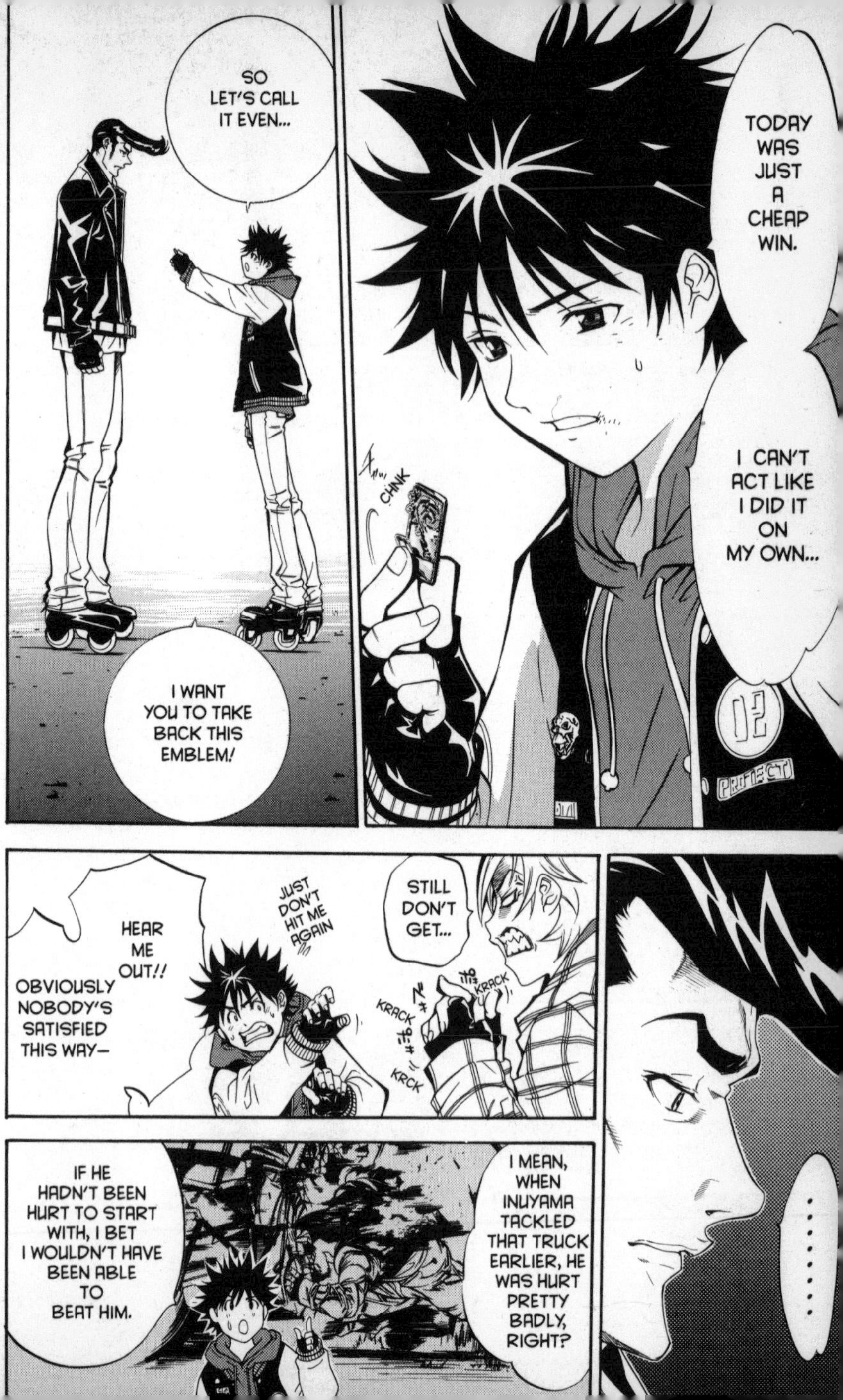
TODAY WAS JUST A CHEAP WIN.
I CAN'T ACT LIKE I DID IT ON MY OWN...
CHINK
SO LET'S CALL IT EVEN...
I WANT YOU TO TAKE BACK THIS EMBLEM!
......
STILL DON'T GET...
KRACK
KRACK
KRCK
JUST DON'T HIT ME AGAIN
HEAR ME OUT!!
OBVIOUSLY NOBODY'S SATISFIED THIS WAY—
I MEAN, WHEN INUYAMA TACKLED THAT TRUCK EARLIER, HE WAS HURT PRETTY BADLY, RIGHT?
IF HE HADN'T BEEN HURT TO START WITH, I BET I WOULDN'T HAVE BEEN ABLE TO BEAT HIM.

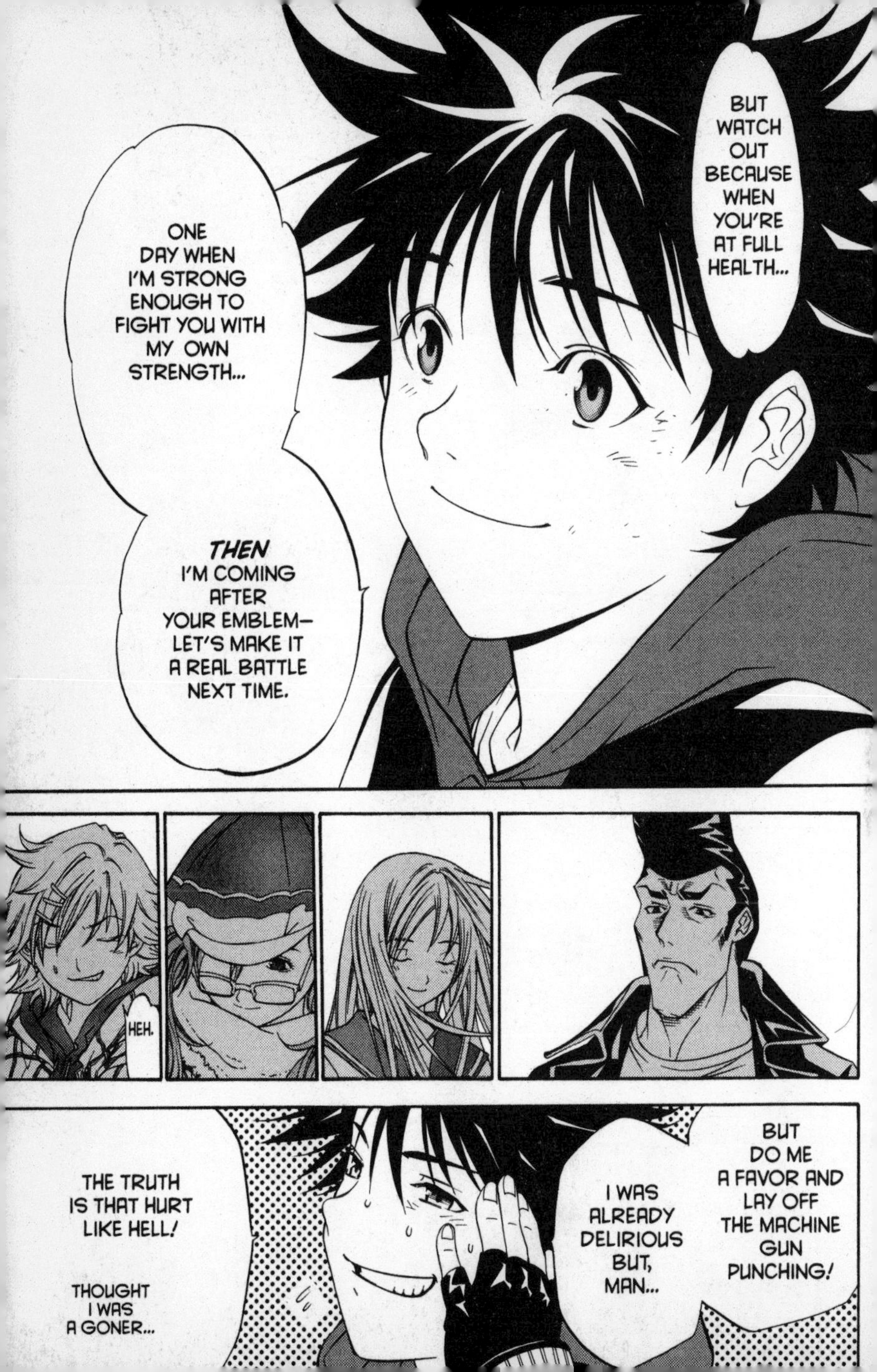
BUT WATCH OUT BECAUSE WHEN YOU'RE AT FULL HEALTH...
ONE DAY WHEN I'M STRONG ENOUGH TO FIGHT YOU WITH MY OWN STRENGTH...
THEN I'M COMING AFTER YOUR EMBLEM— LET'S MAKE IT A REAL BATTLE NEXT TIME.
HEH.
BUT DO ME A FAVOR AND LAY OFF THE MACHINE GUN PUNCHING!
I WAS ALREADY DELIRIOUS BUT, MAN...
THE TRUTH IS THAT HURT LIKE HELL!
THOUGHT I WAS A GONER...

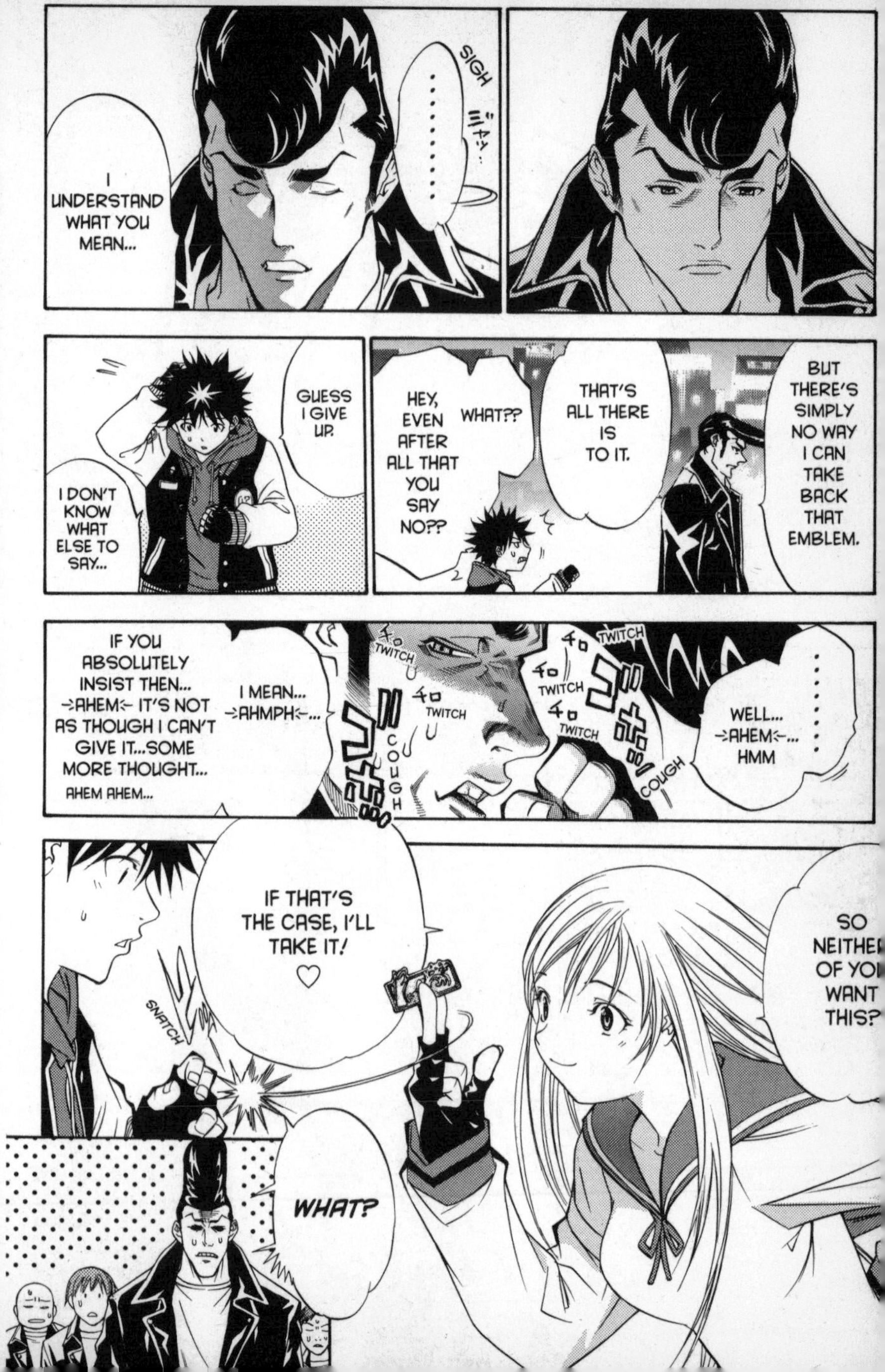
SIGH
......
I UNDERSTAND WHAT YOU MEAN...
BUT THERE'S SIMPLY NO WAY I CAN TAKE BACK THAT EMBLEM.
THAT'S ALL THERE IS TO IT.
WHAT??
HEY, EVEN AFTER ALL THAT YOU SAY NO??
GUESS I GIVE UP.
I DON'T KNOW WHAT ELSE TO SAY...
......
WELL... →AHEM←... HMM
TWITCH
TWITCH
COUGH
TWITCH
TWITCH
TWITCH
COUGH
I MEAN... →AHMPH←...
IF YOU ABSOLUTELY INSIST THEN... →AHEM← IT'S NOT AS THOUGH I CAN'T GIVE IT...SOME MORE THOUGHT...
AHEM AHEM...
SO NEITHE OF YO WANT THIS?
IF THAT'S THE CASE, I'LL TAKE IT! ♡
SNATCH
WHAT?

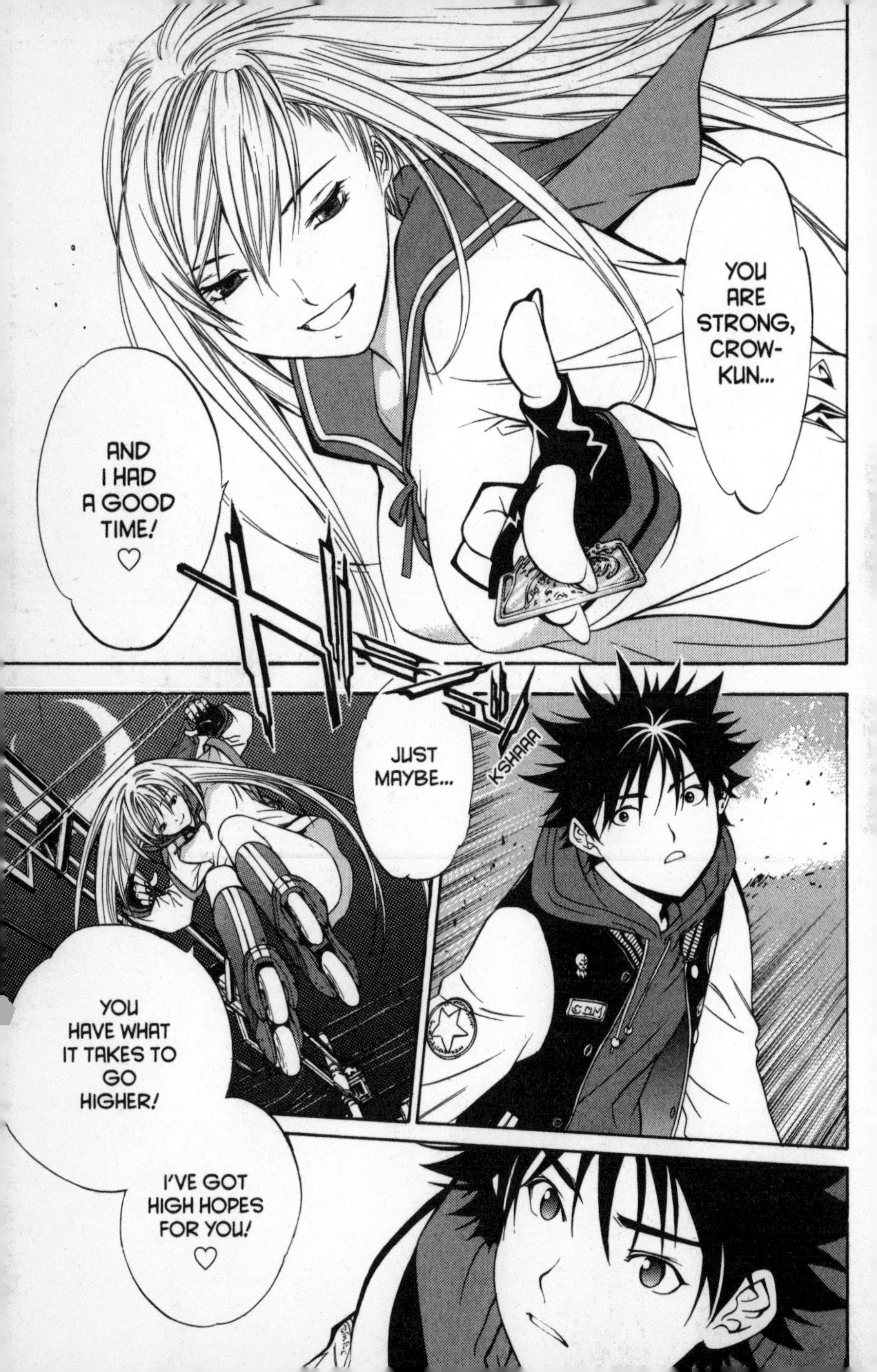
YOU ARE STRONG, CROW-KUN...
AND I HAD A GOOD TIME! ♡
KSHAAA
JUST MAYBE...
YOU HAVE WHAT IT TAKES TO GO HIGHER!
I'VE GOT HIGH HOPES FOR YOU! ♡

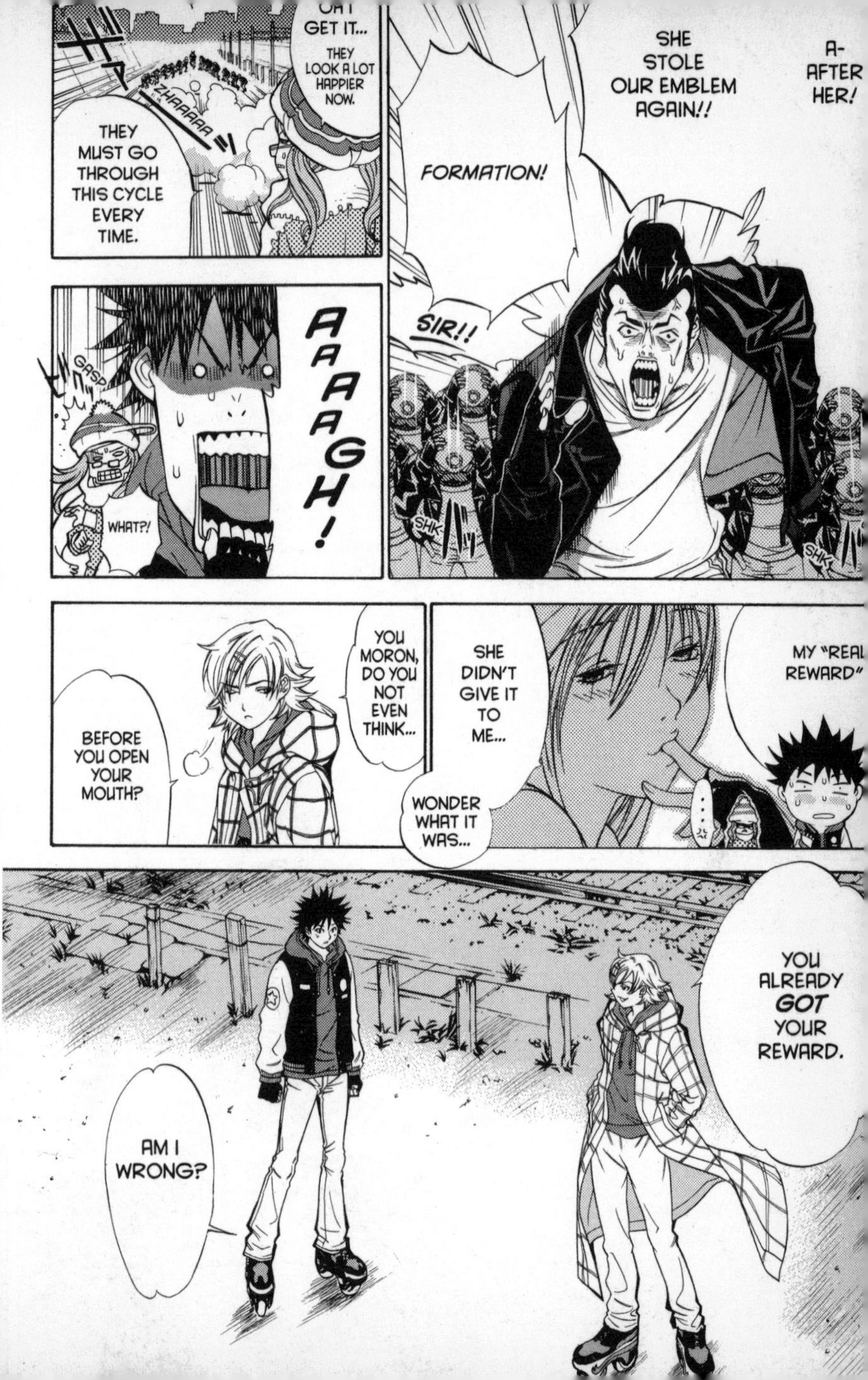
A- AFTER HER!
SHE STOLE OUR EMBLEM AGAIN!!
FORMATION!
SIR!!
SHK
SHK
GET IT...
THEY LOOK A LOT HAPPIER NOW.
ZHAAAAA
THEY MUST GO THROUGH THIS CYCLE EVERY TIME.
AAAAGH!
GASP
WHAT?!
MY "REAL REWARD"
SHE DIDN'T GIVE IT TO ME...
WONDER WHAT IT WAS...
YOU MORON, DO YOU NOT EVEN THINK...
BEFORE YOU OPEN YOUR MOUTH?
YOU ALREADY GOT YOUR REWARD.
AM I WRONG?

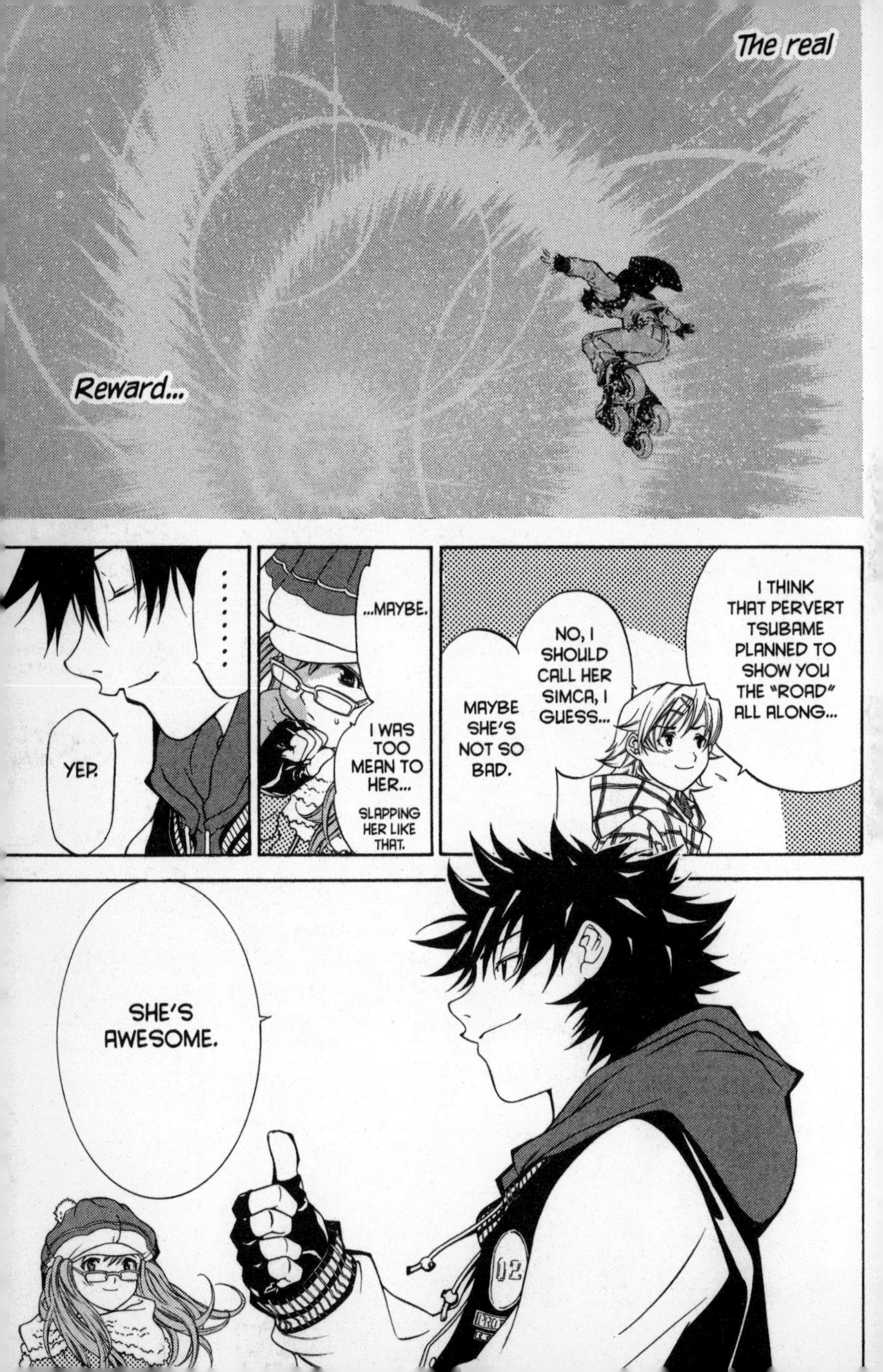
The real
Reward...
I THINK THAT PERVERT TSUBAME PLANNED TO SHOW YOU THE "ROAD" ALL ALONG...
NO, I SHOULD CALL HER SIMCA, I GUESS...
MAYBE SHE'S NOT SO BAD.
...MAYBE.
I WAS TOO MEAN TO HER...
SLAPPING HER LIKE THAT.
....
YEP.
SHE'S AWESOME.

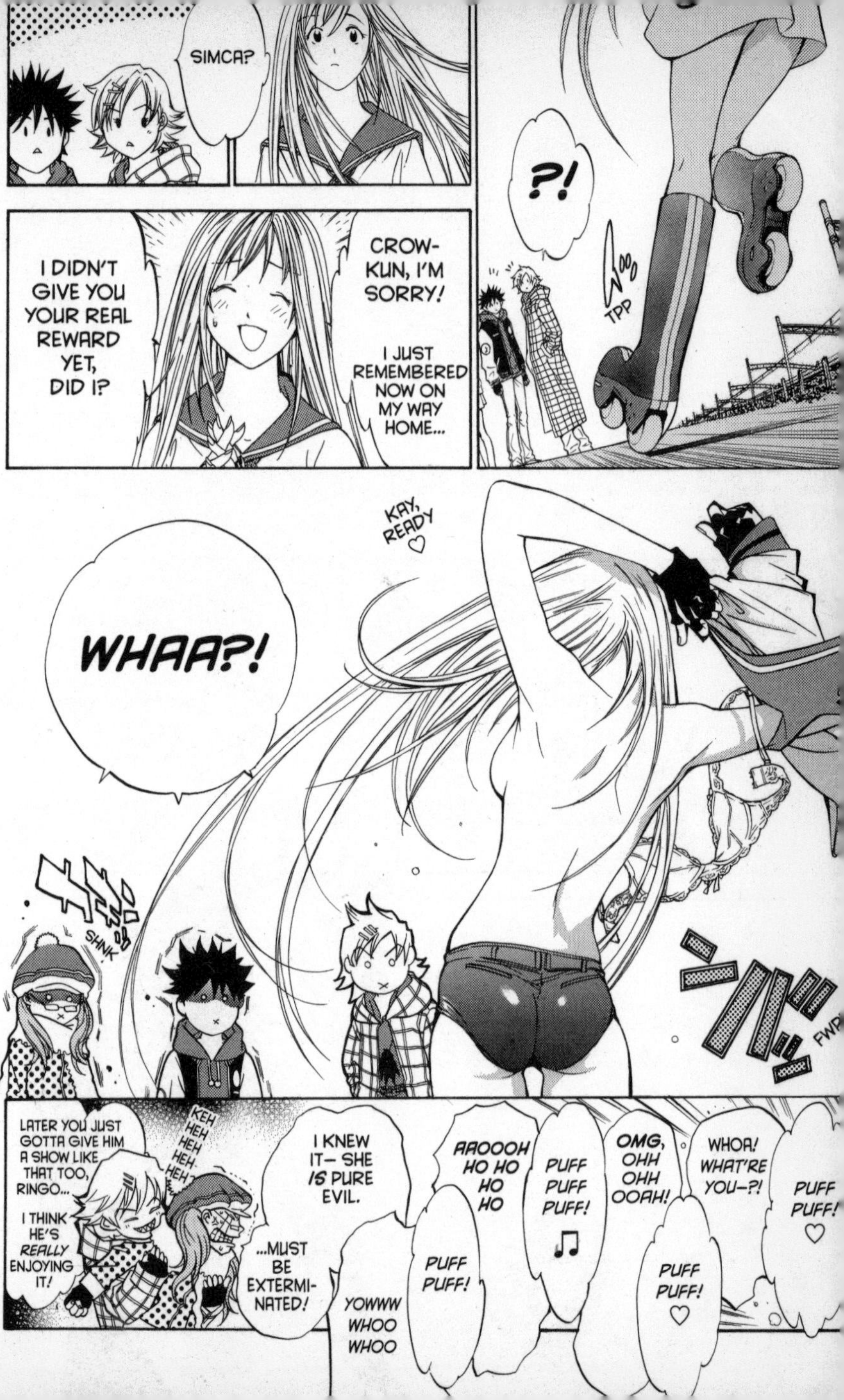
?!
TPP
SIMCA?
CROW-KUN, I'M SORRY!
I JUST REMEMBERED NOW ON MY WAY HOME...
I DIDN'T GIVE YOU YOUR REAL REWARD YET, DID I?
KAY, READY ♡
WHAA?!
FWP
SHNK
PUFF PUFF! ♡
WHOA! WHAT'RE YOU–?!
PUFF PUFF! ♡
OMG, OHH OHH OOAH!
PUFF PUFF PUFF! ♫
AAOOOH HO HO HO HO
PUFF PUFF!
YOWWW WHOO WHOO
I KNEW IT– SHE IS PURE EVIL.
...MUST BE EXTERMINATED!
KEH HEH HEH HEH HEH
LATER YOU JUST GOTTA GIVE HIM A SHOW LIKE THAT TOO, RINGO...
I THINK HE'S REALLY ENJOYING IT!

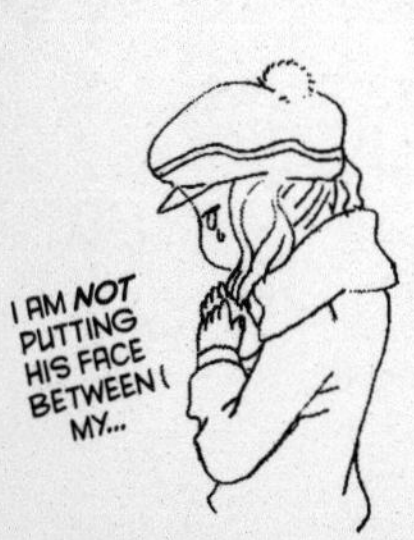
I AM *NOT* PUTTING HIS FACE BETWEEN MY...

CHIWATAROU

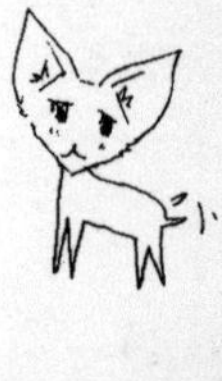

AMONG A VERY SMALL
GROUP OF PEOPLE...
A VERY POPULAR DOG.

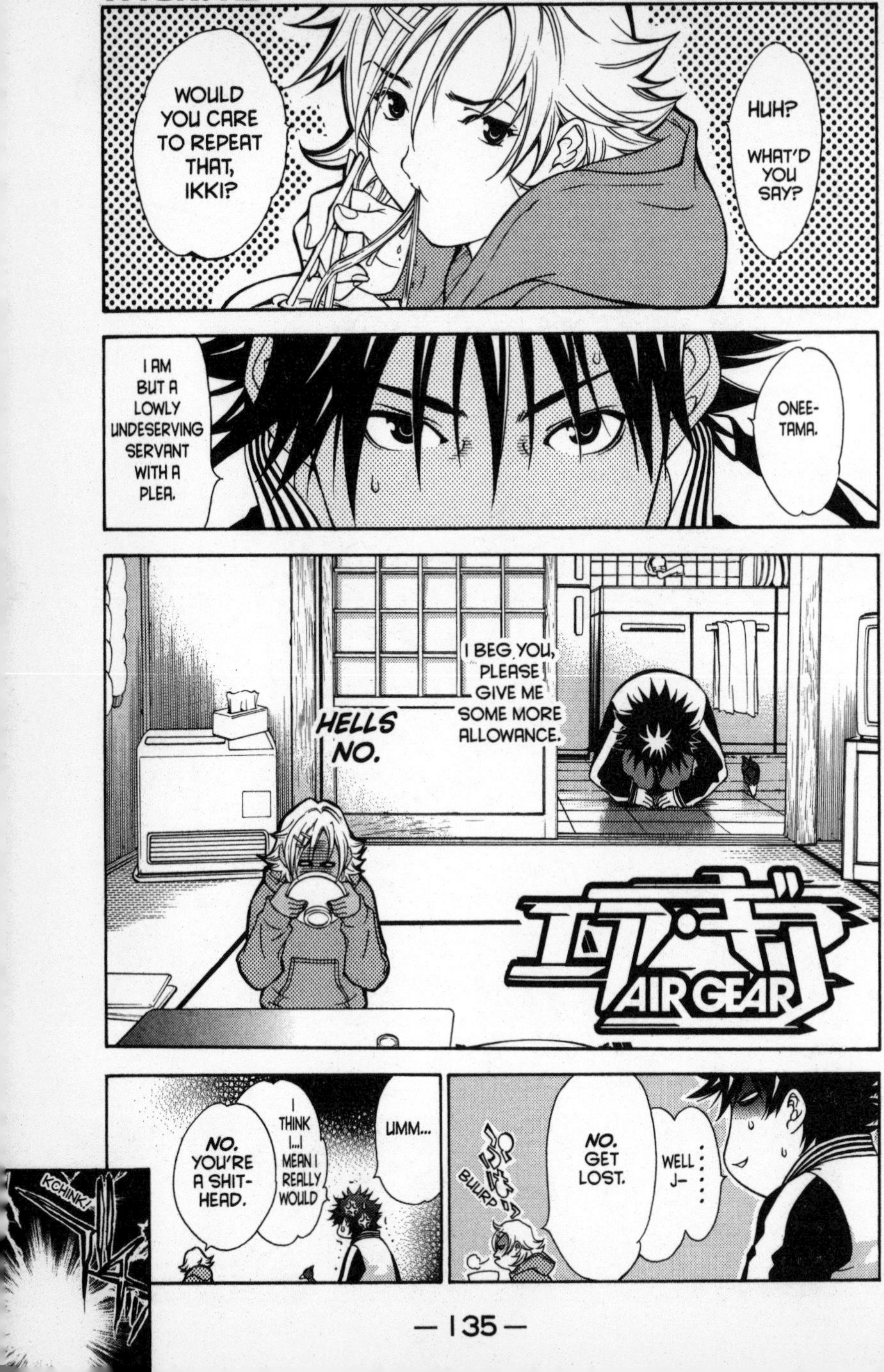
HUH? WHAT'D YOU SAY?
WOULD YOU CARE TO REPEAT THAT, IKKI?
ONEE-TAMA.
I AM BUT A LOWLY UNDESERVING SERVANT WITH A PLEA.
I BEG YOU, PLEASE GIVE ME SOME MORE ALLOWANCE.
HELLS NO.
AIR GEAR
WELL J-......
NO. GET LOST.
BUURP
UMM...
I THINK I...I MEAN I REALLY WOULD
NO. YOU'RE A SHIT-HEAD.
KCHINK!

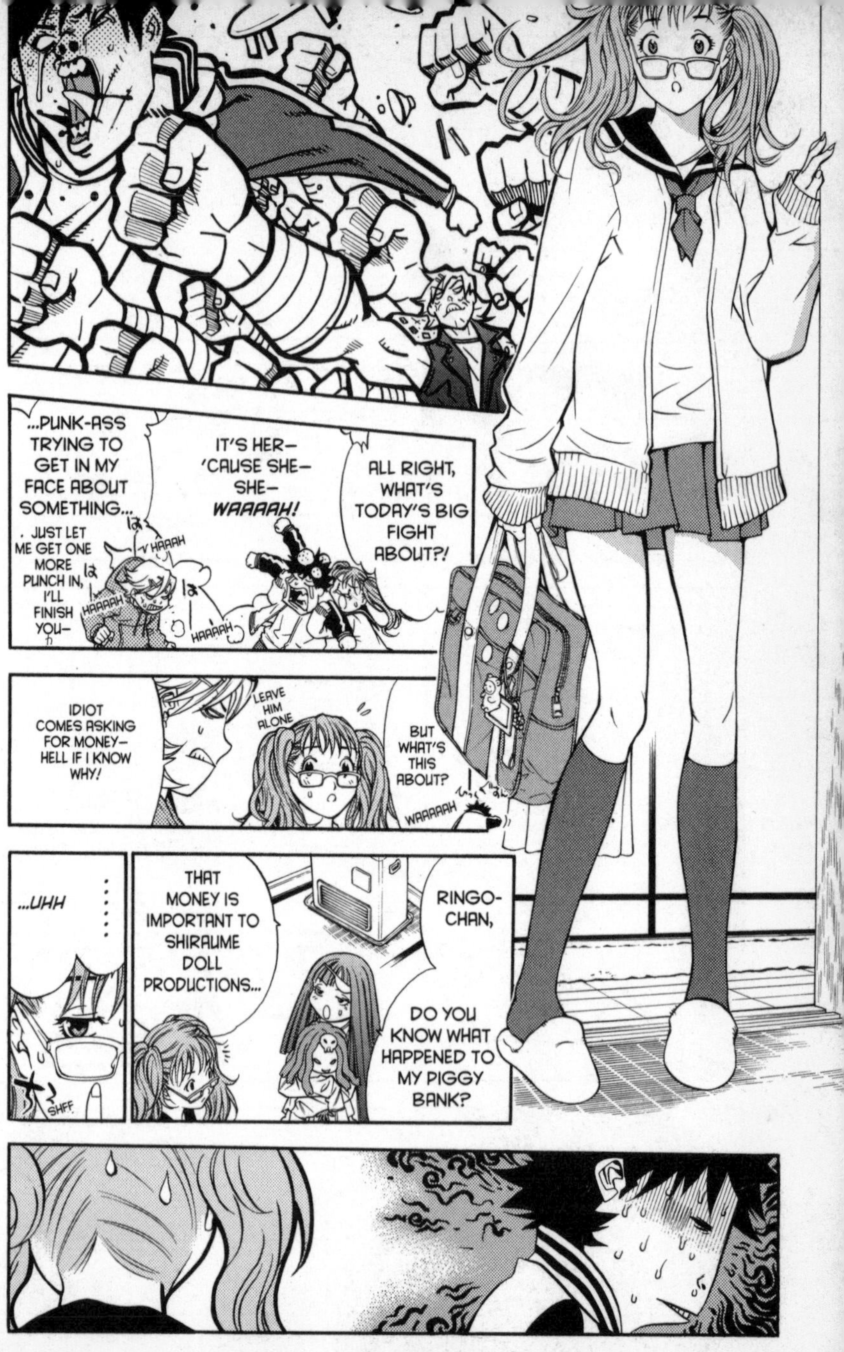
RINGO-CHAN,
DO YOU KNOW WHAT HAPPENED TO MY PIGGY BANK?
ALL RIGHT, WHAT'S TODAY'S BIG FIGHT ABOUT?!
IT'S HER— 'CAUSE SHE— SHE— WAAAAH!
...PUNK-ASS TRYING TO GET IN MY FACE ABOUT SOMETHING...
HAAAAH
HAAAAH
JUST LET ME GET ONE MORE PUNCH IN, I'LL FINISH YOU—
HAAAAH
BUT WHAT'S THIS ABOUT?
WAAAAAH
LEAVE HIM ALONE
IDIOT COMES ASKING FOR MONEY— HELL IF I KNOW WHY!
THAT MONEY IS IMPORTANT TO SHIRAUME DOLL PRODUCTIONS...
......
...UHH
SHFF

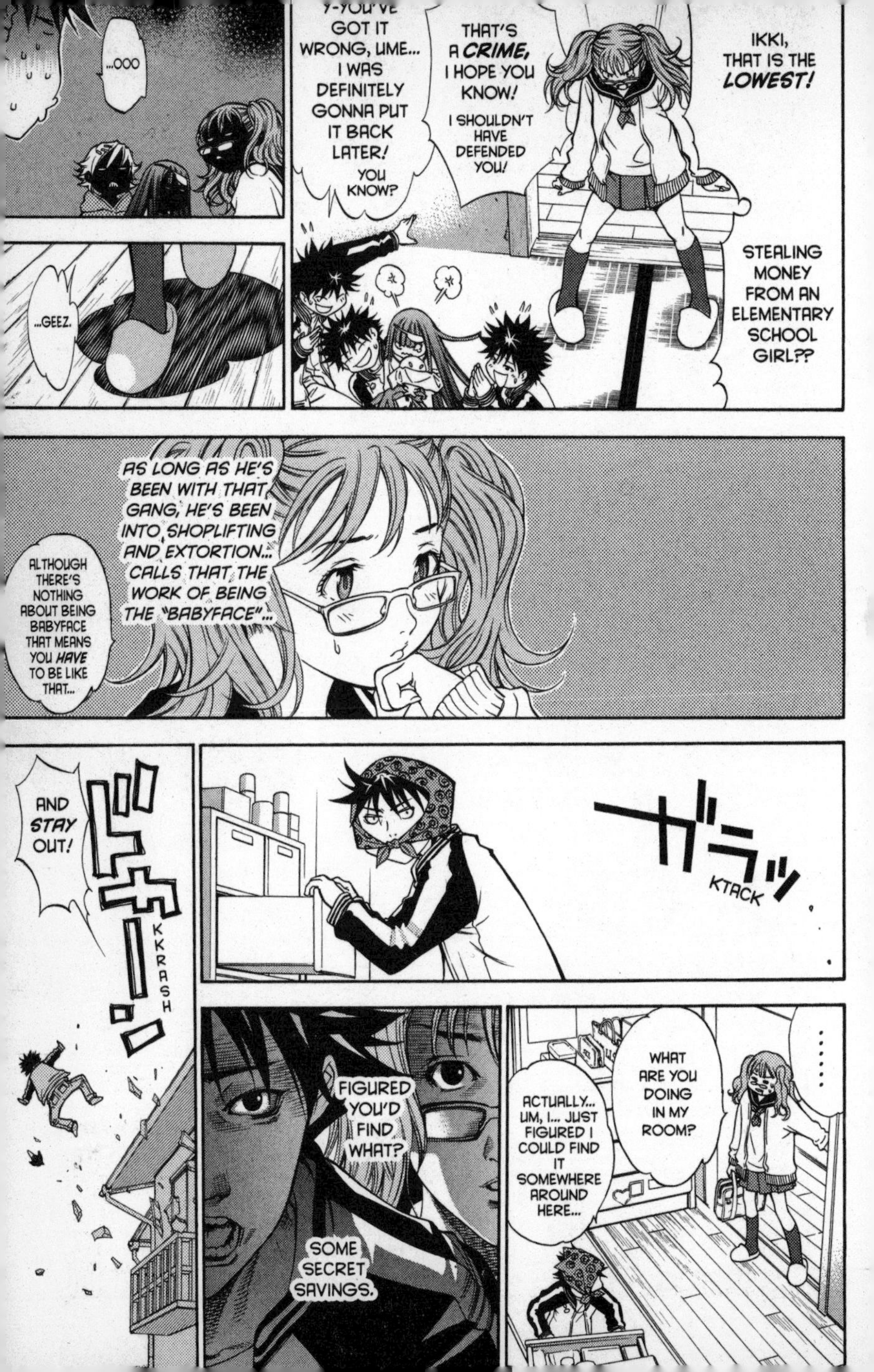
IKKI, THAT IS THE *LOWEST!*
STEALING MONEY FROM AN ELEMENTARY SCHOOL GIRL??
THAT'S A *CRIME,* I HOPE YOU KNOW!
I SHOULDN'T HAVE DEFENDED YOU!
Y-YOU'VE GOT IT WRONG, UME... I WAS DEFINITELY GONNA PUT IT BACK LATER!
YOU KNOW?
...OOO
...GEEZ.
AS LONG AS HE'S BEEN WITH THAT GANG, HE'S BEEN INTO SHOPLIFTING AND EXTORTION... CALLS THAT THE WORK OF BEING THE "BABYFACE"...
ALTHOUGH THERE'S NOTHING ABOUT BEING BABYFACE THAT MEANS YOU *HAVE* TO BE LIKE THAT...
ガラッ
KTACK
......
WHAT ARE YOU DOING IN MY ROOM?
ACTUALLY... UM, I... JUST FIGURED I COULD FIND IT SOMEWHERE AROUND HERE...
FIGURED YOU'D FIND WHAT?
SOME SECRET SAVINGS.
AND *STAY* OUT!
KKRASH

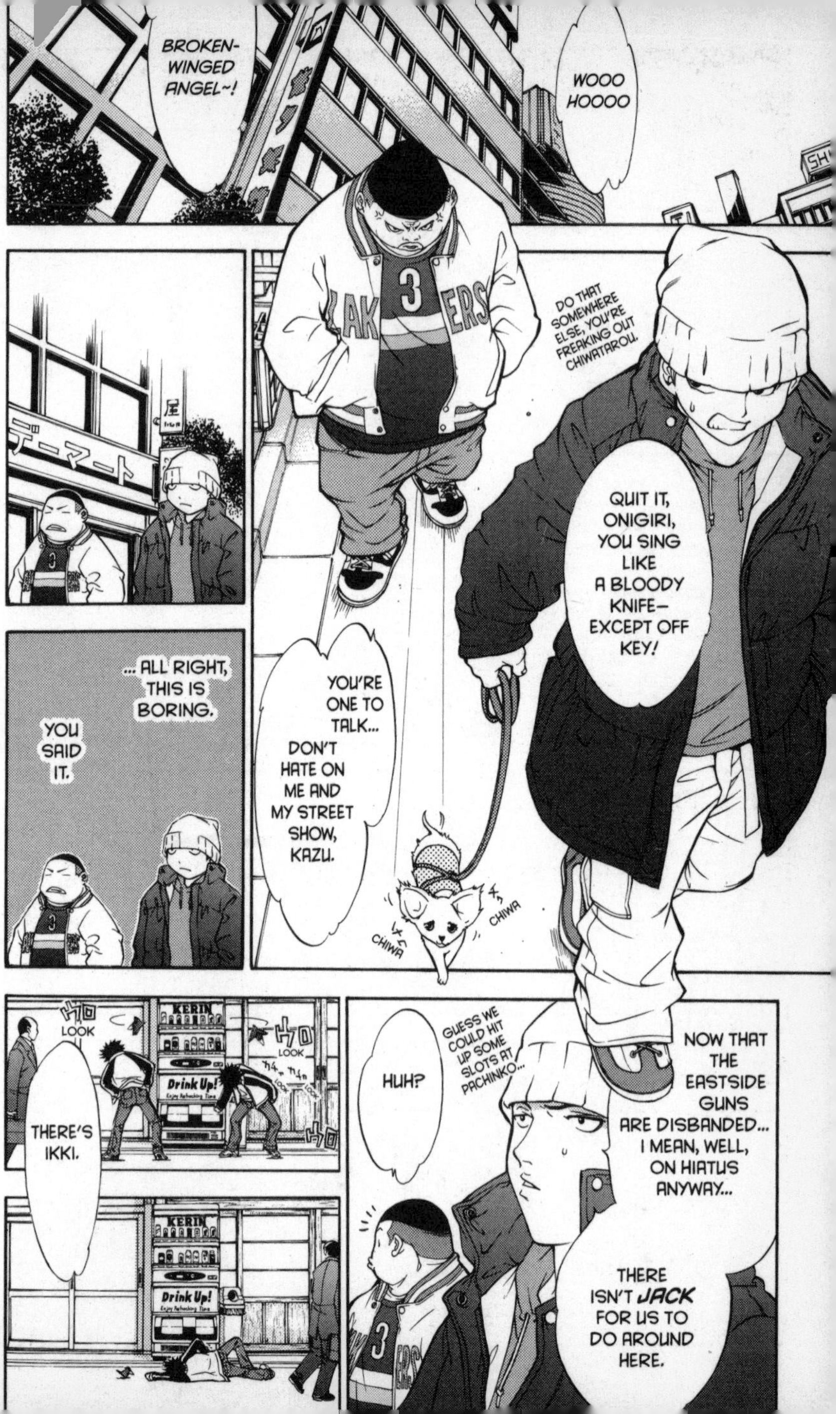
WOOO HOOOO
BROKEN-WINGED ANGEL~!
DO THAT SOMEWHERE ELSE, YOU'RE FREAKING OUT CHIWATAROU.
QUIT IT, ONIGIRI, YOU SING LIKE A BLOODY KNIFE— EXCEPT OFF KEY!
YOU'RE ONE TO TALK... DON'T HATE ON ME AND MY STREET SHOW, KAZU.
CHIWA
CHIWA
... ALL RIGHT, THIS IS BORING.
YOU SAID IT.
NOW THAT THE EASTSIDE GUNS ARE DISBANDED... I MEAN, WELL, ON HIATUS ANYWAY...
GUESS WE COULD HIT UP SOME SLOTS AT PACHINKO...
HUH?
THERE ISN'T JACK FOR US TO DO AROUND HERE.
LOOK
LOOK
LOOK
LOOK
KERIN
Drink Up!
THERE'S IKKI.
KERIN
Drink Up!

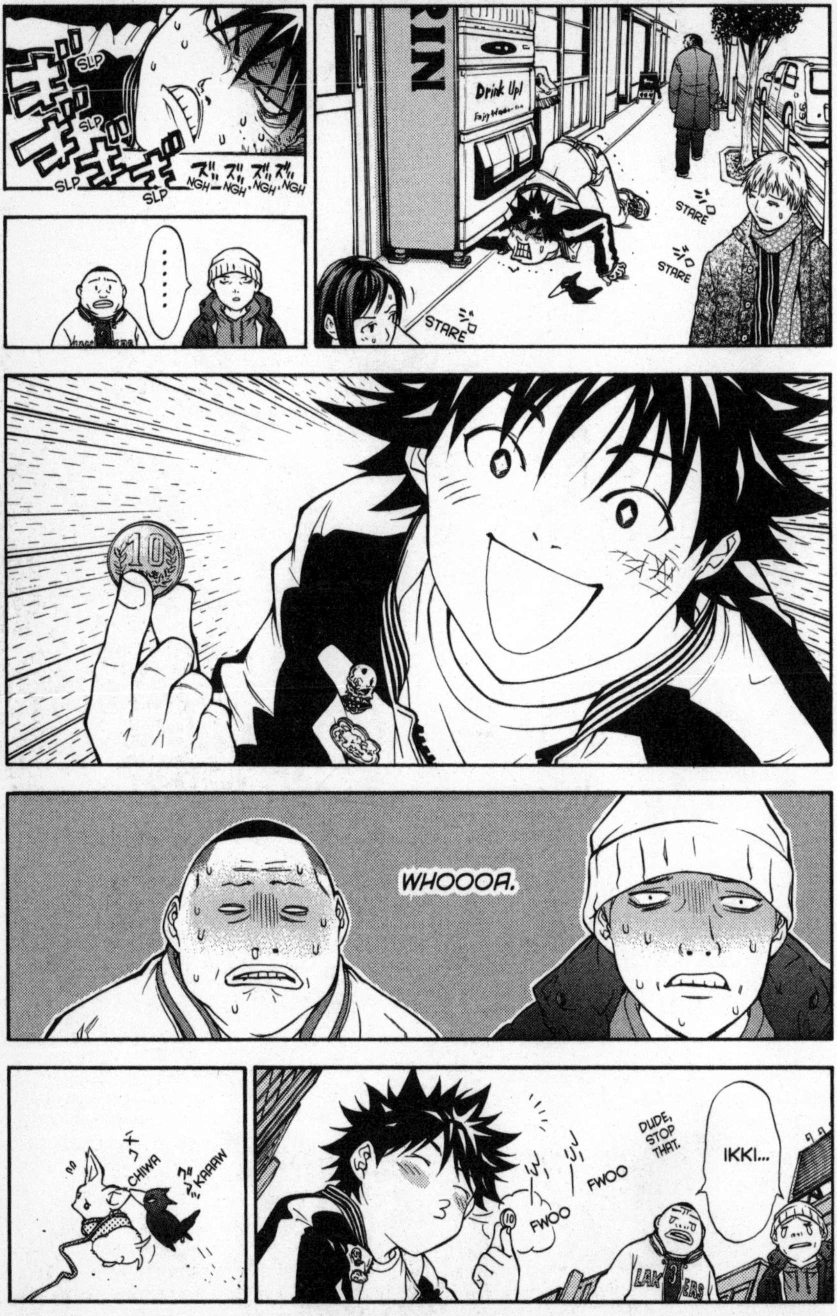
RIN
Drink Up!
STARE
STARE
STARE
SLP
SLP
SLP
SLP
NGH
NGH
NGH
NGH
......
WHOOOA.
IKKI...
DUDE, STOP THAT.
FWOO
FWOO
CHIWA
KRAAW

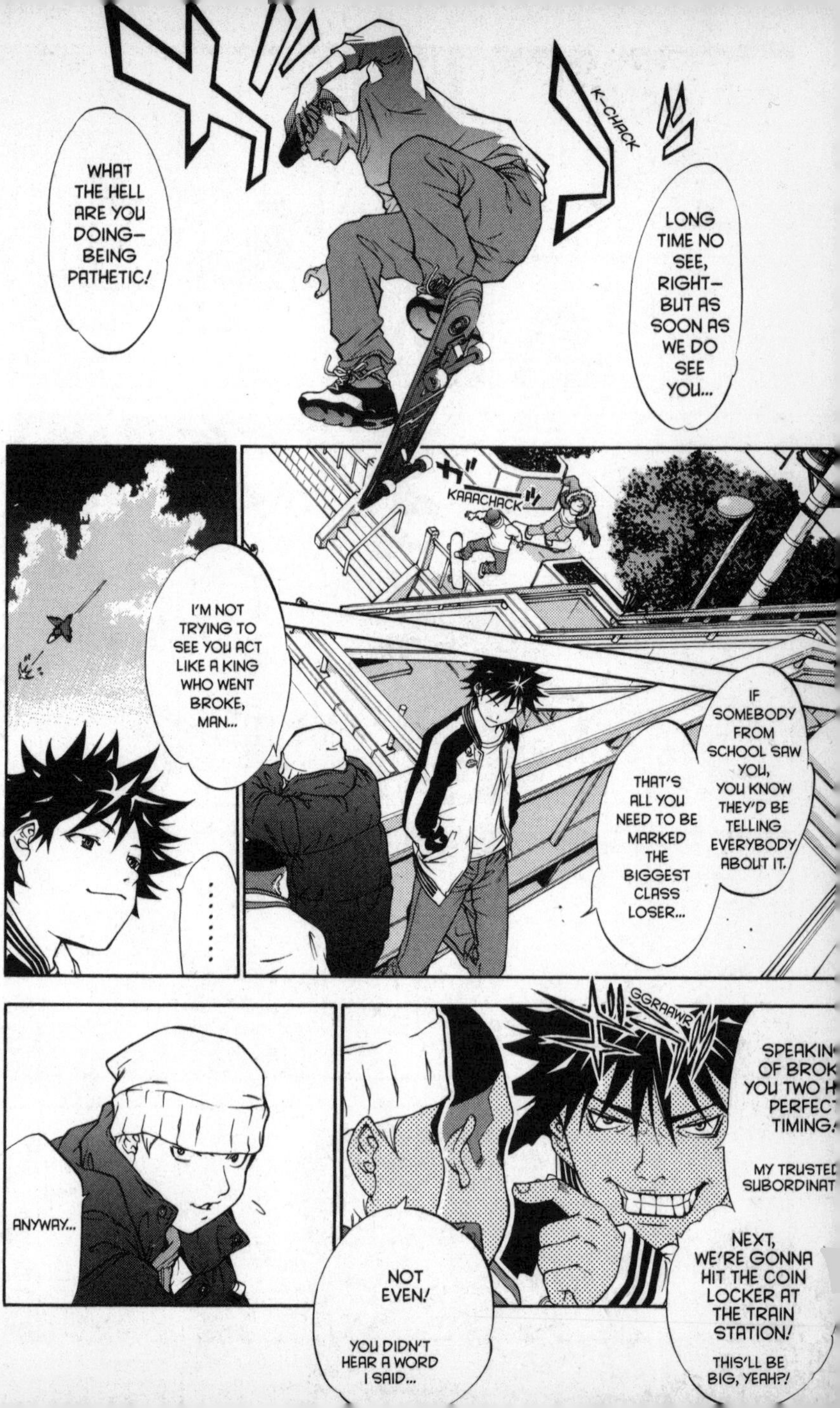
LONG TIME NO SEE, RIGHT— BUT AS SOON AS WE DO SEE YOU...
K-CHACK
WHAT THE HELL ARE YOU DOING— BEING PATHETIC!
KAAACHACK
IF SOMEBODY FROM SCHOOL SAW YOU, YOU KNOW THEY'D BE TELLING EVERYBODY ABOUT IT.
THAT'S ALL YOU NEED TO BE MARKED THE BIGGEST CLASS LOSER...
I'M NOT TRYING TO SEE YOU ACT LIKE A KING WHO WENT BROKE, MAN...
......
GGRAAWR
SPEAKIN OF BROK YOU TWO H PERFEC TIMING!
MY TRUSTED SUBORDINAT
NEXT, WE'RE GONNA HIT THE COIN LOCKER AT THE TRAIN STATION!
THIS'LL BE BIG, YEAH?!
NOT EVEN!
YOU DIDN'T HEAR A WORD I SAID...
ANYWAY...

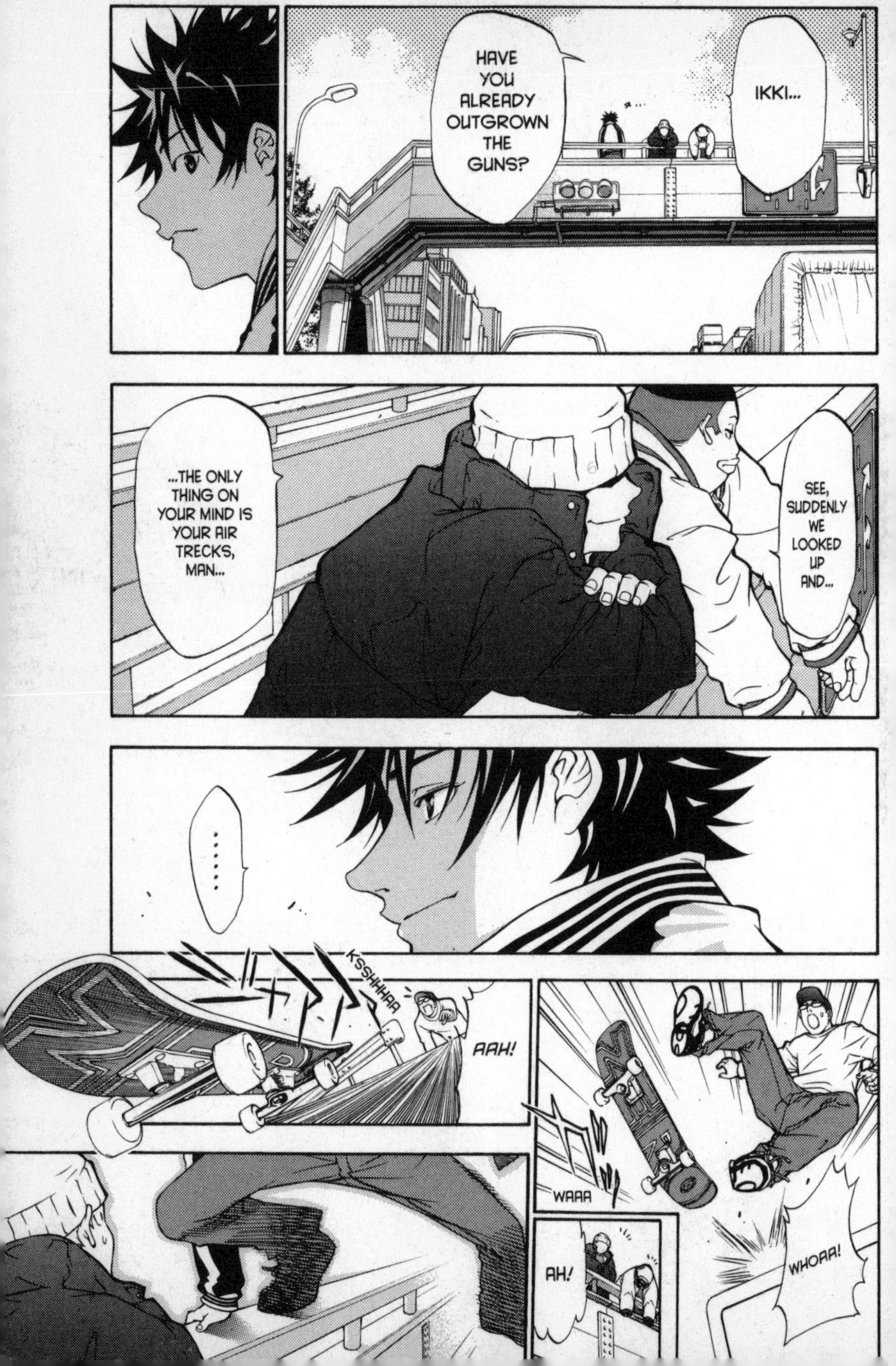
IKKI...
HAVE YOU ALREADY OUTGROWN THE GUNS?
SEE, SUDDENLY WE LOOKED UP AND...
...THE ONLY THING ON YOUR MIND IS YOUR AIR TRECKS, MAN...
......
WAAA
WHOAA!
AH!
KSSHHHAA
AAH!

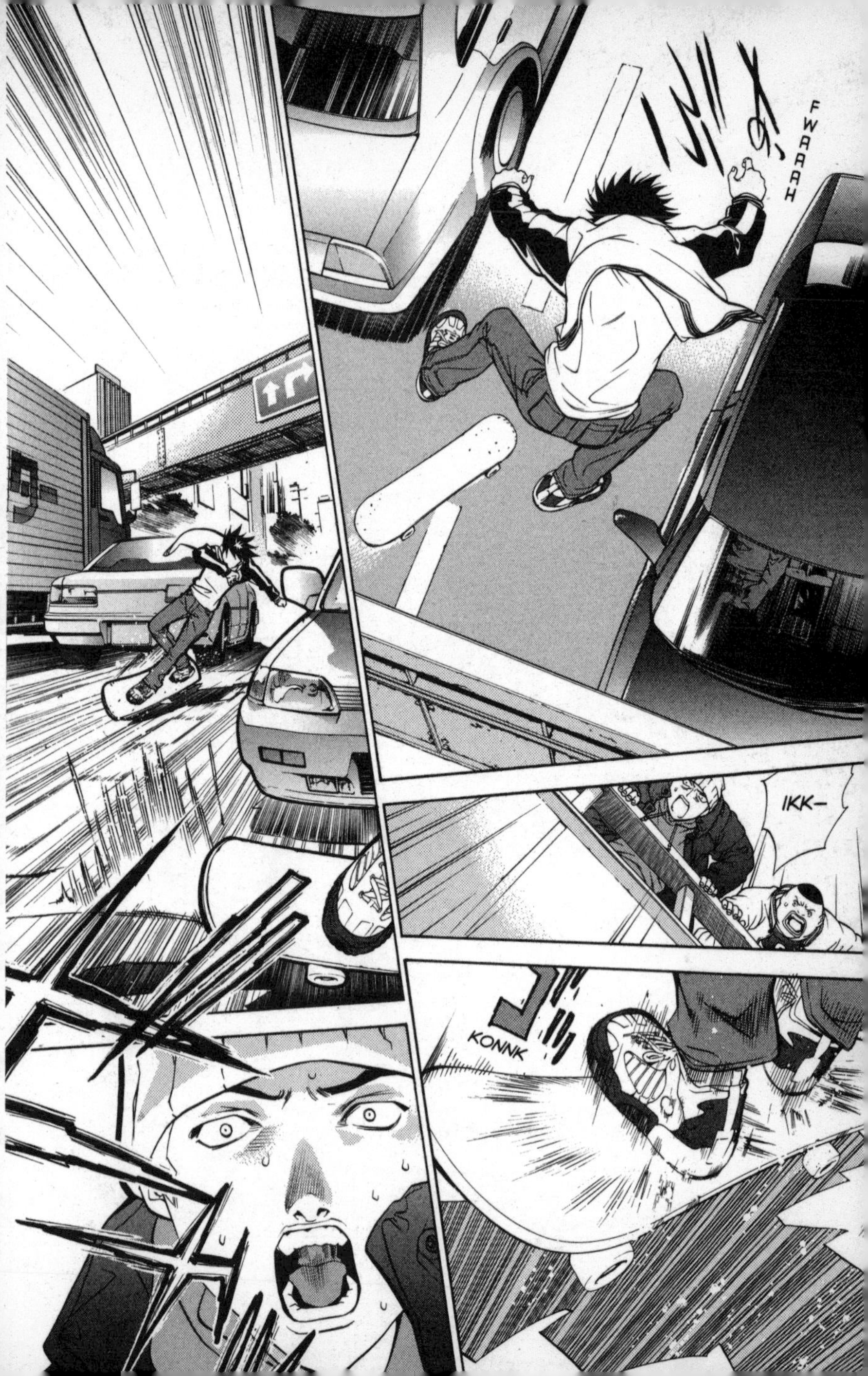
FWAAAAH
IKK—
KONNK

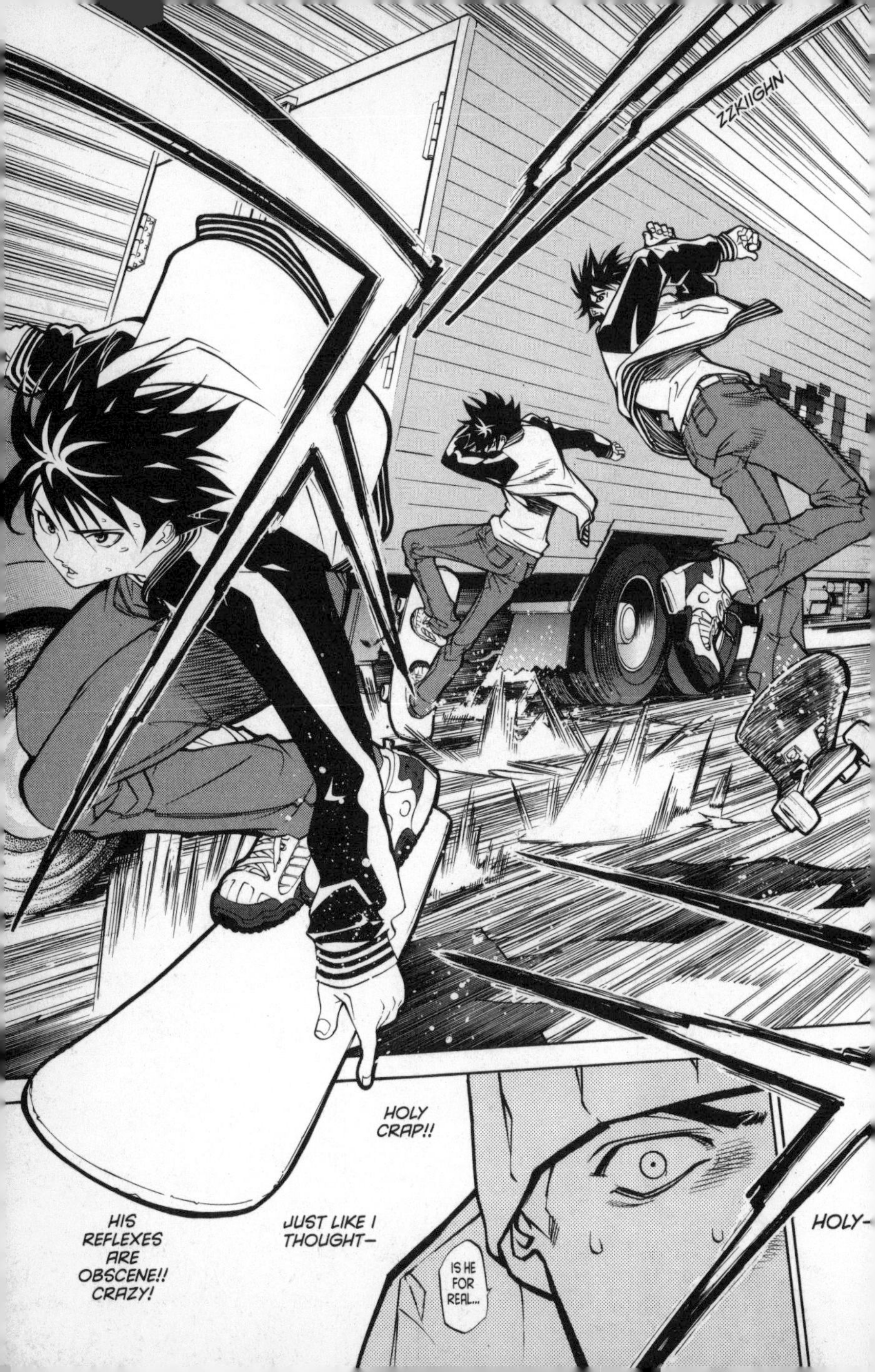
ZZKIIGHN
HOLY-
IS HE FOR REAL...
HOLY CRAP!!
JUST LIKE I THOUGHT—
HIS REFLEXES ARE OBSCENE!! CRAZY!

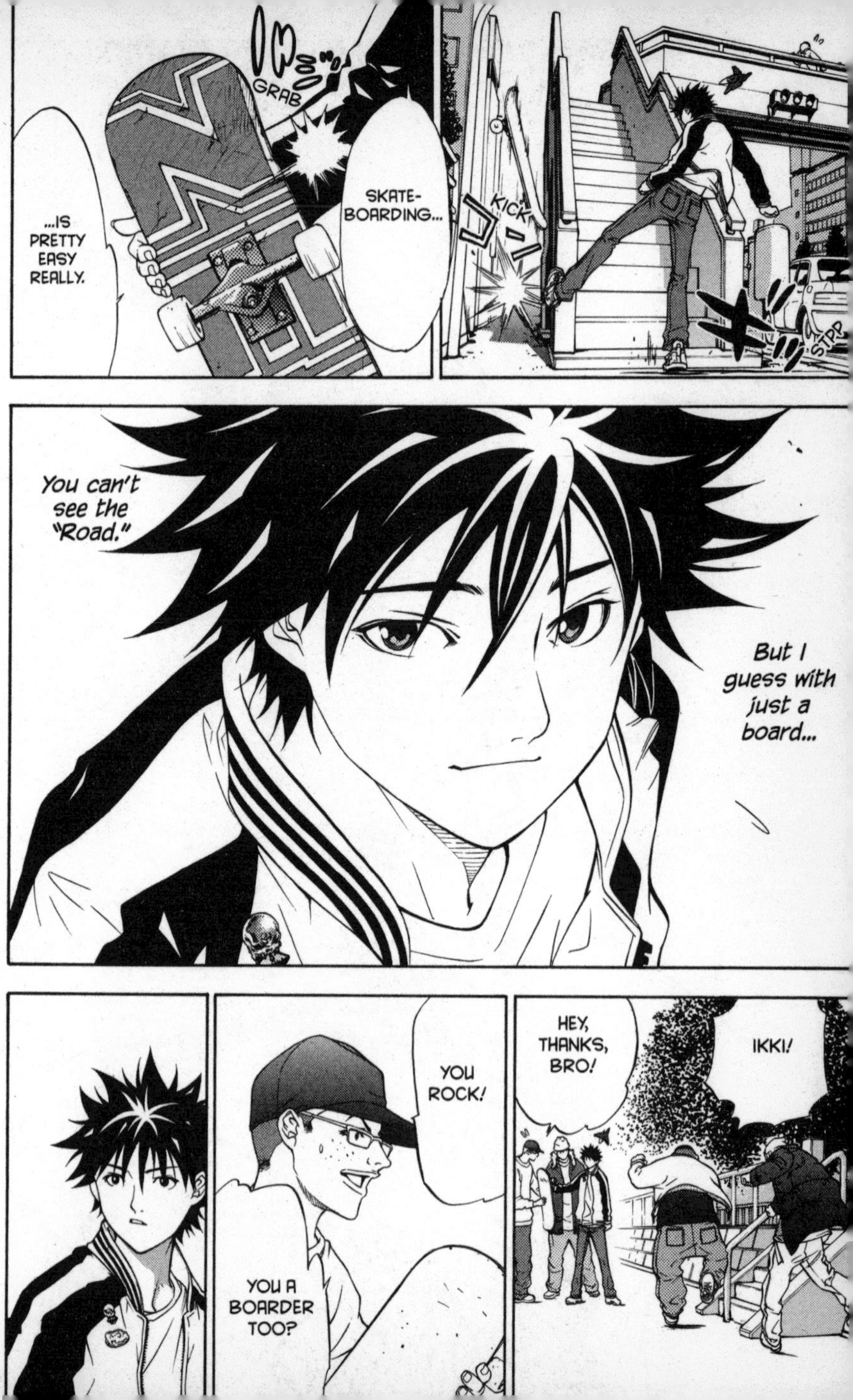
KICK
STPP
GRAB
SKATE-BOARDING...
...IS PRETTY EASY REALLY.
But I guess with just a board...
You can't see the "Road."
IKKI!
HEY, THANKS, BRO!
YOU ROCK!
YOU A BOARDER TOO?

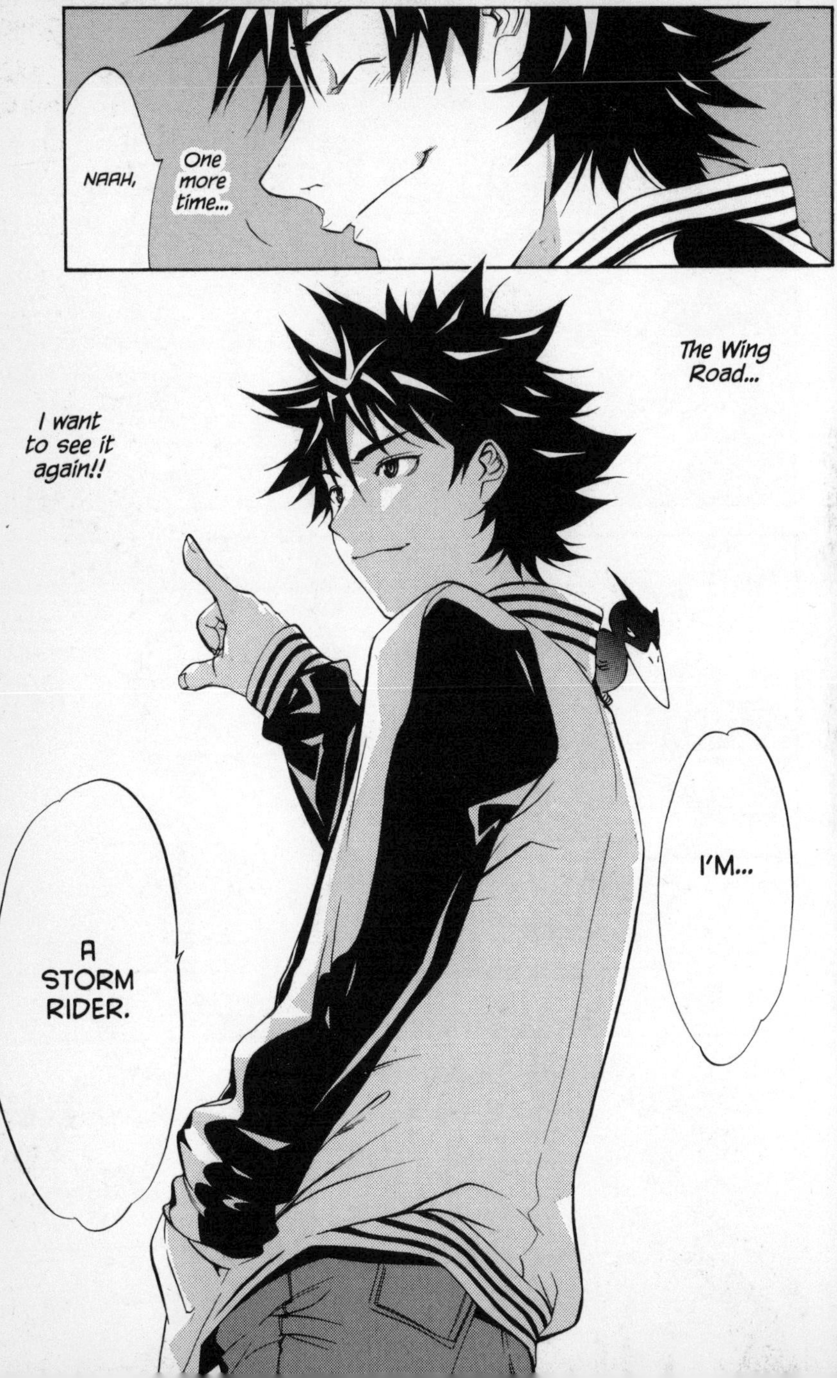
One more time...
NAAH,
The Wing Road...
I want to see it again!!
I'M...
A STORM RIDER.

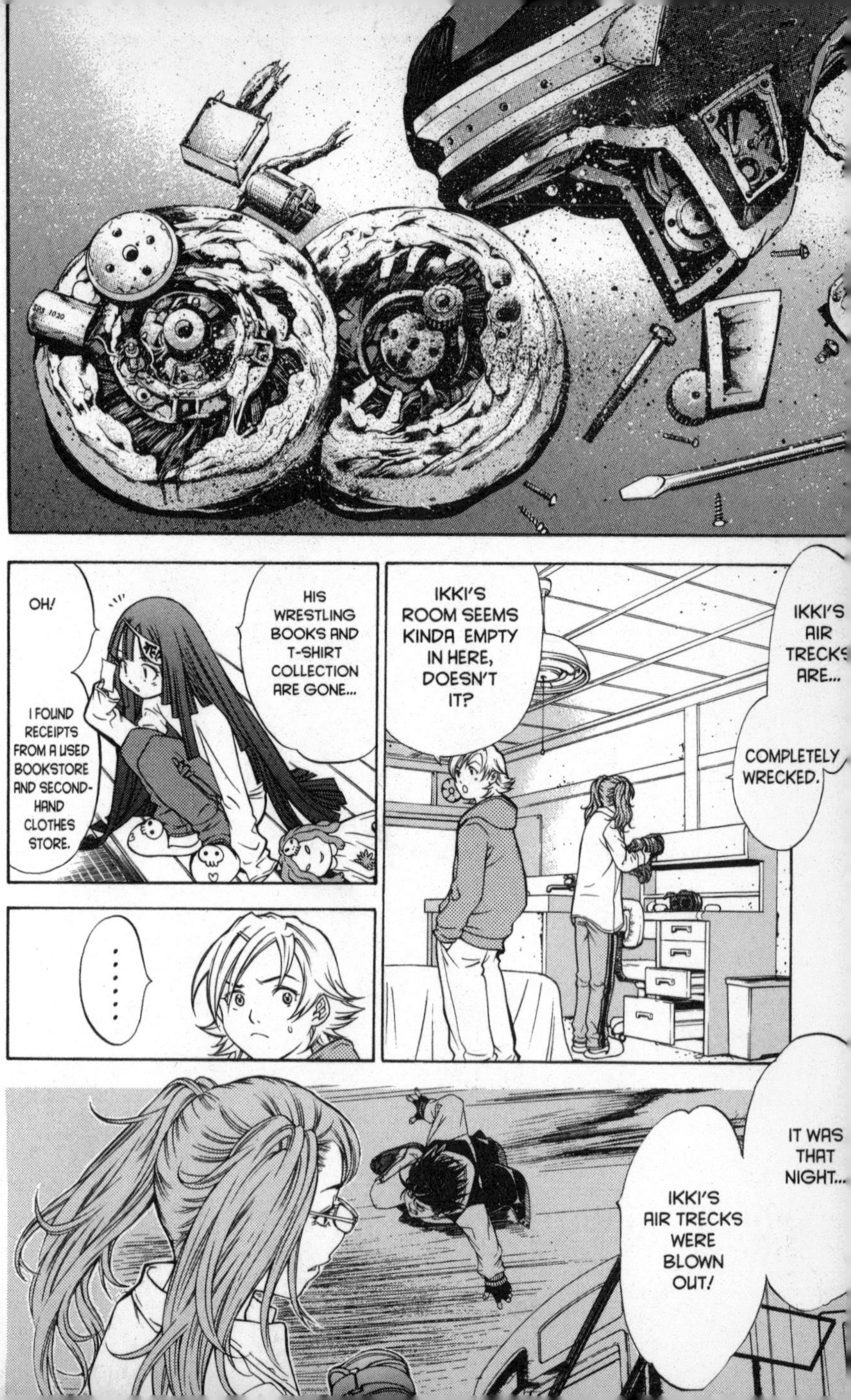
IKKI'S AIR TRECKS ARE...
COMPLETELY WRECKED.
IKKI'S ROOM SEEMS KINDA EMPTY IN HERE, DOESN'T IT?
HIS WRESTLING BOOKS AND T-SHIRT COLLECTION ARE GONE...
OH!
I FOUND RECEIPTS FROM A USED BOOKSTORE AND SECOND-HAND CLOTHES STORE.
......
IT WAS THAT NIGHT...
IKKI'S AIR TRECKS WERE BLOWN OUT!

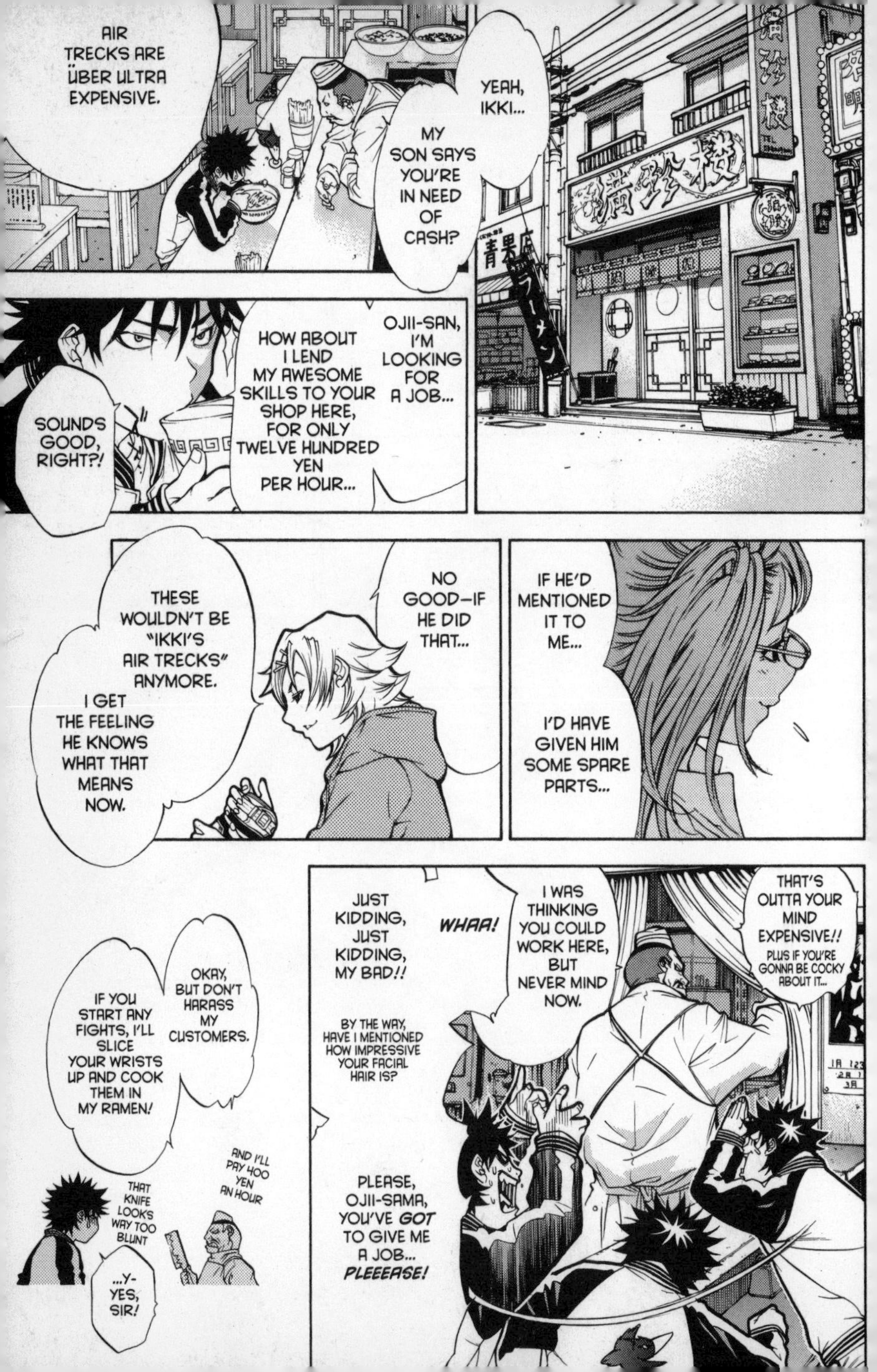
青果店
ラーメン
YEAH, IKKI...
MY SON SAYS YOU'RE IN NEED OF CASH?
AIR TRECKS ARE ÜBER ULTRA EXPENSIVE.
OJII-SAN, I'M LOOKING FOR A JOB...
HOW ABOUT I LEND MY AWESOME SKILLS TO YOUR SHOP HERE, FOR ONLY TWELVE HUNDRED YEN PER HOUR...
SOUNDS GOOD, RIGHT?!
IF HE'D MENTIONED IT TO ME...
I'D HAVE GIVEN HIM SOME SPARE PARTS...
NO GOOD—IF HE DID THAT...
THESE WOULDN'T BE "IKKI'S AIR TRECKS" ANYMORE.
I GET THE FEELING HE KNOWS WHAT THAT MEANS NOW.
THAT'S OUTTA YOUR MIND EXPENSIVE!!
PLUS IF YOU'RE GONNA BE COCKY ABOUT IT...
I WAS THINKING YOU COULD WORK HERE, BUT NEVER MIND NOW.
WHAA!
JUST KIDDING, JUST KIDDING, MY BAD!!
BY THE WAY, HAVE I MENTIONED HOW IMPRESSIVE YOUR FACIAL HAIR IS?
PLEASE, OJII-SAMA, YOU'VE GOT TO GIVE ME A JOB... PLEEEASE!
OKAY, BUT DON'T HARASS MY CUSTOMERS.
IF YOU START ANY FIGHTS, I'LL SLICE YOUR WRISTS UP AND COOK THEM IN MY RAMEN!
AND I'LL PAY 400 YEN AN HOUR
THAT KNIFE LOOKS WAY TOO BLUNT
...Y-YES, SIR!

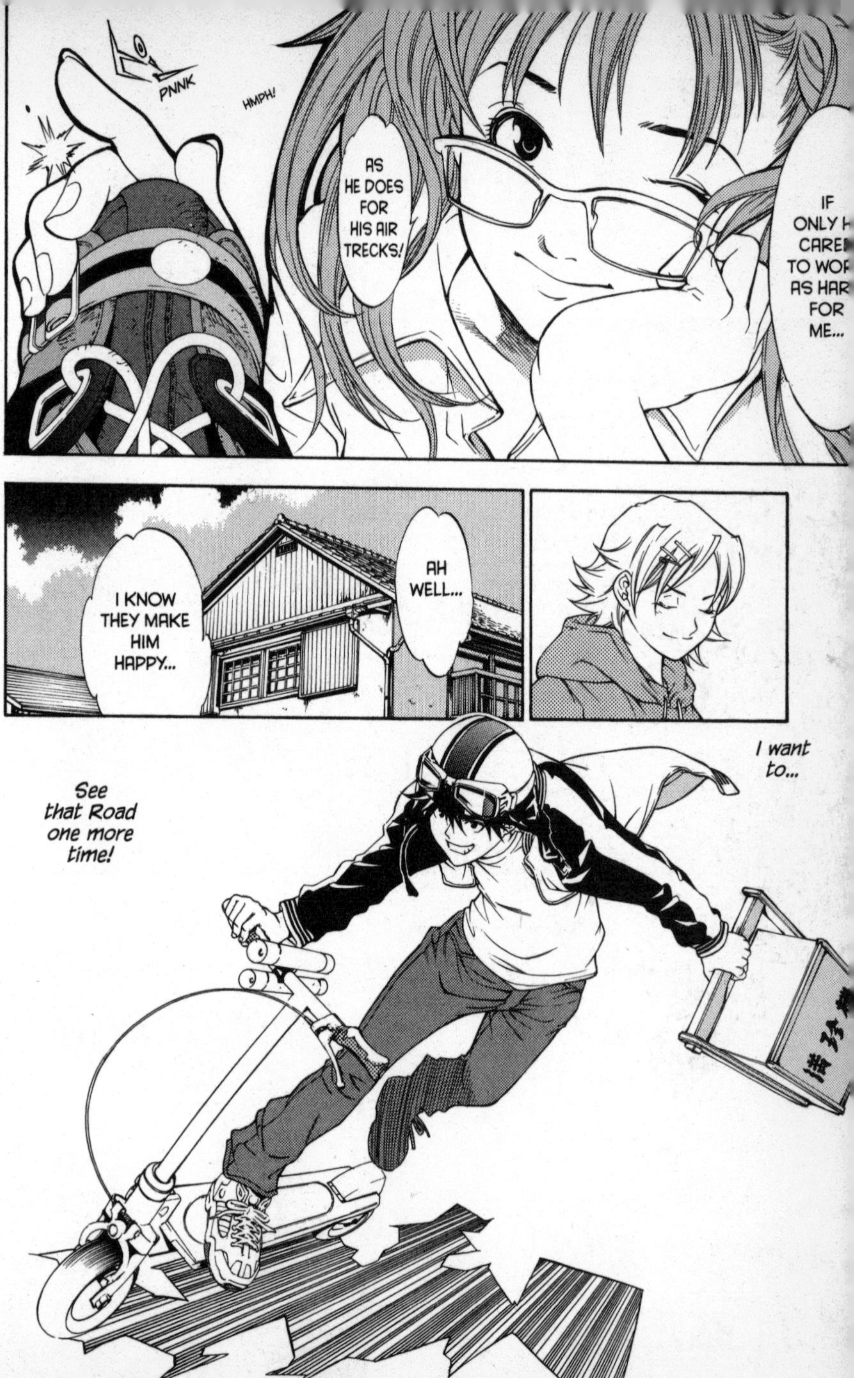
IF ONLY H CARE TO WOR AS HAR FOR ME...
AS HE DOES FOR HIS AIR TRECKS!
HMPH!
PNNK
AH WELL...
I KNOW THEY MAKE HIM HAPPY...
I want to...
See that Road one more time!

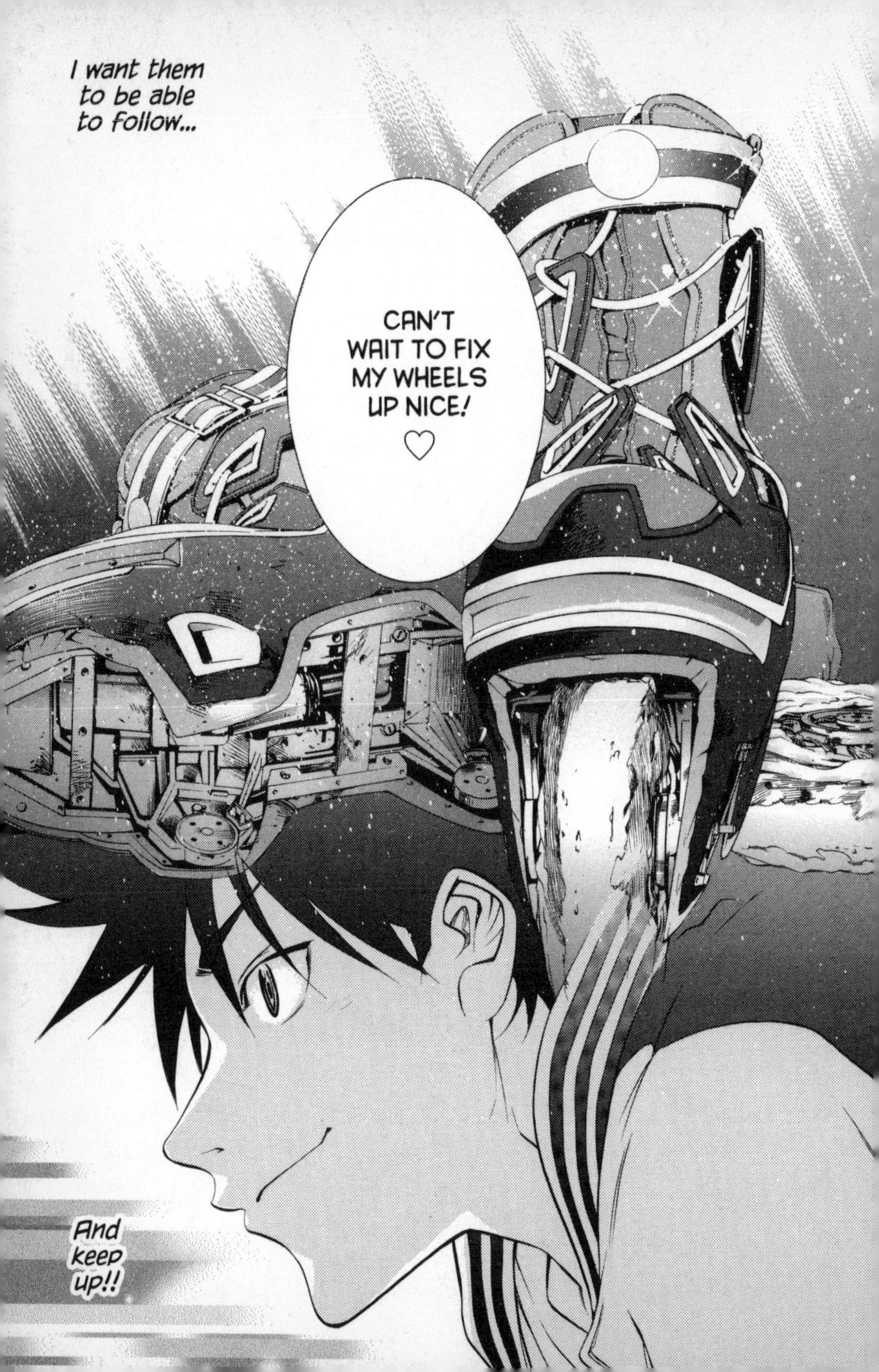
CAN'T WAIT TO FIX MY WHEELS UP NICE! ♡
I want them to be able to follow...
And keep up!!

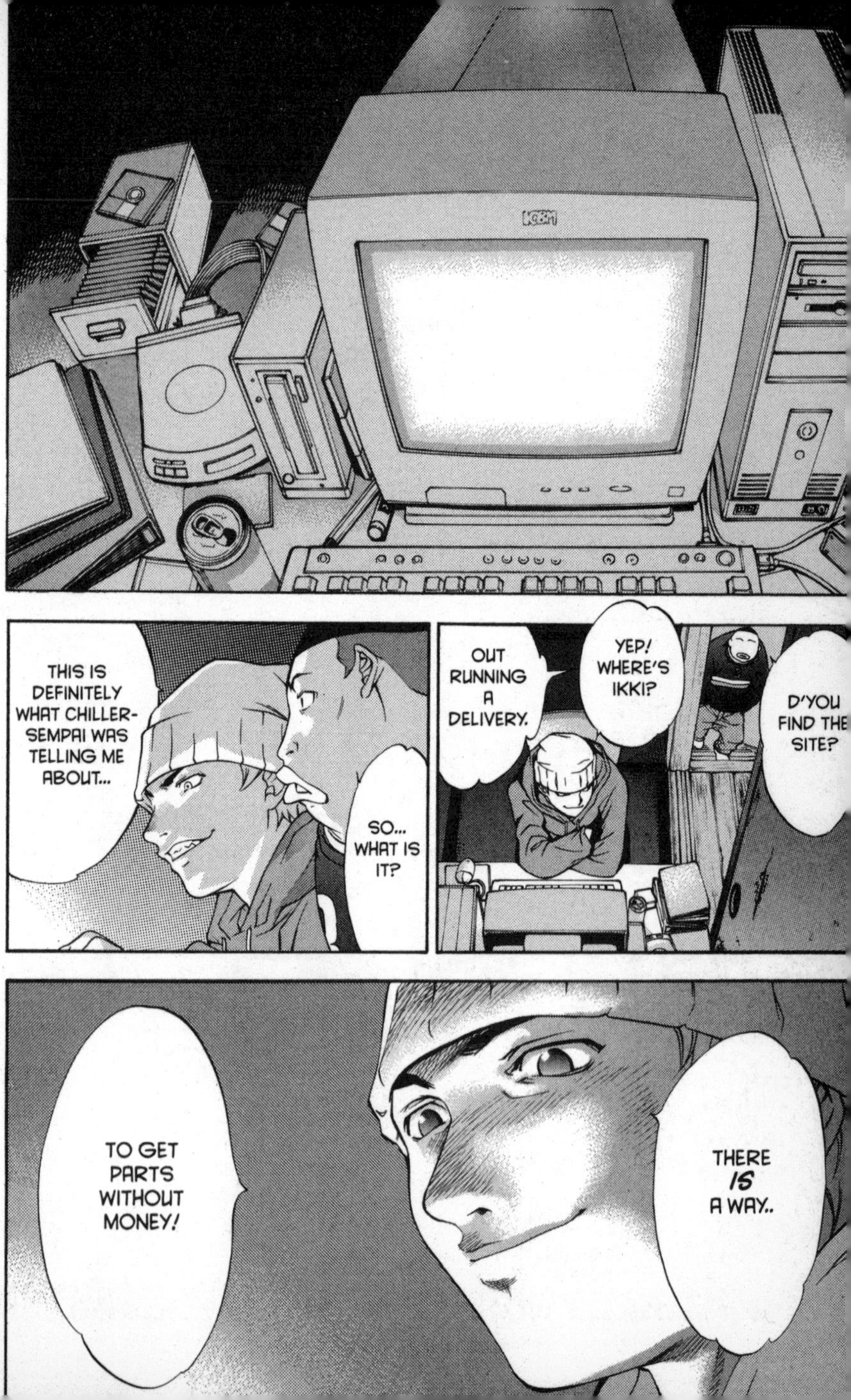
D'YOU FIND THE SITE?
YEP! WHERE'S IKKI?
OUT RUNNING A DELIVERY.
THIS IS DEFINITELY WHAT CHILLER-SEMPAI WAS TELLING ME ABOUT...
SO... WHAT IS IT?
THERE *IS* A WAY..
TO GET PARTS WITHOUT MONEY!

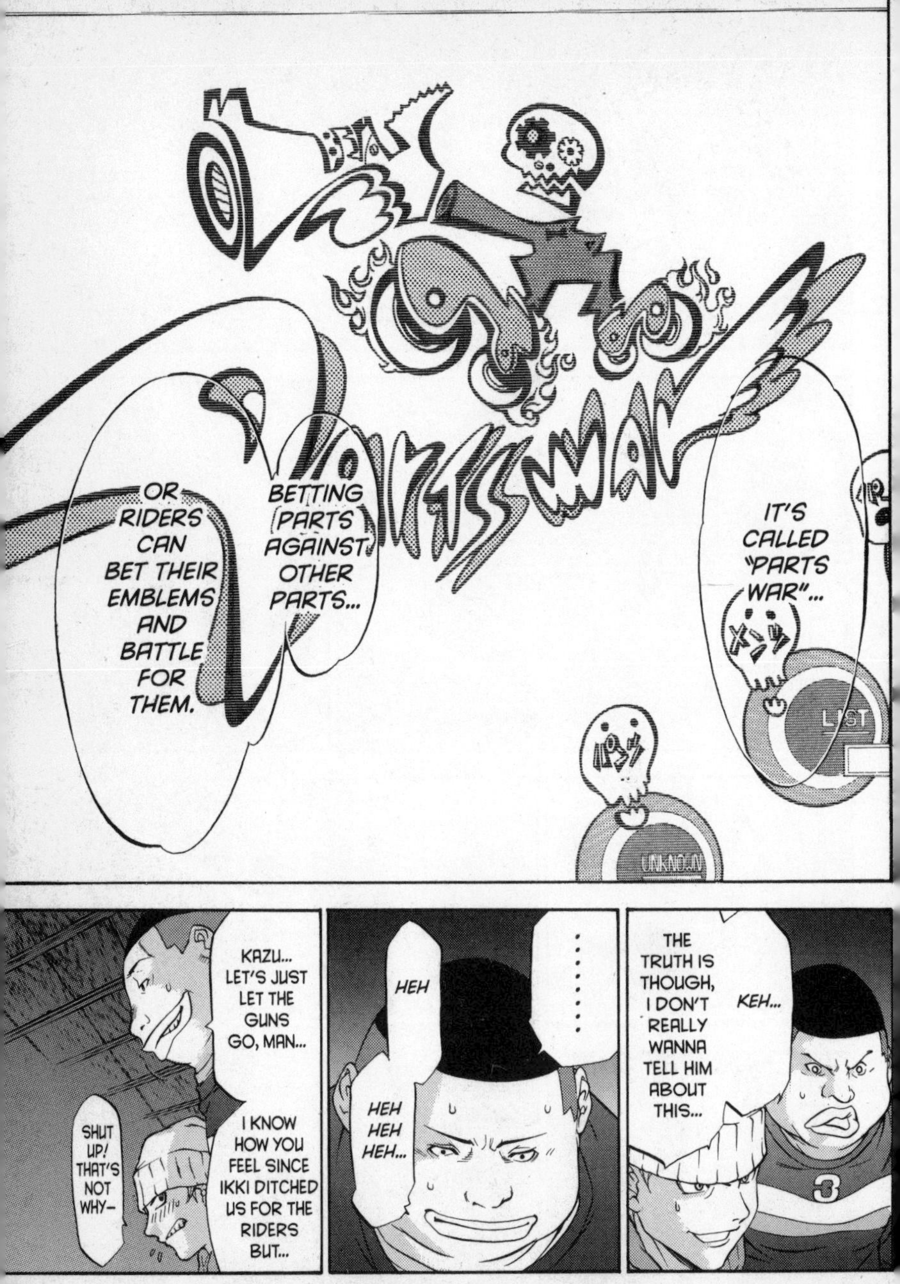
IT'S CALLED "PARTS WAR"...
BETTING PARTS AGAINST OTHER PARTS...
OR RIDERS CAN BET THEIR EMBLEMS AND BATTLE FOR THEM.
LIST
UNKNOWN
KEH...
THE TRUTH IS THOUGH, I DON'T REALLY WANNA TELL HIM ABOUT THIS...
......
HEH
HEH HEH HEH...
KAZU... LET'S JUST LET THE GUNS GO, MAN...
I KNOW HOW YOU FEEL SINCE IKKI DITCHED US FOR THE RIDERS BUT...
SHUT UP! THAT'S NOT WHY—

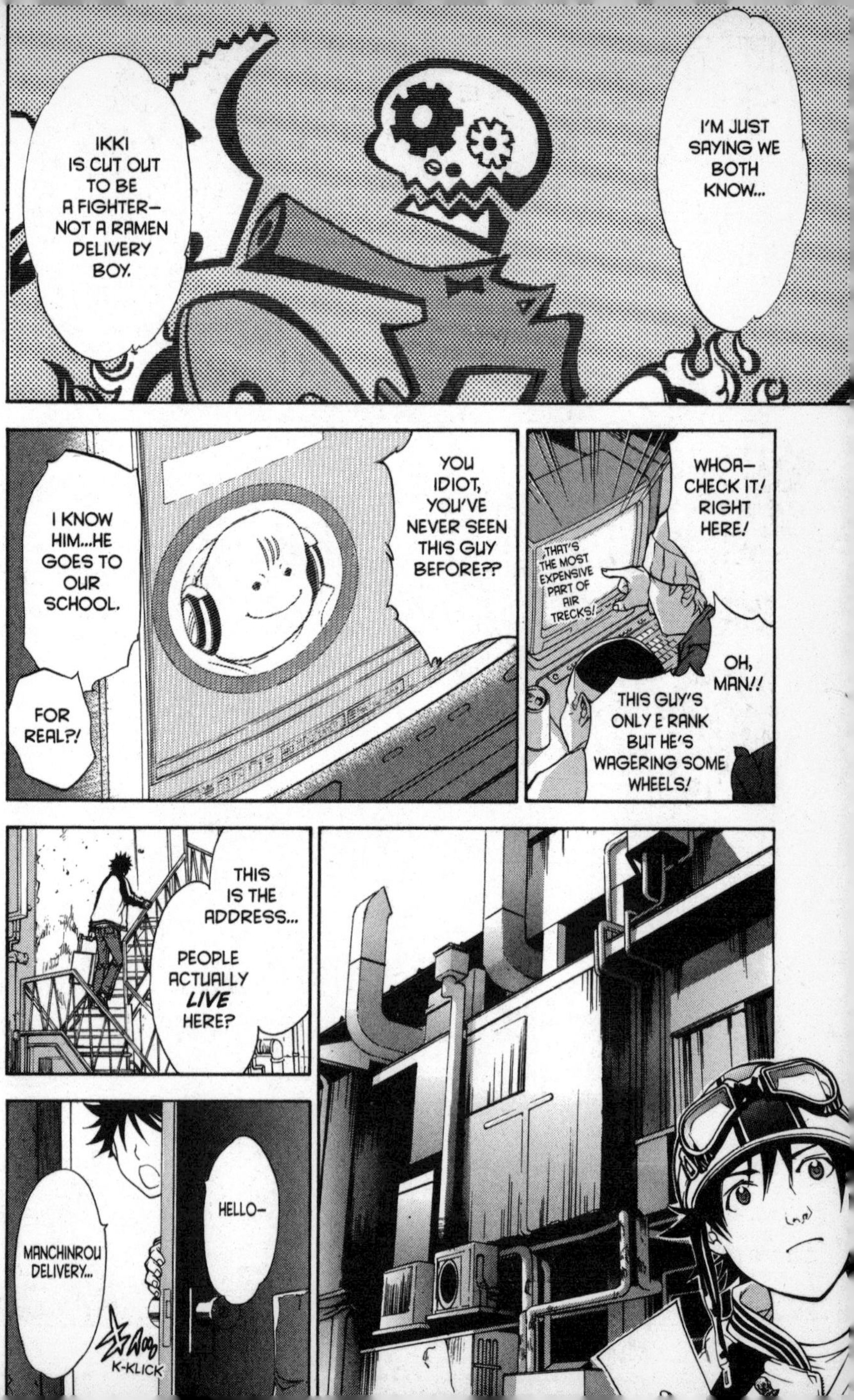
I'M JUST SAYING WE BOTH KNOW...
IKKI IS CUT OUT TO BE A FIGHTER— NOT A RAMEN DELIVERY BOY.
WHOA— CHECK IT! RIGHT HERE!
THAT'S THE MOST EXPENSIVE PART OF AIR TRECKS!
OH, MAN!!
THIS GUY'S ONLY E RANK BUT HE'S WAGERING SOME WHEELS!
YOU IDIOT, YOU'VE NEVER SEEN THIS GUY BEFORE??
I KNOW HIM...HE GOES TO OUR SCHOOL.
FOR REAL?!
THIS IS THE ADDRESS...
PEOPLE ACTUALLY *LIVE* HERE?
HELLO—
MANCHINROU DELIVERY...
K-KLICK

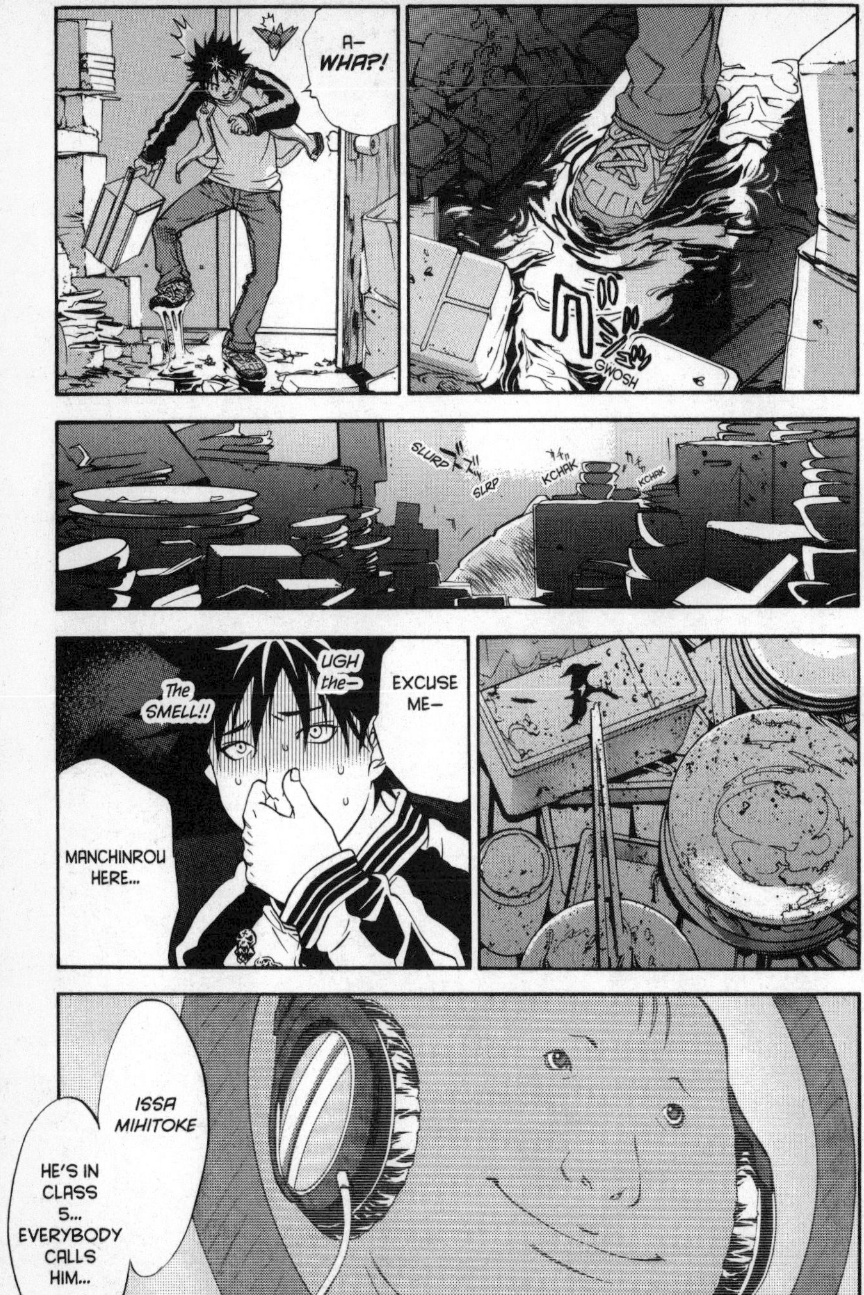
GWOSH
A-
WHA?!
KCHAK
KCHAK
SLRP
SLURP
EXCUSE ME—
UGH the—
The SMELL!!
MANCHINROU HERE...
ISSA MIHITOKE
HE'S IN CLASS 5... EVERYBODY CALLS HIM...

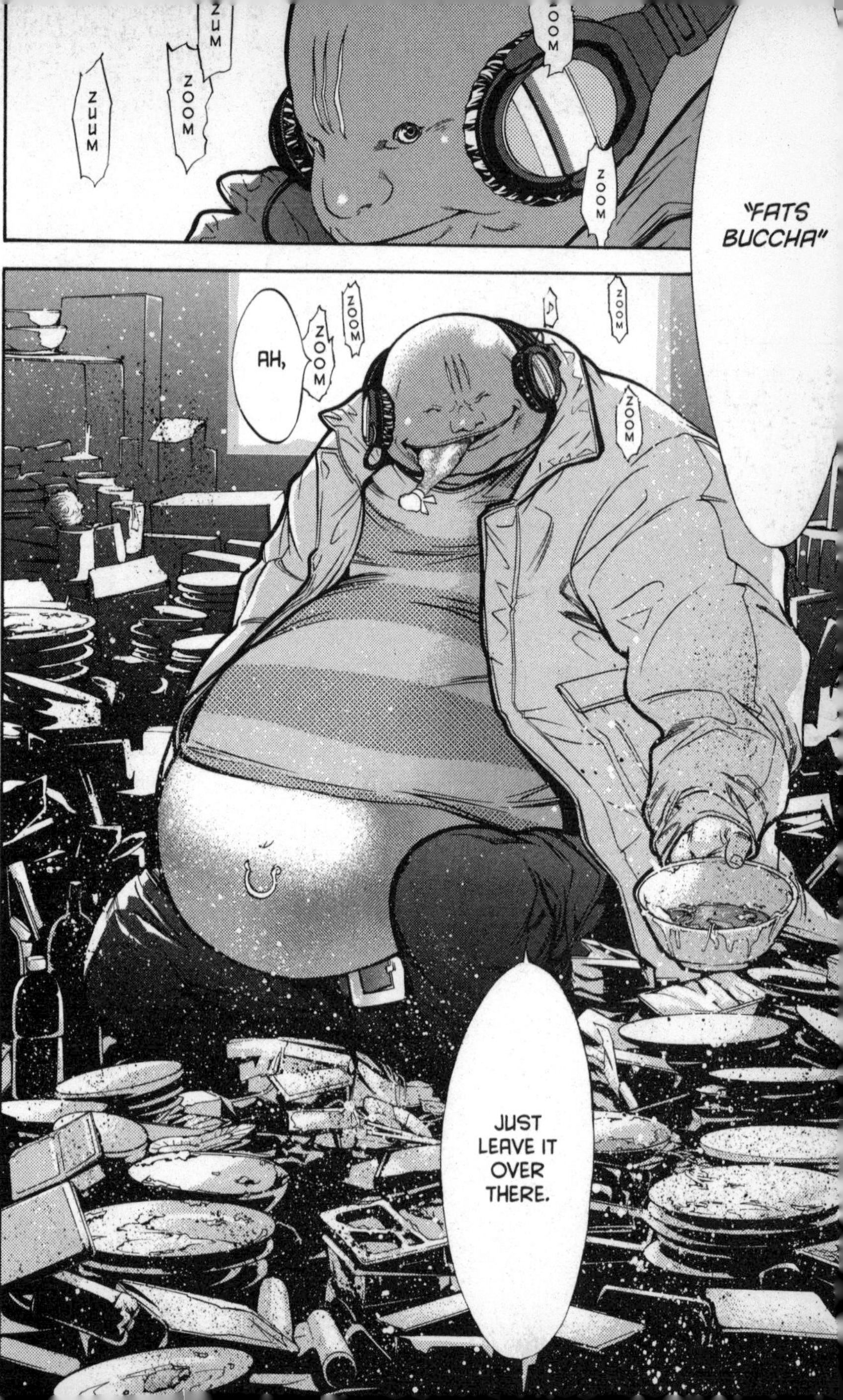
ZOOM
ZOOM
ZUM
ZOOM
ZUUM
"FATS BUCCHA"
ZOOM
♪
ZOOM
ZOOM
ZOOM
AH,
JUST LEAVE IT OVER THERE.

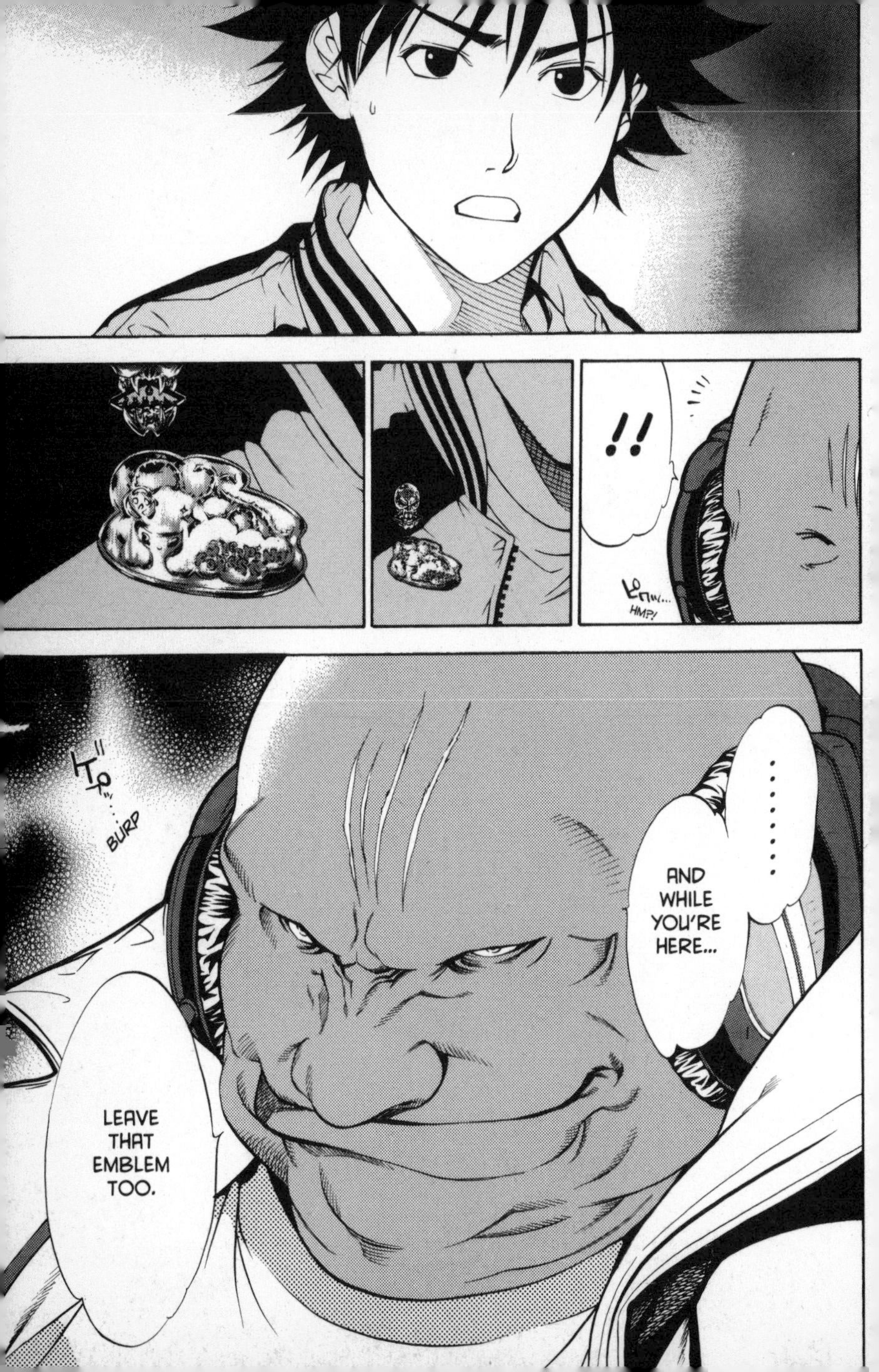
!!
HMP!
....
BURP
AND WHILE YOU'RE HERE...
LEAVE THAT EMBLEM TOO.

RAMEN MADE
WITH SPECIAL
BEEF
SUBSTITUTE

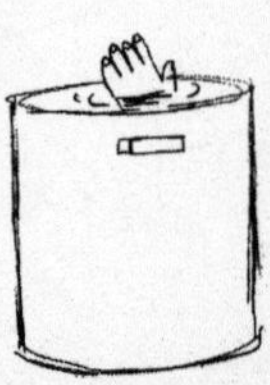

TRUE STORY GUYS, THIS REALLY HAPPENED A LONG TIME AGO. ANY JAPANESE PERSON OVER THIRTY SHOULD REMEMBER IT. (OVER THIRTY IN 2003, I GUESS)

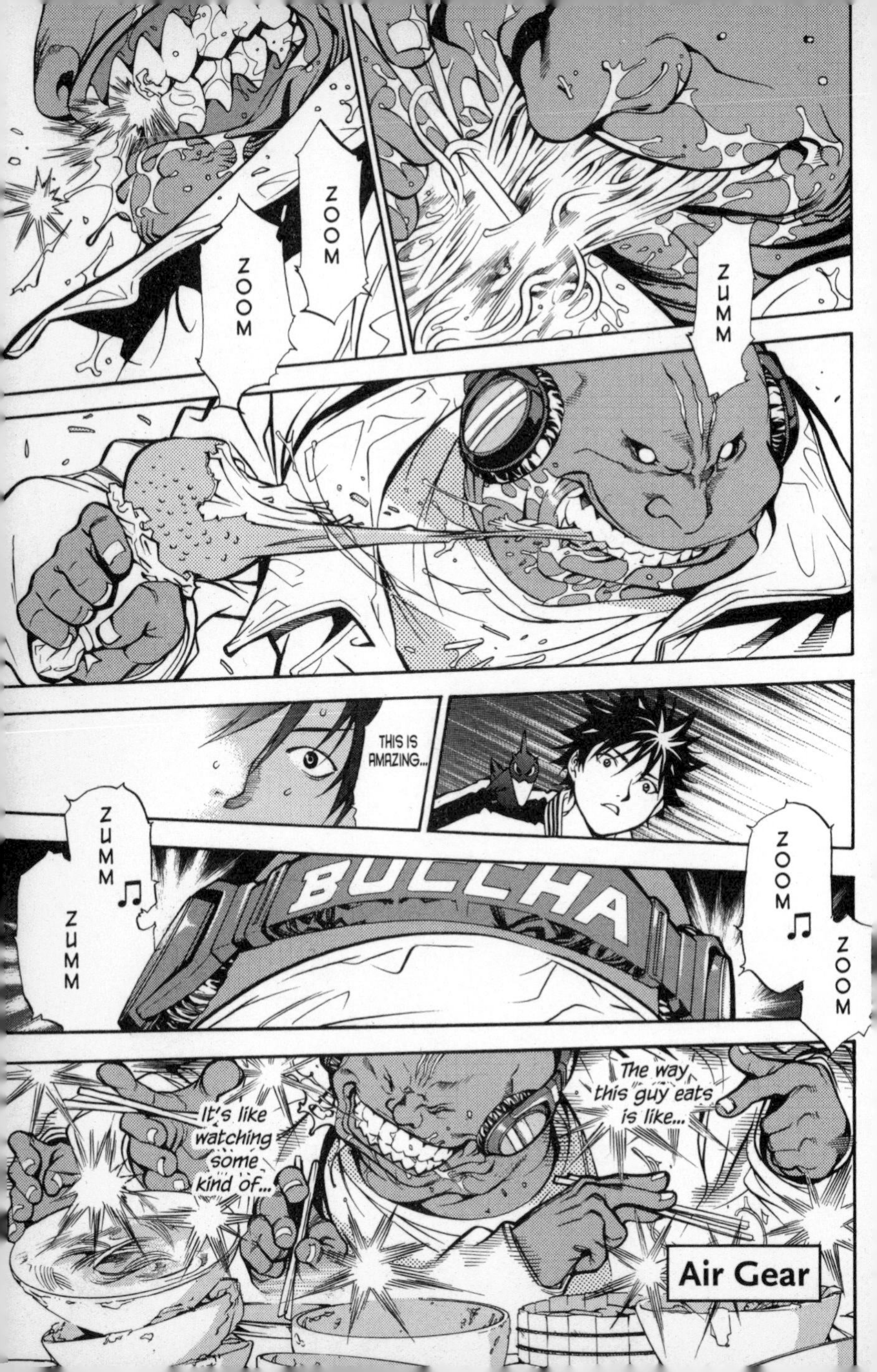

ZUMM
ZOOM
ZOOM
THIS IS AMAZING...
ZOOM ♫
ZOOM
ZUMM ♫
ZUMM
BULLCHA
The way this guy eats is like...
It's like watching some kind of...
Air Gear

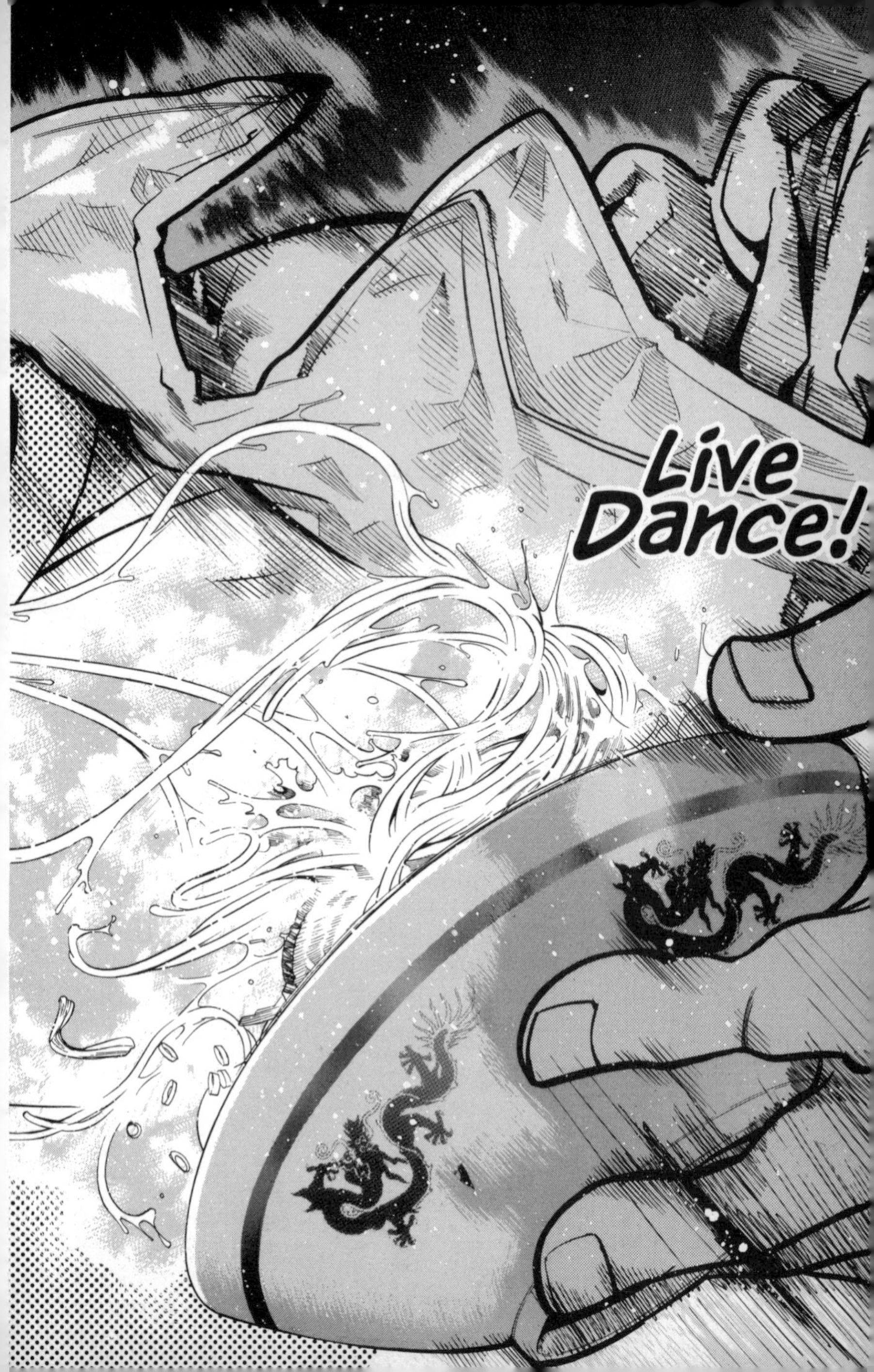
Live Dance!

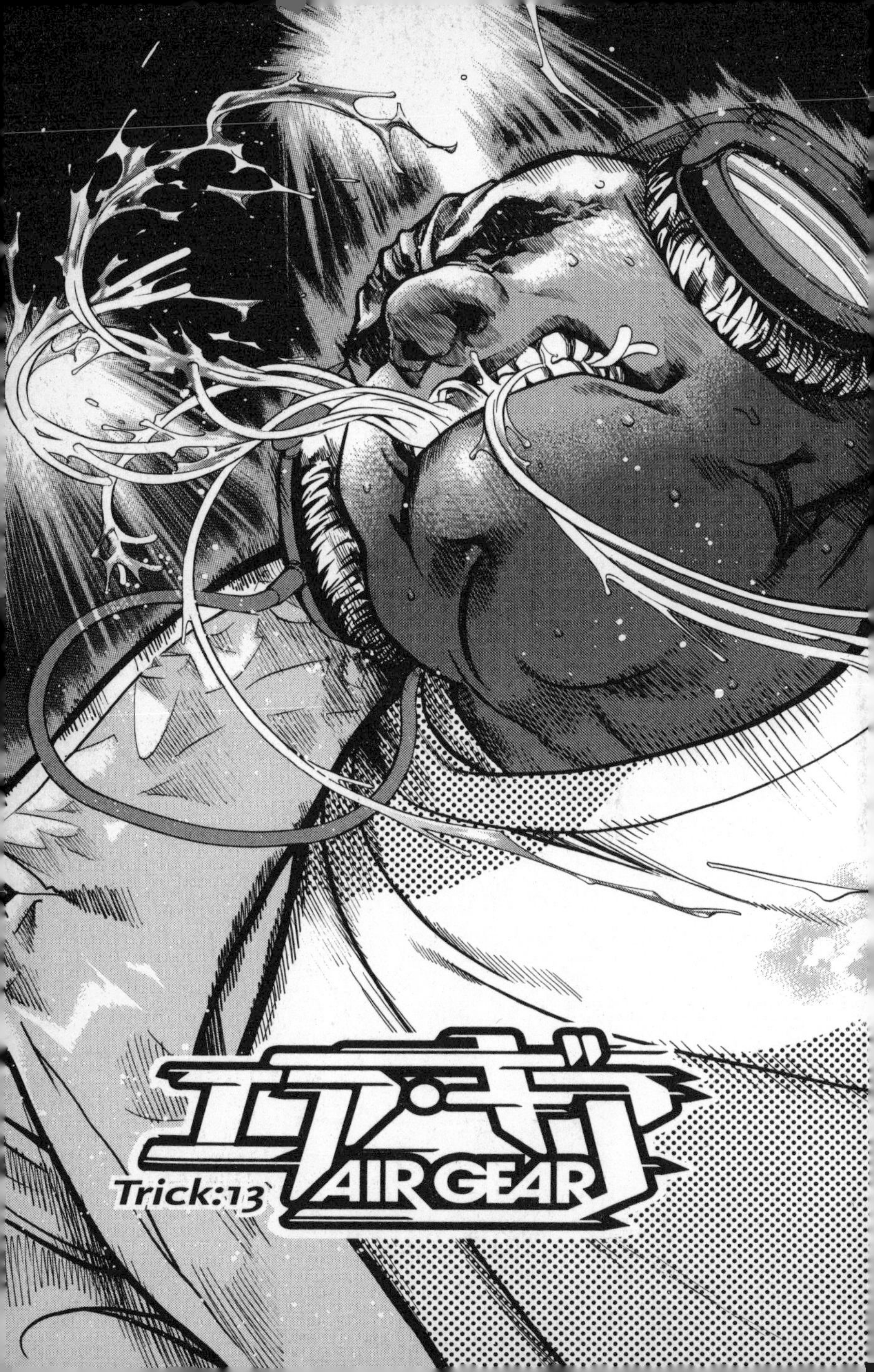
エア・ギア
AIR GEAR
Trick:13

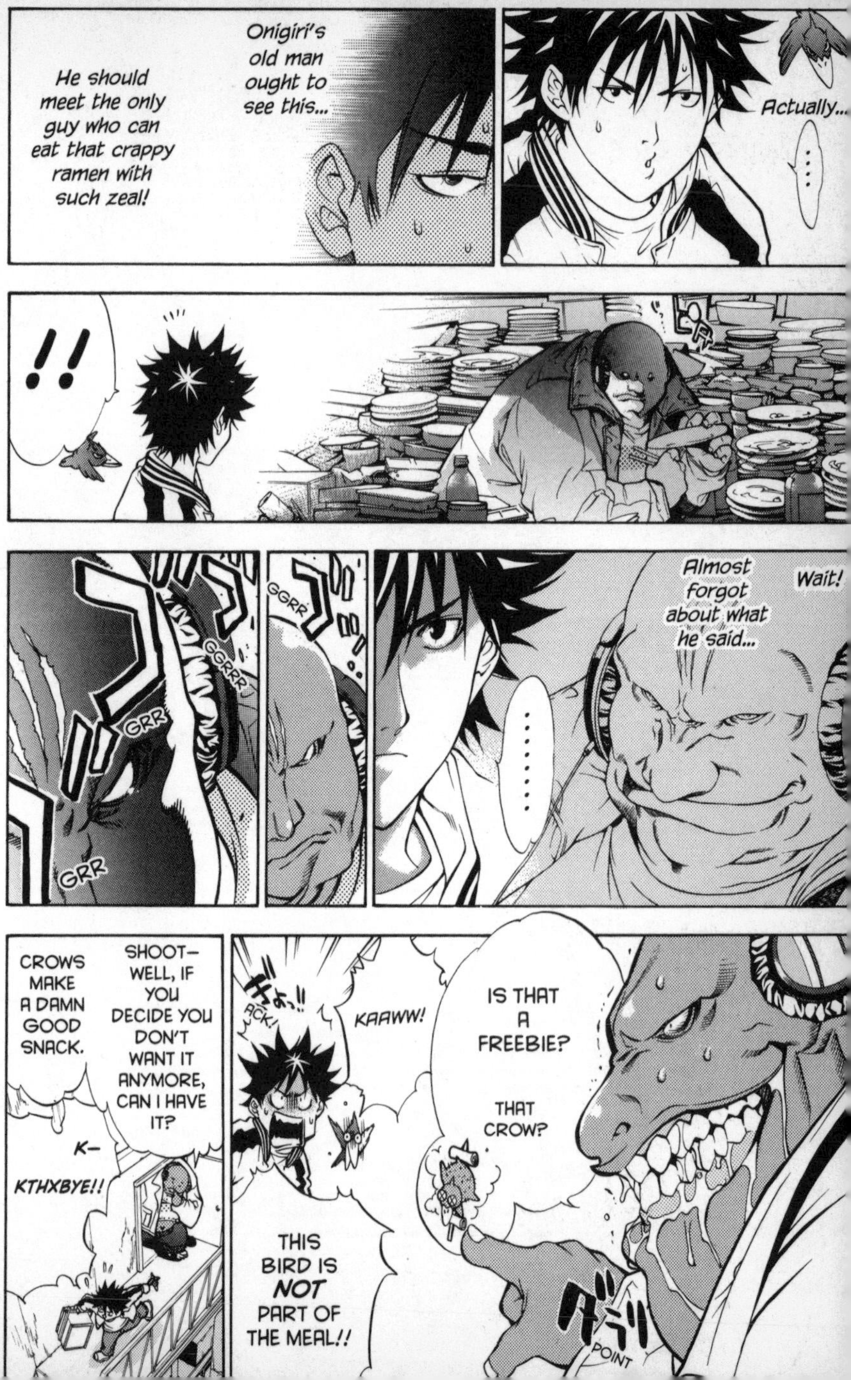
Actually...
....
Onigiri's old man ought to see this...
He should meet the only guy who can eat that crappy ramen with such zeal!
!!
Wait!
Almost forgot about what he said...
....
GGRR
GGRRR
GRR
GRR
IS THAT A FREEBIE?
THAT CROW?
POINT
KAAWW!
ACK!
THIS BIRD IS ***NOT*** PART OF THE MEAL!!
SHOOT— WELL, IF YOU DECIDE YOU DON'T WANT IT ANYMORE, CAN I HAVE IT?
CROWS MAKE A DAMN GOOD SNACK.
K—
KTHXBYE!!

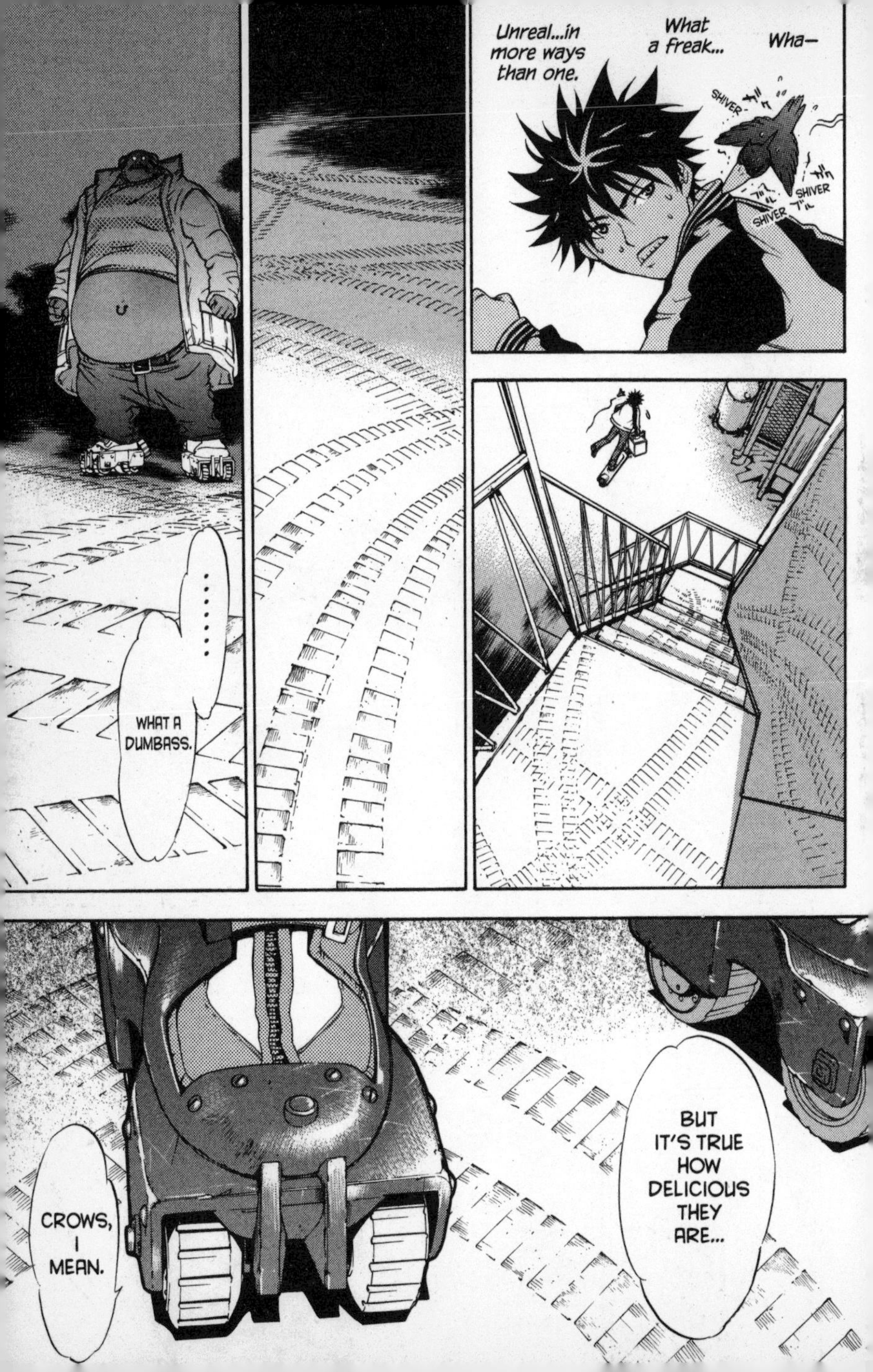
Wha—
What a freak...
Unreal...in more ways than one.
SHIVER
SHIVER
SHIVER
......
WHAT A DUMBASS.
BUT IT'S TRUE HOW DELICIOUS THEY ARE...
CROWS, I MEAN.

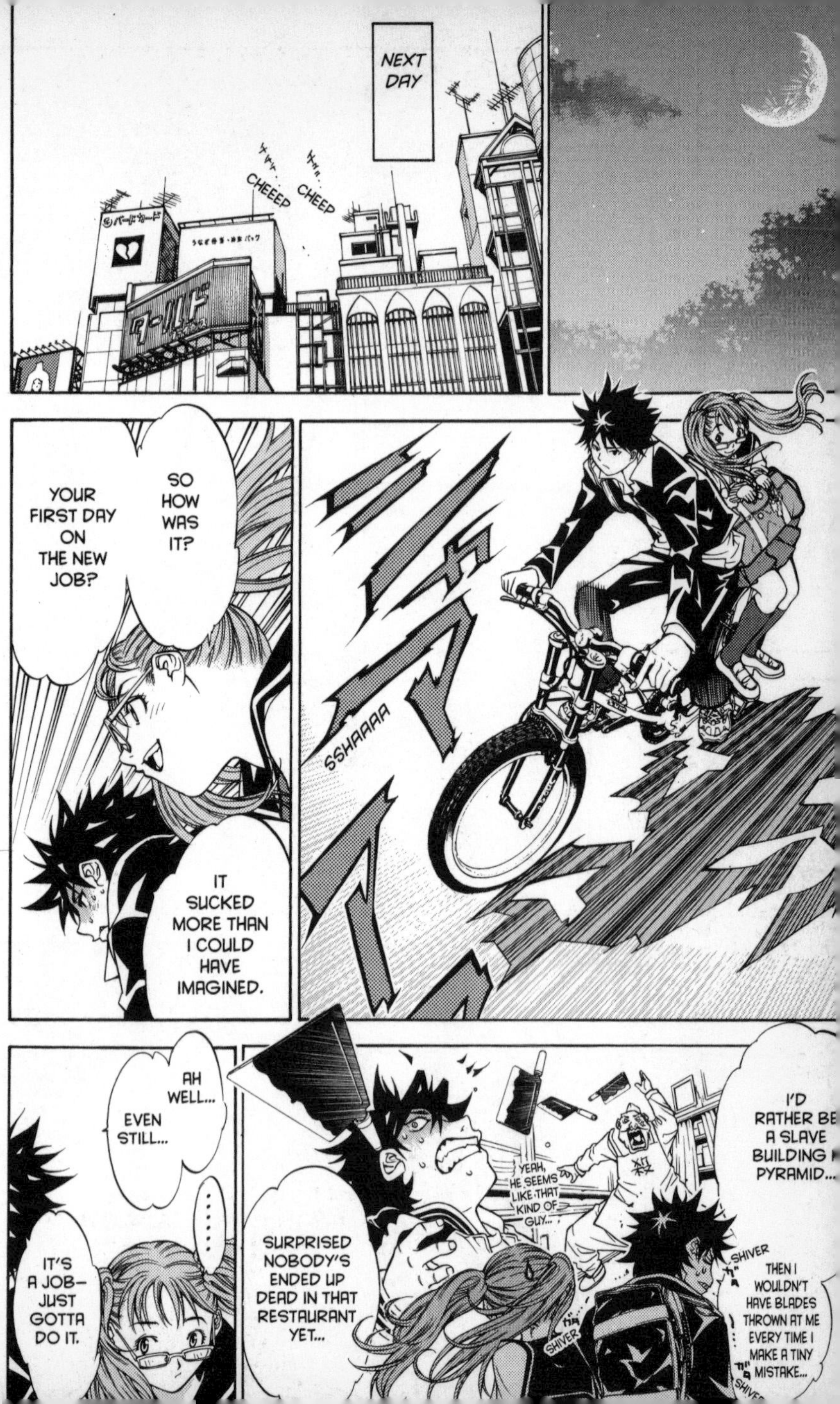
NEXT DAY
CHEEP
CHEEEP
SSHAAAA
SO HOW WAS IT?
YOUR FIRST DAY ON THE NEW JOB?
IT SUCKED MORE THAN I COULD HAVE IMAGINED.
I'D RATHER BE A SLAVE BUILDING PYRAMID...
YEAH, HE SEEMS LIKE THAT KIND OF GUY...
SURPRISED NOBODY'S ENDED UP DEAD IN THAT RESTAURANT YET...
SHIVER
THEN I WOULDN'T HAVE BLADES THROWN AT ME EVERY TIME I MAKE A TINY MISTAKE...
SHIVER
SHIVER
AH WELL...
EVEN STILL...
......
IT'S A JOB— JUST GOTTA DO IT.

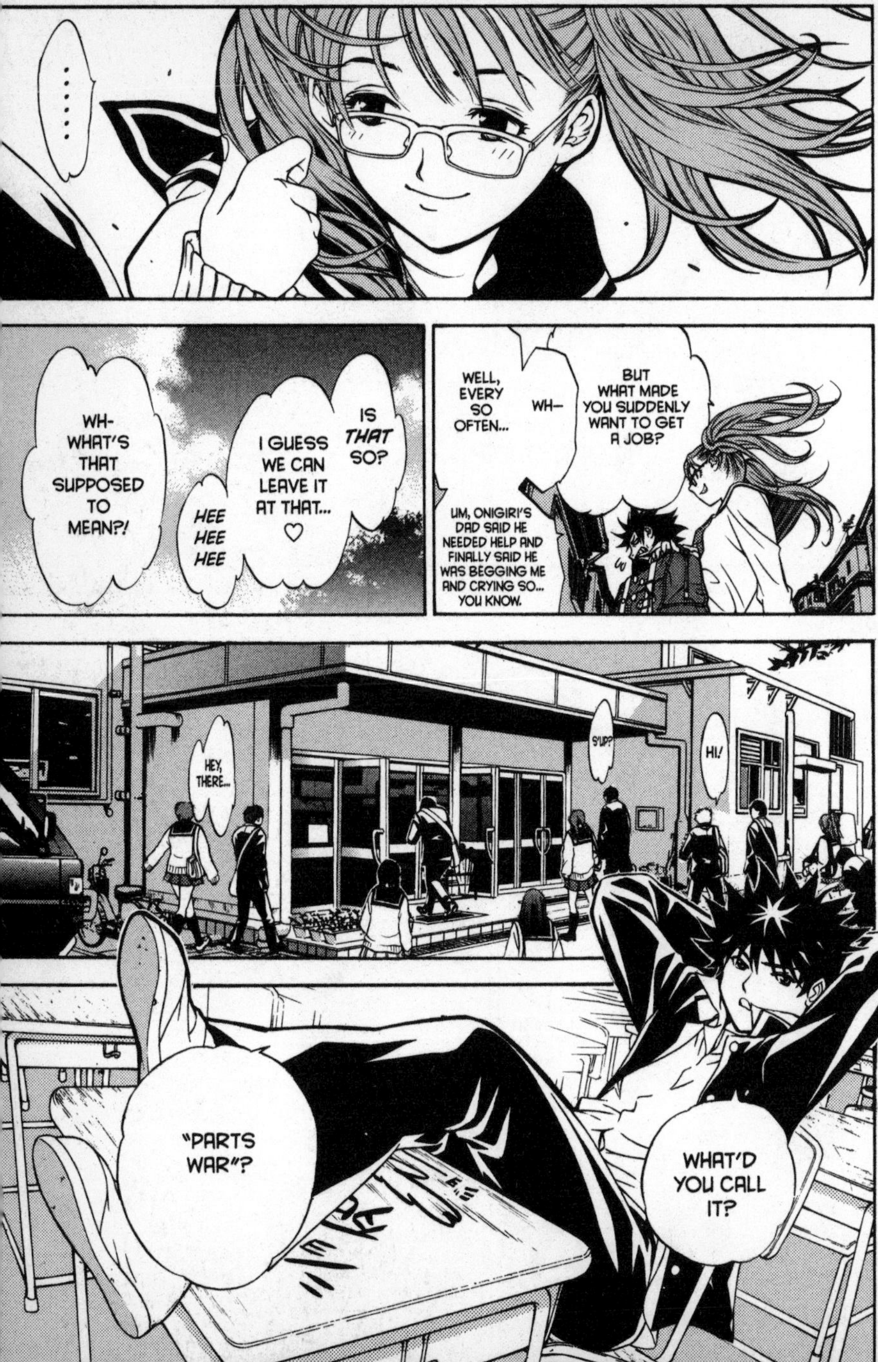
......
BUT WHAT MADE YOU SUDDENLY WANT TO GET A JOB?
WH—
WELL, EVERY SO OFTEN...
UM, ONIGIRI'S DAD SAID HE NEEDED HELP AND FINALLY SAID HE WAS BEGGING ME AND CRYING SO... YOU KNOW.
IS *THAT* SO?
I GUESS WE CAN LEAVE IT AT THAT... ♡
HEE HEE HEE
WH- WHAT'S THAT SUPPOSED TO MEAN?!
HI!
S'UP?
HEY, THERE...
WHAT'D YOU CALL IT?
"PARTS WAR"?

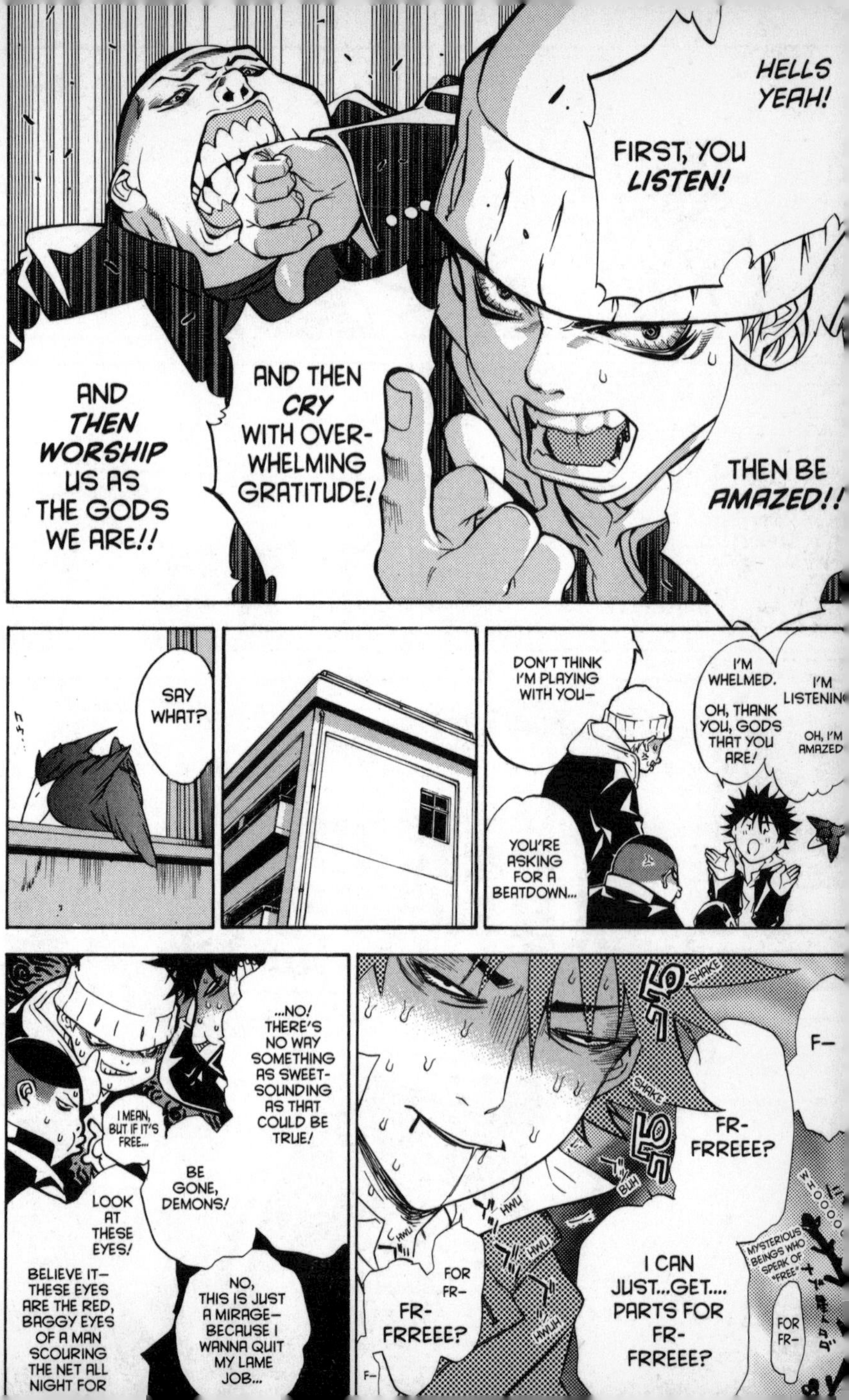
HELLS YEAH!
FIRST, YOU LISTEN!
THEN BE AMAZED!!
AND THEN CRY WITH OVER-WHELMING GRATITUDE!
AND THEN WORSHIP US AS THE GODS WE ARE!!
I'M LISTENING
OH, I'M AMAZED
I'M WHELMED.
OH, THANK YOU, GODS THAT YOU ARE!
DON'T THINK I'M PLAYING WITH YOU—
YOU'RE ASKING FOR A BEATDOWN...
SAY WHAT?
SHAKE
F—
SHAKE
FR-FRREEE?
BUH
WHOOOOO
HWU
HWU
HWU
HWUH
MYSTERIOUS BEINGS WHO SPEAK OF "FREE"
I CAN JUST...GET.... PARTS FOR FR-FRREEE?
FOR FR–
FOR FR–
FR-FRREEE?
F–
...NO! THERE'S NO WAY SOMETHING AS SWEET-SOUNDING AS THAT COULD BE TRUE!
I MEAN, BUT IF IT'S FREE...
BE GONE, DEMONS!
LOOK AT THESE EYES!
NO, THIS IS JUST A MIRAGE— BECAUSE I WANNA QUIT MY LAME JOB...
BELIEVE IT— THESE EYES ARE THE RED, BAGGY EYES OF A MAN SCOURING THE NET ALL NIGHT FOR

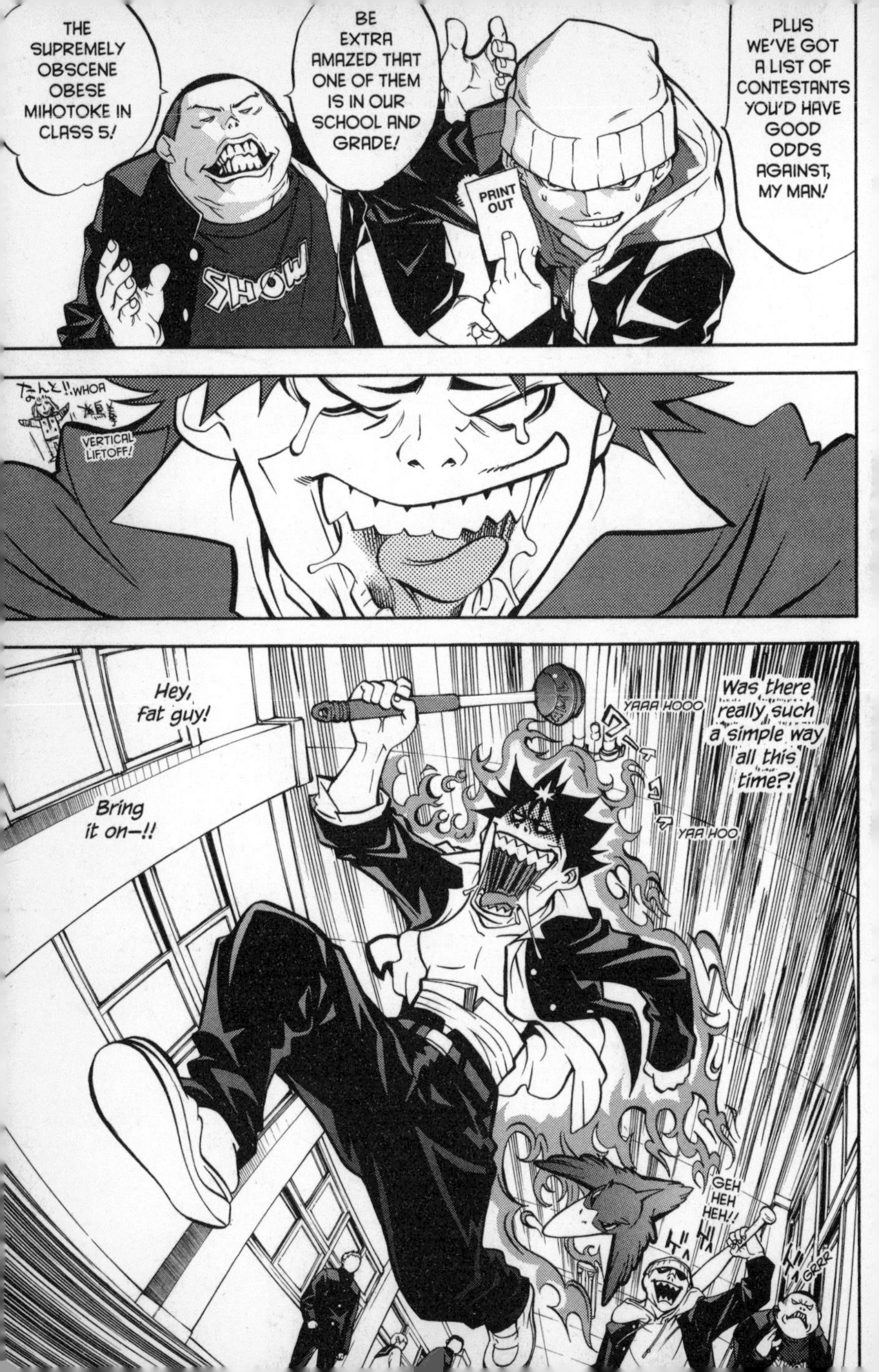
PLUS WE'VE GOT A LIST OF CONTESTANTS YOU'D HAVE GOOD ODDS AGAINST, MY MAN!
PRINT OUT
BE EXTRA AMAZED THAT ONE OF THEM IS IN OUR SCHOOL AND GRADE!
THE SUPREMELY OBSCENE OBESE MIHOTOKE IN CLASS 5!
SHOW
なんと!! WHOA
VERTICAL LIFTOFF!
Was there really such a simple way all this time?!
YAAA HOOO
YAA HOO
Hey, fat guy!
Bring it on—!!
GEH HEH HEH!!
GRRR

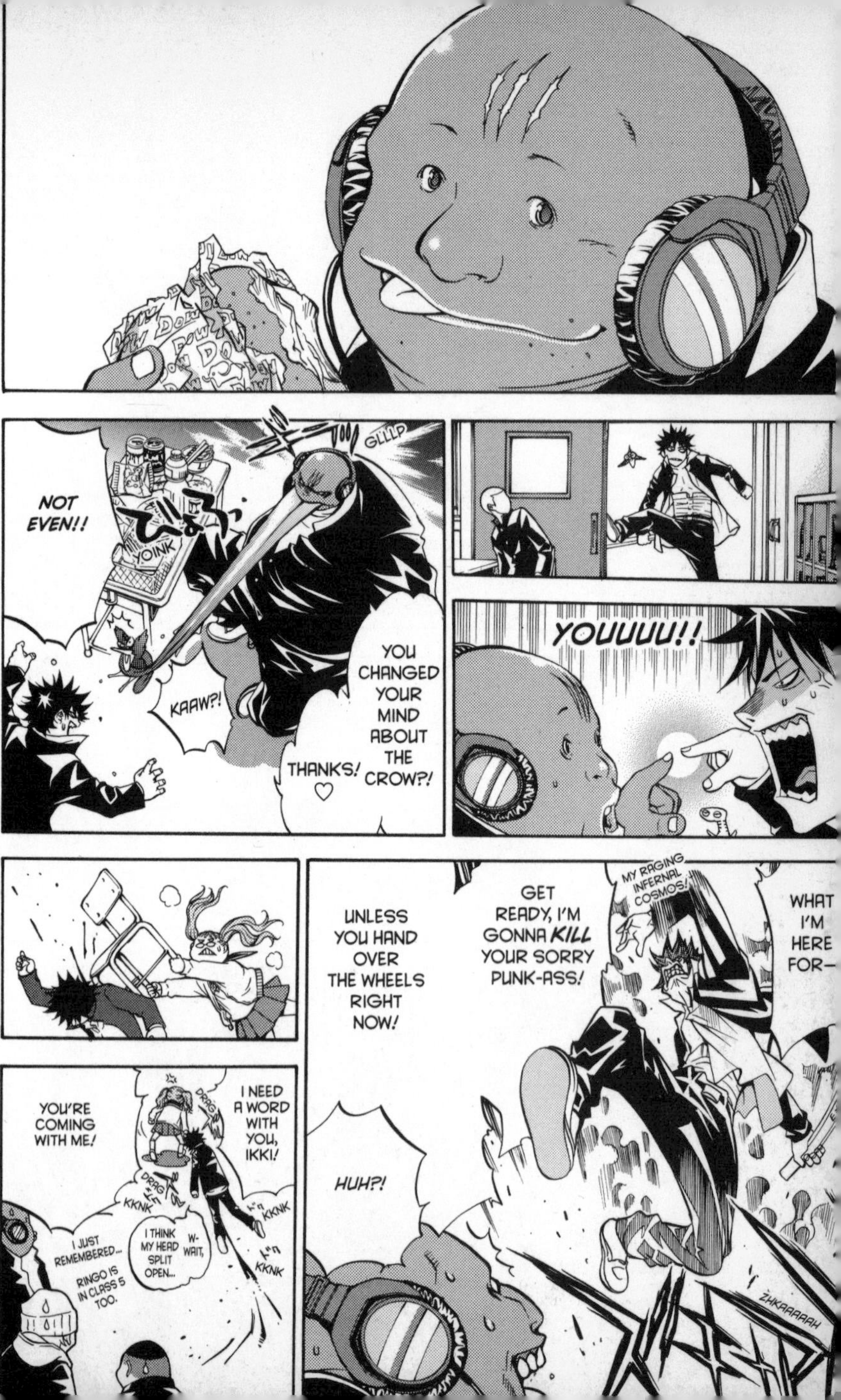

YOUUUU!!
GLLLP
YOU CHANGED YOUR MIND ABOUT THE CROW?!
THANKS! ♡
NOT EVEN!!
YOINK
KAAW?!
WHAT I'M HERE FOR—
MY RAGING INFERNAL COSMOS!
GET READY, I'M GONNA KILL YOUR SORRY PUNK-ASS!
UNLESS YOU HAND OVER THE WHEELS RIGHT NOW!
HUH?!
ZHKAAAAAH
I NEED A WORD WITH YOU, IKKI!
DRAG
YOU'RE COMING WITH ME!
DRAG
KKNK
KKNK
W-WAIT,
KKNK
I THINK MY HEAD SPLIT OPEN...
I JUST REMEMBERED... RINGO IS IN CLASS 5 TOO.

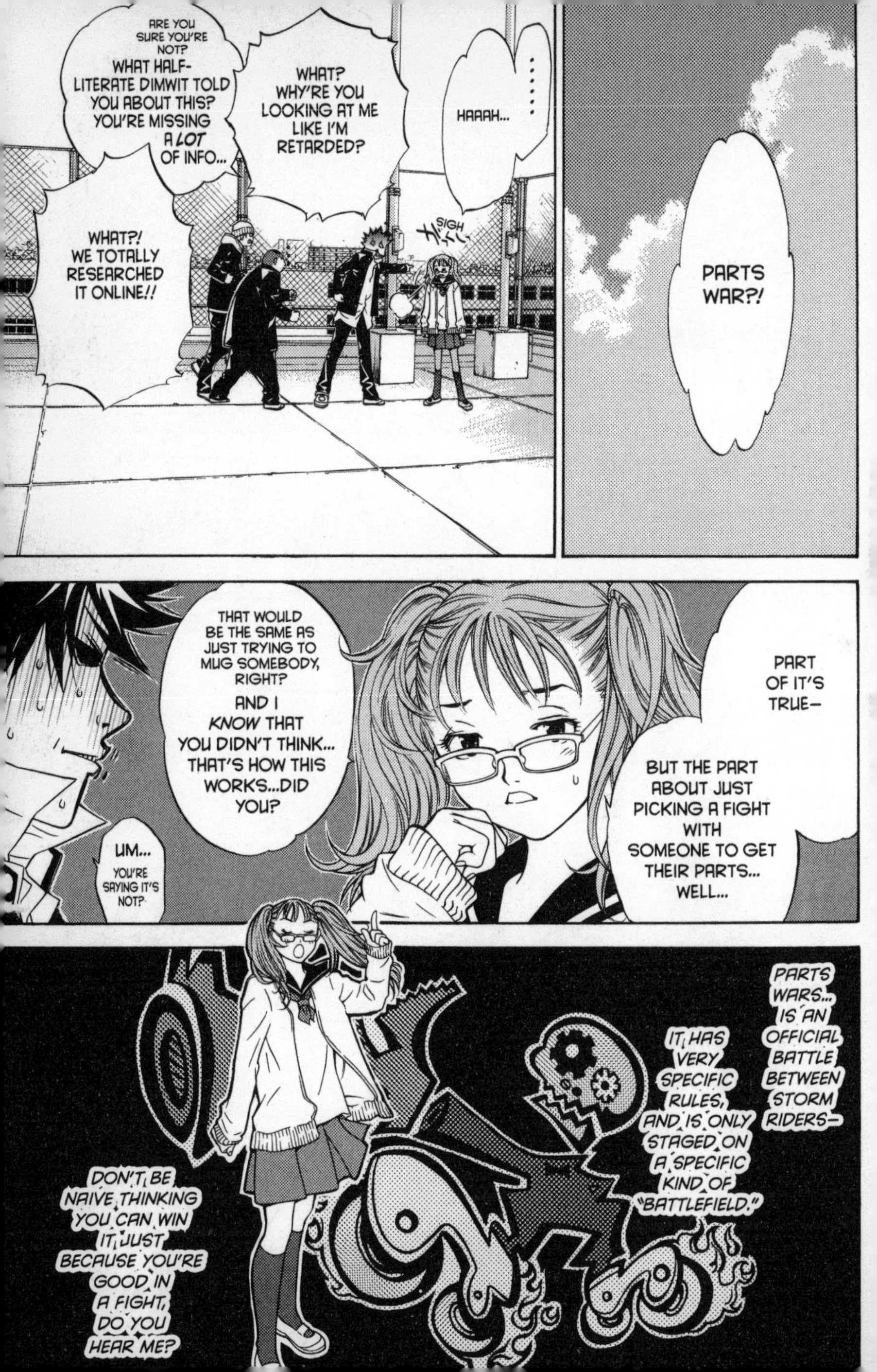
PARTS WAR?!
.....
HAAAH...
SIGH
WHAT? WHY'RE YOU LOOKING AT ME LIKE I'M RETARDED?
ARE YOU SURE YOU'RE NOT? WHAT HALF-LITERATE DIMWIT TOLD YOU ABOUT THIS? YOU'RE MISSING A *LOT* OF INFO...
WHAT?! WE TOTALLY RESEARCHED IT ONLINE!!
PART OF IT'S TRUE—
BUT THE PART ABOUT JUST PICKING A FIGHT WITH SOMEONE TO GET THEIR PARTS... WELL...
THAT WOULD BE THE SAME AS JUST TRYING TO MUG SOMEBODY, RIGHT? AND I *KNOW* THAT YOU DIDN'T THINK... THAT'S HOW THIS WORKS...DID YOU?
UM... YOU'RE SAYING IT'S NOT?
PARTS WARS... IS AN OFFICIAL BATTLE BETWEEN STORM RIDERS—
IT HAS VERY SPECIFIC RULES, AND IS ONLY STAGED ON A SPECIFIC KIND OF "BATTLEFIELD."
DON'T BE NAIVE THINKING YOU CAN WIN IT JUST BECAUSE YOU'RE GOOD IN A FIGHT, DO YOU HEAR ME?

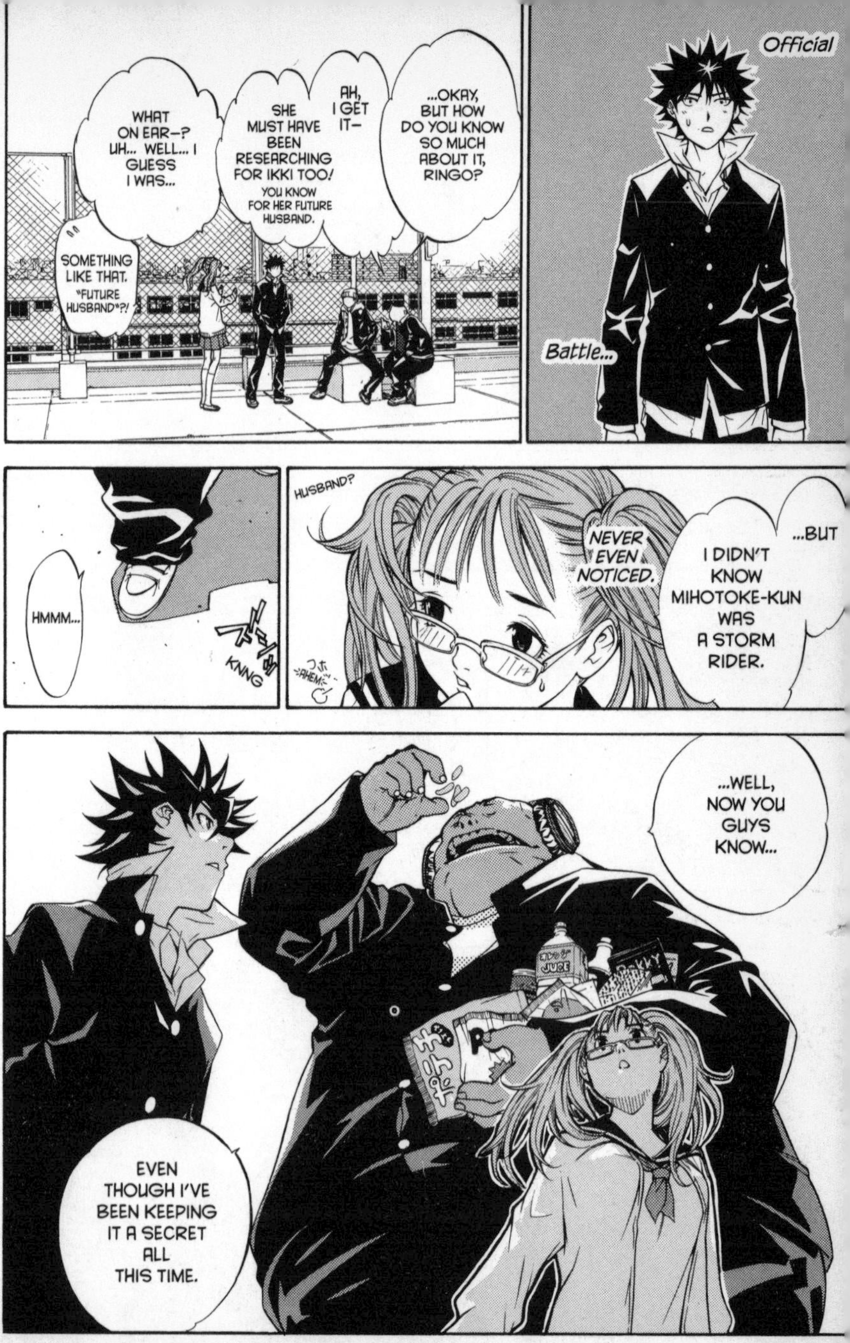
Official
Battle...
...OKAY, BUT HOW DO YOU KNOW SO MUCH ABOUT IT, RINGO?
AH, I GET IT—
SHE MUST HAVE BEEN RESEARCHING FOR IKKI TOO!
YOU KNOW FOR HER FUTURE HUSBAND.
WHAT ON EAR—? UH... WELL... I GUESS I WAS...
SOMETHING LIKE THAT.
"FUTURE HUSBAND"?!
...BUT I DIDN'T KNOW MIHOTOKE-KUN WAS A STORM RIDER.
NEVER EVEN NOTICED.
HUSBAND?
AHEM
KNNG
HMMM...
...WELL, NOW YOU GUYS KNOW...
EVEN THOUGH I'VE BEEN KEEPING IT A SECRET ALL THIS TIME.

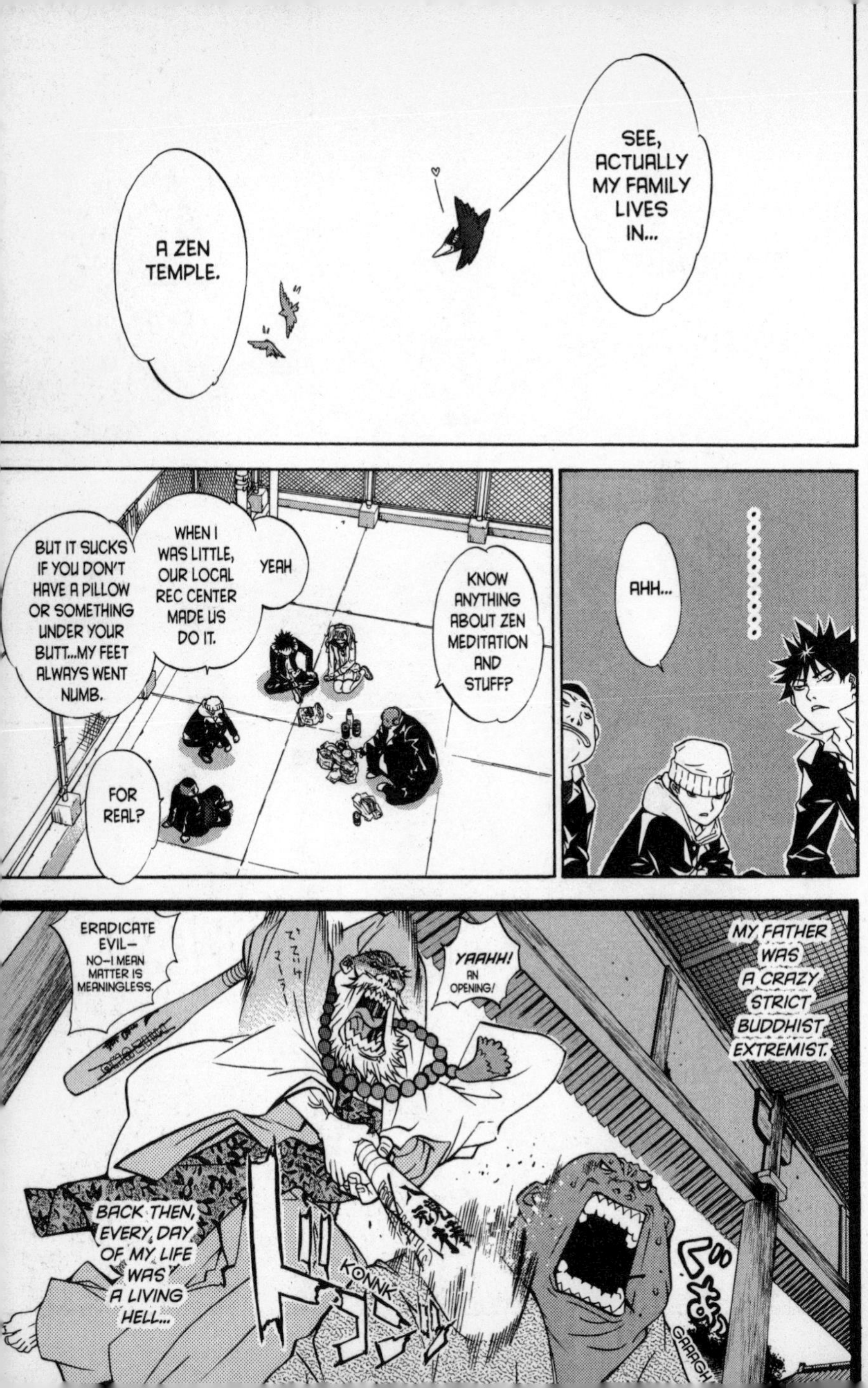
SEE, ACTUALLY MY FAMILY LIVES IN...
A ZEN TEMPLE.
......
AHH...
KNOW ANYTHING ABOUT ZEN MEDITATION AND STUFF?
YEAH
WHEN I WAS LITTLE, OUR LOCAL REC CENTER MADE US DO IT.
BUT IT SUCKS IF YOU DON'T HAVE A PILLOW OR SOMETHING UNDER YOUR BUTT...MY FEET ALWAYS WENT NUMB.
FOR REAL?
MY FATHER WAS A CRAZY STRICT BUDDHIST EXTREMIST.
YAAHH! AN OPENING!
ERADICATE EVIL— NO—I MEAN MATTER IS MEANINGLESS.
GRAAGH
KONNK
BACK THEN, EVERY DAY OF MY LIFE WAS A LIVING HELL...

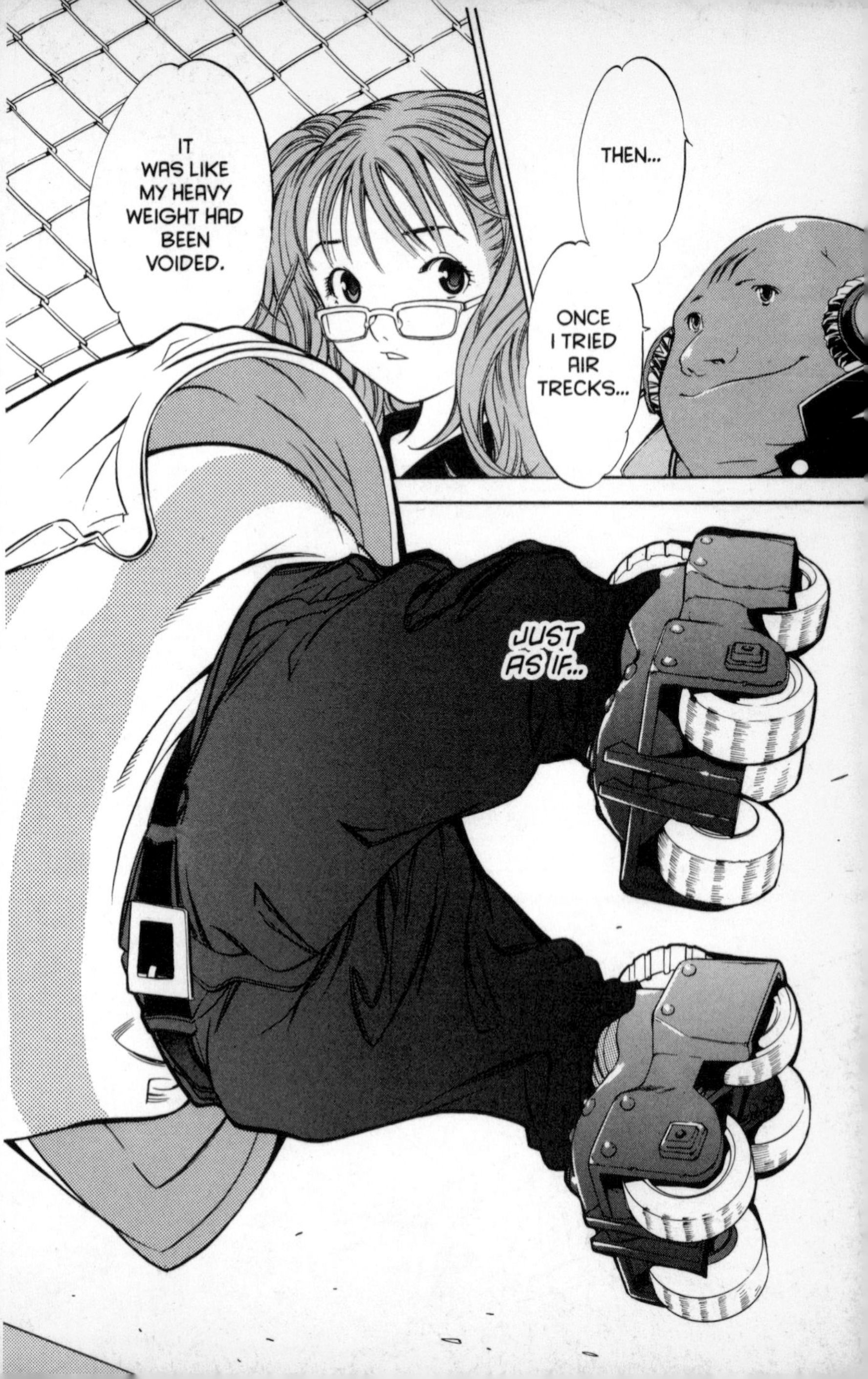
THEN...
ONCE I TRIED AIR TRECKS...
IT WAS LIKE MY HEAVY WEIGHT HAD BEEN VOIDED.
JUST AS IF...

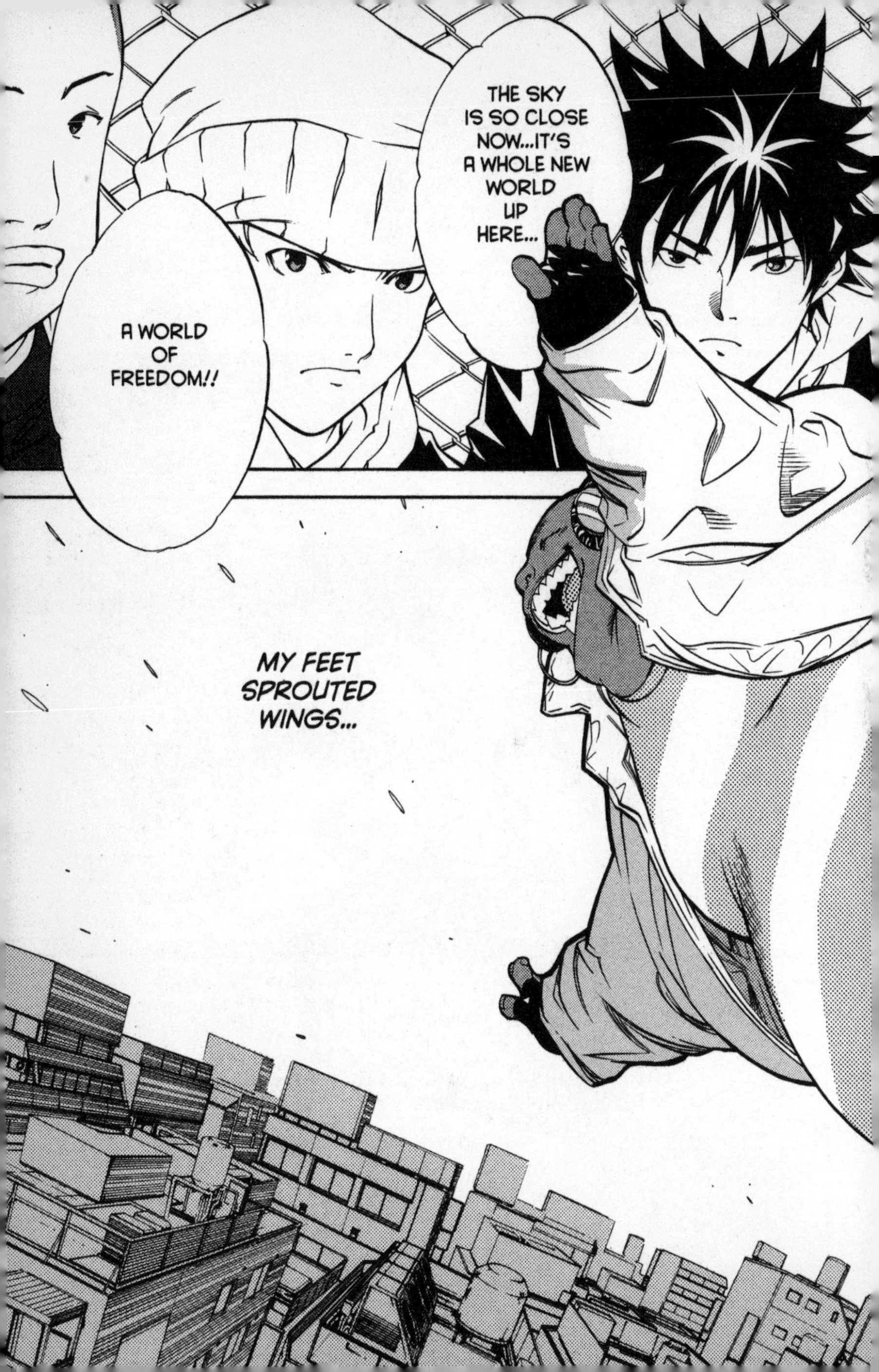
THE SKY IS SO CLOSE NOW...IT'S A WHOLE NEW WORLD UP HERE...
A WORLD OF FREEDOM!!
MY FEET SPROUTED WINGS...

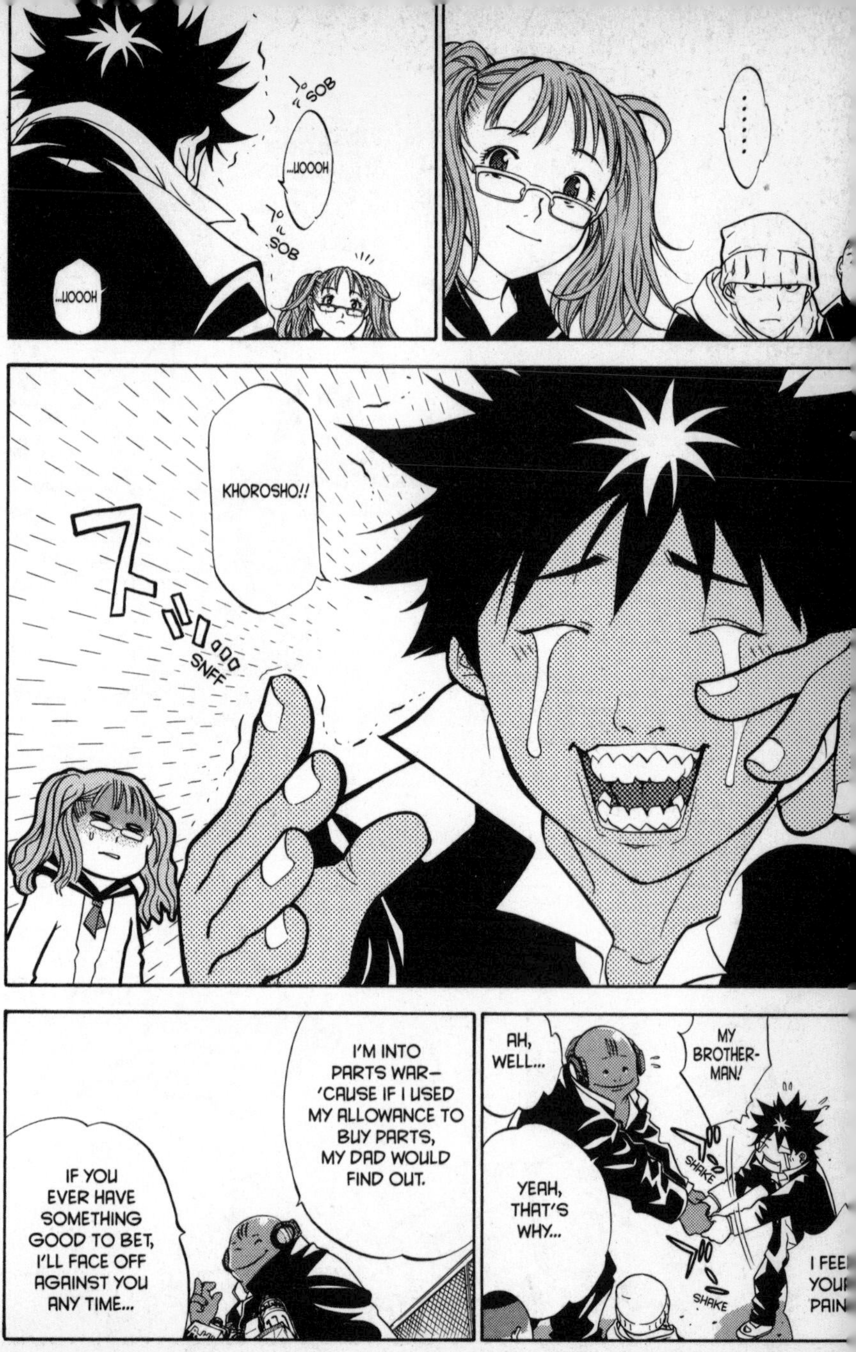
......
SOB
HOOOH...
SOB
HOOOH...
KHOROSHO!!
SNFF
MY BROTHER-MAN!
AH, WELL...
SHAKE
SHAKE
YEAH, THAT'S WHY...
I FEE YOUR PAIN
I'M INTO PARTS WAR— 'CAUSE IF I USED MY ALLOWANCE TO BUY PARTS, MY DAD WOULD FIND OUT.
IF YOU EVER HAVE SOMETHING GOOD TO BET, I'LL FACE OFF AGAINST YOU ANY TIME...

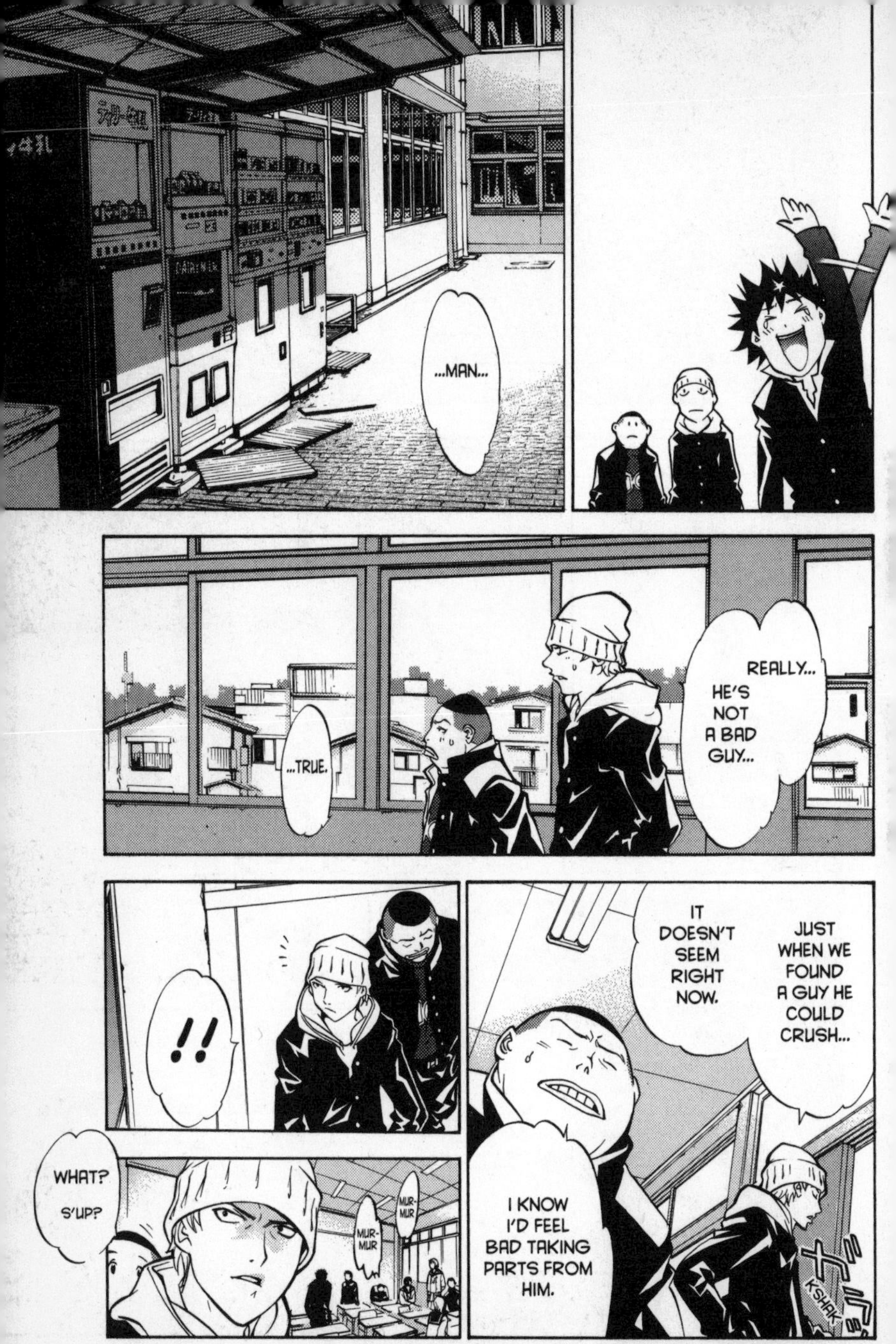
...MAN...
REALLY... HE'S NOT A BAD GUY...
...TRUE.
JUST WHEN WE FOUND A GUY HE COULD CRUSH...
IT DOESN'T SEEM RIGHT NOW.
I KNOW I'D FEEL BAD TAKING PARTS FROM HIM.
KSHAK
!!
MUR-MUR
MUR-MUR
WHAT?
S'UP?

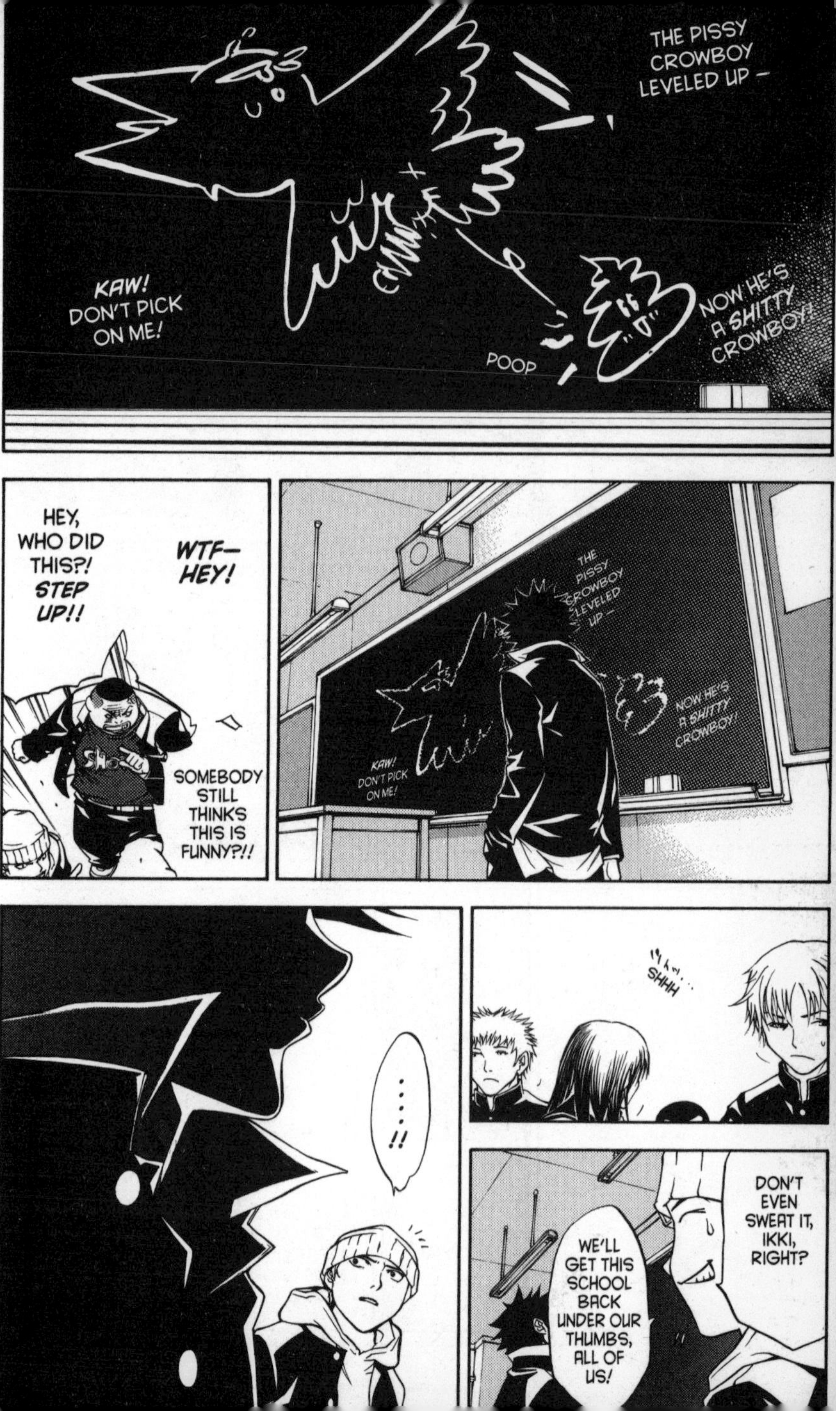
THE PISSY CROWBOY LEVELED UP–
NOW HE'S A SHITTY CROWBOY!
POOP
KAW! DON'T PICK ON ME!
THE PISSY CROWBOY LEVELED UP–
NOW HE'S A SHITTY CROWBOY!
KAW! DON'T PICK ON ME!
WTF— HEY!
HEY, WHO DID THIS?! STEP UP!!
SOMEBODY STILL THINKS THIS IS FUNNY?!!
SHHH...
DON'T EVEN SWEAT IT, IKKI, RIGHT?
WE'LL GET THIS SCHOOL BACK UNDER OUR THUMBS, ALL OF US!
......!!

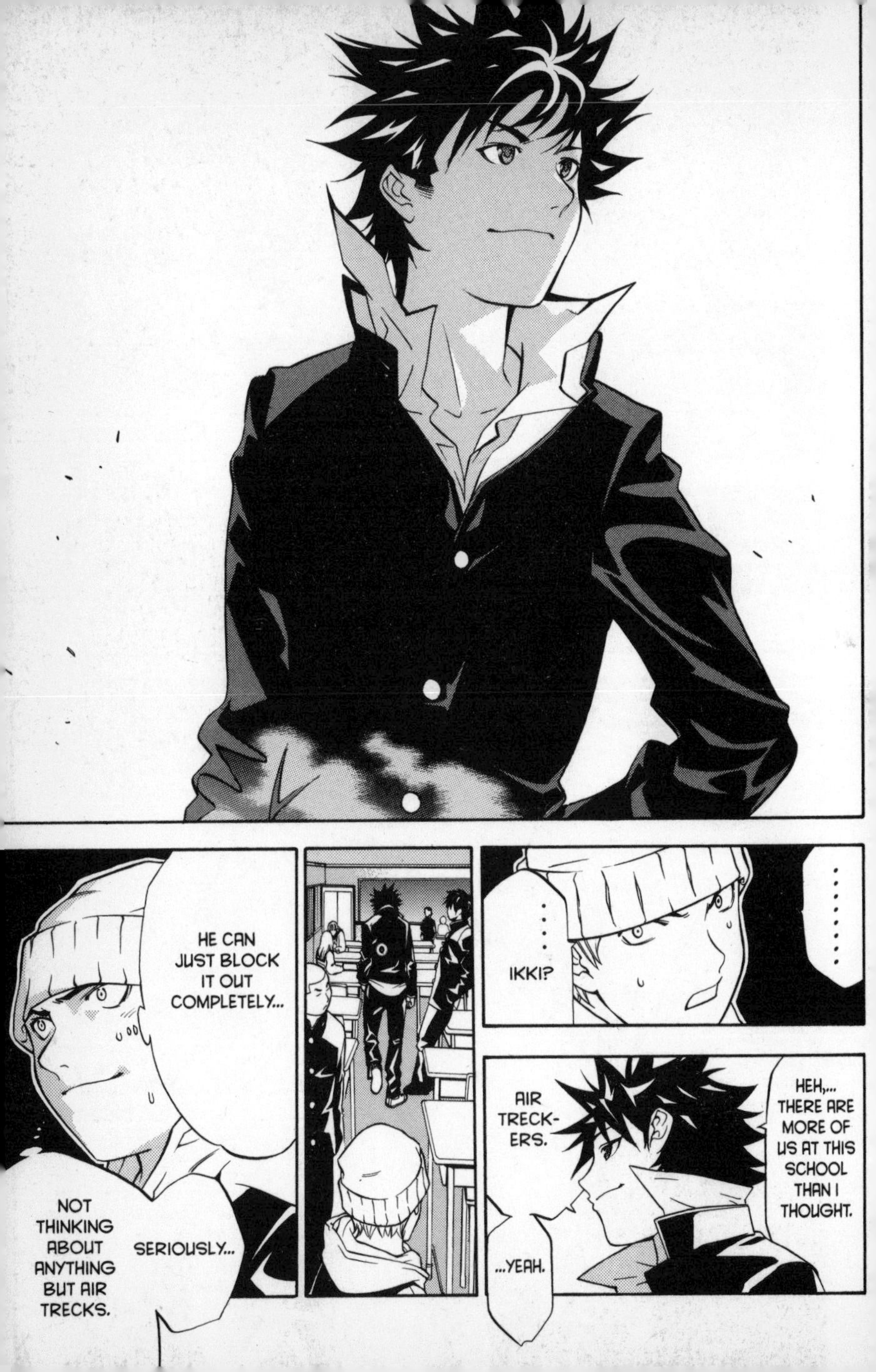
......
....
IKKI?
HEH,... THERE ARE MORE OF US AT THIS SCHOOL THAN I THOUGHT.
AIR TRECK-ERS.
...YEAH.
HE CAN JUST BLOCK IT OUT COMPLETELY...
NOT THINKING ABOUT ANYTHING BUT AIR TRECKS.
SERIOUSLY...

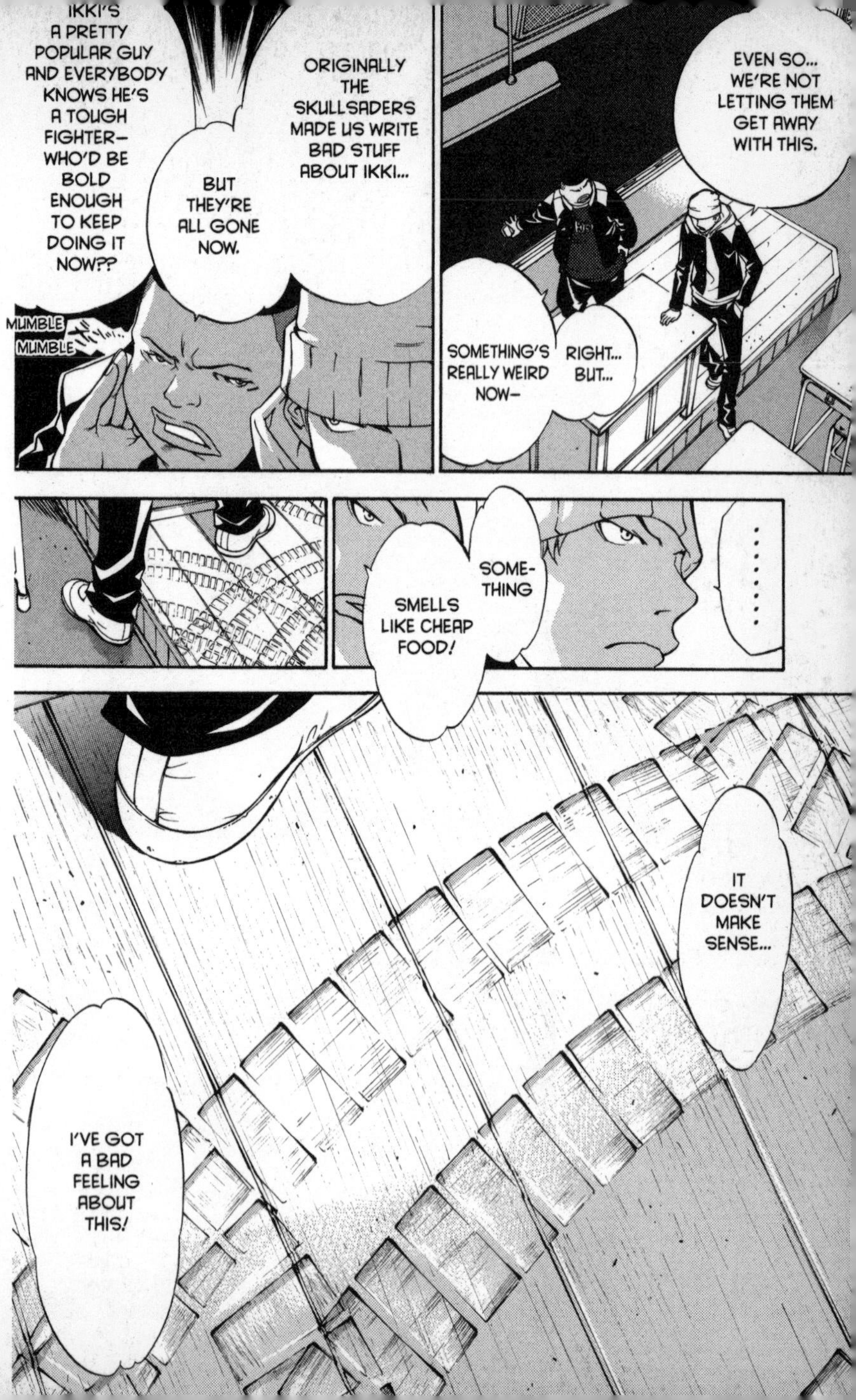
EVEN SO... WE'RE NOT LETTING THEM GET AWAY WITH THIS.
RIGHT... BUT...
SOMETHING'S REALLY WEIRD NOW—
ORIGINALLY THE SKULLSADERS MADE US WRITE BAD STUFF ABOUT IKKI...
BUT THEY'RE ALL GONE NOW.
IKKI'S A PRETTY POPULAR GUY AND EVERYBODY KNOWS HE'S A TOUGH FIGHTER—WHO'D BE BOLD ENOUGH TO KEEP DOING IT NOW??
MUMBLE MUMBLE
......
SOMETHING SMELLS LIKE CHEAP FOOD!
IT DOESN'T MAKE SENSE...
I'VE GOT A BAD FEELING ABOUT THIS!

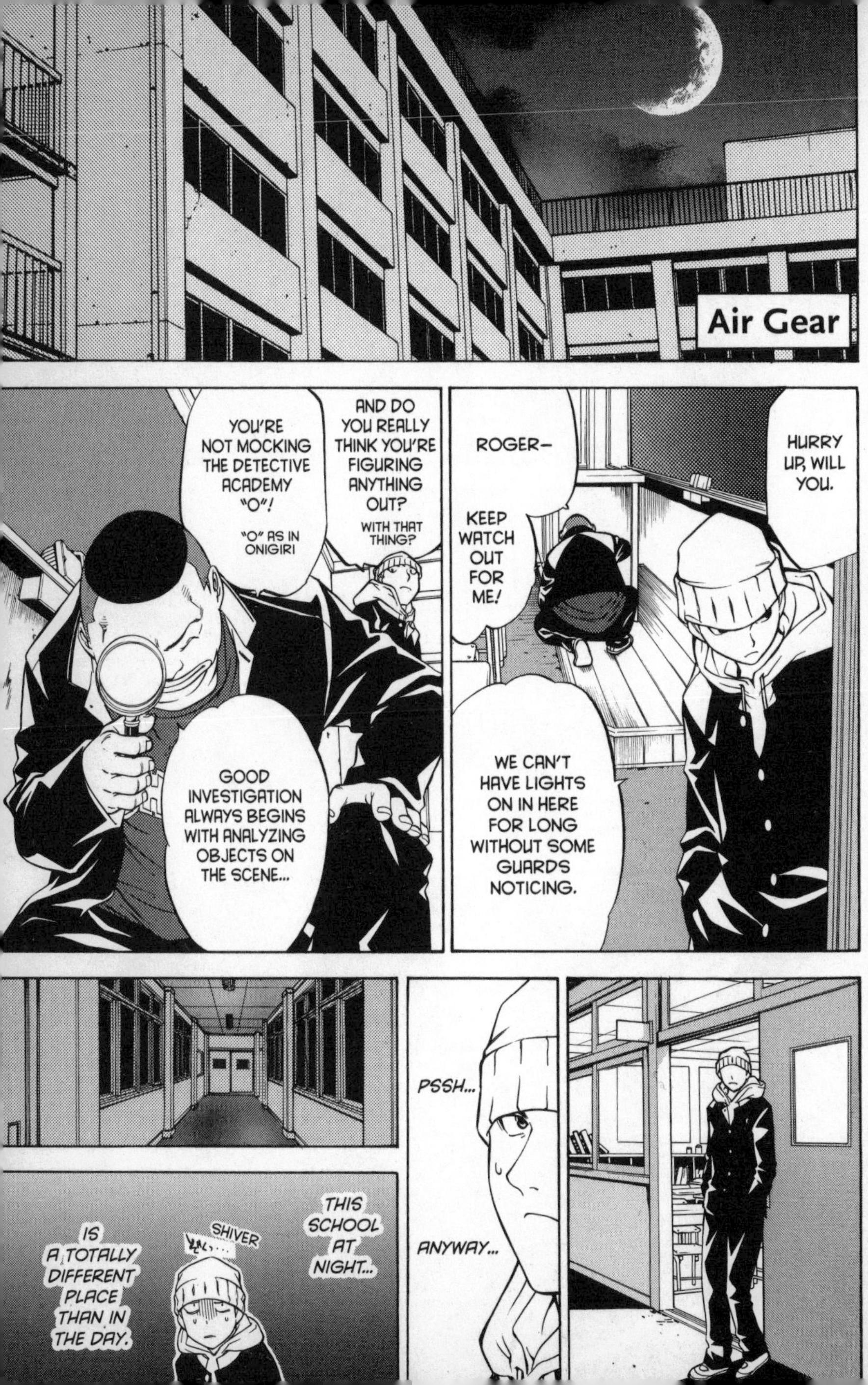
Air Gear
HURRY UP, WILL YOU.
ROGER—
KEEP WATCH OUT FOR ME!
WE CAN'T HAVE LIGHTS ON IN HERE FOR LONG WITHOUT SOME GUARDS NOTICING.
AND DO YOU REALLY THINK YOU'RE FIGURING ANYTHING OUT?
WITH THAT THING?
YOU'RE NOT MOCKING THE DETECTIVE ACADEMY "O"!
"O" AS IN ONIGIRI
GOOD INVESTIGATION ALWAYS BEGINS WITH ANALYZING OBJECTS ON THE SCENE...
PSSH...
ANYWAY...
THIS SCHOOL AT NIGHT...
SHIVER
IS A TOTALLY DIFFERENT PLACE THAN IN THE DAY.

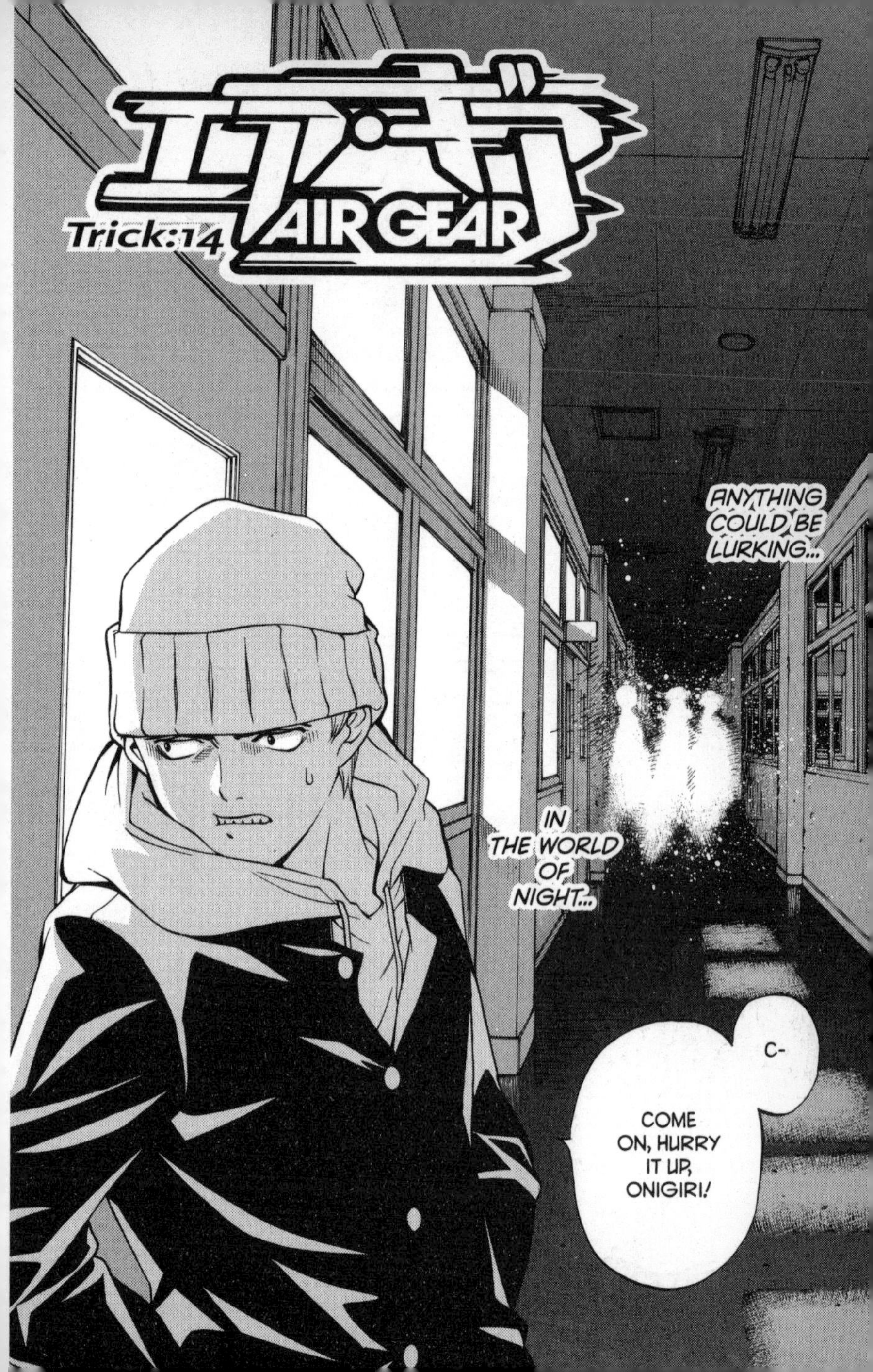
AIR GEAR
Trick:14
ANYTHING COULD BE LURKING...
IN THE WORLD OF NIGHT...
C-
COME ON, HURRY IT UP, ONIGIRI!

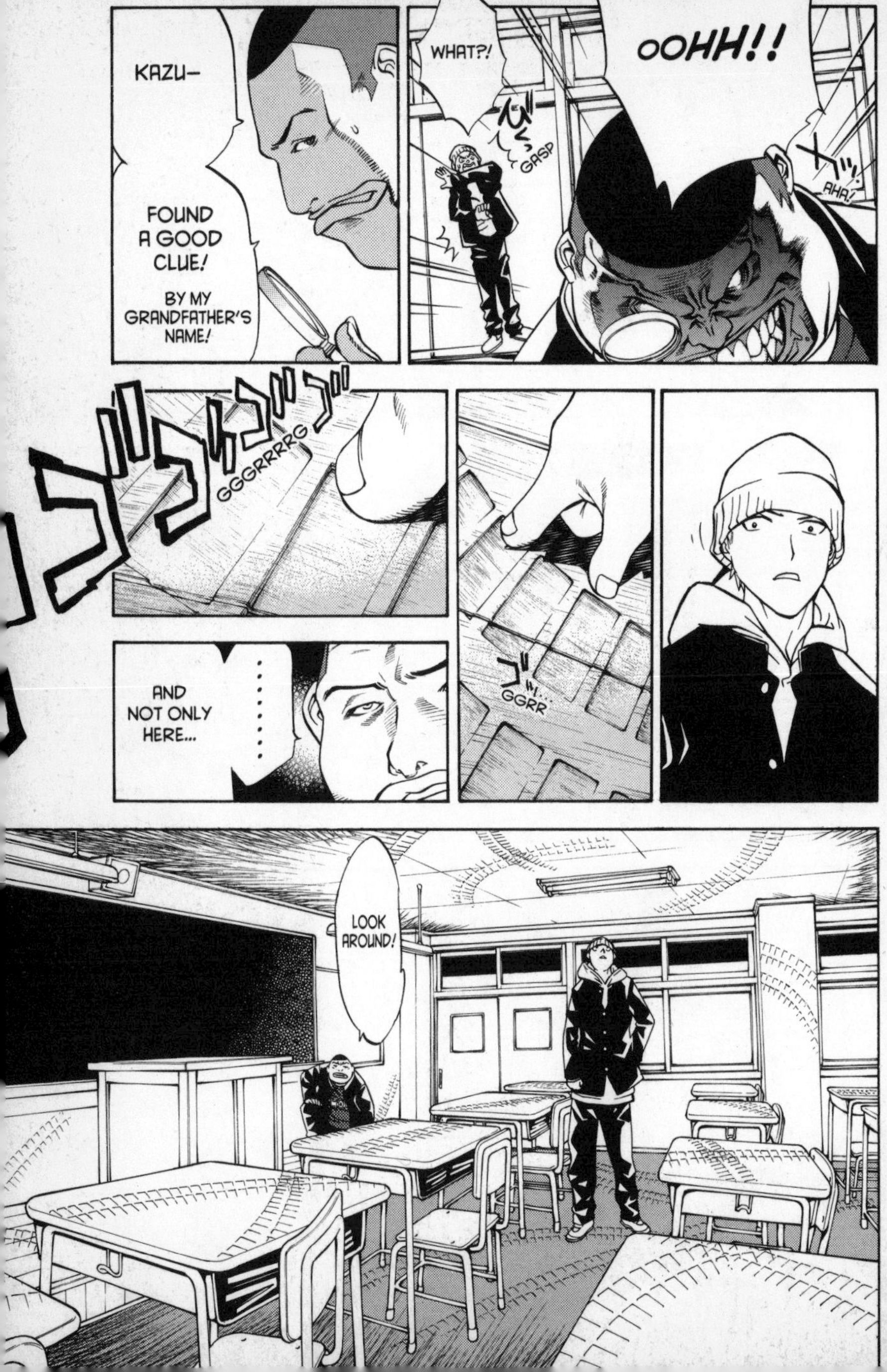
OOHH!!
WHAT?!
GASP
AHA!
KAZU—
FOUND A GOOD CLUE!
BY MY GRANDFATHER'S NAME!
GGRR
GGGRRRRG
AND NOT ONLY HERE...
......
LOOK AROUND!

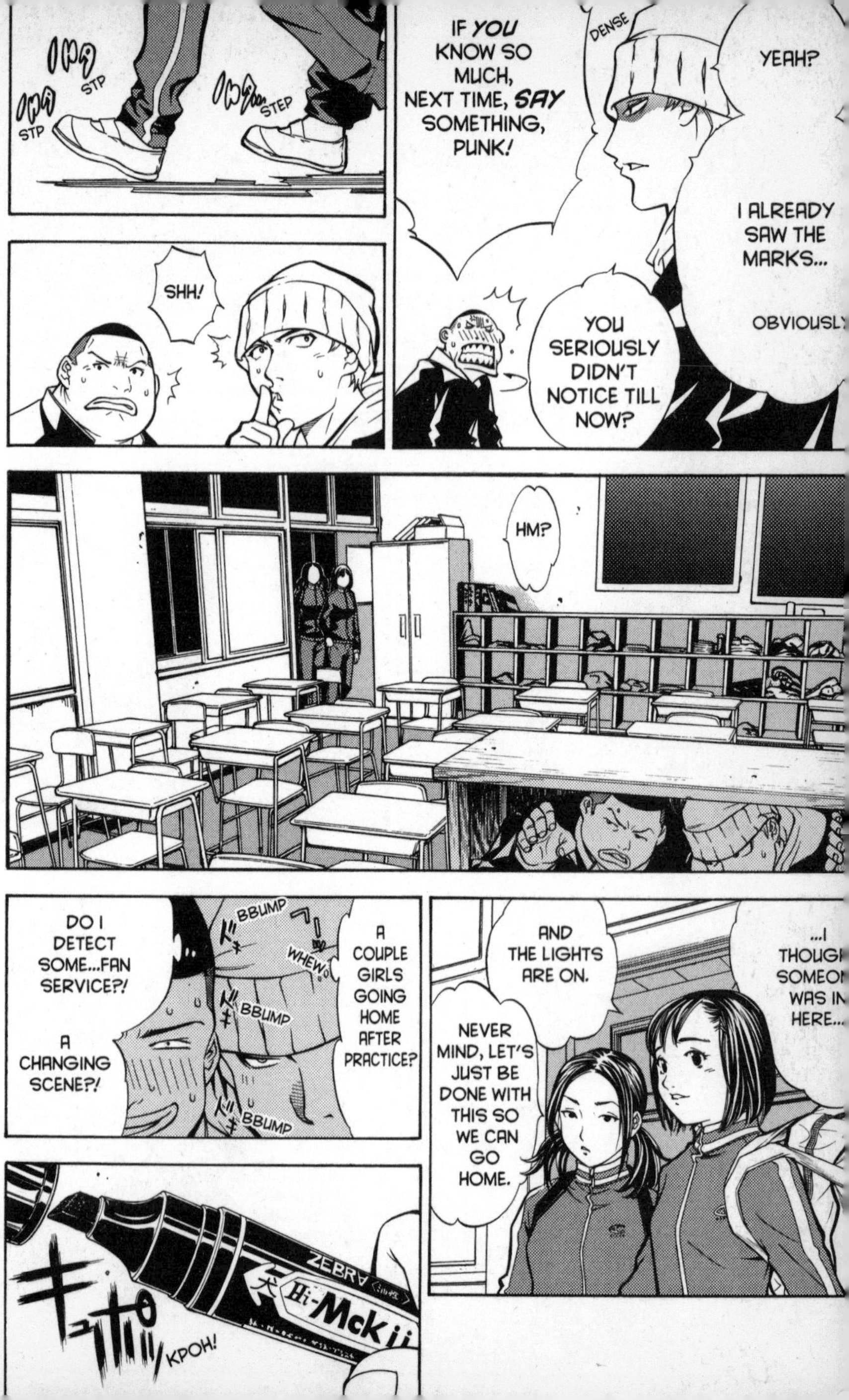
DENSE
YEAH?
I ALREADY SAW THE MARKS...
OBVIOUSLY
YOU SERIOUSLY DIDN'T NOTICE TILL NOW?
IF *YOU* KNOW SO MUCH, NEXT TIME, ***SAY*** SOMETHING, PUNK!
STP
STP
STEP
SHH!
HM?
...I THOUG SOMEO WAS IN HERE...
AND THE LIGHTS ARE ON.
NEVER MIND, LET'S JUST BE DONE WITH THIS SO WE CAN GO HOME.
A COUPLE GIRLS GOING HOME AFTER PRACTICE?
WHEW
BBUMP
BBUMP
DO I DETECT SOME...FAN SERVICE?!
A CHANGING SCENE?!
BBUMP
ZEBRA
Hi-McKii
KPOH!

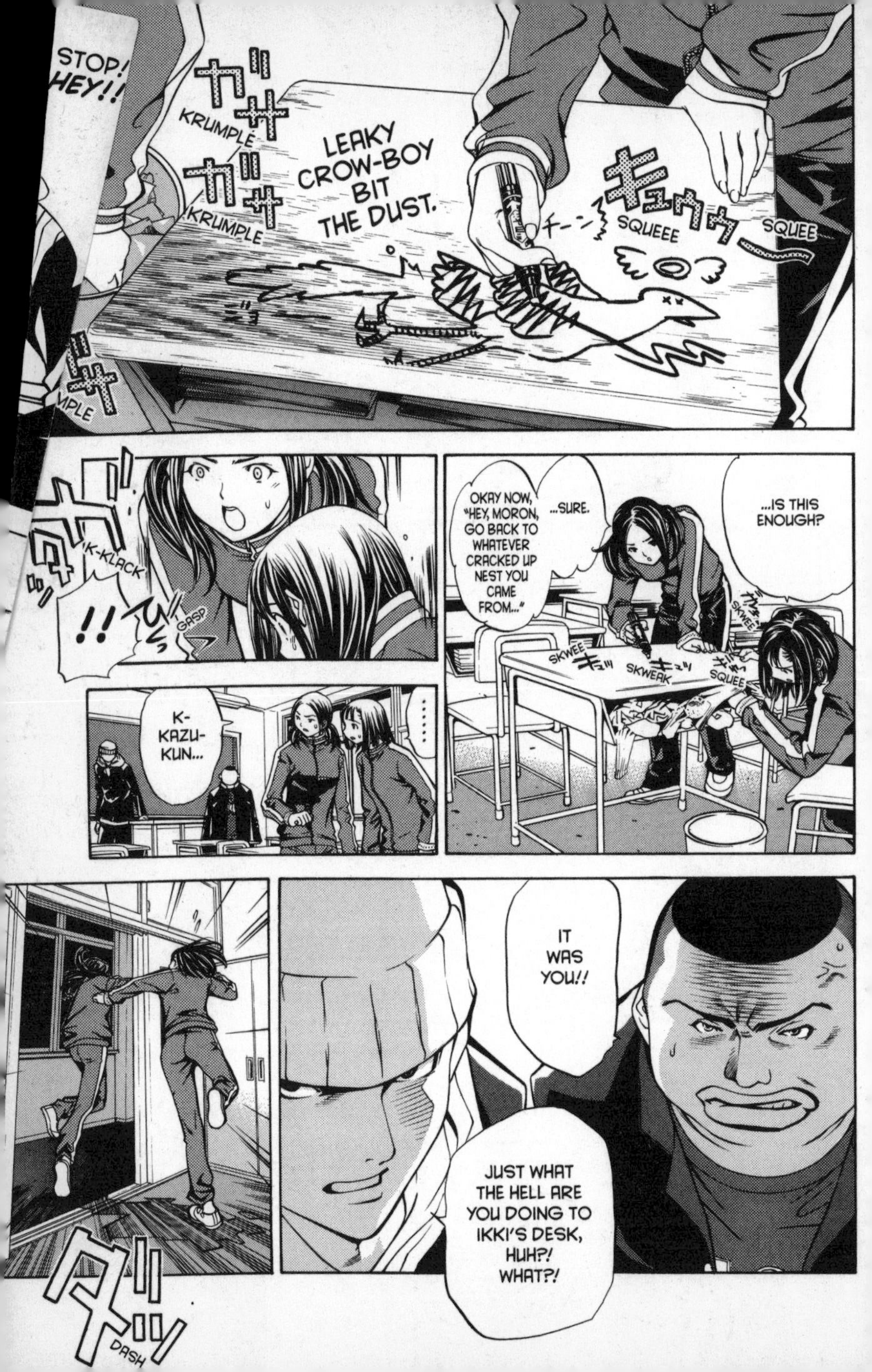
SQUEE
SQUEEE
LEAKY CROW-BOY BIT THE DUST.
KRUMPLE
KRUMPLE
STOP! HEY!!
MPLE
...IS THIS ENOUGH?
...SURE.
OKAY NOW, "HEY, MORON, GO BACK TO WHATEVER CRACKED UP NEST YOU CAME FROM..."
SKWEE
SQUEE
SKWEAK
SKWEE
K-KLACK
GASP
!!
......
K-KAZU-KUN...
IT WAS YOU!!
JUST WHAT THE HELL ARE YOU DOING TO IKKI'S DESK, HUH?! WHAT?!
DASH

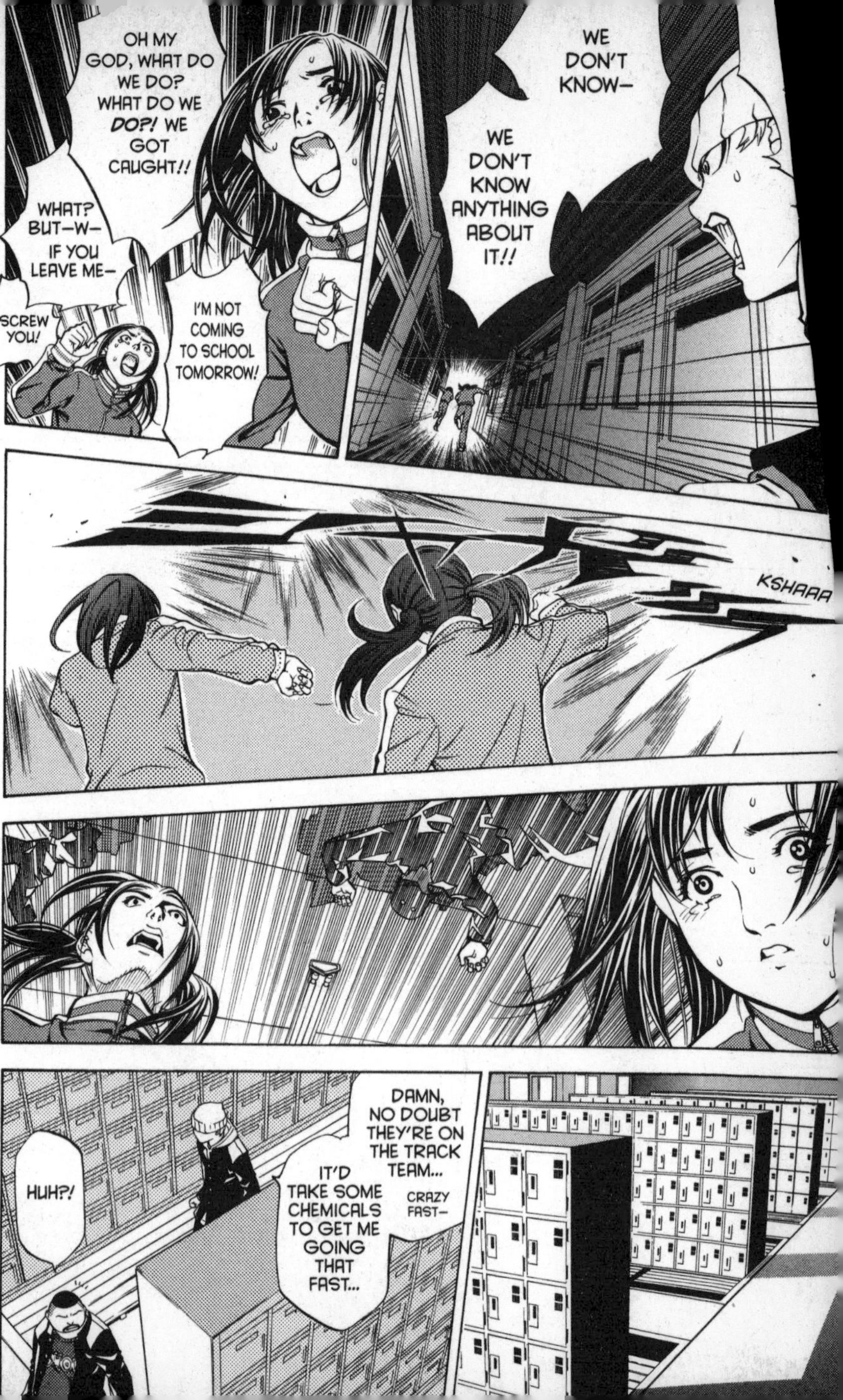
WE DON'T KNOW—
WE DON'T KNOW ANYTHING ABOUT IT!!
OH MY GOD, WHAT DO WE DO? WHAT DO WE DO?! WE GOT CAUGHT!!
WHAT? BUT—W— IF YOU LEAVE ME—
I'M NOT COMING TO SCHOOL TOMORROW!
SCREW YOU!
KSHAAA
DAMN, NO DOUBT THEY'RE ON THE TRACK TEAM...
CRAZY FAST—
IT'D TAKE SOME CHEMICALS TO GET ME GOING THAT FAST...
HUH?!

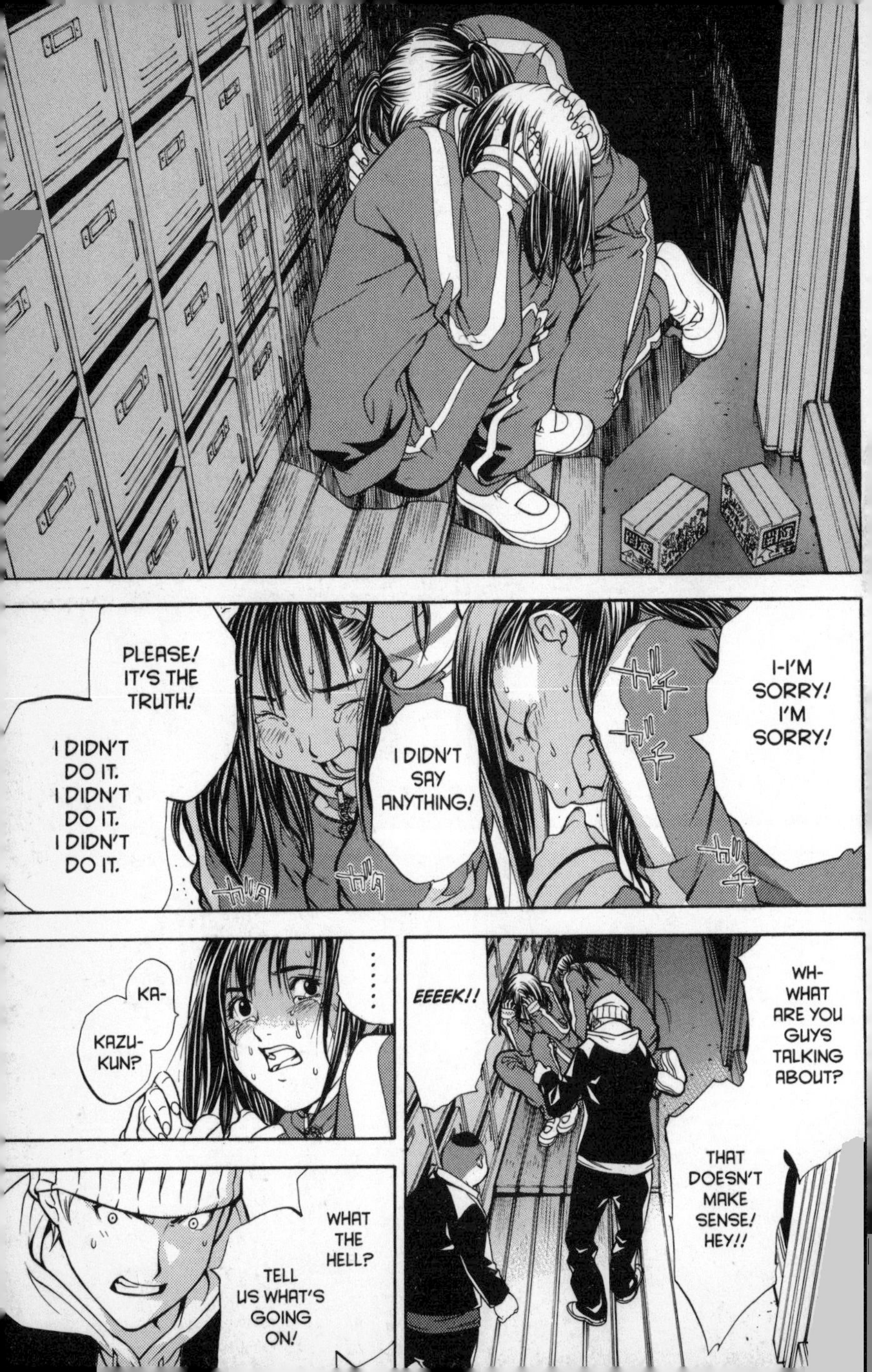
I-I'M SORRY! I'M SORRY!
I DIDN'T SAY ANYTHING!
PLEASE! IT'S THE TRUTH!
I DIDN'T DO IT. I DIDN'T DO IT. I DIDN'T DO IT.
WH- WHAT ARE YOU GUYS TALKING ABOUT?
EEEEK!!
THAT DOESN'T MAKE SENSE! HEY!!
......
KA- KAZU- KUN?
WHAT THE HELL?
TELL US WHAT'S GOING ON!

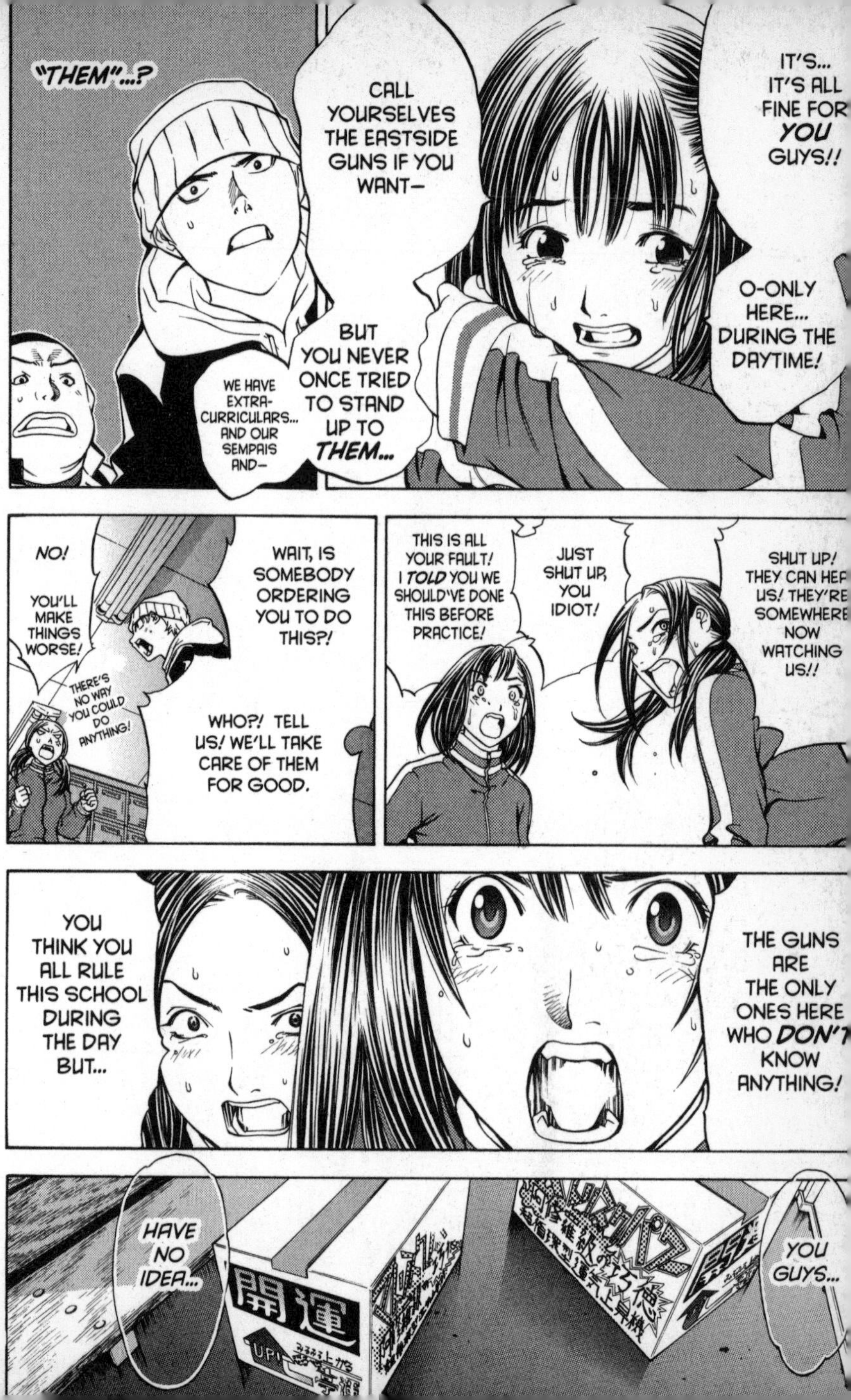
IT'S... IT'S ALL FINE FOR *YOU* GUYS!!
O-ONLY HERE... DURING THE DAYTIME!
CALL YOURSELVES THE EASTSIDE GUNS IF YOU WANT—
BUT YOU NEVER ONCE TRIED TO STAND UP TO *THEM*...
WE HAVE EXTRA-CURRICULARS... AND OUR SEMPAIS AND—
"THEM"...?
SHUT UP! THEY CAN HE US! THEY'RE SOMEWHERE NOW WATCHING US!!
JUST SHUT UP, YOU IDIOT!
THIS IS ALL YOUR FAULT! I *TOLD* YOU WE SHOULD'VE DONE THIS BEFORE PRACTICE!
WAIT, IS SOMEBODY ORDERING YOU TO DO THIS?!
WHO?! TELL US! WE'LL TAKE CARE OF THEM FOR GOOD.
NO!
YOU'LL MAKE THINGS WORSE!
THERE'S NO WAY YOU COULD DO ANYTHING!
THE GUNS ARE THE ONLY ONES HERE WHO *DON'T* KNOW ANYTHING!
YOU THINK YOU ALL RULE THIS SCHOOL DURING THE DAY BUT...
YOU GUYS...
HAVE NO IDEA...
開運
UP!

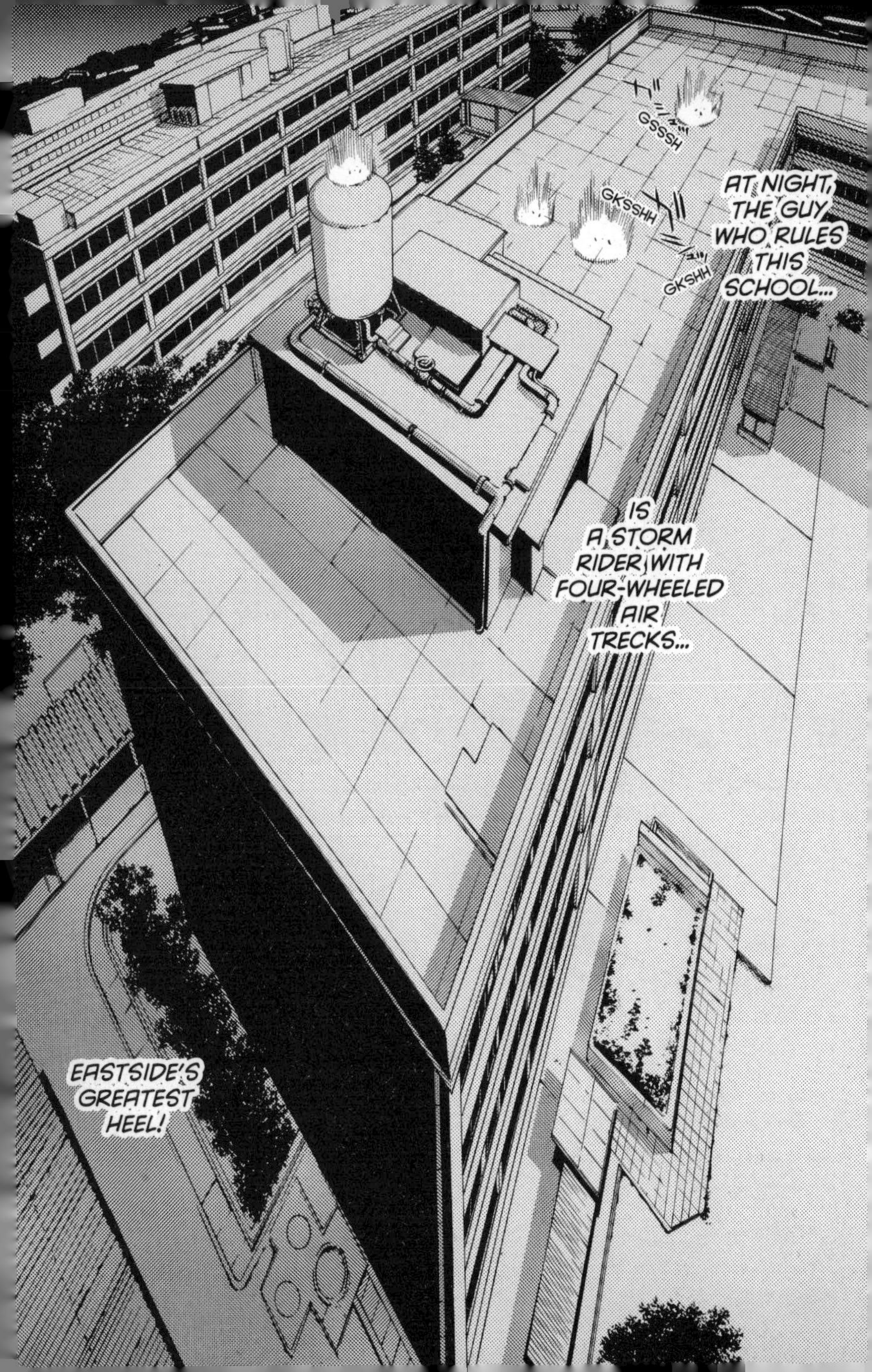
GSSSH
AT NIGHT, THE GUY WHO RULES THIS SCHOOL...
GKSSHH
GKSHH
IS A STORM RIDER WITH FOUR-WHEELED AIR TRECKS...
EASTSIDE'S GREATEST HEEL!

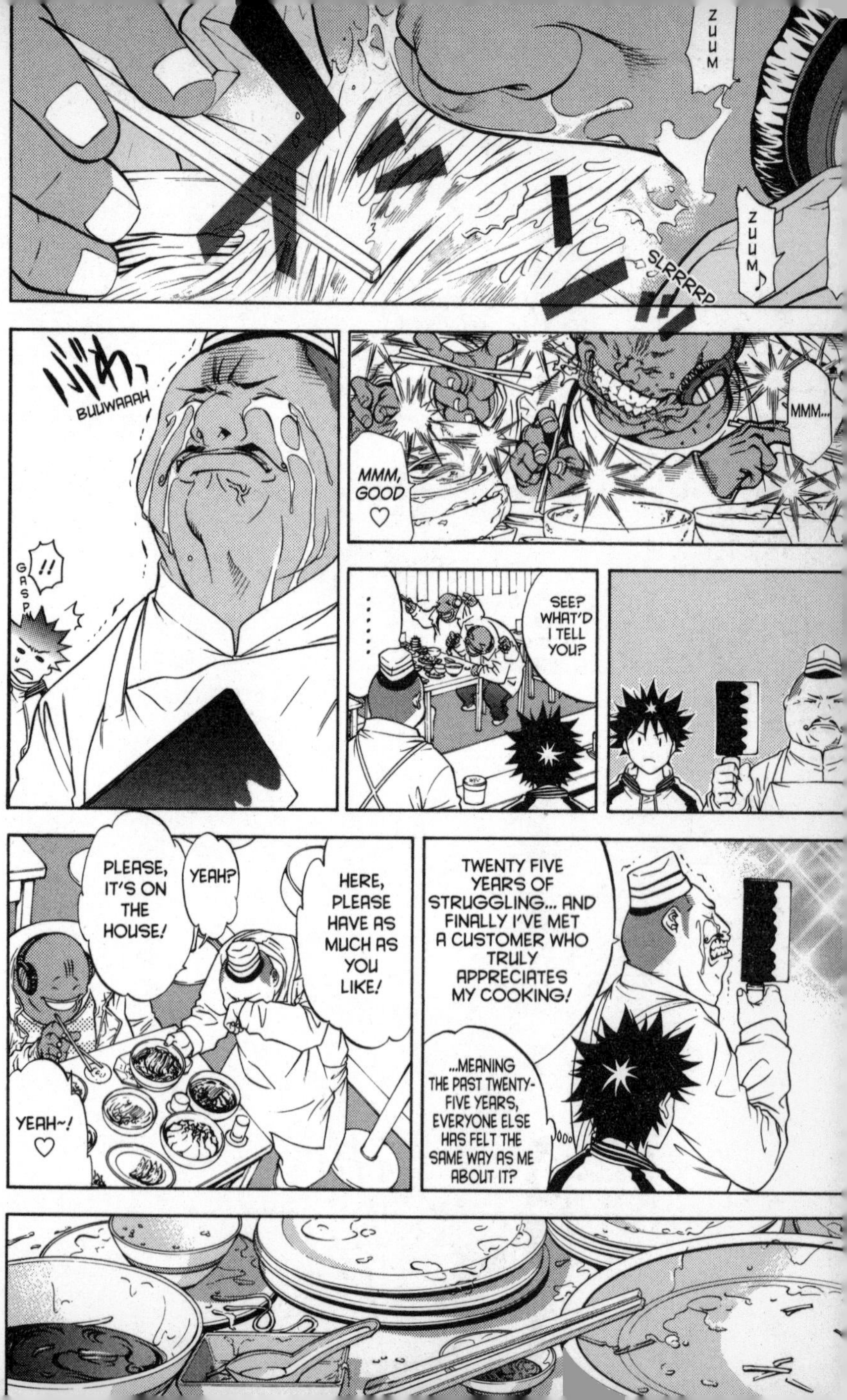
ZUUM
ZUUM♪
SLRRRRP
MMM...
MMM, GOOD ♡
ぶわっ
BUUWAAAH
GASP
!!
SEE? WHAT'D I TELL YOU?
......
TWENTY FIVE YEARS OF STRUGGLING... AND FINALLY I'VE MET A CUSTOMER WHO TRULY APPRECIATES MY COOKING!
...MEANING THE PAST TWENTY-FIVE YEARS, EVERYONE ELSE HAS FELT THE SAME WAY AS ME ABOUT IT?
HERE, PLEASE HAVE AS MUCH AS YOU LIKE!
YEAH?
PLEASE, IT'S ON THE HOUSE!
YEAH~! ♡

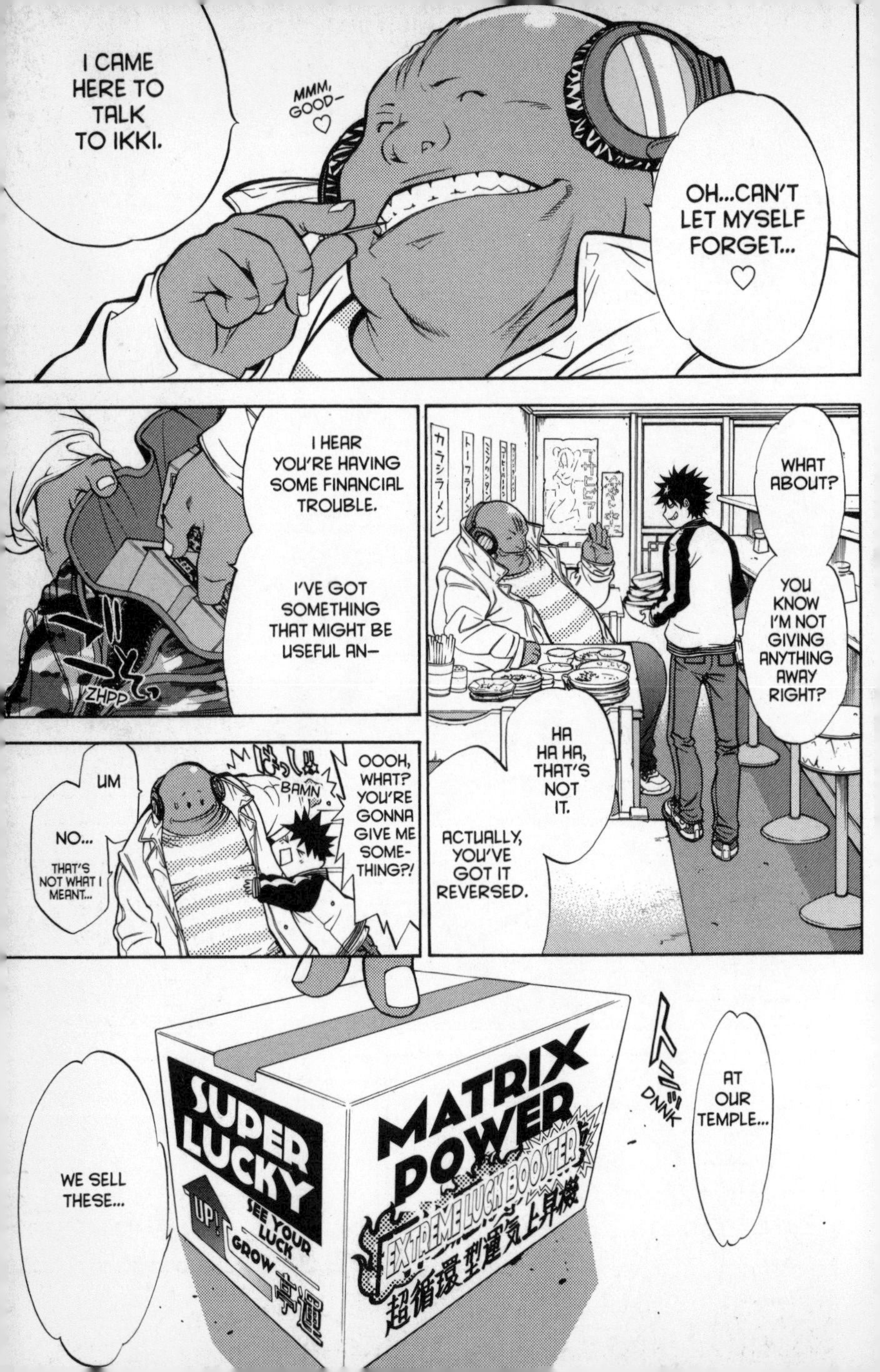
OH...CAN'T LET MYSELF FORGET... ♡
MMM, GOOD– ♡
I CAME HERE TO TALK TO IKKI.
カラシラーメン
トーフラーメン
WHAT ABOUT?
YOU KNOW I'M NOT GIVING ANYTHING AWAY RIGHT?
HA HA HA, THAT'S NOT IT.
ACTUALLY, YOU'VE GOT IT REVERSED.
I HEAR YOU'RE HAVING SOME FINANCIAL TROUBLE.
I'VE GOT SOMETHING THAT MIGHT BE USEFUL AN–
ZHPP
OOOH, WHAT? YOU'RE GONNA GIVE ME SOME-THING?!
BAMN
UM
NO...
THAT'S NOT WHAT I MEANT...
AT OUR TEMPLE...
DNNK
MATRIX POWER
EXTREME LUCK BOOSTER
超循環型運気上昇機
SUPER LUCKY
UP!
SEE YOUR LUCK GROW
WE SELL THESE...

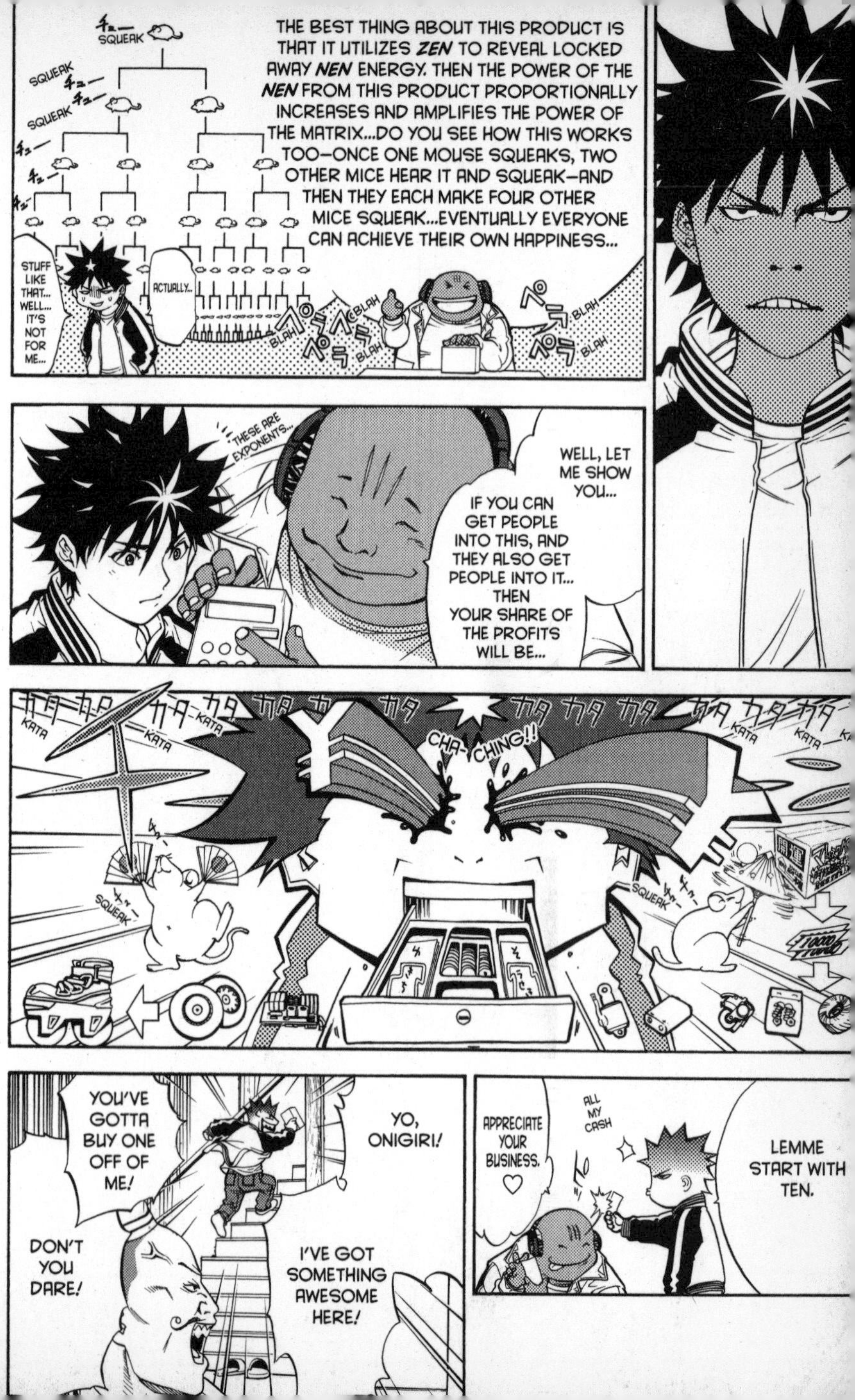
THE BEST THING ABOUT THIS PRODUCT IS THAT IT UTILIZES *ZEN* TO REVEAL LOCKED AWAY *NEN* ENERGY. THEN THE POWER OF THE *NEN* FROM THIS PRODUCT PROPORTIONALLY INCREASES AND AMPLIFIES THE POWER OF THE MATRIX...DO YOU SEE HOW THIS WORKS TOO—ONCE ONE MOUSE SQUEAKS, TWO OTHER MICE HEAR IT AND SQUEAK—AND THEN THEY EACH MAKE FOUR OTHER MICE SQUEAK...EVENTUALLY EVERYONE CAN ACHIEVE THEIR OWN HAPPINESS...
チュー
SQUEAK
SQUEAK
SQUEAK
BLAH
BLAH
BLAH
BLAH
BLAH
ACTUALLY...
STUFF LIKE THAT... WELL... IT'S NOT FOR ME...
WELL, LET ME SHOW YOU...
IF YOU CAN GET PEOPLE INTO THIS, AND THEY ALSO GET PEOPLE INTO IT... THEN YOUR SHARE OF THE PROFITS WILL BE...
THESE ARE EXPONENTS...
KATA
KATA
KATA
KATA
KATA
CHA-CHING!!
SQUEAK
SQUEAK
LEMME START WITH TEN.
ALL MY CASH
APPRECIATE YOUR BUSINESS. ♡
YO, ONIGIRI!
YOU'VE GOTTA BUY ONE OFF OF ME!
I'VE GOT SOMETHING AWESOME HERE!
DON'T YOU DARE!

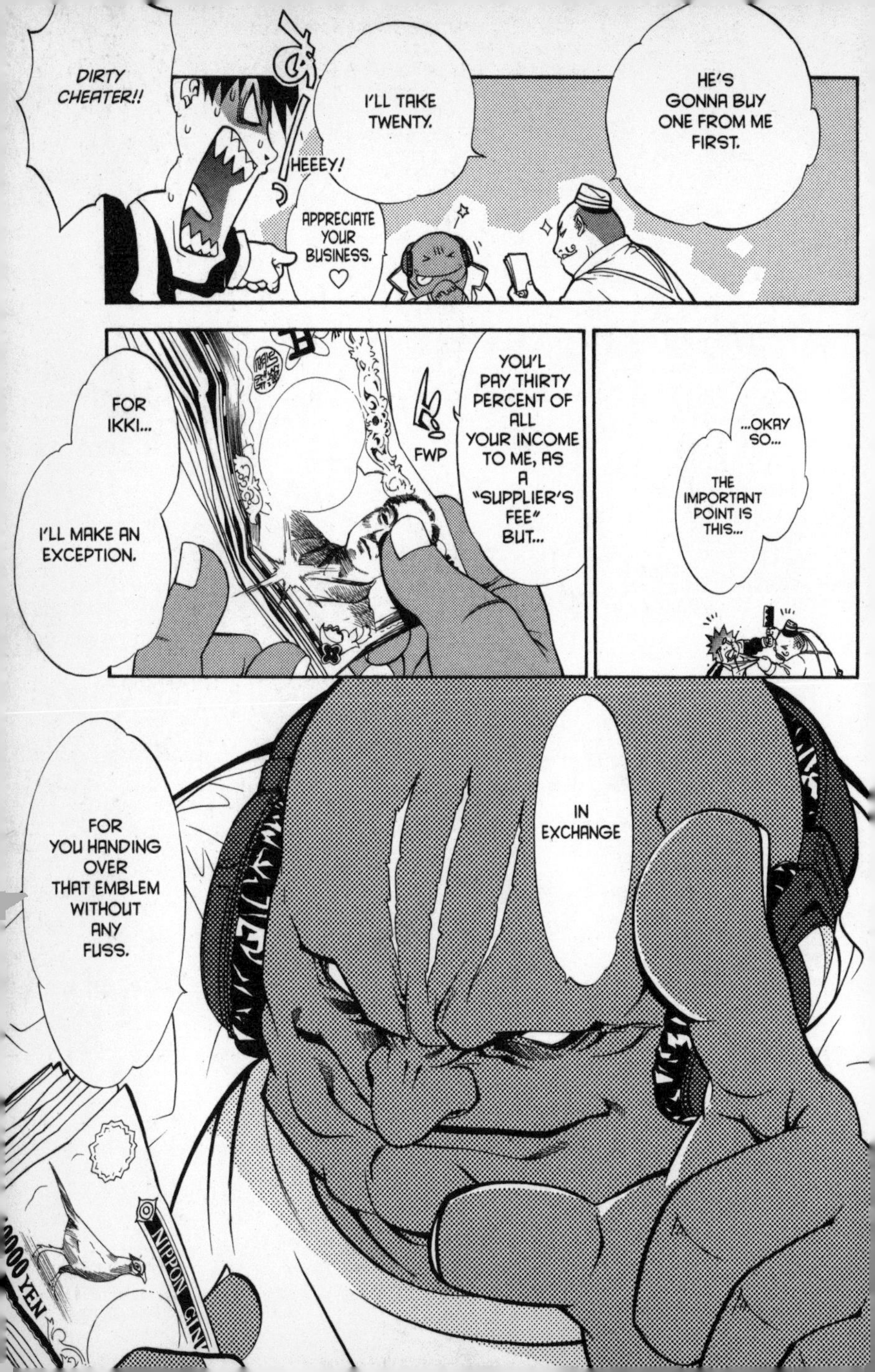
HE'S GONNA BUY ONE FROM ME FIRST.
I'LL TAKE TWENTY.
APPRECIATE YOUR BUSINESS. ♡
HEEEY!
DIRTY CHEATER!!
...OKAY SO...
THE IMPORTANT POINT IS THIS...
YOU'L PAY THIRTY PERCENT OF ALL YOUR INCOME TO ME, AS A "SUPPLIER'S FEE" BUT...
FWP
FOR IKKI...
I'LL MAKE AN EXCEPTION.
IN EXCHANGE
FOR YOU HANDING OVER THAT EMBLEM WITHOUT ANY FUSS.

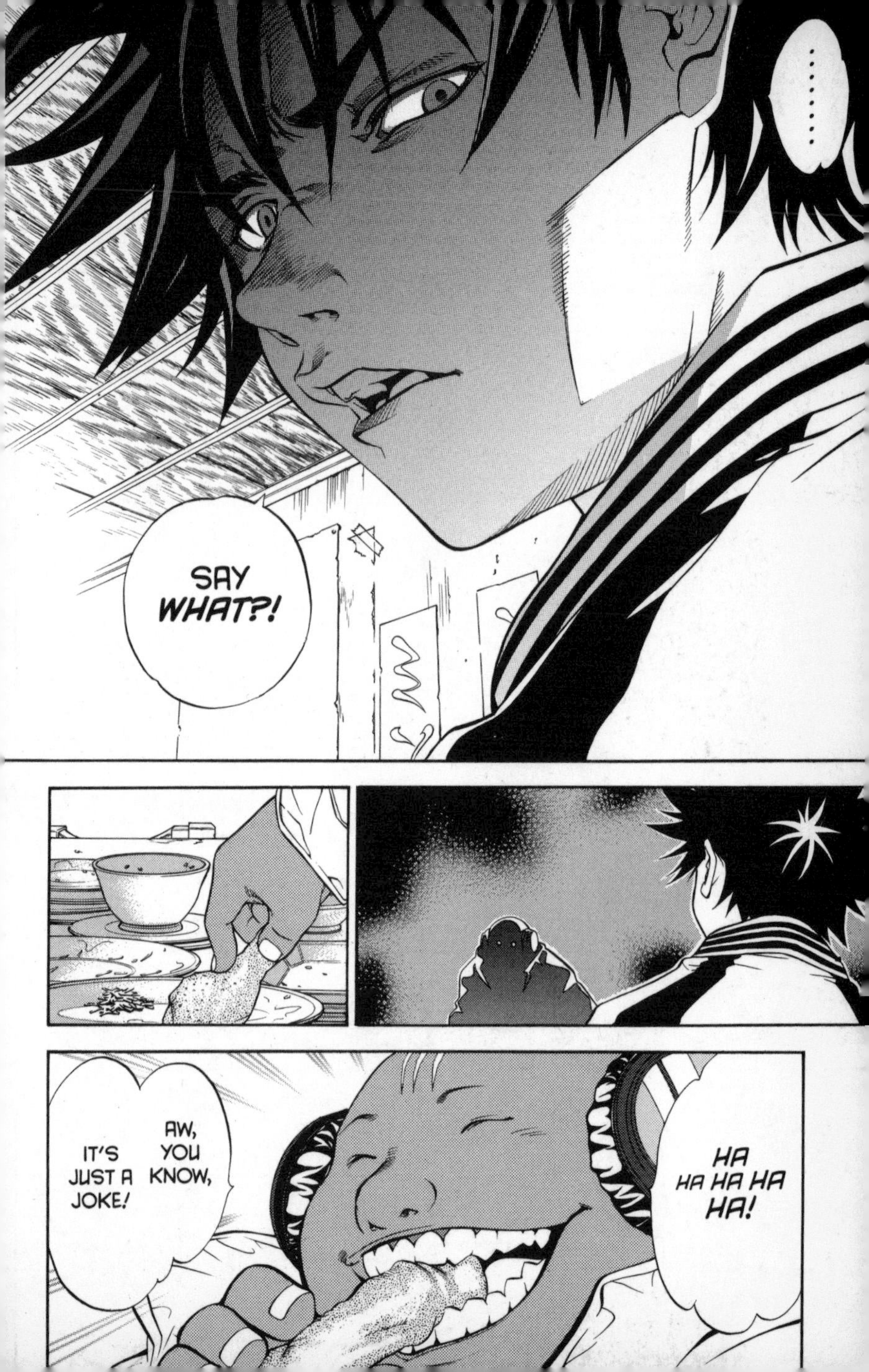
......
SAY WHAT?!
HA HA HA HA HA!
AW, YOU KNOW,
IT'S JUST A JOKE!

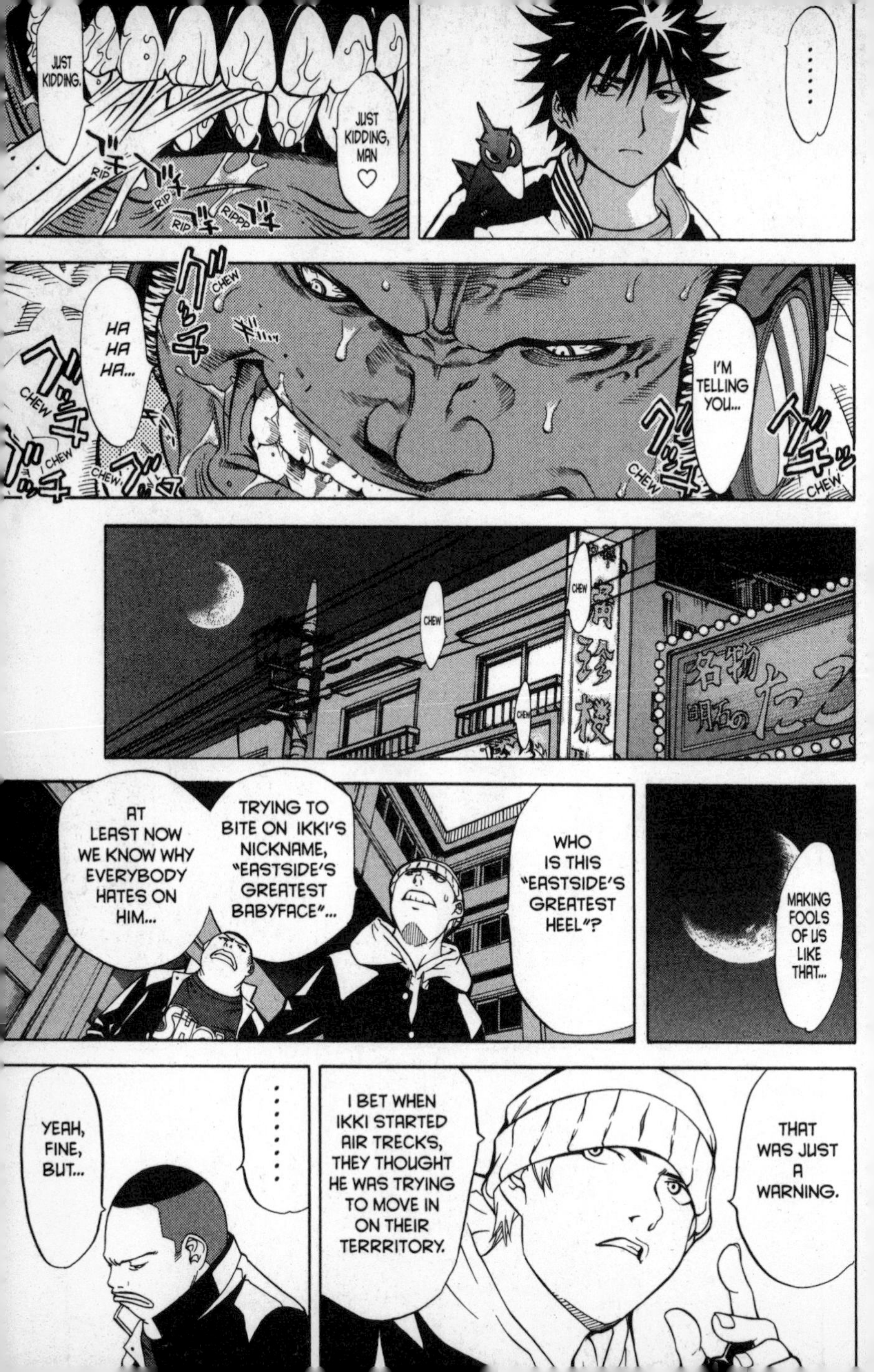
……
JUST KIDDING, MAN ♡
JUST KIDDING.
RIP
RIP
RIPPP
RIP
I'M TELLING YOU...
CHEW
CHEW
CHEW
HA HA HA...
CHEW
CHEW
CHEW
CHEW
CHEW
CHEW
MAKING FOOLS OF US LIKE THAT...
WHO IS THIS "EASTSIDE'S GREATEST HEEL"?
TRYING TO BITE ON IKKI'S NICKNAME, "EASTSIDE'S GREATEST BABYFACE"...
AT LEAST NOW WE KNOW WHY EVERYBODY HATES ON HIM...
THAT WAS JUST A WARNING.
I BET WHEN IKKI STARTED AIR TRECKS, THEY THOUGHT HE WAS TRYING TO MOVE IN ON THEIR TERRITORY.
……
YEAH, FINE, BUT...

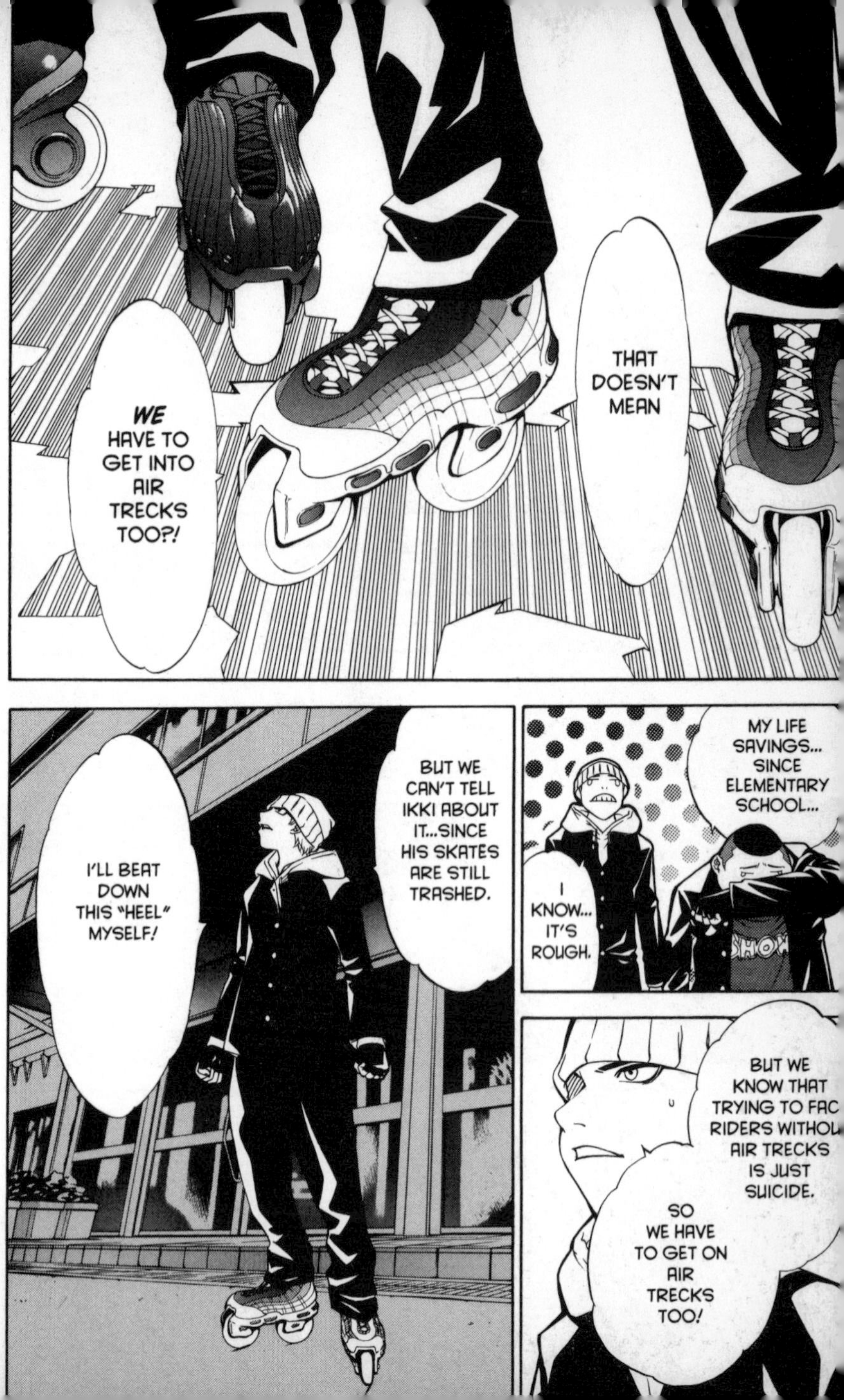
THAT DOESN'T MEAN
WE HAVE TO GET INTO AIR TRECKS TOO?!
MY LIFE SAVINGS... SINCE ELEMENTARY SCHOOL...
I KNOW... IT'S ROUGH.
BUT WE KNOW THAT TRYING TO FAC RIDERS WITHOU AIR TRECKS IS JUST SUICIDE.
SO WE HAVE TO GET ON AIR TRECKS TOO!
BUT WE CAN'T TELL IKKI ABOUT IT...SINCE HIS SKATES ARE STILL TRASHED.
I'LL BEAT DOWN THIS "HEEL" MYSELF!

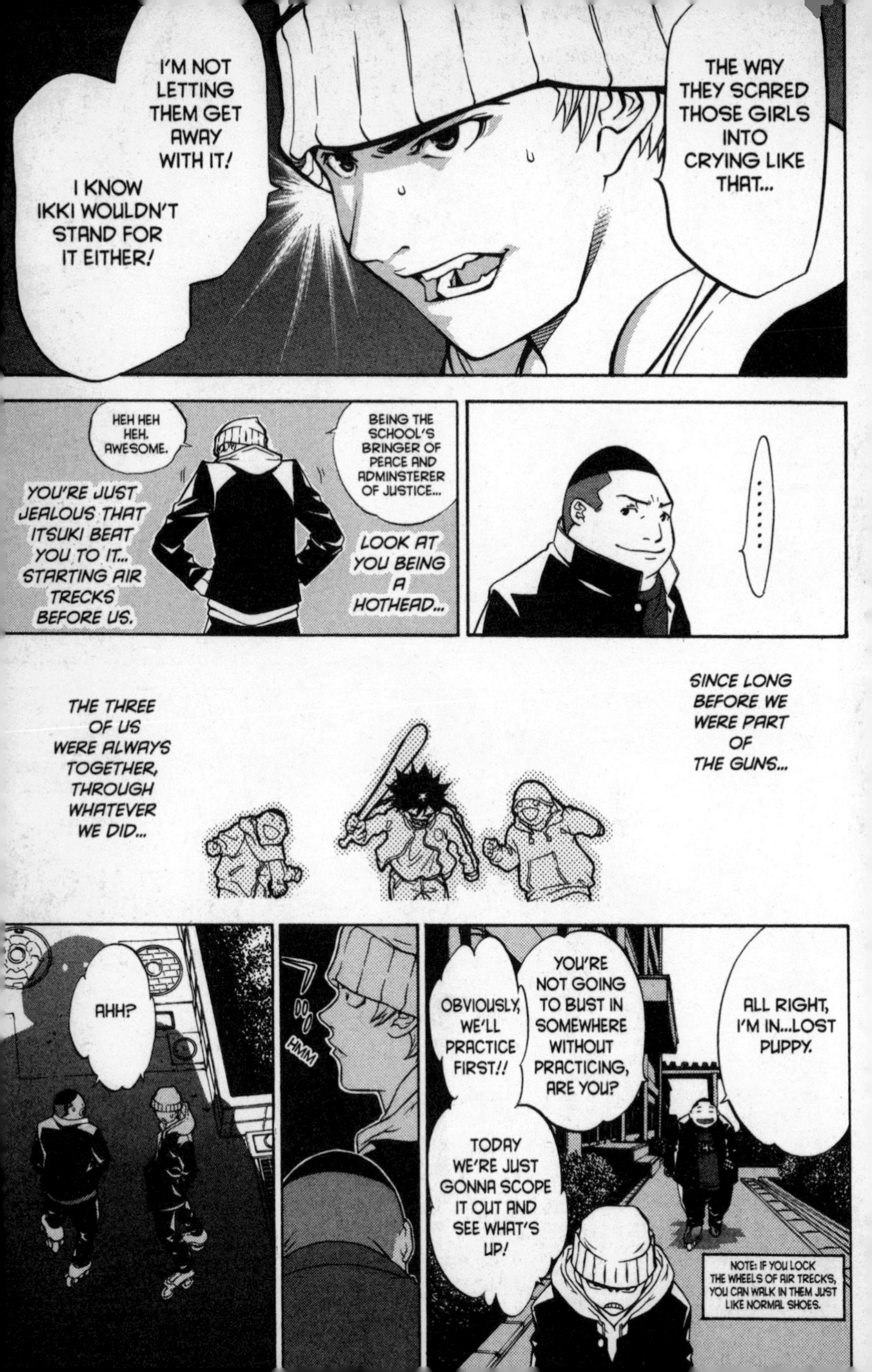
THE WAY THEY SCARED THOSE GIRLS INTO CRYING LIKE THAT...
I'M NOT LETTING THEM GET AWAY WITH IT!
I KNOW IKKI WOULDN'T STAND FOR IT EITHER!
......
BEING THE SCHOOL'S BRINGER OF PEACE AND ADMINSTERER OF JUSTICE...
LOOK AT YOU BEING A HOTHEAD...
HEH HEH HEH. AWESOME.
YOU'RE JUST JEALOUS THAT ITSUKI BEAT YOU TO IT... STARTING AIR TRECKS BEFORE US.
SINCE LONG BEFORE WE WERE PART OF THE GUNS...
THE THREE OF US WERE ALWAYS TOGETHER, THROUGH WHATEVER WE DID...
ALL RIGHT, I'M IN...LOST PUPPY.
YOU'RE NOT GOING TO BUST IN SOMEWHERE WITHOUT PRACTICING, ARE YOU?
OBVIOUSLY, WE'LL PRACTICE FIRST!!
TODAY WE'RE JUST GONNA SCOPE IT OUT AND SEE WHAT'S UP!
NOTE: IF YOU LOCK THE WHEELS OF AIR TRECKS, YOU CAN WALK IN THEM JUST LIKE NORMAL SHOES.
HMM
AHH?

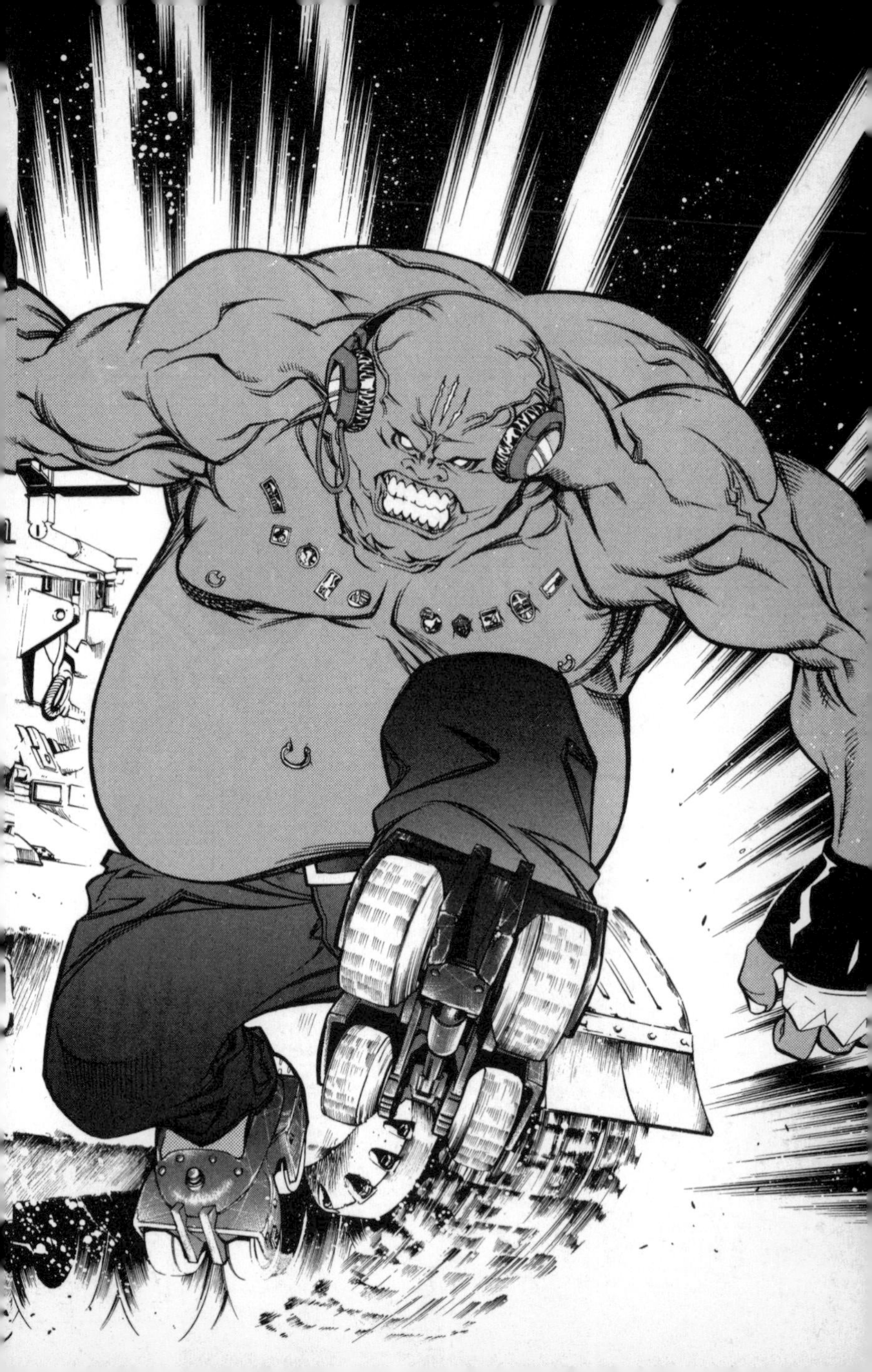

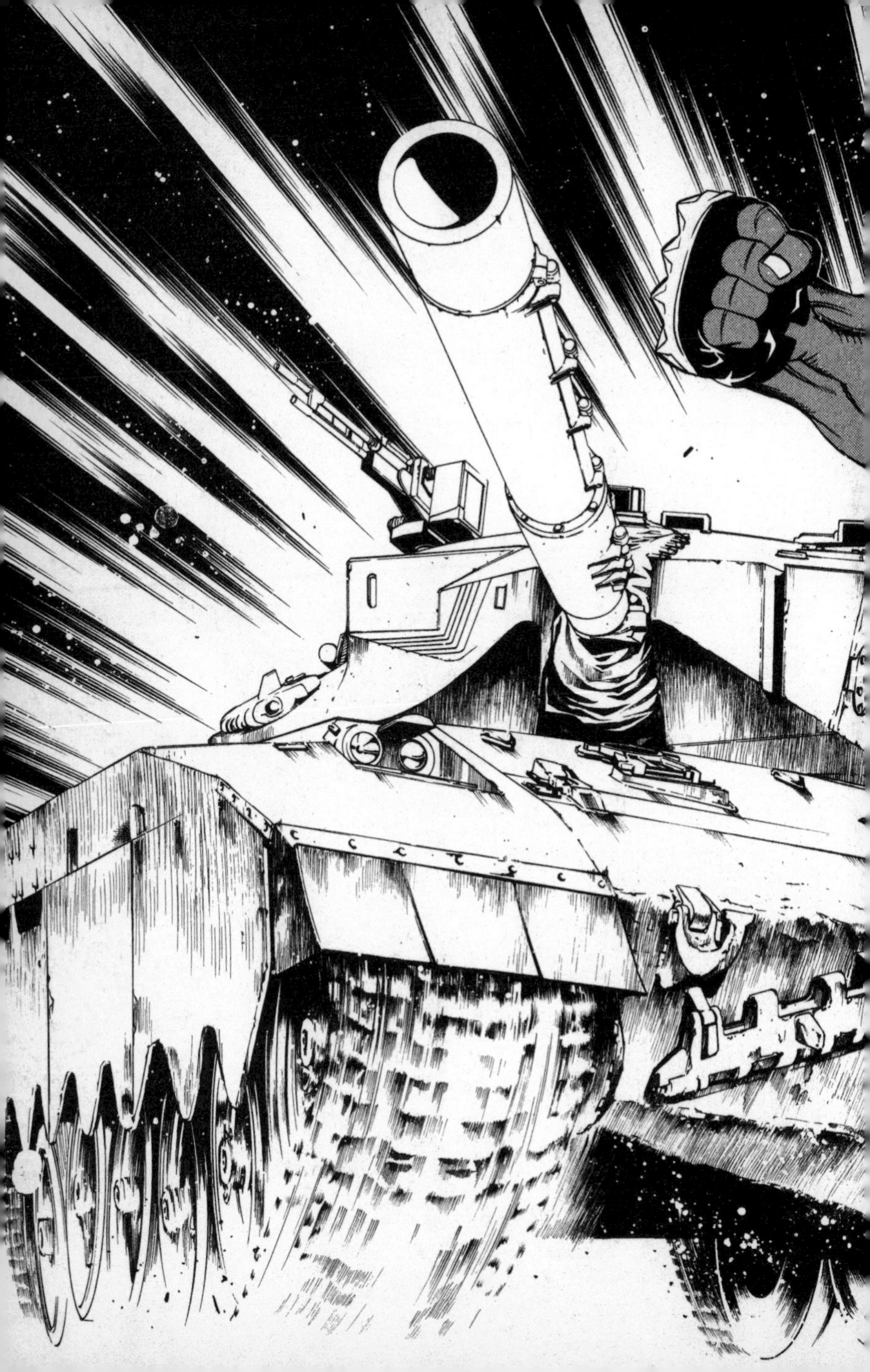

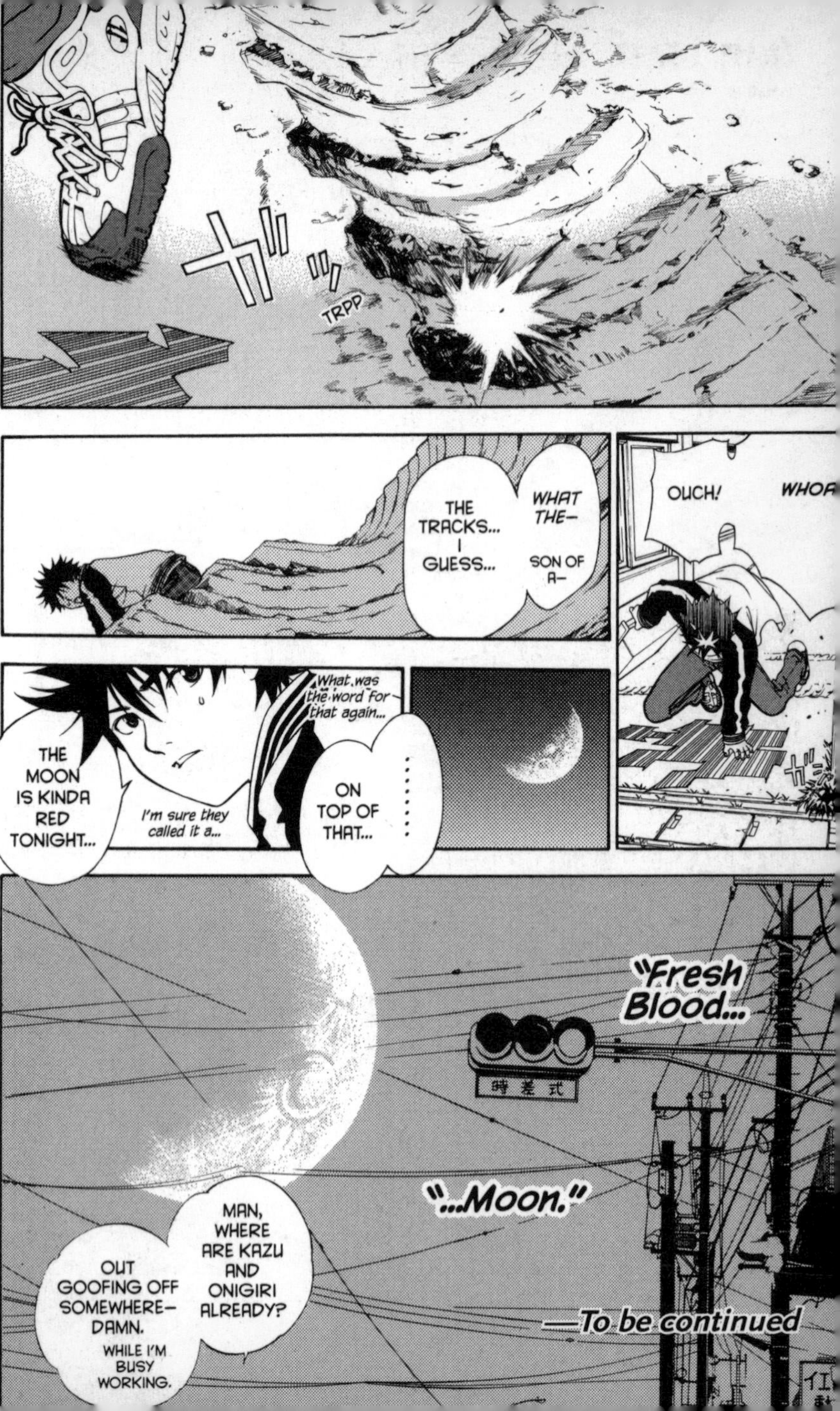
TRPP
WHOA
OUCH!
WHAT THE— SON OF A—
THE TRACKS... I GUESS...
......
ON TOP OF THAT...
What was the word for that again...
THE MOON IS KINDA RED TONIGHT...
I'm sure they called it a...
"Fresh Blood...
"...Moon."
時差式
MAN, WHERE ARE KAZU AND ONIGIRI ALREADY?
OUT GOOFING OFF SOMEWHERE— DAMN. WHILE I'M BUSY WORKING.
—To be continued

ANALYSIS: THESE ARE AIR TRECKS, CHECK IT!

What are Air Trecks?

Generally speaking, at the basic level all Air Trecks are constructed with three major components: Wheel Motor, Air (or Hydrolic) Cushion System, Power Injection System (Like Electrical injectors for power control).

The Braking Systems vary by brand, make, and model but almost all of them are equipped with a power lock switch on the outer sole of the skate (this allows them to override the skates' acceleration so they perform as normal). Only a few models use a deceleration system to come to a complete stop. Most skaters use a technique called a Spin-Turn Stop instead anyway.

Speed skates always have more wheels than normal inline skates, but with Air Trecks that is not always the case. Air Trecks are customizable and various combinations of parts as well as balance can shift their speed tremendously regardless of the number of wheels they have.

What gives the Air Trecks the ability to "fly" is their Cushion System. However the maker-issued specs say that most skates are able to withstand impact from no more than 5-6 meters. In this book, the skaters perform lots of daring jumps which show the true potential of the skates, but if one of them were to not land properly or miss their landing altogether, they would be in truly grave danger.These uses for the skates were never detailed in the manuals, but were created by the thrill seekers who call themselves "Storm Riders."

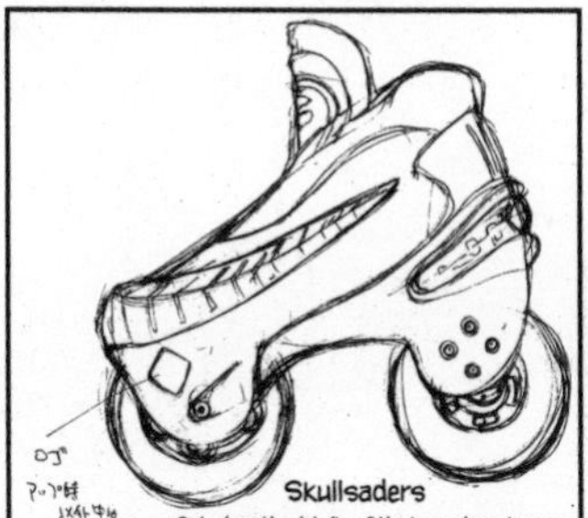
Skullsaders

Only draw the details of the logo when close up. The rest of the time draw just the basic shape.

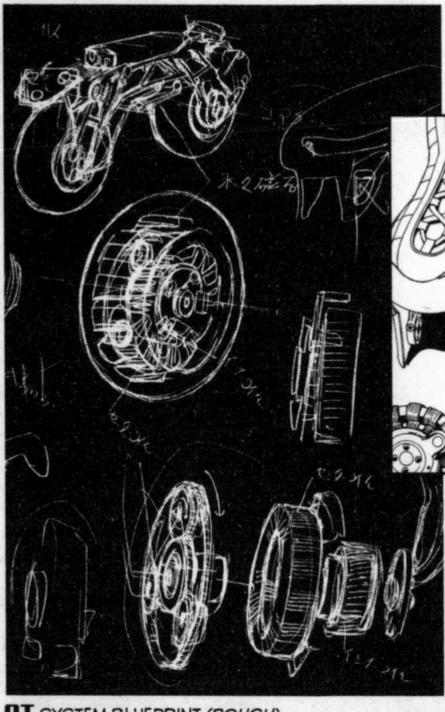
AT SYSTEM BLUEPRINT *(ROUGH)*

These concepts were drawn early with intentions of revising the minor details later.

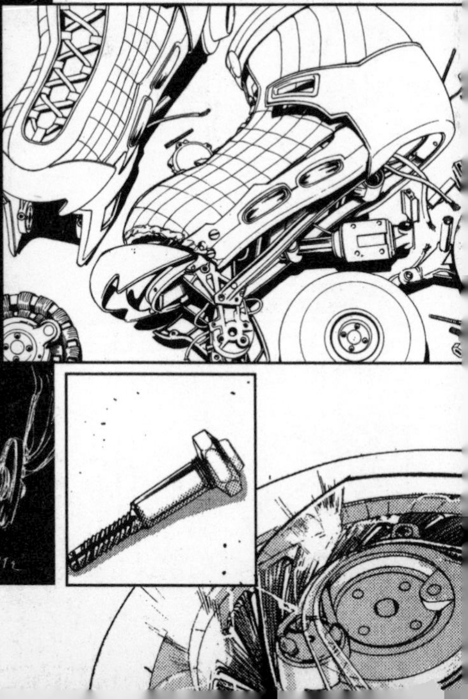

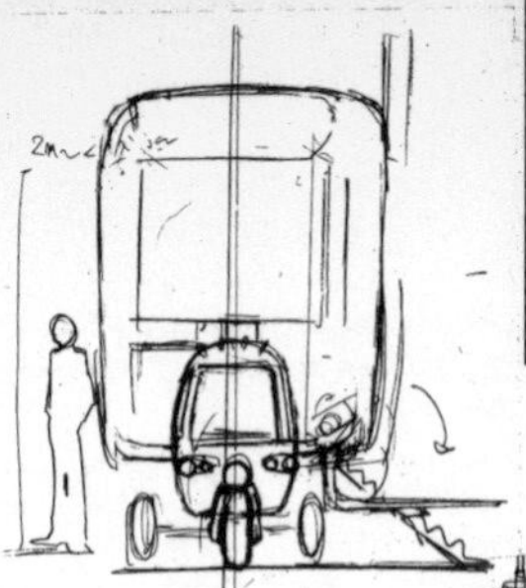

SHOP: In this volume Mikan mentions that normal Air Treck parts can be bought at the local sporting goods store. But when you really want to customize your skates, countless independent merchants (such as the Glam Slum) are available to give you what you're looking for. When a rider says they're headed to the "Shop," that's the kind of place they're talking about.

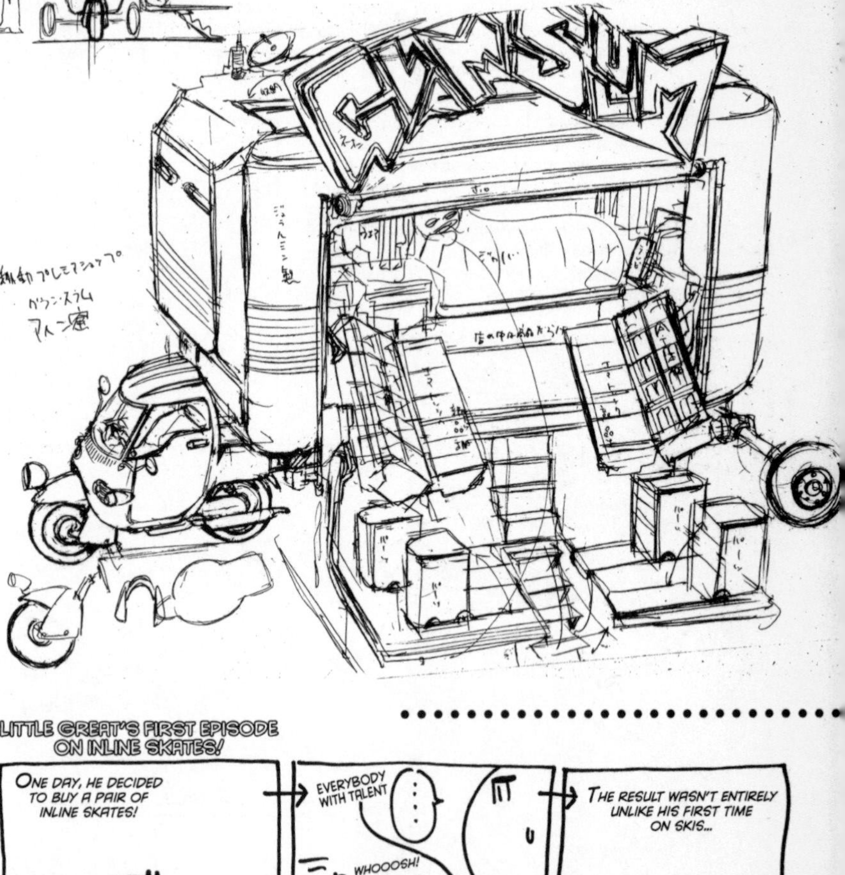

LITTLE GREAT'S FIRST EPISODE ON INLINE SKATES!

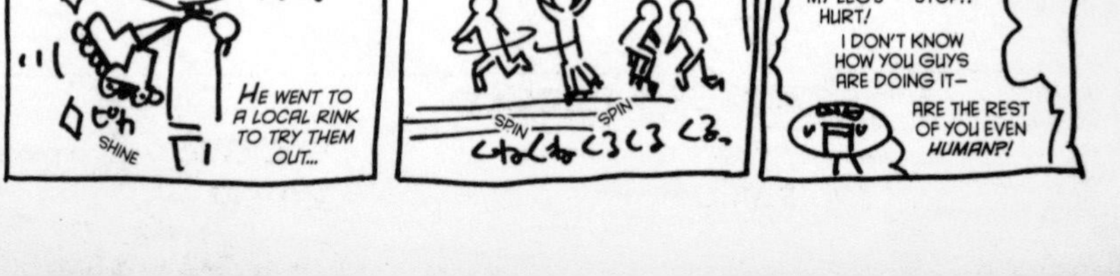
ONE DAY, HE DECIDED TO BUY A PAIR OF INLINE SKATES!
ピカ
SHINE
ピカ
SHINE
HE WENT TO A LOCAL RINK TO TRY THEM OUT...
EVERYBODY WITH TALENT
WHOOOSH!
SPIN
SPIN
THE RESULT WASN'T ENTIRELY UNLIKE HIS FIRST TIME ON SKIS...
AAACK, MY LEGS HURT!
I CAN'T STOP!!
I DON'T KNOW HOW YOU GUYS ARE DOING IT—
ARE THE REST OF YOU EVEN HUMAN?!

staff

竹井　心 *Takei Kokoro*

唐沢千晶 *Karasawa Chiaki*

辰己正博 *Tatsumi Masahiro*

小林俊一 *Kobayashi Shunichi*

田仕雅淑 *Tashi Masayoshi*

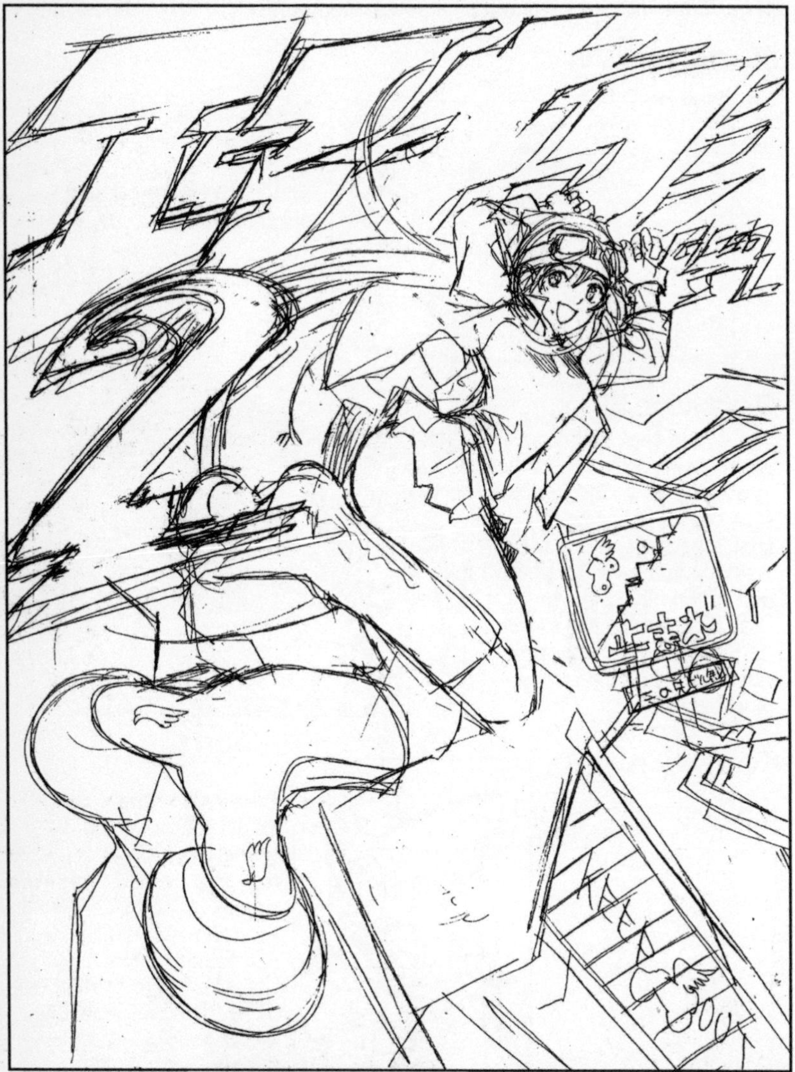

special thanks

石神由紀子 *Ishigami Yukiko*

pacific

屋代川隆史 *Yashirogawa Takashi*

青木　優 *Aoki Yu*

Translation Notes

Japanese is a tricky language for most Westerners, and translation is often more art than science. For your edification and reading pleasure, here are notes on some of the places where we could have gone in a different direction in our translation of the work, or where a Japanese cultural reference is used.

Mochi, page 25

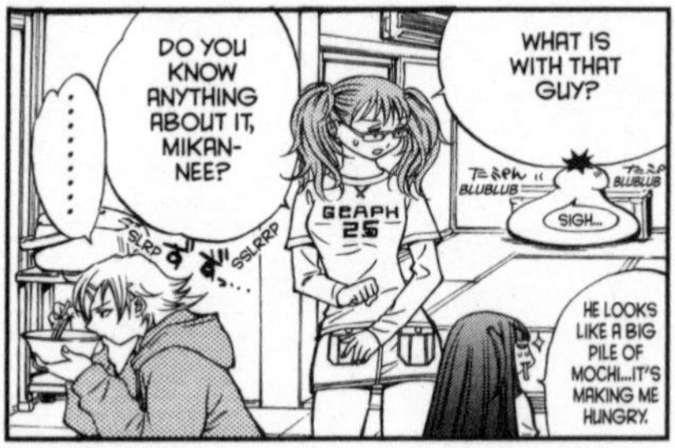
WHAT IS WITH THAT GUY?
SIGH...
BLUBLUB
BLUBLUB
DO YOU KNOW ANYTHING ABOUT IT, MIKAN-NEE?
....
SSLRRP
SLRP
HE LOOKS LIKE A BIG PILE OF MOCHI...IT'S MAKING ME HUNGRY.

Ume is talking about a kind of Japanese sweet. It's made by pounding rice into a putty, and in this scene, Itsuki has about the same consistency.

Gold, page 27

The sound that rings out when Mikan delivers her kick is a solid "KNNGK" written with the kanji for "gold"—that's because a Japanese boy doesn't refer to them as his "family jewels"... that kick was to the *kintama* or "golden orbs"—though obviously the pain is beyond language.

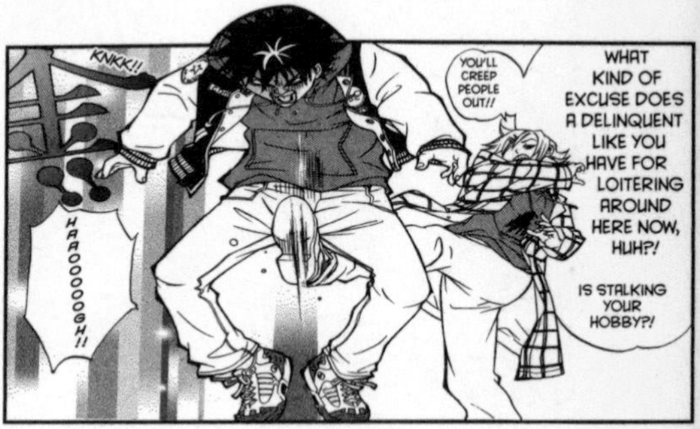
WHAT KIND OF EXCUSE DOES A DELINQUENT LIKE YOU HAVE FOR LOITERING AROUND HERE NOW, HUH?!
IS STALKING YOUR HOBBY?!
YOU'LL CREEP PEOPLE OUT!!
KNKK!!
HAAOOOOOOGH!!

Konjyou, page 34

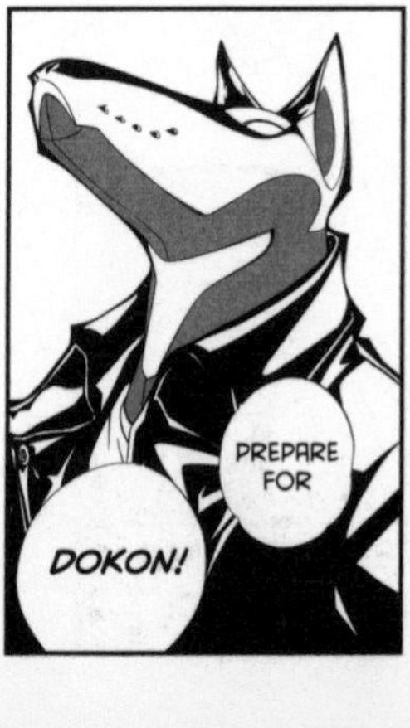
PREPARE FOR
DOKON!

"*Konjyou* Punch" describes an attack going up against something rough or painful—Inuyama calls his mutually violent attack *DOKON,* although written with the kanji for "soul"... Not surprisingly, the artist also draws the sound of head-butting someone while wearing a big helmet mask as "DO-KON".

Omamori, page 39

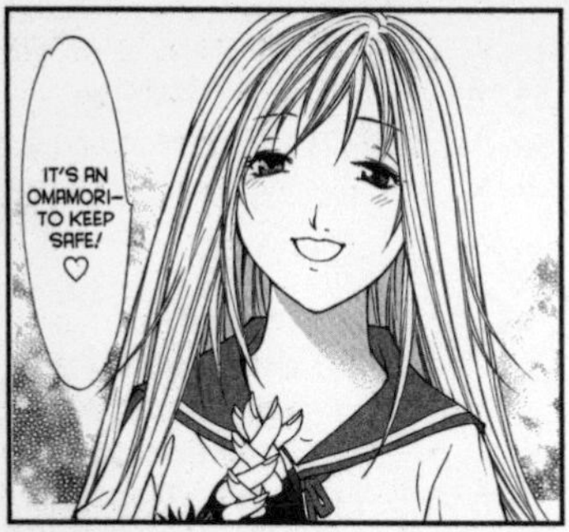
IT'S AN OMAMORI— TO KEEP SAFE! ♡

Simca offers Itsuki an *omamori*. . . a kind of good luck charm, which is meant to protect the holder. But as she bolts later, Itsuki realizes that the roles have reversed and he is being used to protect it.

Sobatto, page 50

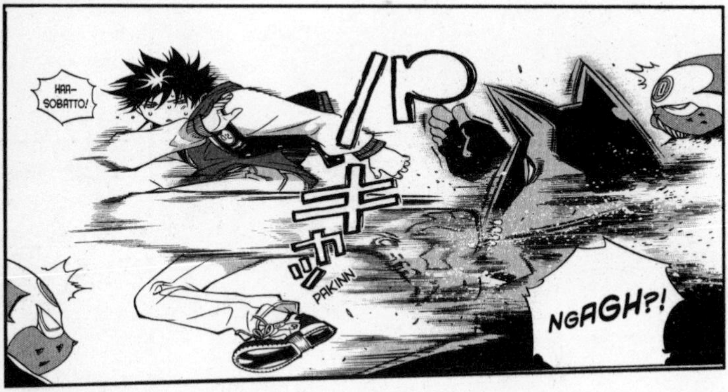
HAA- SOBATTO!
PAKINN
NGAGH?!

Itsuki attacks here with a pro-wrestling move called a *sobatto*. . . He probably says it out loud to indicate that, unlike last time, this move is deliberate!

Bowlingual, page 51

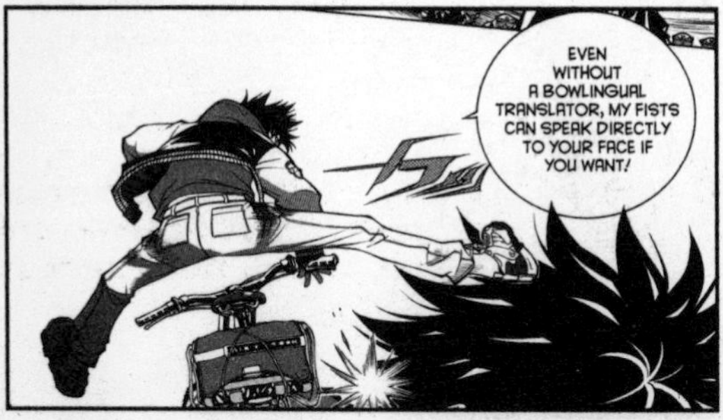
EVEN WITHOUT A BOWLINGUAL TRANSLATOR, MY FISTS CAN SPEAK DIRECTLY TO YOUR FACE IF YOU WANT!

The Bowlingual is a popular toy in Japan— a device that attaches to a dog's collar, around the throat, and "translates" noises the dog makes into human words.

OTOKO!, page 62

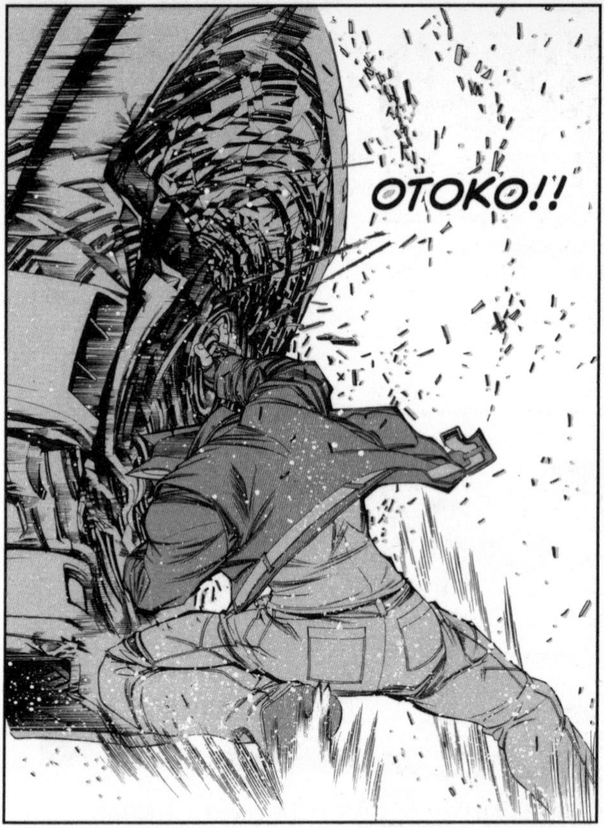
OTOKO!!

Inuyama demonstrates his manliness by knocking a speeding truck off course, shouting *OTOKO!* It's written with the Chinese kanji for MAN, as opposed to the Japanese kanji, meant to show that he is truly a man among men.

TTD PLATOON, page 101

The move Mikan and Rika pull on Itsuki is called a "TTD PLATOON," which is a wrestling move just like the one demonstrated in the diagram.

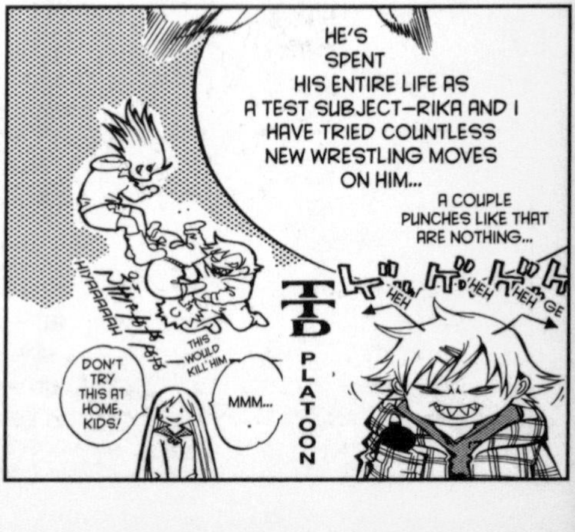
HE'S SPENT HIS ENTIRE LIFE AS A TEST SUBJECT—RIKA AND I HAVE TRIED COUNTLESS NEW WRESTLING MOVES ON HIM...
A COUPLE PUNCHES LIKE THAT ARE NOTHING...
HEH HEH HEH GE
TTD PLATOON
MMM...
THIS WOULD KILL HIM
HIYAAAAAAH
DON'T TRY THIS AT HOME, KIDS!

Onee-tama, page 135

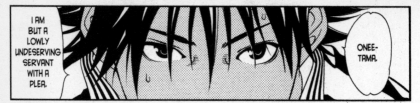

ONEE-TAMA.
I AM BUT A LOWLY UNDESERVING SERVANT WITH A PLEA.

Itsuki calls Mikan *Onee-tama,* which is similar in meaning to *Onee-sama* (a respectful "big sister") but it sounds uncharacteristically adorable coming from him.

Pachinko, page 138

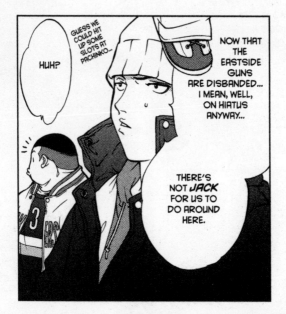

NOW THAT THE EASTSIDE GUNS ARE DISBANDED... I MEAN, WELL, ON HIATUS ANYWAY...
GUESS WE COULD HIT UP SOME SLOTS AT PACHINKO...
HUH?
THERE'S NOT JACK FOR US TO DO AROUND HERE.

Kazu and Onigiri are bored now that their gang is busted up, but Kazu suggests they hit "Pachinko"—that's a very VERY common form of gambling using a machine that's similar to a slot machine, except with less player control. They come in an endless assortment of themes, and the big Pachinko Parlors in certain towns are famous hangouts for gang members and Yakuza.

10 yen, page 139

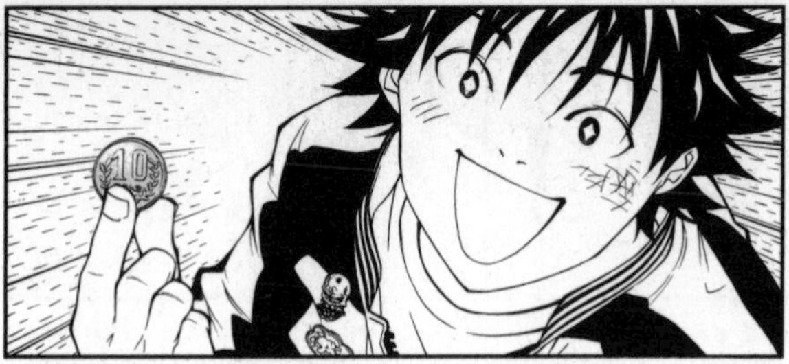

Itsuki finally gets a ten yen coin. That's worth about $0.08. He better collect a lot of them!

Khorosho, page 172

Itsuki calls Mihotoke his *khorosho* which comes from Russian. It literally means "good" and in this case indicates that he relates to his "brother man."

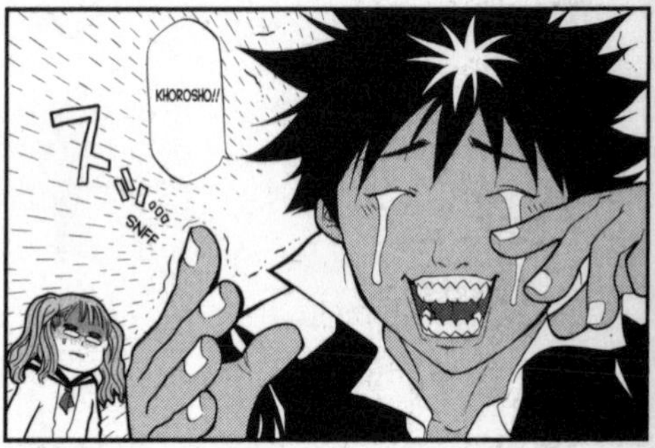
KHOROSHO!!
SNFF

Detective Academy "O," page 177

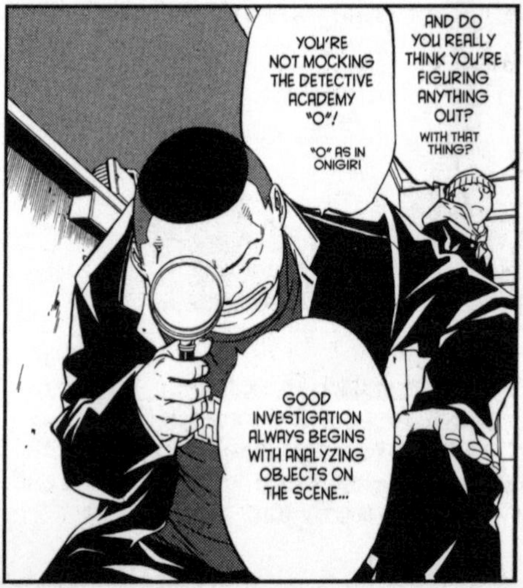
AND DO YOU REALLY THINK YOU'RE FIGURING ANYTHING OUT?
WITH THAT THING?
YOU'RE NOT MOCKING THE DETECTIVE ACADEMY "O"!
"O" AS IN ONIGIRI
GOOD INVESTIGATION ALWAYS BEGINS WITH ANALYZING OBJECTS ON THE SCENE...

Onigiri refers to himself as Detective Academy "O"—a reference to Detective Academy "Q," the popular teenage mystery comic and TV show.

Heel, page 185

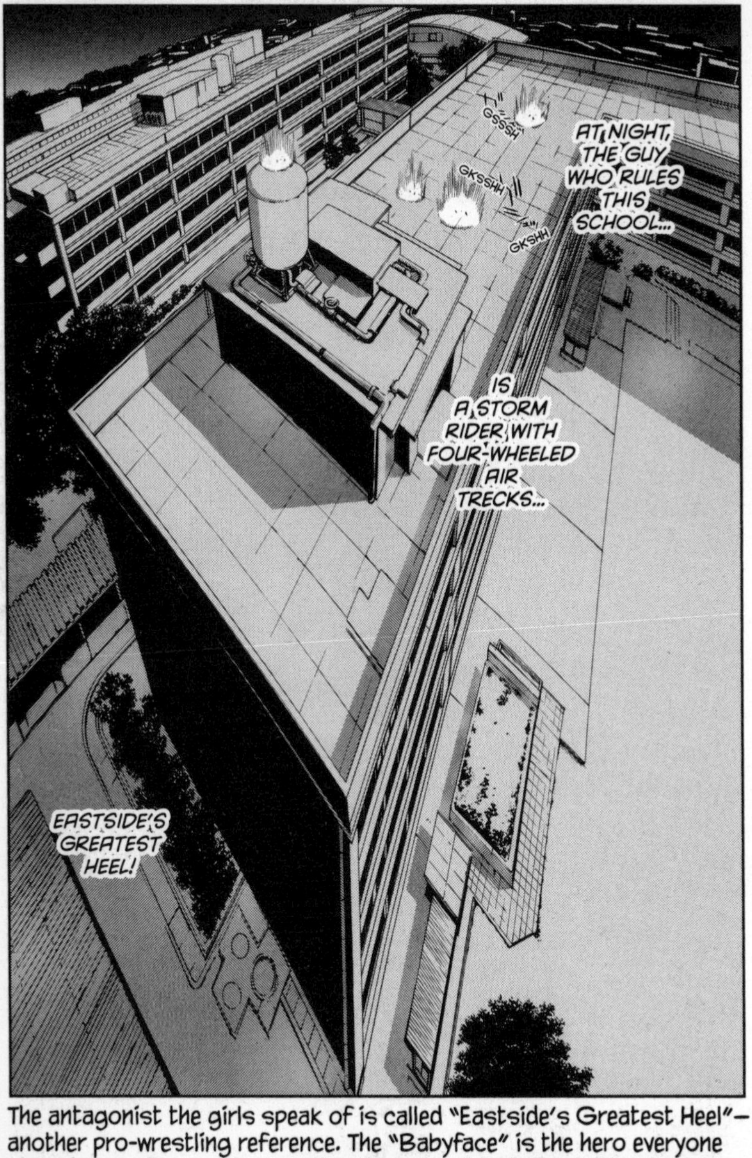
AT NIGHT, THE GUY WHO RULES THIS SCHOOL...
GSSSH
GKSSHH
GKSHH
IS A STORM RIDER WITH FOUR-WHEELED AIR TRECKS...
EASTSIDE'S GREATEST HEEL!

The antagonist the girls speak of is called "Eastside's Greatest Heel"—another pro-wrestling reference. The "Babyface" is the hero everyone should cheer for, and in wrestling the opposite of that is the "heel." It's written with the kanji meaning "King of the Night."

Air Gear volume 3 is available now!
Here is a preview from that volume in Japanese.

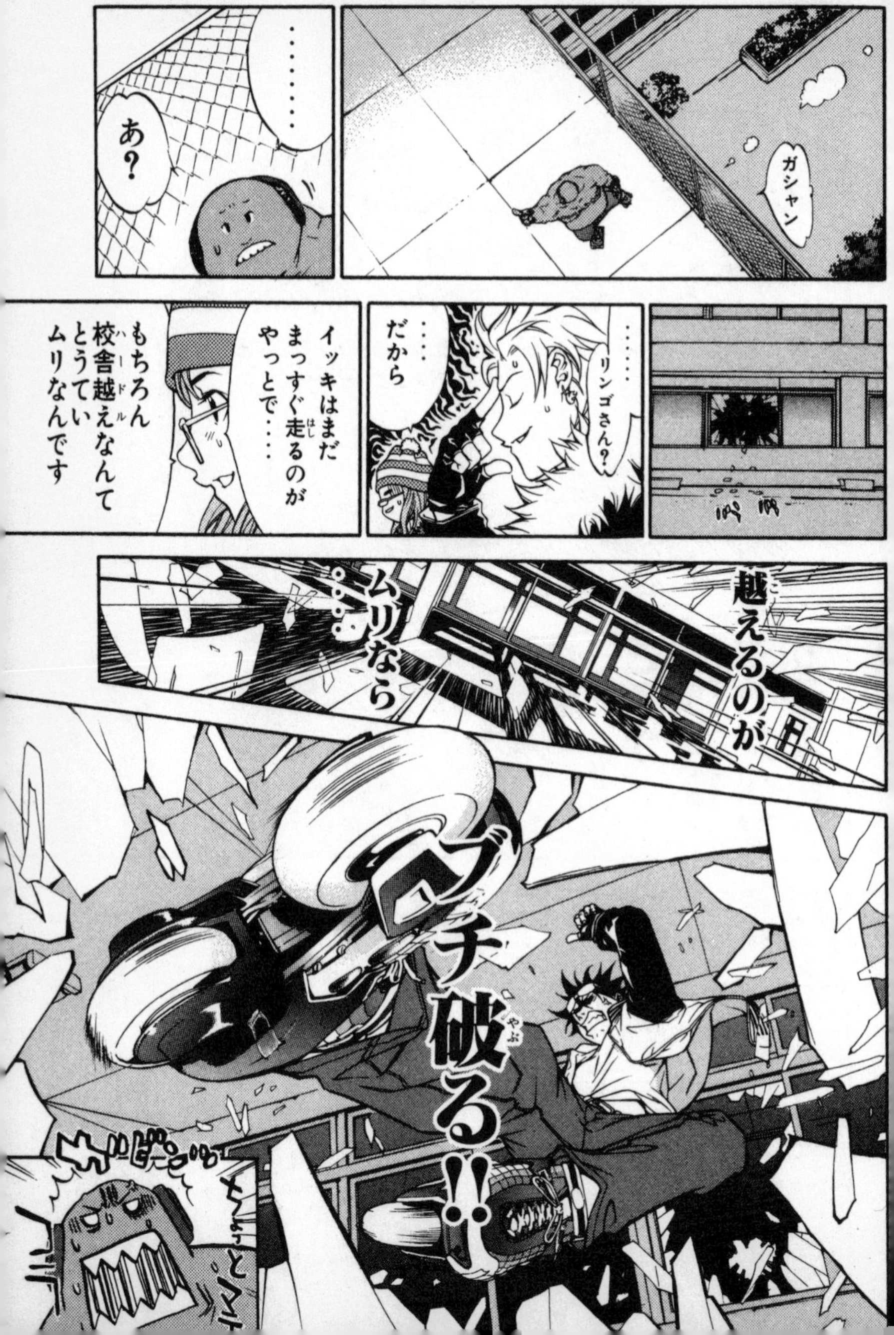
ガシャン
……
あ?
……リンゴさん?
……だから
イッキはまだ まっすぐ走るのが やっとで……
もちろん 校舎越えなんて とうてい ムリなんです
越えるのが ムリなら……
ブチ破る!!
ちょっとマテ

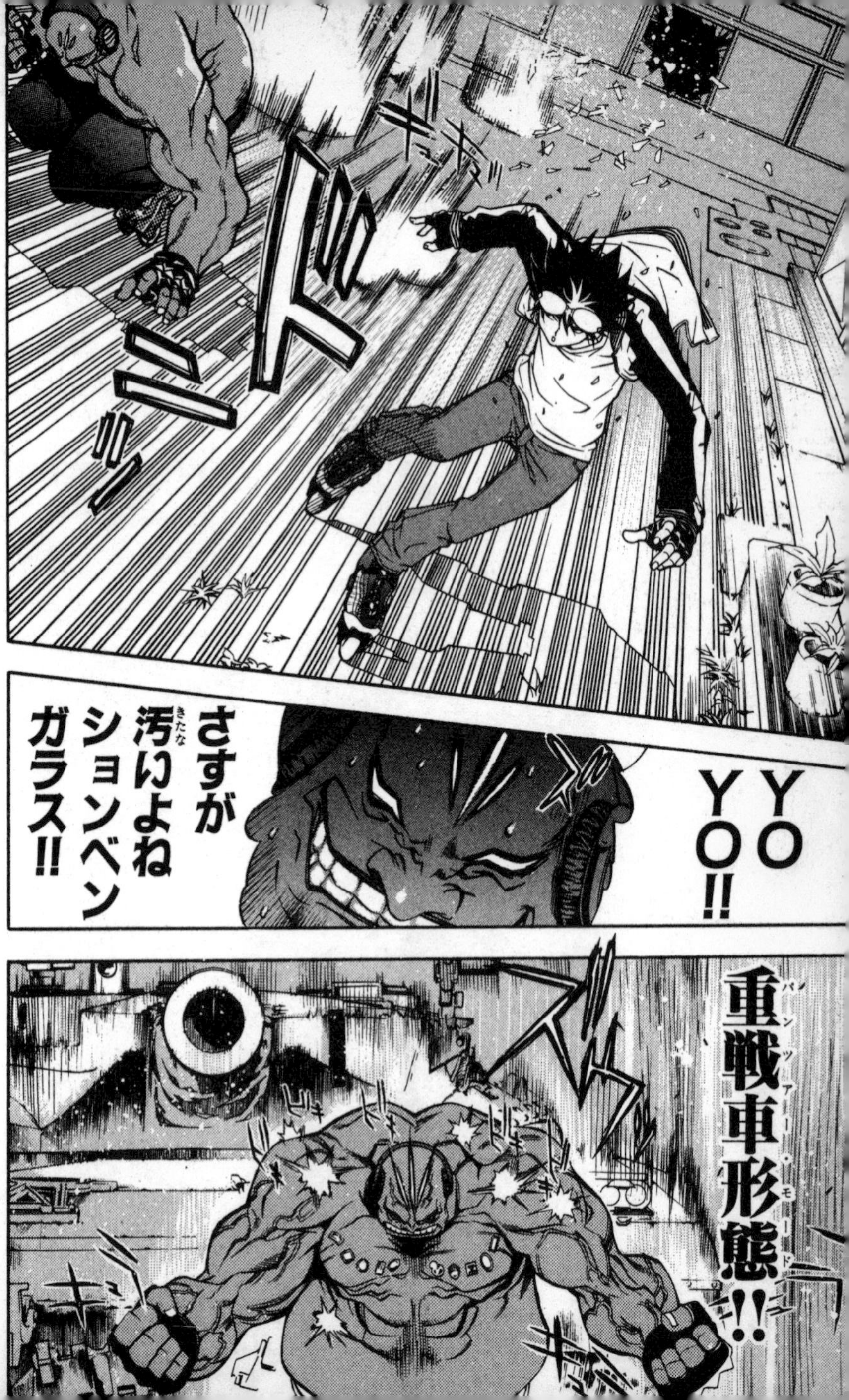
YO YO!!
さすが汚いよねションベンガラス!!
重戦車形態!!

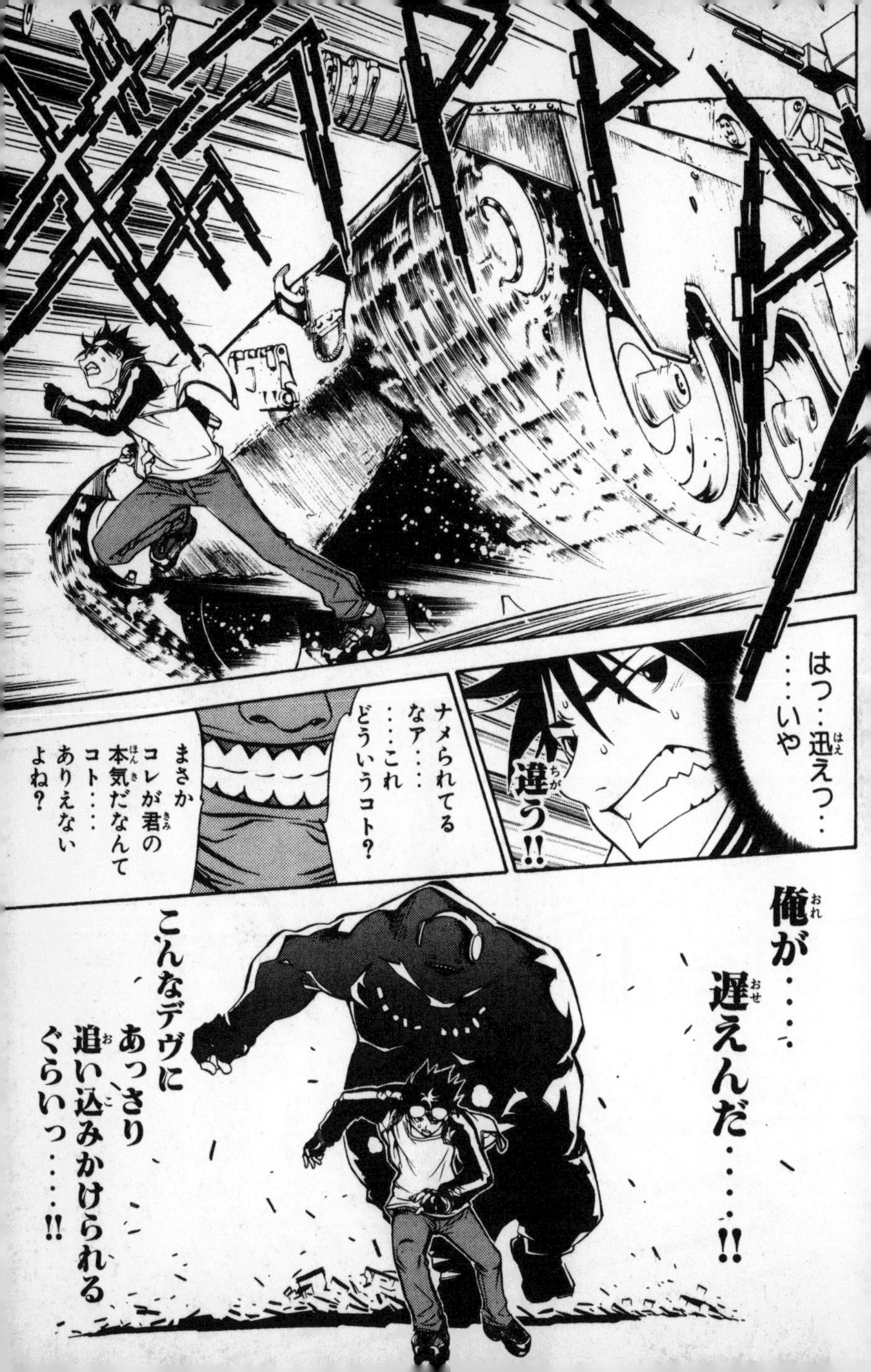
はっ…迅えっ……いや
違う!!
ナメられてるなア……これどういうコト?
まさかコレが君の本気だなんてコト……ありえないよね?
俺が……遅えんだ……!!
こんなデヴにあっさり追い込みかけられるぐらいっ……!!

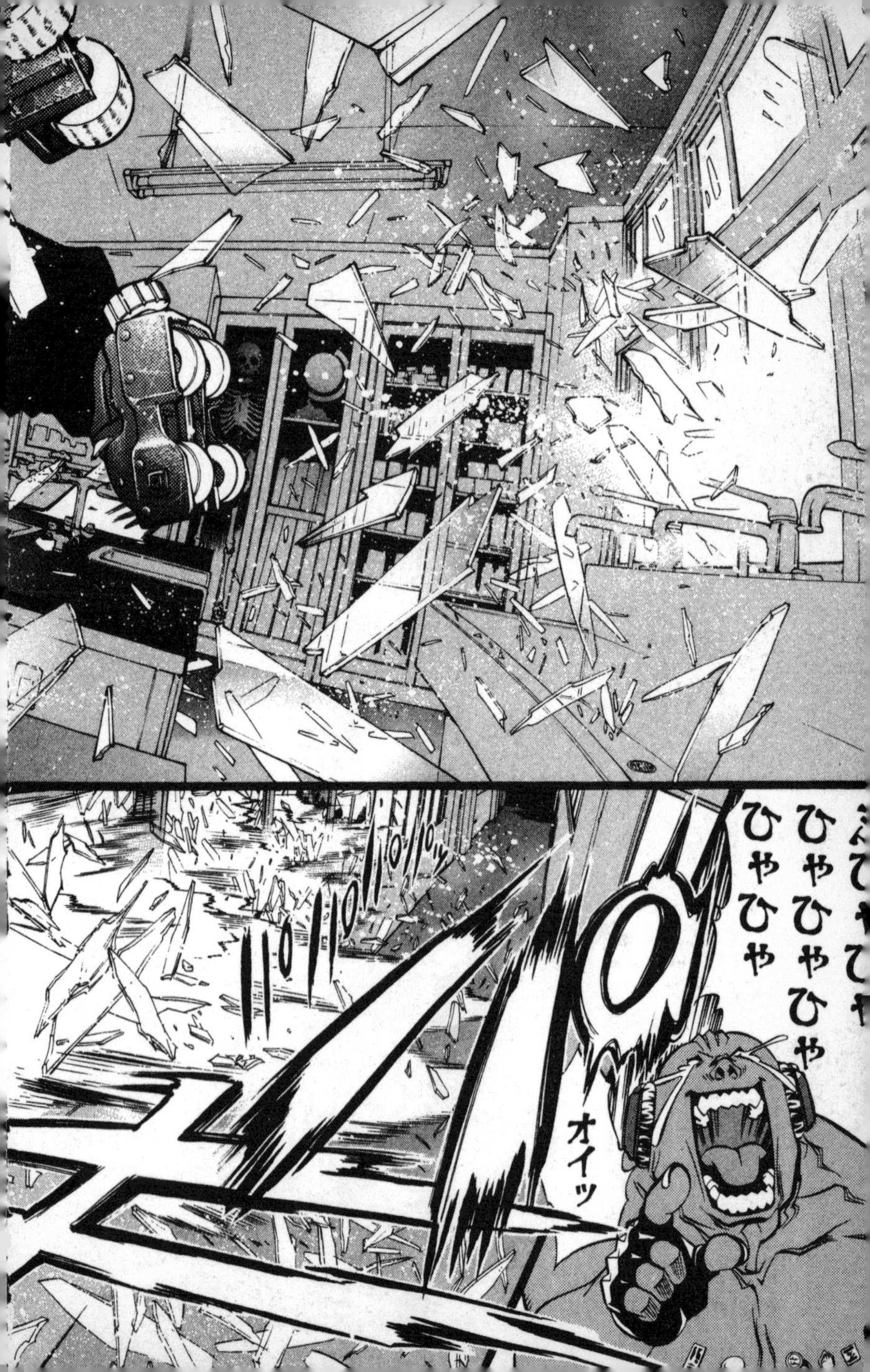
ひゃひゃひゃ
ひゃひゃ
オイッ

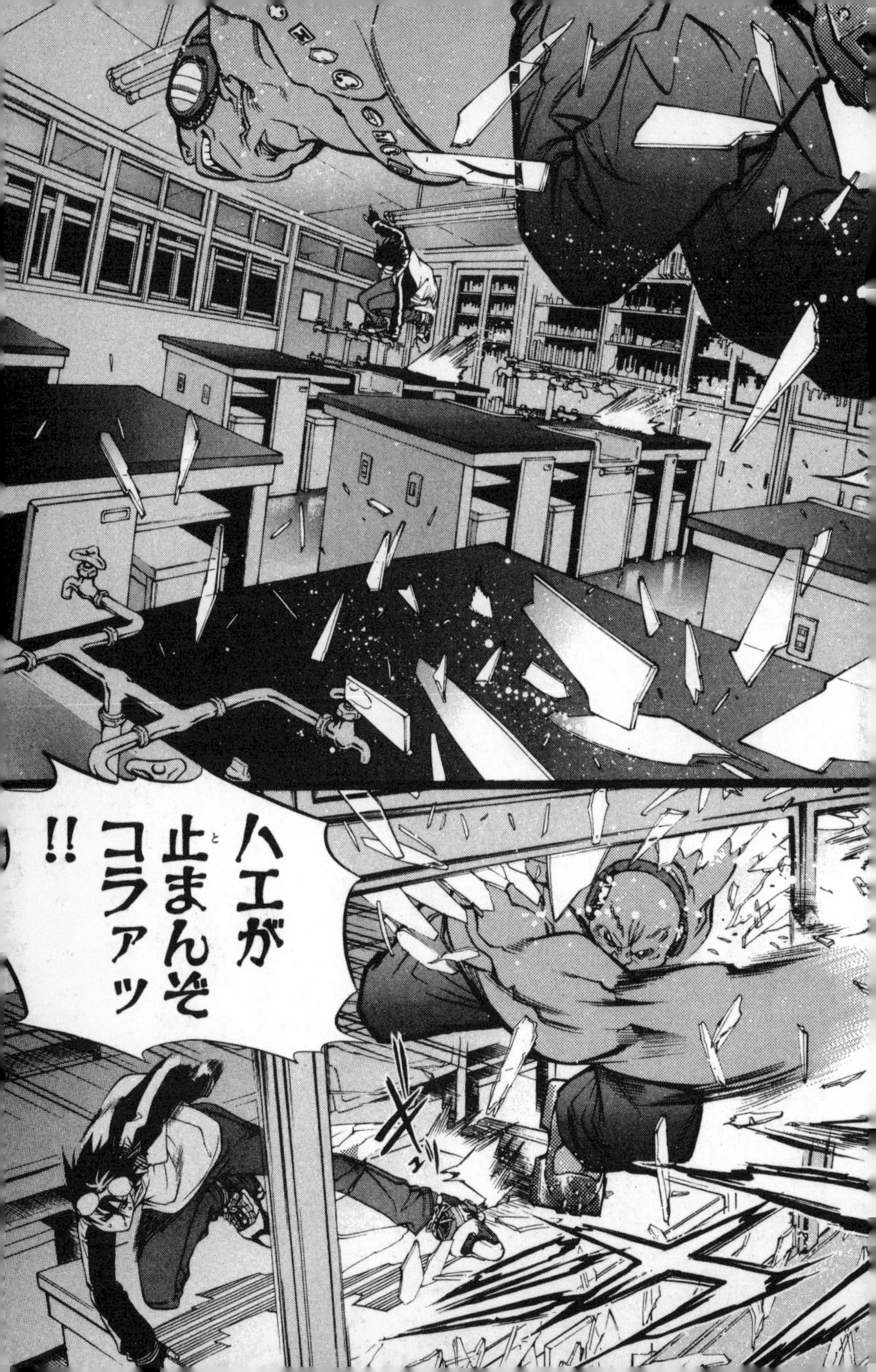
ハエが止まんぞコラァッ!!

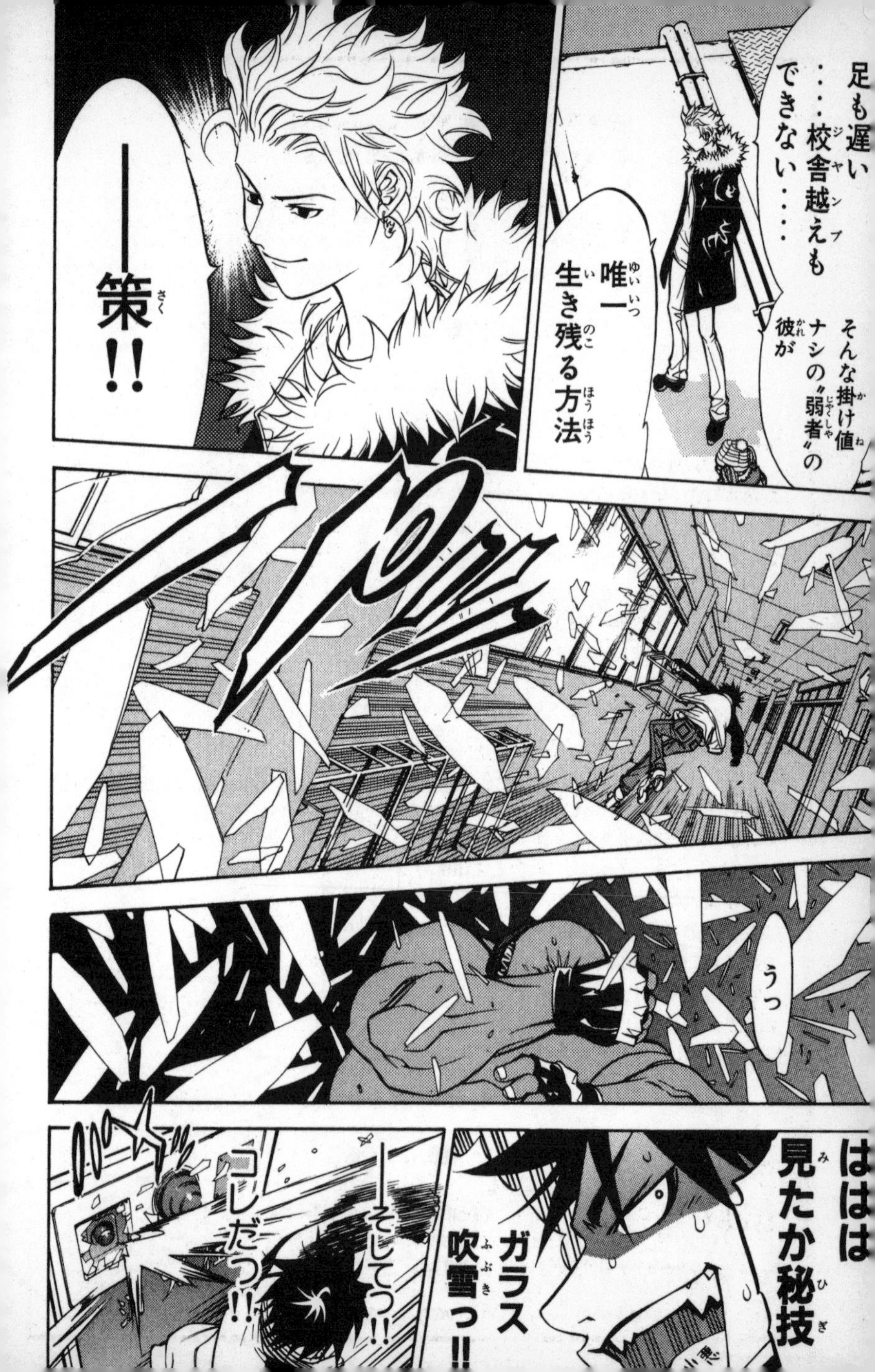
足も遅い……校舎越えもできない……
そんな掛け値ナシの"弱者"の彼が
唯一生き残る方法
——策!!
うっ
ははは見たか秘技
ガラス吹雪っ!!
——そしてっ!!
コレだっ!!

Eternal Sabbath Vol. 1

BY FUYUMI SORYO

WHO WANTS TO LIVE FOREVER?

Ryousuke Akiba calls himself ES, a code name taken from a mysterious scientific experiment. Ryousuke will live to be at least two centuries old and possesses strange mental powers—he can enter people's minds and learn their darkest secrets; he can rearrange their memories so that complete strangers treat him like family. He doesn't do it out of malice, but for survival. Now he wanders Tokyo for reasons known only to him. No one recognizes him for what he is . . . except Dr. Mine Kujyou, a researcher at Touhou Medical University. Dr. Kujyou lives for her work, but she's about to meet someone who challenges everything she knows about science: ES, possessor of the Eternal Sabbath gene. But is he the only one?

Ages: 16 +

Special extras in each volume! Read them all!

KURO GANE

BY KEI TOUME

AN EERIE, HAUNTING SAMURAI ADVENTURE

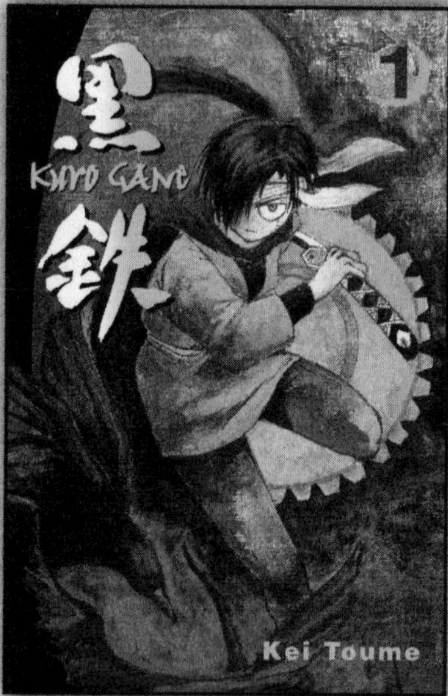
1
黒
KURO GANE
鉄
Kei Toume

Teen: Ages 13+

Avenging his father's murder is a matter of honor for the young samurai Jintetsu. But it turns out that the killer is a corrupt government official—and now the powers that be are determined to hunt Jintetsu down. There's only one problem: Jintetsu is already dead.

Torn to pieces by a pack of dogs, Jintetsu's ravaged body has been found by Genkichi, outcast and master inventor. Genkichi gives the dead boy a new, indestructible steel body and a talking sword—just what he'll need to face down the gang that's terrorizing his hometown and the mobster who ordered his father's hit. But what about Otsuki, the beautiful girl he left behind? Steel armor is defense against any sword, but it can't save Jintetsu from the pain in his heart.

Special extras in each volume! Read them all!

DEL REY

VISIT WWW.DELREYMANGA.COM TO:

- Read sample pages
- View release date calendars for upcoming volumes
- Sign up for Del Rey's free manga e-newsletter
- Find out the latest about new Del Rey Manga series

NEGIMA!™

BY KEN AKAMATSU

Negi Springfield is a ten-year-old wizard teaching English at an all-girls Japanese school. He dreams of becoming a master wizard like his legendary father, the Thousand Master. At first his biggest concern was concealing his magic powers, because if he's ever caught using them publicly, he thinks he'll be turned into an ermine! But in a world that gets stranger every day, it turns out that the strangest people of all are Negi's students! From a librarian with a magic book to a centuries-old vampire, from a robot to a ninja, Negi will risk his own life to protect the girls in his care!

Ages: 16+

Special extras in each volume! Read them all!

DEL REY

VISIT WWW.DELREYMANGA.COM TO:
• View release date calendars for upcoming volumes
• Sign up for Del Rey's free manga e-newsletter
• Find out the latest about new Del Rey Manga series

Pastel

by Toshihiko Kobayashi

I LOVE YUU

Poor 16-year-old Mugi Tadano is left heartbroken after his girlfriend moves away. A summer job at his friend Kazuki's beachside snack bar/hotel seems like the perfect way to get his mind off the breakup. Soon Kazuki sets Mugi up on a date with a girl named Yuu, who's supposed to be...well...a little less than perfect. But when Yuu arrives, she's not the monster that either of the boys had imagined. In fact, Yuu is about the cutest girl that Mugi has ever seen. But after Mugi accidentally walks in on Yuu while she's in the bath, Yuu is furious. When Mugi goes to apologize the next day, he learns that Yuu has left the island. Mugi vows to search high and low for her, but will he ever see the beautiful Yuu again?

Ages: 16 +

Special extras in each volume! Read them all!

BY AKIRA SEGAMI

MISSION IMPOSSIBLE

The young ninja Kagetora has been given a great honor—to serve a renowned family of skilled martial artists. But on arrival, he's handed a challenging assignment: teach the heir to the dynasty, the charming but clumsy Yuki, the deft moves of self-defense and combat.

Yuki's inability to master the martial arts is not what makes this job so difficult for Kagetora. No, it is Yuki herself. Someday she will lead her family dojo, and for a ninja like Kagetora to fall in love with his master is a betrayal of his duty, the ultimate dishonor, and strictly forbidden. Can Kagetora help Yuki overcome her ungainly nature . . . or will he be overcome by his growing feelings?

Ages: 13 +

Special extras in each volume! Read them all!

THE WALLFLOWER

YAMATONADESHIKO SHICHIHENGE

BY TOMOKO HAYAKAWA

It's a beautiful, expansive mansion, and four handsome, fifteen-year-old friends are allowed to live in it for free! But there is one condition—within three years the young men must take the owner's niece and transform her into a proper lady befitting the palace in which they all live! How hard can it be?

Enter Sunako Nakahara, the horror-movie-loving, pock-faced, frizzy-haired, fashion-illiterate hermit who has a tendency to break into explosive nosebleeds whenever she sees anyone attractive. This project is going to take far more than our four heroes ever expected; it needs a miracle!

Ages: 16 +

Special extras in each volume! Read them all!

BY MINORU TOYODA

"We have been telling all the people we meet to read this manga!"
—CLAMP, creators of Tsubasa

A fun, romantic comedy, Love Roma is about the simple kind of relationships we all longed for when we were young. It's a story of love at first sight—literally. When Hoshino sees Negishi for the first time, he asks her to be his girlfriend. Shocked, Negishi nevertheless agrees to allow Hoshino to walk her home, while he explains why he is in love with her. Touched, Negishi begins to feel something for this strange young boy from her school.

Ages: 16+

Special extras in each volume! Read them all!

TOMARE!

You are going the wrong way!

Manga is a completely different
type of reading experience.

To start at the *beginning*, go to the *end*!

That's right! Authentic manga is read the traditional Japanese
way—from right to left. Exactly the *opposite* of how American
books are read. It's easy to follow: Just go to the other end of
the book, and read each page—and each panel—from right side
to left side, starting at the top right. Now you're experiencing
manga as it was meant to be.